AMTA Monograph Series

AMERICAN
MUSIC
THERAPY
ASSOCIATION

Effective Clinical Practice in Music Therapy:
Music Therapy for Children, Adolescents, and Adults with Mental Disorders

Barbara J. Crowe, Monograph Editor
Cynthia Colwell, Series Editor

IBSN: 1-884914-18-7

Monograph Editor: **Barbara J. Crowe**
                         Arizona State University
                         Tempe, Arizona

Series Editor: **Cynthia Colwell**
                         University of Kansas
                         Lawrence, Kansas

Copyright Information: **© by American Music Therapy Association, Inc.,** 2007
                         8455 Colesville Rd., Suite 1000
                         Silver Spring, Maryland 20910 USA
                         www.musictherapy.org
                         info@musictherapy.org

Technical Assistance: **Wordsetters**
                         Kalamazoo, Michigan

Cover Design & Typesetting: **Angie K Elkins, MT-BC**

Printed in the United States of America

List of Contributing Authors

Diane Austin, DA, ACMT, LCAT
New York University, Private Practice
New York, New York

Barbara J. Crowe, MMT, MT-BC
Arizona State University
Tempe, Arizona

Erin Bullard, MT-BC, NMT
Glendale Uptown Home
Philadelphia, Pennsylvania

Flossie Ierardi, MM, MT-BC, LPC
Drexel University Hahnemann Creative Arts in Therapy Music Therapy Program
Philadelphia, Pennsylvania

Gary Johnson, MME, MT-BC, NMT
Colmery O'Neil Veteran Affairs Medical Center; VA
Eastern Kansas Health Care System
Topeka, Kansas

Roberta Wigle Justice, MM, MT-BC, FAMI
Eastern Michigan University
Ypsilanti, MI

Vaughn Kaser, MCAT, MT-BC
Atascadero State Hospital
Atascadero, California

Teresa Leite, PhD, CMT
Lusiada University of Lisbon, Portugal
Portuguese Music Therapy Association
European Music Therapy Confederation
Lisbon, Portugal

Paul Nolan, MCAT, MT-BC, LPC
Drexel University Hahnemann Creative Arts in Therapy Music Therapy Program
Philadelphia, Pennsylvania

Anne B. Parker, MA, MHSA, MT-BC, FAMI
Private Practice
Tucson, Arizona

Kirsten A. Peterson, MBA, MT-BC
Arizona Rhythm Connection
Casa Grande, AZ

Laurie Rugenstein, MMT, MT-BC, LPC, FAMI
Naropa University
Boulder, Colorado

Sammi Siegel, PhD, MT-BC
Private Practice
Birmingham, Michigan

Rick Soshensky, MA, MT-BC, NRMT
Northeast Center for Special Care
Lake Katrine, New York

Carylbeth Thomas, MA, ACMT, LMHC
Lesley University
Berklee College of Music
Community Music Center of Boston
Boston, Massachusetts

Acknowledgments

We wish to thank the authors for their contributions and their on-going input into this book. We appreciate their willingness to generously share their expertise. We also want to thank Hope Smith at Wordsetters and Angie Elkins for their diligence in bringing this book to publication.

— Barbara J. Crowe
— Cynthia Colwell

Contents

x

Section 1:

Introduction to Mental Disorders and History of Music Therapy for the Population

CHAPTER 1

History of Mental Disorders and Music Therapy
Barbara J. Crowe

Definition of Mental Disorders

This client population is defined by the American Psychiatric Association in its *Diagnostic and Statistical Manual of Mental Disorders (DSM-IV)* (1994) as

> *a clinically significant behavioral or psychological syndrome or pattern that occurs in an individual and that is associated with present distress (e.g., a painful symptom) or disability (i.e., impairment) in one or more important area of functioning or with a significantly increased risk of suffering death, pain, disability, or an important loss of freedom. (American Psychiatric Association [APA], 1994, p. xxi)*

These symptoms do not constitute an expected reaction to an event like the death of a loved one but must "currently be considered a manifestation of a behavioral, psychological, or biological dysfunction in the individual" (APA, 1994, pp. xxi–xxii). The client must be manifesting a significant impairment in social or occupational functioning to be considered mentally disordered. Clients with mental disorders have variously been labeled mentally ill, emotionally disturbed, behaviorally disordered, and having a psychiatric disorder. Though the term identifying these clients is *mentally disordered*, it is hard to classify these as mental disorders only as most have physical causes or results. These disorders are loosely grouped into three categories: psychotic disorders, mood disorders, and what used to be referred to as neurotic or situational/reactive disorders, though this is not an official category in the *DSM-IV* (APA, 1994).

Characteristics of the Population

All mental disorder diagnoses are grouped by predominance of symptoms.

Psychotic Disorders

Psychotic disorders are characterized by clear and obvious breaks with reality and severe impairment in all aspects of functioning—physical/motor, cognitive, perception, behavior, and speech. They constitute a long-term, chronic health problem requiring a series of hospitalizations and therapeutic interventions, including psychotropic medications. Psychotic disorders are recognized to have an organic biochemical or structural cause or predisposition. The organic cause predisposes the client to a disorder, while environmental factors may worsen or trigger the manifestation of that disorder. Psychotic disorders include schizophrenia, schizophreniform disorder, schizoaffective disorder, and delusional disorder.

Symptoms characteristic of psychotic disorders are grouped into areas of disability as follows:

- Thought disorders, including delusions such as paranoid delusions (an unshakable personal belief that is obviously untrue), loose associations (ideas shift from one subject to another or to unrelated topics), and bizarre associations (perseveration, blocking, clanging) causing bizarre speech patterns and disruption in ability to communicate
- Perceptual distortions, including hallucinations (response to a sensory input that does not exist) and distorted perceptions (extreme over- or underreaction to sensory input)
- Affect problems, including blunting of affect (severe reduction in intensity of emotional expression), flat affect (no emotional expression), and inappropriate affect (contradictory emotions)
- Disturbances in sense of self, including disturbed self-concept, loss of ego boundaries, and extreme disturbance of body image
- Disturbance in volition (ability to initiate action)
- Social withdrawal
- Psychomotor behavior, including decreased response to environmental cues, catatonic state (immobility), lack of motor coordination, bizarre or ritualistic behaviors (pacing, spitting, biting), and stereotyped movement patterns (muscle spasms, facial grimacing, tics)
- Disruption in personality, including irritability, confusion, and loss of ability to care for self

Mood Disorders

Mood disorders are characterized by a disturbance of mood, defined as a prolonged emotional state that colors a person's whole psychic life. Causes of mood disorders include genetic predisposition, chemical imbalance in the brain, chronic physical illness, and substance abuse. The severity of mood disorder symptoms varies greatly and some, the major affective disorders, also display psychotic symptoms. Mood disorder diagnoses include manic episode, major depressive episode (psychotic), mixed episode, hypomanic episode, major depressive disorder, dysthymic disorder, bipolar disorder, and cyclothymic disorder. All mood disorders involve the symptoms of depression or elation (mania) or combinations of these symptoms:

- Manic features, including excessive elevation in mood, increased sociability and/or superficial, manipulative relationships, inflated self-esteem, lack of personal insight, hyperactivity, lack of self-control, pressure of speech (rapid speech with little content), labile affect, rigid and/or controlling personality, and hostility
- Depressive features, including melancholy and sad affect, mental and motor retardation, labile affect, loss of interest in activities, suicide ideas and attempts, depersonalization

(feeling like a stranger in your own body), severe impairment in social functioning, short attention span, and very poor self-esteem

Situational/Reactive Disorders (Formerly Neurosis)

Earlier versions of the DSM grouped this wide range of disorders first under the category of "neurosis" and then as situational/reactive disorders, because it was believed that they did not have organic causes. With the writing of the *DSM-IV* (APA, 1994), organic causes were recognized in more of these disorders than previously known. The disorders in this loose category all involve an observed reaction or complaint that does not constitute a clean break with reality. Symptoms usually involve psychological discomfort (including worry, anxiety, pain, fears, and phobia), social or occupational inefficiency, or behavioral acting out. They involve normal human psychological reactions to stress that become enduring or recurring beyond normal reactions or occur when the stressor is removed. These disorders are grouped by predominance of symptom as follows:

- *Anxiety disorders* where anxiety is the predominant symptom, including panic attack. Anxiety symptoms include sweating, heart palpitations, trembling, chest pain, lightheadedness, derealization (feelings of unreality), fear of dying, and paresthesias (numbness or tingling sensation). Specific disorders include agoraphobia, panic disorder, specific phobia, social phobia, obsessive-compulsive disorder, posttraumatic stress disorder, acute stress disorder, and generalized anxiety disorder.

- *Somatoform disorders*, which involve the presence of physical symptoms suggesting a physical disorder but with no known organic cause and strong evidence that symptoms are linked to psychological factors. Specific disorders include somatization disorder (formally hysteria), conversion disorder, pain disorder, hypochondriasis, and body dysmorphic disorder.

- *Factitious disorders* occur when physical symptoms are faked.

- *Dissociative disorders*, which involves disruption in the usually integrated functions of consciousness, memory, identity, or perception of the environment. Specific disorders include dissociative amnesia, dissociative fugue, dissociative identity disorder (formally multiple personality disorder), and depersonalization disorder.

- *Sexual and gender identity disorders*, which include sexual dysfunction disorders, paraphilias, and gender identity disorders.

- *Eating disorders*, including anorexia nervosa and bulimia nervosa.

- *Sleep disorders*, which involve severe disruption in sleep patterns.

- *Impulse-control disorders* involving a failure to resist an impulse, drive, or temptation harmful to self or others. Specific disorders include intermittent explosive disorder, kleptomania, pyromania, pathological gambling, and trichotillomania (hair pulling).

- *Adjustment disorders* involving marked distress and impairment in social and occupational functioning.

- *Personality disorders*, occurring when a personality trait becomes inflexible and maladaptive. Clients with this disorder usually have constricted affect, cold and aloof personalities, and impairment in interpersonal relationships. Specific disorders include paranoid personality disorder, schizoid personality disorder, schizotypal personality disorder, antisocial personality disorder, borderline personality disorder, histrionic personality disorder, narcissistic personality disorder, avoidant personality disorder, dependent personality disorder, and obsessive-compulsive personality disorder.

- *Substance-related disorders* are related to ingesting a substance (drugs or alcohol), to side effects of medications, and to toxic exposure to substances. The diagnostic focus is on a pattern of dependence, pathological use, impairment in social or occupational functioning, and physical dependence with withdrawal (APA, 1994).

History of Mental Disorders

Mental illness has been recognized in human beings since the beginning of human culture. The early people in hunter/gatherer societies believed it was caused by magical or religious forces such as spirit possession or the action of curses (Tyson, 1981). The earliest therapeutic interventions for mental disorders involved the rituals, ceremonies, and spirit exorcisms of shamans (Harner, 1980). By the time of the great Greek civilization, a shift was made to discovering the causation for disease. For the Greeks, health, including mental health, was a condition of perfect harmony or equilibrium (Boxberger, 1962). For them, mental illness was a state of disharmony between the physical and the psychological nature of humans (Tyson, 1981). Treatment consisted of finding the means to restore the person to harmony. During the European Middle Ages, patients with a mental illness were again thought to be possessed by demons (Davis & Gfeller, 1992). Disease, particularly mental disease, was seen as a punishment for sin requiring harsh treatment. The mentally ill were tortured, confined in cages, beaten, and forcibly isolated from society (Tyson, 1981).

In 1840, the United States census created a classification of "mental illness" and designed two categories of disorders—idiocy and insanity. This was the beginning of viewing mental illness as a medical disorder. In 1880, seven categories of mental diseases were established, including mania, melancholia, monomania, paresis, dementia, epilepsy, and dispomania (APA, 1994, p. xvii). In 1952, the American Psychiatric Association created the first edition of the *Diagnostic and Statistical Manual of Mental Disorders (DSM)*. A third edition was published in 1980, and the current fourth edition in 1994. With each edition the categories of mental illness were changed, disorders were added or eliminated, and the labels for various mental disorders altered.

Treatment of Mental Disorders

The earliest "treatments" for mental illness involved rituals, exorcisms, torture, and imprisonment. Until the mid-1900s, treatment for mental illness involved long-term hospitalization in a mental hospital, psycho-surgery like lobotomy, sensory stimulation like ice baths and hot wraps, invasive procedures like electroshock and insulin shock therapy, restraint like confinement in straight jackets or padded cells, and recreational activities like crafts and sports. With the widespread acceptance of the work of Sigmund Freud in the early 1900s, treatment for mental illness shifted to psychotherapy and psychoanalytic techniques. In the early 1950s, the first psychotropic medication, chlorpromazine, was introduced (Smeltekop & Houghton, 1990). These medications "made the patient more accessible to treatment and gave evidence that treatment, or at least maintenance, of emotional problems could be done quickly and efficiently and outside the institutional setting" (Wilson, 1990, p. 88). In 1946, the federal National Mental

Health Act was passed providing support for the development of community facilities for psychiatric treatment. In 1955, the United States Congress called for an evaluation of the mental health system and established the Joint Commission on Mental Illness and Health. In 1961, they published a 5-year study setting forth an action for mental health. The movement away from large mental hospitals and toward community-based treatment culminated in 1963 with the passage of Public Law 88-164, which funded the construction of community mental health centers to provide patient evaluation and diagnosis and a wide-range of therapeutic interventions, rehabilitation, and aftercare (Braswell, 1968). In the 1960s, psychiatric treatment shifted to an emphasis on relationships and from strict psychotherapy to a counseling model (Braswell, 1968; Tyson, 1981). Currently, a number of therapeutic approaches or models of treatment for mental disorders theorize both the cause of a mental disorder and the best method for alleviating symptoms.

Organic Model

An organic or bio-medical model of treatment for mental disorders is based on the assumption that chemical imbalance or structural abnormalities of the brain cause mental illness. Treatment in this model would require a means to normalize brain chemicals or minimize the effect of structural abnormalities (Scovel & Gardstrom, 2002). The ever-increasing types of psychotropic medications available for a variety of mental disorders speak to the prevalence of this model.

Systematic-Cybernetic Model

The systematic-cybernetic model sees mental illness as a function of the interactions within relationships and social systems—families, culture, society. Mental disorders arise as responses to relationship problems, as ineffective solutions to those problems, as a means for exercising control, and as a way to structure interactions (Gallo, 1999). Treatment in this model addresses these problems in relationships and helps the client learn more adaptive means of interaction.

Behavioral Model

The behavioral model focuses on external behavior and its relationship to the environment or context. This model assumes that all behaviors, including the symptoms of a mental disorder, are learned. Treatment involves extinguishing a maladaptive behavior and learning new, more appropriate behavior through techniques of positive and negative reinforcement, reward, punishment, and behavioral extinction (Scovel & Gardstrom, 2002).

Cognitive Model

The cognitive model focuses on the internal dialogues or scripts that shape a person's reactions and beliefs. A cognitive approach to therapy for mental disorders is based on the discovery and elimination of internal designs, like language, that are maladaptive or untrue. The belief in this model is that if you change how you think, you will change how you feel and act (Wilber, 1996).

Developmental Model

The developmental model assumes that there are stages of emotional development that all individuals must move through in order for psychological development and mental health to occur. Mental illness constitutes a stop or arrest at one stage of development due to trauma. The various mental disorders are seen as originating in a specific level of development. Treatment in this model involves discovering the point of developmental arrest and helping the client move through the normal developmental sequence.

Psychodynamic Model

The psychodynamic model assumes the causes of a mental disorder are psychological and usually involve the suppression of emotions, memories of traumatic events, and unconscious motivations for behavior and reactions. It uses a wide variety of techniques and approaches that help an individual make psychological changes and adjustments that lead to more adaptive mental health through uncovering of unconscious material, emotional catharsis, and insight development (Bruscia, 1998). (See section on Music Psychotherapy in Chapter 6.)

Humanistic Model

The humanistic model recognizes that human behavior is complicated and unique. It is a psychological model that includes areas of human experience not often included in other psychological models—love, self-growth, creativity, higher values, consciousness development, meaning in life, ego-transcendence, and altruism. Therapists and researchers in the humanistic model believe that the scientific method is not an appropriate model for investigation of human responses and experiences (Ruud, 1978). The therapeutic emphasis is on good communication skills and reflective listening.

Transpersonal Model

An outgrowth of the humanistic model, the transpersonal model assumes that human development can go beyond "normal" ego functioning and that a higher stage of development beyond the ego level is possible. In transpersonal therapy, the goal is to integrate spiritual experience within a larger understanding of human development (Crowe, 2004). (See section on Transpersonal Music Therapy in Chapter 6 for further information.)

History of the Use of Music Therapy for Persons with Mental Disorders

There are historical accounts of the use of music for persons with mental disorders since the earliest human civilizations. Early hunter/gatherer cultures used chant, repetitive drumming and rattling, and healing songs for all illnesses, including those we would now classify as mental disorders (Harner, 1980). As Boxberger (1962) notes, "Medicine was a function of religion: the close relationship of music to the temple rituals indicates why it was so intimately bound up with medical practices in the cultures of ancient peoples" (p. 138). The Old Testament account of David playing the harp for King Saul during attacks of melancholy shows that the Hebrew people believed music had the power to affect emotions and feelings. The ancient Egyptians, Babylonians, Sumerians, and other great cultures of the ancient world also used music as part of medical practice (Boxberger, 1962).

Of particular interest to Western thought were the practices of the ancient Greeks. Music was prescribed to cure mental illness, because it was believed to directly influence emotion and develop character (Davis & Gfeller, 1992). Pythagoras believed that using music in a prescribed manner made a significant contribution to health, especially mental health, since singing and playing instruments were a part of the necessary emotional catharsis (Meinecke, 1948). As Boxberger (1962) notes, the word *catharsis* meant medicine that was administered with the aid of music. Aristotle referred to music as a form of psychotherapy (Tyson, 1981), and the healing temples of Aesculapius, where an ecstatic experience to awaken the power of the soul was created through chant, music, and instruments, were established to cure nervous disorders (Boxberger, 1962). Learning from the Greeks, Roman physicians used music to cure mental disorders. The Roman physician, Aschepeades, treated insanity through harmonious sounds (Boxberger, 1962). Various Greek and Roman writers—Asclepiades, Xenocrates, Clesus, Caelius Aurelianus, and Boethius—reported numerous ways in which music was used in the treatment of mental and nervous problems (Tyson, 1981).

In the Middle Ages in Europe, specific modes were used to influence behavior, including the symptoms of mental illness (Tyson, 1981). During the Renaissance, original Greek writings were re-discovered, including the beliefs about the health benefits of music. During this time music was widely used as a remedy for melancholy, despair, and madness and was used as a preventative measure to enhance emotional health (Davis & Gfeller, 1992). Reflecting the prevailing culture, Shakespeare mentions the use of music in curing mental illness in several of his plays—physicians using music to calm King Lear and to sooth King Henry IV (Boxberger, 1962). In the Baroque era, Kircher developed a theory of temperaments and affections where personality characteristics were linked with certain styles of music. This evolved into a more formalized treatment for mental illness using music. In 1651, Burton wrote a book entitled *Anatomy of Melancholy*, in which he advocated the use of music as a treatment (Gfeller & Davis, 1992).

This trend toward a formalized use of music in the treatment of mental illness was reflected in various publications in the late 1700s and through the 1800s. In 1789 an article appeared in *Columbian Magazine* entitled "Music Physically Considered." This author made a case for the use of music to influence and regulate emotional conditions and stated that music was a "proven" therapeutic agent because of its influence on emotion. In the early 1800s psychiatrist Benjamin Rush advocated the use of music to treat mental diseases. Two of his students wrote dissertations on the subject. Atlee wrote "An Inaugural Essay on the Influence of Music in the Cure of Disease," and Matthews wrote "On the Effects of Music in Curing and Palliating Disease" (Davis & Gfeller, 1992). Burton (1852) stressed the use of music as a remedy for melancholy (Boxberger, 1962). Other articles appeared throughout this time. These included an article by Whittaker in 1874 entitled "Music as Medicine" that concluded that music had the greatest effect on mild forms of mental illness, an article by Edwards in 1878 entitled "Music as Mind Medicine" reporting on "lunatics" reactions to music, and one by Beardsley in 1882 entitled "The Medical Uses of Music," advocating the use of music to treat nervous and mental disorders (Davis & Gfeller, 1992). Davis and Gfeller also report on two significant publications in the history of music for mental disorders. An article by Blumer appeared in the 1892 issue of *The American Journal of Insanity* reporting on a program at Utica State Hospital where musicians were hired to play for patients as part of "moral" treatment. This is the first report of an ongoing music program in an American hospital. In 1899, James L. Corning published an article entitled "The Use of Musical Vibration Before and During Sleep—Supplementary Employment of Chromatoscopic Figures—A Contribution to the Therapeutics of Emotion." This research study was the first reported attempt to systematically record the effects of music on mental illness.

By the early 1900s a large hospital music movement had begun (Van de Wall, 1926, 1936; Vescelius, 1918). As Boxberger (1963) notes, music was used more in mental hospitals than in other hospitals. The early use of music in hospitals was recreational and involved musical instruction, performance, and entertainment. Music programs included bands and choruses, drum and bugle corps, and talent shows (Wilson, 1990). Early examples of the use of music therapy for patients with mental illness include the work of Van de Wall (1926), Altschuler (1939, 1941a, 1941b, 1944a, 1944b, 1948), Eby (1943), and Conway (1949). Willem Van de Wall in particular pioneered music in mental hospitals and established the first such program at Allentown State Hospital for Mental Diseases in the late 1920s (Davis & Gfeller, 1992). By 1948, Schullian and Schoen had published a book, *Music and Medicine*, that included chapters by Altschuler on experiments with music as a therapeutic agent and by Van de Wall on music in hospitals. In 1944, Van de Wall was appointed chairman of the Committee for the Use of Music in Hospitals to oversee the development of music therapy programs in psychiatric hospitals (Davis & Gfeller, 1992). Music therapy as a professional discipline evolved from these early uses of music in psychiatric hospitals (Tyson, 1981).

An early music therapy program was established at the Veterans Administration Hospital in Topeka, Kansas (Michel, 1976). This program consisted of large group experiences on the patient wards to alter mood and modify destructive physical activity and also of music teaching at the bedside conducted by music teachers and musicians (Tyson, 1981). After the Second World War, music therapy practice shifted toward therapeutic and rehabilitation goals (Wilson, 1990). With the development of psychotropic medications, goals for music therapy shifted again to work on psychological needs, establishment of interpersonal relationship, and increased self-esteem (Gaston, 1968). In the book, *Music and Your Emotions* (Gutheil, 1952), a case was presented for the use of music as a psychotherapeutic agent. In that book, Gilman and Paperte (1952) report on the effects of specific music in relation to mental patients at the Army Medical Center. They saw music as an adjunct to psychiatric treatment to increase attention span, provide diversion, modify mood, stimulate imagery, relieve tension, foster self-expression, and stimulate socialization (Tyson, 1981).

Michel (1959) examined 375 cases of music therapy interventions at the Winter Veterans Administration Hospital in Topeka, Kansas, giving us a snapshot of the state of music therapy at the time. He found that the average length of stay was from 4.41 to 48 months. Typical goals set for music therapy were to decrease narcissistic gratification, increase socialization, release hostility, develop hobby interests, and to "establish compulsive routine defenses" (Michel, 1960, p. 143). Music therapy activities included learning musical instruments, record listening, song writing, and radio programming. Most music therapy sessions were done individually with a patient and emphasized musical instruction. He concludes that "most of the patients were beginners where music instruction on instruments was concerned . . ." (Michel, 1959, p. 173). As one patient commented, "I believe music instruction should be available to all patients. . . . Since leaving the hospital I continue to play my instrument in a dance band" (Michel, 1959, p. 171). Because patient instruction and musical performance were the basis for the therapy, Michel makes a plea for more information on the musical background of patients. The music therapy theory developed by Gaston and Sears (Sears, 1968) reflects this performance and musical instruction emphasis for music therapy interventions during this period of time. However, Miles (1958) wrote a groundbreaking report in *Music Therapy 1957* on a true psychotherapeutic approach to music therapy with an individual client. By 1968, numerous reports of music therapy practice and research in psychiatry had appeared (Conrad, 1962; Darbes & Shrift, 1957; Dollins, 1957; Michel, 1952, 1955; Sommer, 1958). Panels on psychiatric music therapy were conducted at music therapy conferences (Michel, 1953). By 1965, Michel reported that state mental hospitals were the largest employers of music therapists (Wilson, 1990).

In general, music therapy approaches and services reflect the ongoing changes in mental health care (Wilson, 1990).

Music and medicine cannot, therefore, be considered other than as part of the social phenomena of civilization. The role of Music in therapy is conditioned by the prevailing physical and socio-cultural environment in which it operates and the practice of music therapy is influenced by the prevailing philosophy of the ear. (Boxberger, 1963, p. 135)

During the late 1960s and into the 1970s, mental health treatment shifted to community-based programs, length of stay decreased, and an emphasis on several therapeutic models—behaviorism and psychotherapy—emerged.

In 1968, Unkefer defined mental disorder as a behavioral disorder and music therapy as a means to "induce, elicit, or persuade better behavior patterns" (pp. 231–232). As he further notes, "Whether directly or indirectly by means of music, the chief aim of the music therapist is *change of behavior* in his patients" (Unkefer, 1968, p. 232). Typically, a music therapy program consisted of individual lessons and practice, small ensembles, and large choral and instrumental groups. In addition to behavioral change, the goals were to stimulate patient interest in music as a meaningful cultural activity, direct energies into music making as a means for growth toward health, increase socialization through group experiences and aesthetic reactions, and develop a sense of achievement and self-worth as a support to ego development (Thompson, 1968).

The shift to community-based and day treatment for persons with mental illness shortened the length of stay for patients and emphasized music therapy activities to enhance socialization, re-establish coping skills, and learn appropriate means of emotional expression. Clemetson and Chen (1968) report on a music therapy program in day treatment that consisted of dance groups; instrumental ensembles emphasizing melodica, autoharp, and guitar; music appreciation groups; rhythm groups; classes in drum rudiments; and community singing. Though there is still emphasis on performance and skill building, there is a shift away from orchestral and band instruments to the more easily approached instruments like guitar and autoharp that could be learned in the shorter amount of time available. The establishment of the Cleveland Music School Settlement was a move toward community music therapy for the mentally ill (Michel, 1976), as was the establishment of the Community Music Center by Florence Tyson (McGuire, 2004).

The 1970s also saw extensive development of a psychotherapeutic approach in music therapy (Bruscia, 1998). Wilson (1968) noted that a shift began in the late 1960s away from the instruction/ achievement-centered approach in music therapy to psychotherapy. The development of the Bonny Method of Guided Imagery and Music reflects this shift in emphasis (Bonny & Savary, 1973), as does the rise of psychodynamic improvisational music therapy techniques (Bruscia, 1987).

Current practice in music therapy for individuals with mental disorders is applied in all the therapeutic models summarized above. Music therapists work with adults, adolescents, and children with mental disorders in large state and county facilities, private psychiatric hospitals, community-based programs, behavioral health units of general hospitals, community music schools, drug and alcohol treatment facilities, group homes and half-way houses, special education programs, forensic psychiatric facilities including prisons, and in private practice (Wilson, 1990). This book is our attempt to summarize current music therapy practice with adults, adolescents, and children with mental disorders. It covers assessment of clients and eligibility for services, music therapy treatment interventions, specific music therapy practice with adults—chronic and psychotic; nonpsychotic including mood disorders, personality disorders, anxiety, etc.; substance abuse; eating disorders; acute care; and community-based services. It also addresses work with adolescents and children with mental disorders.

References

Altschuler, I. A. (1939). Rational music therapy of the mentally ill. Music Teachers National Association Proceedings, 33, 153–157.

Altschuler, I. A. (1941a). The part of music in re-socialization of mental patients. Occupational Therapy and Rehabilitation, 20(2), 75–86.

Altschuler, I. A. (1941b). The role of music in re-socialization of mental patients. American Journal of Physical Medicine, 20, 75–86.

Altschuler, I. A. (1944a). Four years experience with music as a therapeutic agent at the Eloise hospital. American Journal of Psychology, 111(7), 792–794.

Altschuler, I. A. (1944b). Music in the treatment of neurosis, theoretical consideration and practical experiences. Music Teachers National Association Proceedings, 68, 154–163.

Altschuler, I. A. (1948). A psychiatrist's experiences with music as a therapeutic agent. In D. M. Schullian & M. Schoen (Eds.), Music and medicine (pp. 266–281). New York: Henry Schuman, Inc.

American Psychiatric Association (APA). (1994). Diagnostic and statistical manual of mental disorders (4th ed.). Washington, DC: Author.

Bonny, H. L., & Savary, L. M. (1973). Music and your mind: Listening with a new consciousness. New York: Harper & Row.

Boxberger, R. (1962). Historical bases for the use of music in therapy. In E. R. Schneider (Ed.), Music therapy 1961 (pp. 125–166). Lawrence, KS: National Association for Music Therapy.

Boxberger, R. (1963). An historical study of the National Association for Music Therapy. In E. H. Schneider (Ed.), Music therapy 1962 (pp. 133–197). Lawrence, KS: National Association for Music Therapy.

Braswell, C. (1968). Development of music therapy in the community: Overview. In E. T. Gaston (Ed.), Music in therapy (pp. 346–349). New York: Macmillan.

Bruscia, K. E. (1987). Improvisational models of music therapy. Springfield, IL: Charles C. Thomas.

Bruscia, K. E. (1998). The dynamics of music psychotherapy. Gilsum, NH: Barcelona.

Burton, R. (1852). The anatomy of melancholy. Philadelphia: J. W. Moore.

Clemetson, B. C., & Chen, R. (1968). Music therapy in a day-treatment program. In E. T. Gaston (Ed.), Music in therapy (pp. 394–400). New York: Macmillan.

Conrad, J. (1962). A music therapy program for short-term psychiatric patients. Bulletin of NAMT, 11(3), 7–12.

Conway, J. L. (1949). A rhythm band for mental patients. American Journal of Occupational Therapy, 3, 246–249.

Crowe, B. J. (2004). Music and soulmaking: Toward a new theory of music therapy. Lanham, MD: Scarecrow Press.

Darbes, A., & Shrift, D. (1957). The effect of music therapy on three groups of hospitalized psychiatric patients as measured by some clinical and observational methods. Bulletin of NAMT, 6, 7–8.

Davis, W. B., & Gfeller, K. E. (1992). Music therapy: An historical perspective. In W. B. Davis, K. E. Gfeller, & M. H. Thaut (Eds.), An introduction to music therapy: Theory and practice (pp. 16–37). Dubuque, IA: William C. Brown.

Dollins, C. N. (1957). The use of background music in a psychiatric hospital to increase group conversational frequency. In E. T. Gaston (Ed.), Music therapy 1956 (pp. 229–230). Lawrence, KS: Allen Press.

Eby, J. (1943). The value of music in a psychiatric institution. Occupational Therapy and Rehabilitation, 22, 31–35.

Gallo, F. P. (1999). Energy psychology: Explorations at the interface of energy, cognition, behavior, and health. Boca Raton, FL: CRC Press LLC.

Gaston, E. T. (1968). Music in therapy. New York: Macmillan.

Gilman, L., & Paperte, F. (1952). Music as a psychotherapeutic agent. In E. A. Gutheil (Ed.), Music and your emotions (pp. 25–55). New York: Liveright.

Gutheil, E. A. (Ed.). (1952). Music and your emotions. New York: Liveright.

Harner, M. (1980). The way of the shaman. New York: Bantam Books.

McGuire, M. G. (2004). Psychiatric music therapy in the community: The legacy of Florence Tyson. Gilsum, NH: Barcelona.

Meinecke, B. (1948). Music and medicine in classical antiquity. In D. Schullian & M. Schoen (Eds.), Music and medicine (pp. 47–95). New York: Henry Schuman.

Michel, D. E. (1952). A study of the sedative effects of music for acutely disturbed patients in a mental hospital. In E. G. Gilliland (Ed.), Music therapy 1951 (pp. 182–183). Lawrence, KS: National Association for Music Therapy.

Michel, D. E. (1953). Music in mental hospitals panel: Philosophy and theory. In E. G. Gilliland (Ed.), Music therapy 1952 (pp. 36–69). Lawrence, KS: National Association for Music Therapy.

Michel, D. E. (1955). Some applications of group therapy methods with music therapy. In E. T. Gaston (Ed.), Music therapy 1954 (pp. 205–208). Lawrence, KS: National Association for Music Therapy.

Michel, D. E. (1959). A survey of 375 cases in music therapy at a mental hospital. In E. H. Schneider (Ed.), Music therapy 1958 (pp. 166–176). Lawrence, KS: National Association for Music Therapy.

Michel, D. E. (1960). Concluding report: A survey of 375 case records in music therapy. In E H. Schneider (Ed.), Music therapy 1959 (pp. 137–152). Lawrence, KS: National Association for Music Therapy.

Michel, D. E. (1976). Music therapy: An introduction to therapy and special education through music. Springfield, IL: Charles C. Thomas.

Miles, C. (1958). The treatment of a hospitalized adolescent patient by the method of individual music therapy. In E. T. Gaston (Ed.), Music therapy 1957 (pp. 65–80). Lawrence, KS: Allen Press.

Ruud, E. (1978). Music therapy and its relationship to current treatment theories. St. Louis, MO: Magnamusic Baton.

Schullian, D., & Schoen, N. (Eds.). (1948). Music and medicine. New York: Henry Schuman.

Scovel, M. A., & Gardstrom, S. C. (2002). Music therapy within the context of psychotherapeutic models. In R. F. Unkefer & M. H. Thaut (Eds.), Music therapy in the treatment of adults with mental disorders (3rd ed.) (pp. 117–132). St. Louis, MO: MMB Music.

Sears, W. (1968). Processes in music therapy. In E. T. Gaston (Ed.), Music in therapy (pp. 30–46). New York: Macmillan.

Smeltekop, R. A., & Houghton, B. A. (1990). Music therapy and psychopharmacology. In R. F. Unkefer (Ed.), Music therapy in the treatment of adults with mental disorders (pp. 109–125). New York: Schirmer Books.

Sommer, D. T. (1958). The effect of background music on frequency of interaction in group psychotherapy. In E. T. Gaston (Ed.), Music therapy 1957 (pp. 167–168). Lawrence, KS: Allen Press.

Thompson, M. F. (1968). Music therapy for the criminally insane and the psychopath. In E. T. Gaston (Ed.), Music in therapy (pp. 259–267). New York: Macmillan.

Tyson, F. (1981). Psychiatric music therapy: Origins and development. New York: Fred Weidner and Sons.

Unkefer, R. F. (1968). Adult behavior disorders. In E. T. Gaston (Ed.), Music in therapy (pp. 231–237). New York: Macmillan.

Van de Wall, W. (1926). A systematic music program for mental hospitals. American Journal of Psychiatry, 6, 279–291.

Vescelius, E. A. (1918). Music and health. The Musical Quarterly, 4(3), 376–401.

Wilber, K. (1996). A brief history of everything. Boston: Shambhala.

Wilson, A. E. (1968). Music in the treatment and education of emotionally disturbed children. In E. T. Gaston (Ed.), Music in therapy (pp. 293–313). New York: Macmillan.

Wilson, B. L. (1990). Music therapy in hospital and community programs. In R. F. Unkefer (Ed.), Music therapy in the treatment of adults with mental disorders (pp. 126–144). New York: Schirmer Books.

CHAPTER 2

Assessment
Barbara J. Crowe

Assessment is recognized as an integral part of any therapeutic intervention (Bruscia, 1988). In music therapy, the American Music Therapy Association specifies areas of assessment in their *Standards of Clinical Practice* (AMTA, 2004) for all clinical specialties. As Bruscia (1988) notes, "Assessment is that part of the therapy process concerned with understanding a client, his or her condition and therapeutic needs" (p. 5). It is a process of gathering information on the client, analyzing that information, and drawing conclusions about a person's needs, problems, and abilities (Cohen & Gericke, 1972). Assessment is first done before treatment begins so that the information generated can be used to set goals and objectives (treatment outcomes), determine treatment protocols and interventions, and determine the most appropriate means of evaluating the client's progress to accurately assess and evaluate music therapy as a treatment modality (Isenberg-Grzeda, 1988; Wilson, 2002). Assessment continues on an ongoing basis throughout the treatment process (Cassity & Cassity, 1994). A true therapeutic assessment cannot be a vague process of trial and error, but instead must be a specific, goal-oriented, and comprehensive process that allows therapists to measure the results of their treatment (Cohen & Gericke, 1972). An assessment *process* or *system*, not just a standardized assessment form, must be developed (Cohen, Averbach, & Katz, 1978). As Bruscia (1988) notes, "The therapist must organize and control the methods of obtaining data so that the client's responses cannot be attributed to extraneous influence or chance" (p. 8). He also writes that a clinically effective assessment must have clearly defined objectives, be administered by a qualified therapist, have unique clinical advantages, use effective means of data collection, produce reliable (consistent) data, lead to valid conclusions (it measures what it says it measures), and be ethical (Bruscia, 1988, p. 5). A true assessment becomes an essential part of clinical accountability for music therapy (Layman, Hussey, & Laing, 2002).

Functioning Areas to be Assessed—Domains of Functioning

A music therapy assessment judges functioning in both musical behaviors and nonmusical behaviors—general functioning outside the music environment. The *Standards of Clinical Practice* established by the American Music Therapy Association (2004) specifies the following areas of assessment for adults in mental health treatment:

- Motor functioning
- Sensory processing, planning, and task execution
- Substance use or abuse
- Reality orientation
- Emotional states
- Vocational states
- Educational background
- Client's use of music
- Developmental level
- Coping skills
- Infection control precautions (p. 21)

Davis (1992) addresses eight functional domains needed for a music therapy assessment for clients with mental disorders:

- Medical, including the client's diagnosis and past and present health status
- Cognitive, including comprehension, attention span, memory ability, and problem-solving skills
- Social, including self-expression, self-control, and quality and quantity of interactions
- Physical, including range of motion, gross and fine motor skills, motor coordination, strength and endurance, and stereotypical physical mannerisms
- Vocational/educational including work skills
- Emotional, including appropriateness of affect, emotional responses, emotional intelligence, ability to express self, and verbalization
- Communication, including expressive and receptive language and nonverbal communication
- Leisure skills, including recreational interests (pp. 289–290)

Cassity and Cassity (1994) address five functional domains for a music therapy assessment:

- Interpersonal/socialization especially withdrawal behavior, poor leisure skill, and uncooperative behavior
- Affect with special notice of inability to identify or express feelings toward others
- Cognitive abilities, including low self-esteem, poor problem solving, memory difficulties, and disorientation
- Behavior, including attention problems and poor eye contact
- Physical, including motor coordination and speech and language difficulties

Codding (2002) identifies four areas of nonmusical functioning needed for a music therapy assessment:

- Physical/motor
- Cognitive/academic
- Social/emotional
- Play/leisure

Chase (2002) identifies five nonmusical functioning domains that should be addressed for a music therapy assessment:

- Motor domain with subareas
  1. gross motor, including locomotor ability, nonlocomotor movement (movement of torso and upper body), and balance

2. fine motor involving finger skills, grasp, and grip strength

3. perceptual-motor abilities, including eye-hand coordination, the ability to target motor response based on visual or auditory input (e.g., hitting a drumhead or strumming a guitar)

4. psychomotor skills, including rhythmic movement response to music

- Communication domain with subareas

    1. speech and vocal characteristics, including expressive and receptive language, articulation, phonation (loudness and pitch level, voice quality, rate of speech, and unusual or stereotypical language)

    2. nonverbal communication, including body language, gestures, facial expressions, nonverbal vocalizations, and use of sign language

- Cognitive domain with subareas

    1. comprehension of words, language, song lyrics

    2. body awareness, including appropriate use of the body for expression

    3. laterality and directionality, including use of a dominant hand, knowledge of directions, and body position in space

    4. visual perception, including distortions and misperceptions, perception and discrimination, and hyper- or hyposensitivity

    5. auditory perception, including recognition of sound sources, perception and discrimination, distortions, hyper- or hyposensitivity

- Affective domain with subareas

    1. facial expression, including appropriate expressions and use of facial expression

    2. range of affect, including affective style (labile, blunted, flat, etc.)

    3. appropriate emotional responses, including over or under reaction and congruence of expression and content

- Social domain with subareas

    1. awareness of self, others, and the environment

    2. interactions and interpersonal relationships, including ability to appropriately interact with peers and authority figures

    3. ability to participate in groups (Chase, 2002, pp. 21-22)

Music therapists (Adelman, 1985; Cassity & Cassity, 1995) have addressed a specific form of treatment for individuals with mental disorders, Multimodal Behavior Therapy. This approach requires assessment and treatment in seven specific areas:

- Behavior
- Affect
- Sensorium, including sensory impression and perceptions
- Imagery as internal representations of self and world, including self-image and body-image
- Cognition as client's cognitive structure and internal "scripts" concerning self;
- Interpersonal relations
- Substance use

For a complete overview of this approach in music therapy practice and assessment, see Cassity and Cassity (1995), *Multimodal Psychiatric Music Therapy of Adults, Adolescents, and Children: A Clinical Manual.*

Other professionals from a number of disciplines often assess these nonmusical domains of functioning. The question often arises, "Why does the music therapist need to assess these aspects of functioning?" A number of writers contend that there are a number of reasons a music therapy assessment should be done to assess these functional domains (Bruscia, 1987; Pavlicevic, 1995; Wigram, 1999). First, music is basic human behavior, and clients often react differently in musical situations because of music's attractiveness. The symbolic and nonverbal nature of music adds valuable information to the overall assessment. Second, the music therapy assessment allows the therapist to see the client from a different and important perspective. Third, a music therapy assessment allows the therapist to observe the client's response to auditory yet nonverbal stimuli. Fourth, client responses to music reveal healthy or unhealthy social and emotional behavior. The music therapy assessment gives the client a multisensory awareness not possible in other forms of assessment (Bruscia, 1988; Michel & Rohrbacher, 1982; Wilson, 2002). Bruscia (1987) outlines the specific ways in which a music therapy assessment can assess the intricacies of the client's social functioning. Information about the client is revealed intramusically (within the music produced by the client), intrapersonally (within the client's personality or between the client and his music), intermusically (between the client's music and the music of others), and interpersonally (between the client and other people). The music therapy assessment supplements information from other professional reports with questions or tasks specific to the music therapy process (Davis, 1992).

Music as a Domain of Functioning for Assessment

As specified in the AMTA *Standards of Clinical Practice* (2004), musical response and behavior is an important domain of functioning for a music therapy assessment. The music therapy assessment, "will also determine the client's responses to music, music skills, and musical preferences" (AMTA, 2004, p. 18). Chase (2002) elaborates on these areas of musical assessment breaking them down into four subareas:

- Vocal, including tone matching; ability to hold tonal center; singing, humming, or chanting on pitch; singing words; and duplicating whole melodies
- Percussion/rhythm, including accurately duplicating rhythm patterns from auditory and visual stimuli, identifying changes in rhythms, ability to hear and duplicate tempo changes, and ability to appropriately use rhythm instruments
- Preference, including client's musical choices; genre preference; preferences of musical styles, instruments, and sound; and overall response to music
- Music perception, including discrimination of melodic and rhythmic patterns, timbre, dynamics, and harmonic structure (p. 22)

Cassity and Cassity (1994) add assessment of ability to play musical instruments, locomotor and nonlocomotor movement to music, and ability and willingness to improvise both vocally and instrumentally. Musical background and training and experiences with music and music making are also mentioned as important to the music therapy assessment (Codding, 2002; Davis, 1992). Cassity and Cassity (1994) detail a number of music activities or experiences that can be used to assess musical skills and interests of clients. These include listening to music with discussion, instrumental and vocal improvisation, music composition and songwriting, instrumental and vocal performance, interpretive drawing to music, musical games, and structured and creative movement to music.

The Assessment Process

An assessment *process* for music therapy for clients with mental disorders can and should involve a number of methods—informal, formal, and standardized (Chase, 2002). An informal music therapy assessment process does not have written accountability. A formal music therapy assessment process is a systematic process, which is administered in a similar manner each time it is used and measures designated areas of skill, response, or behavior. A standardized assessment is usually a test that has been scientifically verified through research and that can be used by various music therapists with similar results (Chase, 2002, pp. 9–10). Informal and formal methods of music therapy assessment are most commonly used for clients with mental disorders since few specific assessment tools in this area exist in music therapy (Layman et al., 2002). The following is a summary of the most common methods of assessment in music therapy practice.

Interviews with Clients and/or Family Members

Interviewing the client and possibly family members is the most common form of assessment in music therapy for clients with mental disorders (Wilson, 2002). An interview is used to determine the client's musical taste and preference, musical skills and background, general interests, perception of problems, and stress inducers. Interviews can be unstructured or structured. In an unstructured interview, an informal means of assessment, the therapist engages the client in a general discussion about issues, concerns, interests, and preferences. Formal or structured interviews with predetermined questions provide more consistency of information from client to client. An assessment interview can be conducted orally or a written questionnaire might be used (Wilson, 2002). Musical preferences can also be determined using a music rating scale. Usually a written form is created containing a continuum rating scale ("strongly dislike" through "strongly like"). Short musical excerpts from a variety of musical genres are played, and the client marks his or her response to each example on the rating sheet.

Observation of Client

Observations of clients can be naturalistic or structured and used both as formal or informal means of assessment. During naturalistic observations, the music therapist observes the client in a natural setting or during the course of a normal day's activities. Such observations can be done while the client is on the unit, during recreational activities, at meals, and in other therapy situations. The music therapist would be observing the client's behavior, emotional responses, interactions with others, coping skills, and motor response, behavior, and ability (Bruscia, 1988). A structured or contrived observation involves conducting a music therapy session with specific activities and tasks to be observed (Wilson, 2002). Various music therapy interventions are used for structured observations, including free instrumental improvisation, singing, movement to music, songwriting/lyric composition, playing rhythm instruments/drums, imagery to music, and exploration of musical instruments, particularly electronic instruments (Cassity & Theobold, 1990). This use of "assessment sessions" in music therapy is a common practice (Jensen, 1999; Stige,

1999). A structured assessment through observation can be more specified using a behavioral checklist (Bitcon, 2000). This is a predetermined list of behaviors that the music therapist would look for during an observation opportunity (Davis, 1992).

Reviewing Client Records

An important part of client assessment is gathering information from the client's records and other forms of existing information. A large percentage of information needed for client assessment is found in these records (Wilson, 2002). The client records contain reports from other professionals, the results of standardized tests, medical and social history, the admission summary, diagnosis designation, presenting problems, initial recommendations, possible goals, and an overall treatment plan for the client. Of particular interest to the music therapist are the reports from the psychologist/psychiatrist, social worker, occupational therapist, and nursing staff.

Standardized Assessment Tests

A standardized assessment test is used to compare the client's response to the responses of others. To be a standardized assessment tool, the administration procedure, the collection of data, the test items, and the scoring standards must be specified in writing (Wilson, 2002). A true standardized test must be given to a large number of subjects and the results verified through statistical analysis for reliability and validity. Such a test measurement can be used by other music therapists with similar results (Chase, 2002). There are three groups of assessment tests used by music therapists for clients with mental disorders: existing standardized psychological tests, projective music tests, and standardized music therapy assessment tests.

Standardized psychological tests. Wilson (2002) notes that music therapists often use three types of standardized psychological tests:

- Psychological inventory, e.g., The Minnesota Multiphasic Personality Inventory
- Projective test, e.g., Rorschach Test
- Intelligence test, e.g., Wechsler Adult Intelligence Scale (p. 158)

These tests have some limited usefulness since they are not grounded in a music environment.

Gregory (2000) reviewed the *Journal of Music Therapy* to determine what standardized general psychological assessment tests were used by music therapists and reported in *Journal* articles. She finds that the following assessment tests are reported:

- Vineland Social Maturity Scale
- Hamilton Rating Scale for Depression
- Snyder Self-Monitoring Scale
- Valecha and Ostrom Abbreviated Internal/External Locus of Control Scale
- Overall Gorham Brief Psychiatric Rating Scale
- Yalom Group Cohesiveness Scale
- Myers Emotional Disturbance Scale

A great number of standardized psychological tests are available and should be considered by the music therapist as part of his or her assessment process. Many of these tests, however, require specialized training to administer, so that the information may best be obtained from reading the psychologist/ psychiatrist's report of test results.

Projective music tests. There was early interest in the use of a music assessment test to determine clients' personality characteristics, personal issues, and emotional states by "projecting" these onto musical response or product (Crocker, 1956). Early interest in this form of assessment was reported in music therapy publications (Grimmett, 1952; Hahn, 1952; Reinke, 1956) and in psychological journals (Cattell & Anderson, 1953; Cattell & McMichael, 1960; Cattell & Saunders, 1954). Though early results varied and research often failed to duplicate results, interest in projective music tests continued (Greenberg & Fischer, 1971; Healey, 1973; McFarland, 1984; Stein, 1977; Steinberg & Raith, 1985). Currently, the most common use of projective music tests is utilized in improvisatory music therapy (Bruscia, 1987; Pavlicevic, 1995; Pavlicevic & Trevarthen, 1989). (See section on improvisation in Chapter 5 for more detailed information.)

Standardized music therapy assessment tests. There is little research on music therapy assessment tests for clients with mental disorders and few published standardized tests (Cassity & Cassity, 1994). The published, formal music therapy assessment tests for adults, adolescents, and children include the following:

- Music/Activity Therapy Intake Assessment (Braswell et al., 1983, 1986). This is an activity therapy assessment based on Joint Commission requirements for assessing patient needs, interest, life experience, and capacities and deficiencies. It is an interview-based assessment with set questions.
- Improvisational Assessment Profile (Bruscia, 1987). This assessment provides for the "clinical observation, musical analysis, and psychological interpretation of the client's improvisation" (p. 403).
- Music Therapy Assessment for Disturbed Adolescents (Wells, 1988). This test involves clients in three musical tasks—select a song, compose a written story to background music, and instrumental improvisation—to determine specific behavior. It is a designated observation during participation in an activity.
- Psychiatric Music Therapy Questionnaire (Cassity & Cassity, 1995). This is a behavioral interview questionnaire based on multimodal behavioral categories (Adelman, 1985).
- Music Interaction Rating for Schizophrenics (Pavlicevic & Trevarthen, 1989).
- Hamilton Rating Scale for Depression and Rhythmic Competency (Migliore, 1991).
- Music Therapy Effects Scale (Thaut, 1989),
- Patient Evaluation of Treatment (Heaney, 1992),
- Music Psychotherapy Assessment (Loewy, 2000). This involves assessment in 13 areas of inquiry involving structured and improvisatory musical experiences to establish a therapeutic relationship and assess the areas of functioning specified (Chase, 2002).

The Assessment Report

Once the assessment process is completed, the music therapist needs to report his or her findings. The information gathered during informal and formal assessment activities is often reported in narrative descriptions or report form. Transferable language should be used so that other professionals can read and understand the information. Music-specific language, terms, and responses need to be described or defined (Layman et al., 2002). Questionnaires, behavioral checklists, and rating scales may be included directly into the report.

Determining the Assessment Process

Music therapist need to select or create an assessment process for themselves based on a number of factors:

- The client population and overall responses
- The area of functioning to be assessed
- The treatment model within which the music therapy will be conducted (e.g., behavioral, cognitive, etc.)
- The technique, format, or tests used to accomplish the assessment
- The needs, requirements, or constraints of the institution or setting where the assessment will be conducted (Chase, 2002; Isenberg-Grzeda, 1988)

When designing an assessment for clients with mental disorders, music therapists may ask themselves a number of questions to focus their process:

- What do I want to know?
- What areas of client functioning do I want/need to assess?
- What constraints will client functioning and/or disability put on the assessment process?
- What areas of assessment are unique to music therapy? to the setting? to the particular client?
- How does a music-based assessment add important/unusual information to the client's overall assessment?
- What theoretical orientation or therapeutic model shapes this assessment?
- How does predominance of music therapy intervention or approach (GIM, improvisation, etc.) shape the assessment process?
- What are the means for gathering the information? What forms of assessment will be utilized?
- How will this information be used to determine client goals/objectives, activity interventions, and therapeutic approaches?
- How will ongoing evaluations be accomplished?

Goals for Music Therapy for Individuals with Mental Disorders

The assessment information gathered is used to set the long-term goals (treatment outcomes) and short-term objectives or behavioral objectives for the client. A behavioral objective is a specific statement of treatment outcomes to be achieved at specific times or under specific circumstances in therapy. All goals are highly individualized, based on the strengths, weaknesses, abilities, and needs of the client as determined by the assessment. A goal is a statement of what the client will know, be able to do, verbalize, perform, or look like after the music therapy intervention is completed.

> *Goals or therapeutic outcomes are descriptions of what the client or group of clients will know and be able to do after therapeutic intervention, and represent a standard for judging whether the goal(s) has been achieved and when the termination of treatment is appropriate. (Wolfe & O'Connell, 1999, p. 38)*

Specific goals for various clients and client groups are addressed in subsequent sections. Generally, typical long-term goals for individuals with mental disorders may include, but are not limited to:

- increase tolerance for instruction;
- increase attention-span and attention to task;
- improve self-esteem, self-concept, and self-awareness;
- improved reality orientation (responding to, recognizing, and discrimination of sensory input);
- improve reality testing;
- facilitate behavior change—decrease inappropriate behavior, increase appropriate behavior;
- learn and practice new patterns of behavior and response;
- improve body-image and body-awareness;
- improve verbal and nonverbal communication skills;
- promote emotional awareness and release and expression of emotion;
- improve social skills, social behavior, and group behavior;
- re-establish healthy functioning and coping skills;
- uncover repressed memories and emotions;
- promote emotional catharsis;
- develop personal insight and awareness of personal issues;
- develop cognitive and coping strategies;
- develop behavioral and impulse control;
- improve interpersonal relationships;
- increase relaxation and deal appropriately with stress and anxiety (Adelman, 1985; Peters, 2000).

References

Adelman, E. J. (1985). Multimodal therapy and music therapy: Assessing and treating the whole person. Music Therapy, 5(1), 12–21.

American Music Therapy Association (AMTA). (2004). Standards of clinical practice. In A. Elkins (Ed.), AMTA member sourcebook (pp. 18–22). Silver Spring, MD: Author.

Bitcon, C. (2000). Alike and different (2nd ed). Gilsum, NH: Barcelona Publishers.

Braswell, C., Brooks, D., Decuir, A., Humphreys, T., Jacobs, K., & Smith, K. (1983). Development and implementation of a music/activity therapy intake assessment for psychiatric clients. Part I: Initial standardization procedures in data from university students. Journal of Music Therapy, 20(2), 88–100.

Braswell, C., Brooks, D., Decuir, A., Humphreys, T., Jacobs, K., & Smith, K. (1986). Development and implementation of a music/activity therapy intake assessment for psychiatric patients. Part II: Standardization procedures in data from psychiatric patients. Journal of Music Therapy, 23(3), 126–141.

Bruscia, K. E. (1987). Improvisational models of music therapy. Springfield, IL: Charles C. Thomas.

Bruscia, K. E. (1988). Standards for clinical assessment in the arts therapies. The Arts in Psychotherapy, 15(1), 5–10.

Cassity, M. D., & Cassity, J. E. (1994). Psychiatric music therapy assessment and treatment in clinical training facilities with adults, adolescents, and children. Journal of Music Therapy, 31(1), 2–30.

Cassity, M. D., & Cassity, J. E. (1995). Multimodal psychiatric music therapy of adults, adolescents, and children: A clinical manual (2nd ed.). St Louis, MO: MMB Music.

Cassity, M. D., & Theobold, K. A. K. (1990). Domestic violence: Assessment and treatments employed by music therapy. Journal of Music Therapy, 27(4), 179–194.

Cattell, R. B., & Anderson, J. C. (1953). The measurement of personality and behavioral disorders by the IPAT music preference test. Journal of Applied Psychology, 37, 446–454.

Cattell, R. B., & McMichael, R. E. (1960). Clinical diagnosis by the IPAT music preference test. Journal of Consulting Psychology, 24, 333–341.

Cattell, R. B., & Saunders, D. (1954). Musical preferences and personality diagnosis: A factorization of one hundred and twenty themes. Journal of Social Psychology, 39, 3–24.

Chase, K. M. (2002). The music therapy assessment handbook. Columbia, MS: Southern Pen Publishing (www.southernpen.com).

Codding, P. A. (2002). A comprehensive survey of music therapists practicing in correctional psychiatry: Demographics, conditions of employment, service provision, assessment, therapeutic objectives, and related values of the therapist. Music Therapy Perspectives, 20(2), 56–68.

Cohen, G., Averbach, J., & Katz, E. (1978). Music therapy assessment of the developmentally disabled client. Journal of Music Therapy, 15(2), 88–99.

Cohen, G., & Gericke, O. L. (1972). Music therapy assessment: Prime requisite for determining patient objectives. Journal of Music Therapy, 9(4), 161–189.

Crocker, D. B. (1956). Music as a projective technique. In E. T. Gaston (Ed.), Music therapy 1955 (pp. 86–97). Lawrence, KS: National Association for Music Therapy.

Davis, W. B. (1992). The music therapy treatment process. In W. B. Davis, K. E. Gfeller, & M. H. Thaut (Eds.), An introduction to music therapy theory and practice (pp. 287–301). Dubuque, IA: Wm C. Brown.

Greenberg, R., & Fischer, S. (1971). Some differential effects of music in projective and structured psychological tests. Psychological Reports, 28, 817–818.

Gregory, D. (2000). Test instruments used by Journal of Music Therapy authors from 1984–1997. Journal of Music Therapy, 37(2), 79–94.

Grimmett, J. O. (1952). Personality diagnosis through music—An apperceptive dynamic approach to personality diagnosis. Bulletin of NAMT, 1(2), 9–10.

Hahn, M. E. (1952). A proposed technique for investigating the relationship between personality structure and musical preference. Bulletin of NAMT, 1(2), 10.

Healey, B. (1973). Pilot study in the applicability of the music preference test of personality. Journal of Music Therapy, 10(1), 36–45.

Heaney, C. J. (1992). Evaluation of music therapy and other treatment modalities by adult psychiatric inpatients. Journal of Music Therapy, 29(2), 70–86.

Isenberg-Grzeda, C. (1988). Music therapy assessment: A reflection of professional identity. Journal of Music Therapy, 25(3), 156–169.

Jensen, B. (1999). Music therapy with psychiatric in-patients: A case study with a young schizophrenic man. In T. Wigram & J. DeBacker (Eds.), Clinical applications of music therapy in psychiatry (pp. 44–60). London: Jessica Kingsley.

Layman, D. L., Hussey, D. L., & Laing, S. J. (2002). Music therapy assessment for severely emotionally disturbed children: A pilot study. Journal of Music Therapy, 39(3), 11–19.

Loewy, J. (2000). Music psychotherapy assessment. Music Therapy Perspectives, 18(1), 47–58.

McFarland, R. A. (1984). Effects of music upon emotional content of TAT stories. Journal of Psychology, 166, 227–234.

Michel, D. E., & Rohrbacher, M. (Eds.). (1982). The music therapy assessment profile for severely/profoundly handicapped persons, research draft III (0–27 month level). Denton, TX: Texas Woman's University.

Migliore, M. J. (1991). The Hamilton Rating Scale for Depression and Rhythmic Competency: A correlational study. Journal of Music Therapy, 28(4), 211–221.

Pavlicevic, M. (1995). Growing into sound and soundmaking into growth: Improvisation groups with adults. The Arts in Psychotherapy, 22(4), 359–367.

Pavlicevic, M., & Trevarthen, C. (1989). A musical assessment of psychiatric states in adults. Psychopathology, 22, 325–334.

Peters, J. S. (2000). Music therapy: An introduction (2nd ed.). Springfield, IL: Charles C. Thomas.

Reinke, J. H. (1956). The use of unfamiliar music as stimulus for a projective test of personality. In E. T. Gaston (Ed.), Music Therapy 1955 (pp. 224–230). Lawrence, KS: Allen Press.

Stein, J. (1977). Tempo errors and mania. American Journal of Psychiatry, 134(4), 454–456.

Steinberg, R., & Raith, L. (1985). Music psychopathology: Musical tempo and psychiatric disease. Psychopathology, 18, 274–285.

Stige, B. (1999). The meaning of music: From the client's perspective. In T. Wigram & J. DeBacker (Eds.), Clinical applications of music therapy in psychiatry (pp. 61–83). London: Jessica Kingsley.

Thaut, M. H. (1989). The influence of music therapy interventions on self-rated changes in relaxation, affect, and thought in psychiatric prisoner-patients. Journal of Music Therapy, 26(3), 155–166.

Wells, N. F. (1988). An individual music therapy assessment procedure for emotionally disturbed young adolescents. The Arts in Psychotherapy, 15(1), 47–54.

Wigram, T. (1999). Assessment methods in music therapy. A humanistic or natural science framework? Nordic Journal of Music Therapy, 8(1), 7–25.

Wilson, B. L. (2002). Assessment of adult psychiatric clients: The role of music therapy. In R. F. Unkefer (Ed.), Music therapy in the treatment of adults with mental disorders (pp. 155–180). St. Louis, MO: MMB Music.

Wolfe, D. E., & O'Connell, A. (1999). Specifying and recording treatment objectives within a group music therapy setting. Music Therapy Perspectives, 17(1), 37–41.

Section 2:

Treatment Interventions

CHAPTER 3

Music Therapy Interventions for Individuals with Mental Disorders: An Overview
Barbara J. Crowe and Roberta Wigle Justice

There have been several attempts to organize the various music therapy activity interventions utilized for clients with mental disorders. The one cited most frequently is the Wheeler Psychotherapeutic Classifications of Music Therapy Practices (1983).

Wheeler's Psychotherapeutic Classification of Music Therapy Practices

Wheeler (1983) suggests an organization of the music therapy interventions for individuals with mental disorders based on a continuum of procedures to meet the various need levels of patients in psychiatry. Based on the work of Wolberg (1977), she divides interventions into three categories: music therapy as an activity therapy, insight music therapy with re-educative goals, and insight music therapy with re-constructive goals.

Supportive, Activity-Oriented Music Therapy

The first level is labeled supportive, activity-oriented music therapy. At this level, music therapy experiences are generally success-oriented, structured, and socializing in nature. In these interventions, goals are achieved as a direct result of participation in the activity, not on personal insight gained because of that participation. The therapeutic focus is on the here and now—reactions, behaviors, skills.

> *The activities are aimed at strengthening defenses, developing appropriate mechanisms of behavior control, supporting healthy feelings and thoughts, breaking social isolation, providing safe, reassuring reality stimulation, exposing the patient to the influence of basic group dynamics, and diverting the patient from possible neurotic concerns.* (Unkefer & Thaut, 2002, p. 182)

Why a behavior occurs is not important (Wheeler, 1983). According to Lord (1971), the goals achieved in music therapy as activity therapy include

- increase tolerance of instruction;
- decrease avoidance behavior when in a new or challenging activity;
- learn how to achieve success in long-term projects;

- increase attention span and concentration skills;
- develop realistic view of self;
- increase self-esteem;
- decrease inappropriate behaviors;
- increase tolerance of authority figures;
- decrease avoidance behavior in social situations;
- increase awareness, acceptance, and responsibility to other's feelings;
- develop skills in dealing with emotion;
- develop knowledge of ways to avoid social withdrawal.

Interventions on this level of therapy are structured so that the client can "practice" new patterns of behavior and response. The overall emphasis is on developing new coping skills, improving self-confidence, and learning more adaptive responses to emotions rather than on developing personal insight as to the *cause* of the problem. This approach corresponds to the Experiences in Structure in the Sears' music therapy theory continuum (Sears, 1968) and can be considered product-oriented music therapy interventions (Crowe, 2004).

The music therapist's role in these interventions is to establish a positive, fairly directive relationship with the client. The music therapist creates or structures the session to meet the physical, social, cognitive, and emotional functioning level of the client. Hadsell (1993) outlines the elements of external structure (those elements of the environment that are controlled by the therapist) as follows:

- The music, including what music to use, the amount of intrinsic structure provided by beat and rhythm, client familiarity and preference, and presence of other musical elements like timbre, mode, tempo, form
- Time, including session scheduling, session pacing, and amount of time for each intervention
- Space/equipment, including room arrangement, equipment needed, and organization of furniture and equipment placement
- Amount of client decision making, including degree of control maintained by therapist and degree of client input or choice
- Materials used, including age and ability appropriateness, musical preference, and social acceptability
- Direction giving/instructions, including amount of verbal directions, physical modeling, and the form of the directions
- Activity intervention chosen, including choice in type and variety of activities, task analysis of component skills, and sequence of instruction
- Reinforcement, including type used (verbal, tangible, or physical)

Each structural element can be implemented at one of three levels—maximum, where the client has no input; moderate, where the client has some options and limited decision making; and minimum, where the client has autonomy. Examples of music therapy interventions at this level include group singing, drumming experiences, and performance/skill building. Clients best served at this level include people in temporary crisis; those dealing with severe anxiety; individuals with chronic, severe mental disorders like schizophrenia, organic syndromes, or affective disorders; and those dealing with regression and delusions.

Insight Music Therapy With Re-Educative Goals

The second level in Wheeler's hierarchy is labeled re-educative, insight and process-oriented music therapy. According to Wheeler (1983), in insight music therapy with re-educative goals the music elicits emotions or reactions directly related to the therapeutic outcome. Verbal interaction between client and therapist is increased and plays an increasingly important role in the overall therapy achieved. In insight music therapy with re-educative goals, the insights are close to consciousness and are elicited through attention to the present reactions, including personal feelings and interpersonal interactions. Maladaptive behavior may be challenged and new, adaptive patterns of thought, reaction, and behavior learned and practiced during the music therapy activity intervention. "The re-educative therapy experience is aimed at helping the patient reorganize his values and behavioral patterns, acquire new tension- and anxiety-relieving interpersonal attitudes, and, through projection of personal thoughts and feelings in the therapy process, learn to assume responsibility for them" (Unkefer & Thaut, 2002, p. 183). The ability of music to elicit strong, deep emotions is important. In this approach, the music is used to stimulate verbalizations with insight developing through discussion. This approach corresponds to the Sears' Experiences in Self-Organization and Experiences in Relating to Others (Sears, 1968). Music therapists using this approach need the ability to listen empathetically and must have good verbal responding skills (Nolan, 2005). They also need skills in choosing the music for sessions that evoke emotions, images, memories, and reactions. Examples of this level of music therapy include lyric analysis, group therapy experiences (Plach, 1980), and music and storytelling (Borczon, 1997) and can be considered process-oriented music therapy activity interventions (Crowe, 2004).

Insight Music Therapy With Re-Constructive Goals

The third level in the hierarchy is labeled reconstructive, analytical and catharsis- oriented music therapy. In this level, music therapy experiences are used to uncover, relive, or resolve subconscious conflicts. This level of music therapy intervention uses music to elicit that unconscious material, which is, "then worked within an effort to promote reorganization of the personality" (Wheeler, 1983, p. 11). The emotions and images produced relate to present situations or to repressed memories and emotions from past events. The goal is to re-experience and work through past situations that were not processed or resolved completely. "One goal is to achieve insight into how individuals became the way they are" (Wheeler, 1983, p. 11). The music is a critical component in bringing up and expressing the repressed material. The music therapist using interventions on this level needs advanced training in therapeutic techniques and a deep familiarity with the music used as an intervention. Examples of this level of music therapy include The Bonny Method of Guided Imagery and Music (Bonny & Savary, 1990) and Analytical Music Therapy (Priestley, 1975). (See Wheeler's Levels of Music Therapy Experiences found in Figure 3.1.)

Appropriate level of music therapy experiences match the internal needs of the clients, whether inpatient or outpatient. The more internally disorganized an individual is at any given time, the more externally focused an experience needs to be (Priestley, 1975). As an individual's level of internal organization improves, more internally focused music therapy experiences can be helpful. Thus, a person with an illness that has psychotic episodes may need music therapy experiences with a great deal of external structure during those episodes, but may be able to make use of more cognitive or insight oriented music therapy approaches as the symptoms decrease.

WHEELER'S LEVELS OF MUSIC THERAPY EXPERIENCES		
Supportive, activity-oriented music therapy	Re-educative, insight and process-oriented music therapy	Re-constructive, analytically and catharsis-oriented music therapy

Level of Self-Organization of the Client

Extremely Disorganized	Delusional	Confused	Stressed	Fully Organized
External Focus Needed	↔ ↔ ↔		↔	Internal Focus Appropriate

DSM-IV Diagnostic Categories

Active psychosis: Schizophrenia/Mania Brief psychotic episodes (depression, personality disorders)	Depressive disorders Delusional disorders Anxiety disorders Personality disorders	Other mood disorders Anxiety disorders Personality disorders Situational stress

Philosophical Orientations to Psychiatric Treatment

Behavioral Biomedical	Cognitive Cognitive-Behavioral	Humanistic Psychodynamic

Figure 3.1. "Wheeler's Levels of Music Therapy Experiences" (chart by Roberta Wigle Justice).

Unkefer and Thaut (2002) refined this organization somewhat by incorporating Wheeler's (1983) work with the levels of inpatient group therapy developed by Yalom (1983) to create their "taxonomy" of clinical music therapy. Taxonomy is a system of classification of information. Unkefer and Thaut took two prominent systems of organizing approaches or levels of therapy in psychodyanmic work to systematically address various music therapy interventions for specific adult clients with mental disorders. Wheeler's classification of music therapy practices was addressed previously. The work of Yalom delineated the steps of group process and the levels of personal insight possible with clients holding various psychiatric diagnoses. The combination of the pioneering work of these two individuals helped Unkefer and Thaut create a highly specific and complete organization of music therapy interventions for all the diagnoses for adults with mental disorders (pp. 210–247). This taxonomy is an excellent resource for music therapists working with these clients.

References

Bonny, H. L., & Savary, L. M. (1990). Music and your mind (2nd ed.). Barrytown, NY: Station Hill Press.

Borczon, R. (1997). Music therapy group vignettes. Gilsum, NH: Barcelona.

Crowe, B. J. (2004). Music and soulmaking: Toward a new theory of music therapy. Lanham, MD: Scarecrow Press.

Hadsell, N. A. (1993). Levels of external structure in music therapy. Music Therapy Perspectives, 11(2), 61–65.

Lord, W. (1971). Communication of activity therapy rationale. Journal of Music Therapy, 8(2), 68–71.

Nolan, P. (2005). Verbal processing in the music therapy relationship. Music Therapy Perspectives, Special Issue: The Role of the Music Therapist in Music Therapy Process, 23, 18–23.

Plach, T. (1980). The creative use of music in group therapy. Springfield, IL: Charles C. Thomas.

Priestley, M. (1975). Music therapy in action. New York: St. Martin's Press.

Sears, W. (1968). Processes in music therapy. In E. T. Gaston (Ed.), Music in therapy (pp. 30–46). New York: Macmillan.

Unkefer, R. F., & Thaut, M. H. (Eds.). (2002). Music therapy in the treatment of adults with mental disorders: Theoretical bases and clinical interventions (2nd ed.). St. Louis, MO: MMB Music.

Wheeler, B. L. (1983). A psychotherapeutic classification of music therapy practices: A continuum of procedure. Music Therapy Perspectives, 1, 8–16.

Wolberg, L. R. (1977). The technique of psychotherapy (3rd ed.). New York: Grune & Stratton.

Yalom, I. D. (1983). Inpatient group psychotherapy. New York: Basic Books.

CHAPTER 4

Supportive, Activity-Oriented Music Therapy: An Overview
Barbara J. Crowe

Specific music therapy interventions are included in the three areas of Wheeler's (1983) classifications: supportive, activity-oriented interventions; insight music therapy with re-educative goals; and insight music therapy with re-constructive goals. These classifications are described in detail in Chapter 3.

The following activity interventions are product-oriented and are useful for clients with severe forms of mental disorder, such as psychotic disorders.

Musical Instruction

In musical instruction activities, clients learn new musical skills or strengthen existing skills. Musical instruction can be instrumental or vocal and can be conducted either individually or in a small group setting. The music therapist conducts a thorough task analysis of all skills and knowledge needed by the client to learn the playing skill and then structures successive learning tasks emphasizing successful experiences, personal satisfaction, and pleasure for the client. Instruction on voice or any musical instrument is based on client interest and previous instruction and skill level. Instruments that are useful for this intervention include guitar, electric guitar, bass guitar, drum set, African drums/conga drum, piano, electric keyboard/organ, recorder, and harmonica. The goals achieved with this intervention include improved communication, increased frustration tolerance, ego support, and improved musical and interpersonal skills (Unkefer, 1990).

Musical Performance Ensembles

In this intervention, clients play in small ensemble groups using existing or newly acquired music skills. Typical ensembles include performance of a specific genre of music—rock and roll, jazz, blues, country western, Tejano, salsa, Zydeco, hip hop, etc.—and specific ensembles—handbell/tone chime choirs, vocal choirs, etc. Goals for this intervention include learning social skills, exercising responsibility, subordinating personal needs to the needs of the group, following instructions, accepting feedback and criticism, and personal satisfaction and self-esteem from the musical performance. These experiences can lead to community performance as a music therapy intervention. (See section on performance with clients with substance abuse issues in Chapter 10.)

Structured Movement to Music

Structured movement interventions include structured dance (folk and ethnic dancing; popular dancing like waltz, tango, disco, salsa), exercise to music, and structured/rhythmic mirroring to music. Initial experiences should include movement awareness, where the clients express themselves through movement to various rhythm patterns and beat forms; mirroring therapist's movements; and exploring spontaneous movement. Emphasis should be on line dances, circle activities, and individual movement in a group setting. These interventions promote the goals of body awareness, awareness of nonverbal expression of emotions, body usage and coordination, and physical health and stamina.

Group Singing

Group singing can be a form of sing-a-long of familiar songs or true vocal ensembles where vocal skill building is emphasized. These interventions start with songs familiar to the clients, using songbooks to ensure a successful experience, and providing appropriate accompaniment. Songs popular from when the clients were in their teens and early 20s are often used. Unison singing is emphasized and part singing through rounds and partner songs (two different pentatonic songs that can be sung together) is implemented later. Goals achieved with this intervention include group participation, improved social skills, improved physical health through deep breathing, increased attention span and frustration tolerance, and improved self-esteem.

Musical Composition

In this intervention, clients create original music. This can be done through improvisation on Orff instruments or electric keyboards (see section on improvisation in Chapter 5), using computer and computer programs to facilitate the process, or based on a particular form or style of music. Musical terms can be used to focus and structure a composition.

Use of Technology

These interventions emphasize the use of technological devices to facilitate musical performance, composition and songwriting, and musical expression. Useful devices include electric keyboards, drum machines, karaoke machines, sound generating devices like the Midi Creator, microphones with amplifiers, recording technology, and computers and computer programs for sound editing, music writing, and recording (Crowe & Rio, 2004).

Rhythmic Activities

Structured rhythmic activities can include use of hand percussion to accompany songs or for simple rhythmic ensembles, use of Orff chants to direct listening and echoing activities (Bitcon, 2000), use of written charts for playing, and the use of rhythmic ostinato. A version of rhythm band can be used if structured to be age appropriate and emphasizing high musical quality. Rhythm instruments used must be adult-appropriate and of orchestral quality. Rhythm instruments from world music traditions can be useful in bringing a variety of timbres to the experiences. Goals fostered by these interventions include reality orientation, attention to task, energy release and sublimation of emotions, and nonverbal expression of feelings. (See also the section on rhythmic improvisation in this Chapter 5.)

SPECIFIC TECHNIQUES
Drumming Group Experiences
Kirsten A. Peterson

For most people talking comes easily. Making pleasant conversation about the weather or the game last night with someone standing in line at the grocery store is something many people take for granted. We go about our day-to-day lives chatting with people who cross our paths and then we go along our merry way. However, for many people with a mental disorder, conversations do not come easily. People diagnosed with a severe mental disorder like schizophrenia at times have great difficulty with simple conversation. Music therapy provides a means for the patients to express themselves nonverbally. The basic form of this expression is rhythm and, in particular, drumming.

The popularity of the drum circle is increasing in the field of music therapy. For centuries, drumming has been used for rituals, celebrations, and communication. Although rhythm has always existed in the area of healing, new research is just beginning to help us understand why rhythm is a key element to mental health. A basic reason rhythm/drumming contributes to treatment for mental disorders is that rhythm is with us all the time. It is part of our internal body processes—in our heart, blood circulation, and respiration. It is in our gross motor movement—in our feet and in our toes when we hear a song we like. "Rhythm is what keeps you alive," according to Mickey Hart, and "true rhythm dorks are rare" (Hull, 1998, p. 93).

In its most basic form, the drum makes a sound the moment you strike the head. Whether you use a mallet, a stick, or your hand, you have instant sound, instant gratification. The client with a mental disorder, including severely impaired (especially psychotic conditions), does not have to concentrate on playing the right note or using correct technique. They can just focus on the simplicity of striking the drum. It is a form of active participation that is immediately available to any client.

Drumming Groups for Clients With Mental Disorders

Three types of drumming groups are typically useful for patients with mental disorders:
- Goal-specific drumming groups
- Community drum circles

- Hand drumming techniques

Goal-specific drumming groups are structured for a specific purpose and relate to drumming activities other than drum circles and technique-learning groups. Goal-specific drumming in grief and loss groups, substance abuse groups, and general music therapy groups is used when the goals center on building self-esteem. In these groups, the drum is used as the communication tool. The patient has the option to respond verbally, but it is not required. In these groups, a question is presented to the patient, who then answers on the drum. Other members may verbally reflect on what they played. The Health Rhythms Training (Bitman, Stevens, & Bruhn, 2004) sponsored by REMO Drums provides training in this technique. It is an excellent way to work into difficult issues such as low self-esteem, depression, addiction, grief, or loss. It is also an effective way for people to express the "high" of a drug or the coming down after the high without words. Many people relate to what is being played versus what is said. The music therapist uses his or her own skills to develop questions to fit whatever goal being addressed. When using this "goal-specific drumming," the music therapist must be comfortable working with the emotions that may come up. It is important for the therapist to know his or her limits and be willing to ask others for help. Groups can be co-facilitated with other therapists from disciplines such as art therapy, recreational therapy, occupational therapy, and psychology, if possible.

Community drum circles are an opportunity for people of a community to come and drum together. Arthur Hull (1998) describes a community drum circle as "a modern day version of an old-time community social. People come together to sing, dance, play music and socialize" (p. 21). A community drum circle is structured but not controlled, facilitated but not taught. With careful attention, the community always communicates what it needs. Emphasis shifts from refined musical product to play, fun, and enjoyment.

While facilitating a community drum circle in the psychiatric adult population, it is just as important, if not more important, to listen to what the patients are expressing. In facilitating drum circles with the psychotic patient, each week is different from the next. Some weeks, the patients may entrain (come into synchronization) the minute they walk through the door. Other weeks, the entire session may elapse with each member expressing his own rhythm and never connecting with the person sitting across the room. The two most important keys to drumming with patients with mental disorders are to listen and to facilitate what is given. The music therapist can sit in the back with claves beating out 4/4 time, and the clients might never join in. Or the clients may weave the group in and out of 3/4, 6/8, 7/8, or unknown time signatures. At the end, they know where they went. They connected with the people around them without saying a word. This is a powerful tool. Two case studies illustrate this point.

Case Study 1. Patient A had both Axis I and Axis II diagnoses. She suffered from depression as well as some other diagnoses. She loved drumming. As the two music therapists at the hospital doing drumming groups, we both were off work on a Friday, the day we always had community drum circle. This patient was very upset that it would not happen. Other disciplines were involved with drumming, and this time was no exception. The group was left with an art therapist and one of the therapy technicians as well as this patient. Patient A was asked before the therapist's departure if she would be willing to help the others facilitate the circle. From that moment forward, every time this patient came to group, she would be up in the middle dancing and would always do a little facilitation. The other staff later reported that she did a good job facilitating that day. This person, in the hospital for depression among other things, had an hour every week to feel like she had some control. She experienced an increase in self-esteem and probably some feelings of normalcy, if only for a little while. To this day, she wants to know when we are drumming again.

Case Study 2. This case study happened when the music therapist was asked to facilitate a drum circle at the memorial service of one of the patients, also a fellow drummer and a drum circle regular. While in the group, "Joe" would often share rhythms and songs he had learned in his childhood from his culture. The drumming for this memorial service consisted of a short drumming experience at the beginning of the service and a longer one at the end. Around 100 people showed up for this service and the hospital did not have nearly this many instruments. So when introduced, one person kept a steady quiet beat on the buffalo drum while a rhythm was played on the djembe. A couple of other therapists handed out shakers to the inner circle. Everyone was invited to close their eyes, focus on the rhythm, and recall memories of our lost friend. This went on for about three minutes before it was brought to a close, and the service continued with no instruments being played. At the end, the mourners were asked to play and a community drum circle began. For about fifteen minutes, the entire group played with the message to send their thoughts and prayers to Joe. This drum circle was extraordinarily moving, cohesive, and focused. At the end of the group, it was remarked that they sounded great, and one of Joe's greatest friends at the hospital stated, "It's for Joe."

Lastly, the *hand drumming techniques* group is designed to teach basic hand drumming skills. This group actually came out of the community drum circle where a few people in the community drum circle wanted to learn more about specific techniques or rhythms. It is important to remember that the community drum circle is not the place to teach techniques. As stated above, the circle is a place to facilitate. Instead, a separate technique class was offered before the start of the circle. People could come by early and learn a few basic sounds and basic rhythms. Nothing too complicated, but enough to give them tools to experiment with during the next hour drum circle.

Case Study 3. One patient came to the community drum circle only one time. He had well-developed skills and real talent for drumming. This guy could play! But he did not have the djembe technique the therapist was more familiar with. Instead, he was a conga player. He was encouraged to come back to the drum circle, but he never attended group again. He was not comfortable with large groups of people. So instead, a conga was brought to him, and he was asked to teach the therapist some conga techniques. He refused at first, but eventually he did teach a few conga techniques.

How to Get Started

The best way to start is to jump in and facilitate. There are several ways to learn about facilitation. You can always attend one of the many conferences on facilitation techniques (Bitman et al., 2004). There are also written books on facilitation techniques. The two "how to" books that are recommended include, *The Art and Heart of Drum Circles* by Christine Stevens (2003) or *Drum Circle Spirit* by Arthur Hull (1998). Watching facilitators at drum circles is also instructive. Whatever route you choose to begin, know that there are many styles of facilitation. They all have positive points. Find a style that's personally comfortable and jump on in.

"The more you learn, the less you know." This applies to drumming just as much as it does to anything else. There are so many wonderful facilitators doing this type of work every day. The most important advice for a new music therapist is to just get in there and do it. There are always more techniques and more styles out there to learn. Peers and other master facilitators can be great teachers, but the best teachers are the patients engaged in this activity. Hearing their response gives important feedback as to what works and what does not. When the facilitation is effective, great music is the result.

Specific Drum Circle Facilitation Techniques (by Gary Johnson)

When facilitating a rhythm/percussion instrument playing session, the music therapist leads the group through seven general steps:

1. Greet each group member.
2. Do a warm-up. Use egg shakers to introduce basic rhythmic concepts and to increase cognitive arousal.
3. Introduce larger rhythm/percussion instruments, including drums and congas (ask patients to choose between two possible instrument options).
4. Facilitate a group "jam." A "jam" involves a free form of drumming with an organizing steady pulse. Generally, a pulse is set by a player with a large drum while group members improvise in any way they are able around that beat.
5. Shift to a more cognitively challenging application such as a call and response (a 4/4 rhythm is first played by a leader and the group is then encouraged to repeat it).
6. Return to a group "jam." Group members are not required to duplicate any particular pattern.
7. Facilitate a group discussion. What changes in mood and feelings were experienced?

Sessions can be facilitated using these steps as a guide. It is important to begin the session by greeting the group and introducing the facilitator(s). This provides a personal interaction between patient and practitioner. A warm-up with egg shakers, or similar instrumentation, and then adding to or replacing the shakers with larger percussion instruments allows the patient to interact with stronger and louder rhythmic patterns and encourages more active engagement in the group playing or "jamming" experience. The call and response begins with the leader playing a simple 4/4 rhythmic pattern with the group imitating the same pattern. The role of leader can shift to anyone in the group. The second group "jam" and discussion bring closure to the session and provide the opportunity for members to express any changes in feelings and moods.

Relaxation Techniques

Roberta Wigle Justice

Stress is defined as a constraining force or influence (e.g., a physical, chemical, or emotional factor) that causes bodily or mental tension and may be a factor in disease causation. It is also defined as a state resulting from a stress, one of bodily or mental tension resulting from factors that tend to alter an existing equilibrium. This implies changes in one's life. There are major changes and minor changes, positive changes and negative changes. There are, therefore, major stressors and minor stressors, positive stressors and negative stressors in everyone's life. These can be physical, chemical (nutritional), or emotional in nature. Everyone responds to stress with some basic physiological reactions, well known to most people as the fight, flight, or freeze responses. These all have some characteristics in common, and although not everyone responds exactly the same, there are some basic principles that are similar. Muscle tension occurs in most people as a protective response—pulling up and inward. This tension triggers the central nervous system (CNS) to increase heart rate and breathing. Cognitive thoughts related to the stressor also trigger these responses by increasing or modifying them. After the stress goes away or is dealt with, the body returns to a relaxed (theoretically) state and repairs itself.

In general, music for relaxation should have predictability. This means it should be either familiar to and preferred by the listener and have repetitive patterns that will be easily recognizable as consistent and, therefore, safe. Harmonic patterns that are within a culture's normal use will have this quality, as will music with the following general qualities:

- Simple melody or no melody
- Highly structured, repeated, simple harmony
- Pleasing instrumentation and/or nature sounds (to the listener)
- Tempo of music that is slow and consistent by gradually slowing down physically (choosing or playing music that is about 50–70 beats per minute or slightly slower than the heart rate will facilitate this relaxation process)
- Live music having the ability to slow down at the discretion of the player but also is more likely to have inconsistencies, depending on the skill of the player

Specific Relaxation Techniques Accompanied by Music

Clients can engage in several specific techniques to assist in the relaxation process. By far, the most common of these are muscle relaxation techniques. These techniques can be modified to fit client needs by focusing on his or her need for externally structured experiences. Highly disorganized clients (those with psychotic disorders, high levels of agitation, etc.) have a greater need for external structure. Clients with symptoms of depression or anxiety will have periods of disorganization and will need more structure, while clients with good self-organization skills will need less external structure during muscle relaxation techniques.

The first activity in muscle relaxation activities is *stretching* (Figure 4.1). Several basic concepts should be considered when doing stretching to music:

- For relaxation, hold all stretches 8–10 seconds, while letting the muscles loosen and keeping the body in alignment.
- Stretch only to the point of feeling the stretch, never to the point of pain.
- Hold all stretches statically/no bouncing.
- Breathe in when opening the chest, out when curling over, calmly when holding stretches.

LEVELS OF COMPLEXITY OF STRETCHING		
Basic	Average	Intricate
Large muscle groups— bending head forward lifting chin up reaching arms up bending over to touch toes twisting upper back	Adding : muscle groups— tilting head in various angles squeezing elbows together in front and back pointing toes and flexing feet	Adding: small muscle groups— face eyes hands different shoulder stretches circling ankles lower back

Figure 4.1. "Levels of Complexity of Stretching."

Another muscle relaxation technique is *progressive tense/release* (based on Jacobson, 1962) (Figure 4.2). Basic concepts to consider when doing progressive tense/release technique include the following:

- Tense each muscle group and hold it tight for 8–10 seconds.
- Release and let muscle relax and warm up 8–10 seconds.

- Tense again, more gently.
- Release and let relax for twice as long as first tensing.

LEVELS OF COMPLEXITY OF TENSION/RELEASE		
Basic	Average	Intricate
Simple, large muscle groups— legs and feet together arms and hands together stomach and back together	Begin to focus on isolating muscle groups— feet vs. legs calves vs. thighs parts of chest, back hands vs. arms upper and lower arms face vs. back of head	Complex, small muscles— muscles in knees lower back elbows and wrists upper back and neck parts of face (forehead, cheeks, lips, etc.)

Figure 4.2. "Levels of Complexity of Tension/Release."

Autogenic or passive progressive relaxation is another muscle relaxation approach (Schultz & Luthe, 1969) (Figure 4.3). Some basic concepts of this technique should be considered:

- Do not use for people in active psychosis.
- Focus on various muscle groups and relaxation without tensing first using the following:
    (a) repetition of relaxation phrase;
    (b) bringing in relaxing feeling, temperature, color, or energy;
    (c) pacing about 50–60 beats per minutes unless otherwise indicated.

LEVELS OF COMPLEXITY FOR AUTOGENIC RELAXATION		
Basic	Average	Intricate
Not recommended for people in active psychosis For others, focus on simple, large muscle groups	Begin to focus on isolating muscle groups— feet vs. legs calves vs. thighs parts of chest, back hands vs. arms upper and lower arms face vs. back of head	Complex, small muscles— muscles in knees lower back elbows and wrists upper back and neck parts of face (forehead, cheeks, lips, etc.)

Figure 4.3. "Levels of Complexity for Autogenic Relaxation."

Other relaxation techniques include *breathing* (Figure 4.4) and *focused imagination with music* (Figure 4.5).

Basic concepts of *breathing* with musical accompaniment include the following:

- Stressed breathing is rapid and shallow, blowing off carbon dioxide more rapidly than normal and increasing oxygen and glucose in the muscles.
- Heart rate increases to assist the blood to the extremities.
- Breathing should be incorporated into the stretching.
- Holding long, soft hums forces deep breathing (toning).
- Relaxed breathing is generally 12× per minute for an adult.

LEVELS OF COMPLEXITY FOR BREATHING RELAXATION		
Basic	Average	Intricate
Concrete hands on body or "square" breathing*	Focus mind on parts of lung**	Imagine body parts breathing

*"square" breathing
    - Breathe in for a 3-count, hold breath for a 3-count, breathe out for a 3-count, hold for a 3-count; then
    - Increase to 4 counts or slow counts down.
**full lung breathing
    - Breathe into lower lung, letting stomach and abdomen expand and relax;
    - Breathe into middle lung, letting rib cage, front and back, expand and relax;
    - Breathe into upper lung, letting chest and back expand and relax; then
    - Breathe using all three parts in sequence.		

Figure 4.4. "Levels of Complexity for Breathing Relaxation."		

Focused imagination with music includes several basic concepts:

- Focus the thoughts on one imagined scene or situation for one to five minutes.
- Hold the mind from wandering.
- Connect to relaxing sensory stimuli, allowing strengthening of defenses.

LEVELS OF COMPLEXITY FOR FOCUSED IMAGINATION		
Basic	Average	Intricate

Remembering a real place—
    house
    chair
    room
    place outside
	Thinking about a place (real or imagined)—
	    a safe room/house
	    an island
	    a scene from a picture
	    landscape
	    a garden
		Connecting with a deep place inside

Figure 4.5. "Levels of Complexity for Focused Imagination."		

When facilitating focus imagination experiences, have the clients take a minute to imagine any of the situations presented in Figure 4.5. They should use all of the senses to deepen the experience (visual, auditory, tactile, olfactory, and gustatory). The important aspects of any imagined place are its peaceful, calm, deeply relaxing, and safe qualities. It does not have to be light, quiet, or out of doors.

References

Bitcon, C. (2000). Alike and different. *Gilsum, NH: Barcelona.*

Bitman, B., Stevens, C., & Bruhn, K. T. (2004). HealthRhythms: Group empowerment drumming. *Valencia, CA: Remo Drums.*

Crowe, B. J., & Rio, R. (2004). Implications of technology in music therapy practice and research for music therapy education: A review of literature. Journal of Music Therapy, 41*(4), 282–320.*

Hull, A. (1998). Drum circle spirit: Facilitating human potential through rhythm. *Tempe, AZ: White Cliffs Media.*

Jacobson, E. (1962). You must relax. *New York: McGraw-Hill.*

Stevens, C. (2003). The art and heart of drum circles. *Milwaukee, WI: Hal Leonard.*

Unkefer, R. F. (Ed.). (1990). Music therapy in treatment of adults with mental disorders: Theoretical bases and clinical interventions. *New York: Schirmer Books.*

Wheeler, B. L. (1983). A psychotherapeutic classification of music therapy practices: A continuum of procedures. Music Therapy Perspectives, 1, 8–16.

Additional Resources

American Psychiatric Association. (1994). Diagnostic and statistical manual of mental disorders *(4th ed.). Washington, DC: Author.*

Crowe, B. J. (1995). Cost effective activity programs for older adults with dementia. *Tempe, AZ: Rhythm for Life.*

Friedman, R. L. (2000). The healing power of the drum: A psychotherapist explores the healing power of rhythm. *Reno, NV: White Cliffs Media.*

Hart, M., Stevens, J., & Lieberman, F. (1990). Drumming at the edge of magic: A journey into the spirit of percussion. *New York: Harper Collins.*

Redmond, L. (1997). When the drummers were women: A spiritual history of rhythm. *New York: Three Rivers Press.*

Reuer, B., & Crowe, B. J. (1995). Best practice in music therapy utilizing group percussion strategies for promoting volunteerism in the well older adult. *San Diego, CA: San Diego State University Foundation.*

Chapter 5

Insight Music Therapy with Re-educative Goals: An Overview
Barbara J. Crowe

In these interventions, verbal sharing and interaction between client, therapist, and possibly other group members augment the active participation in the intervention. The emphasis is on discovery and exploration of personal thoughts, feelings, and interpersonal reactions.

Use of Songs

Bruscia (1998) believes songs have an important place in insight music therapy for several reasons, including the following:

- People have relationships with songs.
- Songs connect people to times in their lives, people, situations, and emotions.
- Clients have personal associations and meanings with songs.
- Songs can access certain psychological material and emotions.

Songs used in insight music therapy need to be connected to the client and structured to foster verbal expression and discussion. To accomplish this, Bruscia (1998) suggests providing an appropriate context or atmosphere, such as listening with eyes closed, focusing on a topic or issue, or presenting an image prior to experiencing the song. He suggests a number of specific ways to use songs in insight music therapy with re-educative goals. All these interventions include verbal sharing and processing of material expressed.

Song Performance

In song performance, the therapeutic value lies in the client or group singing the song as a form of personal expression. The music therapist supports the process by accompanying or joining the singing. During the performance, the music therapist listens closely to the musical performance (musical elements, voice quality, dynamics, breath support, etc.), not the lyric content, as indicators of the client's emotional state, psychological issues, and mood.

Song Reception

Song reception involves clients' sharing of a song with the therapist or group. Song choices reflect important times and events in the client's life. Songs can be performed live or presented through a recording. This sharing becomes a therapeutic communication between the client and therapist.

Lyric Analysis

Lyric analysis focuses on the lyrics of a song and becomes the basis to discuss therapeutic issues, client concerns, belief systems, and coping skills. The basic procedure for lyric analysis is as follows:

- Introduce the artist and song.
- Have the lyrics written out and present the song either with a live performance or through a recording.
- Give clients cues or questions to focus their listening. (Examples: "Listen to the song and follow along with the lyrics. What line really jumps out at you?" or "What do you think the songwriter was feeling?")
- Urge the clients to focus on both the lyrics and the musical presentation. ("What in the music or performance communicates to you? Does it support the artist's message?")
- Lead the discussion following the song listening, reassuring the clients that there are no right or wrong answers. Everyone's interpretation of the song is correct, because it reflects his or her experience, mood, emotions, and memories.

Song Reminiscence

Song reminiscence involves using songs to elicit memories. In this technique, songs that are determined to be possibly meaningful to the client are presented using recordings or live performance by the music therapist. Through verbal prompting, the client shares what memories the song elicits. This technique is especially useful in life-review activities, where clients remember and evaluate all the significant events of their lives.

Song Collage

Song collage involves assembling and recording a tape or CD of songs that represent or describe the essential nature of the client, the stages of his or her life, significant achievements, and memories and emotions from a lifetime.

Song Improvisation

Song improvisation involves the spontaneous creation of song lyrics, usually to a familiar melody, that relate to a therapeutic issue of the client. The use of a 12-bar blues format with clients improvising lyrics is an example of this intervention. (See the section on vocal music psychotherapy in Chapter 6.)

Song Parody or Cloze Songwriting

This intervention involves rewriting the lyrics of existing songs or filling in the blanks with personal information in song lyrics. An example might be taking the song "My Favorite Things" and having clients list their "favorite things" as new lyrics to the song.

Song Writing

A number of music therapists have written about songwriting as an insight music therapy technique (Clendenon-Wallen, 1991; Edgerton, 1990; Ficken, 1976; Freed, 1989; Goldstein, 1990; Lindberg, 1995; Schmidt, 1983). This intervention involves creating new songs to express a client's concerns, personal issues, and emotional states. The process may involve the client composing both the music and lyrics, the music therapist composing the music with lyrics by the client, or the client improvising a melody and lyrics with the music therapist providing accompaniment. The goals achieved with this intervention include:

- appropriate expression of feelings and emotions;
- improved self-esteem;
- enhanced feelings of accomplishment;
- improved decision-making skills;
- increased self-awareness;
- clarification of personal issues;
- development of problem-solving skills.

Music therapists have suggested a number of ways to facilitate this intervention. Schmidt (1983) suggested the following:

- Determine how much structure clients need to successfully complete the task. What are their musical skills, expressive language abilities, and the emotional content of the song?
- Determine whether client or therapist provides the melodic structure. The activity can start with pre-existing melodies and improvised melodic fragments.
- Facilitate lyric writing by progressing from song parody, filling in the blanks, and adding new verses to existing songs, to using a question-and-answer format or structured exploration of a theme or topic.
- Create the musical settings or determine the melody through "successive steps of approximation" (Schmidt, 1983, p. 6). These steps can include exploring natural speech inflections and rhythms, use of Orff ostinati or pentatonic scales to encourage melodic improvisation, spontaneous singing or scat singing, and structured experiences in melodic formation using resonator bells or Orff instruments.
- Speak lyrics rhythmically and orchestrate them with percussion and melodic instruments, having the therapist present various melodies for the lyrics and letting clients choose the one they like. This can accomplish setting lyrics to music or using predetermined song formats like the 12-bar blues form (Schmidt, 1983, pp. 6–7).
- Use Orff-style accompaniments that do not require musical training to play (Ficken, 1976).

Lindberg (1995) suggests other methods for helping clients create original songs:

- For lyric generating, create words and phrases through brainstorming and free association around key words or phrases describing a topic or concern.
- Lyrics are constructed from the generated lists.
- For melody and accompaniment, the music therapist often does this at first with the clients picking a particular melody or accompaniment style presented to them.
- Songs are recorded and written copies prepared.

Expressive Movement

Expressive movement involves free form, spontaneous movement to music to help the client learn to use music and movement as a means of emotional self-expression and to release feelings of tension and anxiety. These creative movements to music reveal a great deal about a client's feelings, self-esteem, and psychodynamic issues. The music therapist may want to consult with a dance/movement therapist when using this activity intervention.

Structured Affective Listening

In this intervention, listening to and interacting with music forms the basis for therapeutic discussion focused on a client's awareness of issues, coping mechanisms, inappropriate thoughts and responses, problem areas, and emotions and feelings. Clients respond to music in a number of ways, including:

- associations and memories with past experiences, whether pleasant or unpleasant;
- images or mental pictures evoked by the music;
- moods elicited by the music;
- client identification with the music, lyrics, performer, or culture;
- aesthetic reaction.

The goals achieved with this intervention include:

- stimulating expression and discussion of feelings and experiences;
- practicing verbal communication skills;
- providing experiences in cooperative group functioning and tolerance of other's ideas;
- self-discovery;
- enriching listening skills and techniques;
- improving realization of the client's own methods of perceiving and relating to a particular type of experience;
- emotional release and catharsis.

Specific approaches include the following:

- Create a story to music—individually or as a group.
- Choose or draw a picture to music.
- Select emotion words or phrases from a list to describe the music.
- Use open-ended phrases to describe the music, such as, "This music makes me feel _____ _____."
- Use listening prompts for focus discussion, such as, "What animal does the music remind you of?" or "Think of one day in your life that this music reminds you of."
- Create an "album" or CD cover to express something about oneself.
- Illustrate a poem or story with music, improvisation, or sound effects.

SPECIFIC TECHNIQUES

Music Therapy Improvisation for Adult Psychiatric Settings

Paul Nolan and Flossie Ierardi

This section of the chapter attempts to present a clinically based rationale and instructional guide for the music therapist who desires to begin using music therapy improvisational techniques within adult psychiatric settings. The uses of musical materials and experiences presented here are combined from the authors' professional experience as clinicians in adult psychiatry (inpatient and day treatment settings), as educators in a graduate university-based music therapy education program, and as conference presenters and authors. This is an attempt to integrate the authors' experiences of using and teaching music therapy improvisation with treatment goals and approaches from contemporary psychotherapeutic practice used in inpatient psychiatry.

The presentation of methods and suggestions are focused specifically toward short-term inpatient facilities that emphasize helping the patient stabilize and reach a remission from acute symptoms of psychosis, anxiety, and depression. Therefore, improvisation styles and approaches that are typically used to advance higher functioning and human growth are not developed in this section. A greater emphasis is placed upon varieties of musically structured approaches rather than less structured, such as free atonal improvisation. The clinical orientation through which this material is viewed tends to combine psychodynamic schools, influenced by object relations and ego psychology frameworks and also from humanistic theories, specifically those of Abraham Maslow. We believe that the suggestions included in this chapter may be applicable to all current clinical orientations.

From clinical observations it is noted that some individuals with chronic schizophrenia may work better with music therapy methods other than improvisation that incorporate more concrete musical experiences such as singing, ensemble playing, and structured song writing. Improvisation is but one of many available methods of music therapy for the acute, adult inpatient setting and day programs.

Basic Approaches

The topic of music therapy improvisation, also known as *improvisation therapy, clinical musical improvisation,* and *clinical improvisation,* among other terms, is substantiated by a fairly large collection of journal articles and book chapters. For the purposes of this chapter, we focus only on the use of music therapy improvisation assessment and treatment in which both the patient(s) and therapist play music as used in adult inpatient and partial, or day program, settings. For a full review of a wide variety of models of improvisation, the reader is referred to Bruscia's (1987) *Improvisational Models of Music Therapy.*

Within these settings, according to published reports, music therapy improvisation is used primarily in groups (Alvin, 1975; Darnley-Smith, 2002; Langdon et al., 1989; Loth, 2002; Murphy, 1991; Nolan, 1991; Odell-Miller, 1991; Priestley, 1975; Stephens, 1983; Stewart, 2002; Towse & Flower, 1993) and occasionally in individual cases (Boone, 1991; DeBacker & Van Camp, 2002; John, 1995; Nolan, 1994; Pavlicevic, 1995). Regarding the amount and type of structure used, many European authors, especially those trained in England, describe forms of free tonal and atonal improvisation, first developed by Juliette Alvin, a major founding figure of British music therapy. Free atonal improvisation, in her music therapy approach, contains shifts in mood and stylistic aspects depending upon the therapist's response to the music or the sounds of the client. Priestley further modified Alvin's approach for use in inpatient psychiatry (Wigram, Pedersen, & Bonde, 2002). Priestley later developed Analytic Music Therapy generally for higher functioning, noninpatient clients. Although this section cannot provide a review of the literature, the reader is referred to this partial listing of authors who discuss the use of free improvisation within adult psychiatry (Darnley-Smith, 2002; Kortegaard,1993; John, 1995; Metzner, 2004; Pavlicevic, 1997; Stewart 2002; Towse & Flower, 1993). Other structuring approaches include patient initiated, tonally based, with verbal suggestions (Nolan, 1991); drum circle techniques (Justice, 1994); short-term care (Justice, 1994; Loth, 2002; Murphy, 1991; Nolan, 1991; Towse & Flower, 1993); long-term care (Boone, 1991; John, 1995; Kortegaard, 1993; Odell-Miller, 1991; Priestley, 1975; Stewart, 2002); partial hospital or day program (Darnley-Smith, 2002; Odell-Miller, 1991, 2002); and older adults in inpatient settings and mental health day programs (Darnley-Smith, 2002; Odell-Miller, 1995). Clinical areas of focus include developing relatedness and interaction (Pavlicevic, 1995; Stephens, 1983; Towse & Flower, 1993); here-and-now, known as actual (Kortegaard, 1993; Stephens, 1983; Towse & Flower, 1993); and extra musical (symbolic) processes (Kortegaard, 1993; Murphy, 1991; Nolan, 1994; Priestley, 1975; Stephens, 1983) in music therapy improvisation.

Uses of Musical Instruments

Instruments available to patients for improvisation generally include pitched (xylophones, glockenspiel, kalimbas) and nonpitched (hand drums; tambourines; variety of shaking, striking, and scraping instruments) percussion with the music therapist favoring piano and in some cases guitar (Nolan, 1994), cello (Metzner, 2004) and violin (Priestley, 1975). Stephens (1983) suggests the therapist's use of instruments, including large drums that have a range of expressive possibilities for working with musical responses of group members. Guidelines as well as suggestions for complementary skills in improvisation also appear (Bruscia, 1989; Gardstrom, 2001), though suggestions and techniques for using improvisation in this setting are not yet readily available.

Clinical Orientation

It is a common phenomenon in music therapy for adults in inpatient psychiatric settings to demonstrate higher levels of functioning during sessions compared to their general functioning on the unit. Nolan has been quoted as saying that "Arts Therapies attract that which is well within patients" (Pratt, 1992, p. 3). Understanding this seemingly natural phenomenon and directing it toward health care goals requires a studied, tested clinical orientation. Some of the key functions of a clinical orientation are to (a) guide the therapeutic relationship, (b) set the patient's treatment goals, and (c) provide an understanding and a way to respond to the patient's musical expression within the context of his or her musical and psychosocial developmental level.

Group models, presumably the most common format used by music therapists in inpatient and partial hospital settings, attempt "to increase patients' awareness of themselves through their interactions with other group members; to provide patients with improved interpersonal and social skills; to help members adapt to the inpatient setting; and to improve communication between patients and staff" (Kaplan & Sadock, 1998, p. 901). There is limited literature describing group models in music therapy. Although no one approach to group therapy has an exact point-to-point comparison with music therapy approaches, the literature from group therapy can provide important guidance for running successful groups and in avoiding common pitfalls in this setting.

Yalom (1983), one of the most respected researchers and theorists in the field of group therapy, found that therapy group leaders, especially in working with lower functioning patients, need to show direct support, emphasize the here-and-now, and provide structure. These themes seem to be inherent in music therapy improvisation. We believe that the music therapy improvisation approach, as it continues to be developed as a mode of psychotherapy, has an advantage over verbal methods in this setting by using preverbal processes that may be a more readily accessible cognitive style for these patients (Nolan, 1994).

Supportive Psychotherapy

In early music therapy literature, Wheeler (1981) suggests an activity therapy approach for short-term psychiatric inpatient treatment. Since that time, music therapists have also demonstrated music therapy improvisation using insight and noninsight approaches (Nolan, 1997; Pavlicevic, 1995). One such approach to psychotherapy, but not often cited in the music therapy literature by name, is *supportive psychotherapy*.

Supportive psychotherapy uses direct measures, or interventions, to ameliorate symptoms and to ntain, restore, and improve self-image (sense of efficacy), ego function (relation to reality, thinking, affect, defenses, synthetic functions), and adaptive skills (effective functioning).

The objective of supportive psychotherapy is not to change the patient's personality, as in Wheeler's level three insight music therapy with reconstructive goals (Wheeler, 1981), but, "to help the patient cope with symptoms in order to prevent relapse of serious mental illness"(Winston, Rosenthal, & Pinsker, 2004, p. 4). Nolan, in forensic (1983), medical (1991), and inpatient psychiatric (1994) settings, used this model. Within music therapy, this approach encourages a wide range of client responses from a supportive reality contact to insightful self-awareness and is suggested for use by music therapists in this setting.

The role of the music therapist in supportive psychotherapy. Within this approach, it is suggested that the therapist adopt the nurturer rather than confronter role. The short-term relationship provides an opportunity for the music therapist to first reduce the patient's anxiety through the mastery within creative experience in improvisation. The patient may then be encouraged to seek therapy as an outpatient, which may reduce the number of repeated hospitalizations he or she may have to endure.

The Role of Structure in Improvisation

Structure in the context of music therapy improvisation refers to (a) the degree of control, or how many options, exist within the use of the musical elements; (b) the way in which the patient(s) is to use the music and the degree of emphasis upon the interpersonal processes; and (c) the assignment of instruments and musical roles in a group. Increasing the amount of structure within a musical experience is an intervention meant to allow for greater predictability, as well as maximal involvement, by reducing the amount of musical options for lower functioning patients. Using structure as a variable in treatment can be seen as a supportive externalized ego, temporarily providing those ego functions that the patient is less able to access due to symptoms of mental illness. Generally speaking, musical options can be increased as symptoms remit. A good balance between the degree and the type of structure in relation to the patient's capabilities can produce good results. The patient may demonstrate not only reality-based musical behavior but also pleasure within aesthetic involvement, some level of creativity, and attunement with the music, the group, and/or the therapeutic relationship.

The therapist must make ongoing decisions concerning the individual's or group members' needs for adjustments in levels of structure, or ego support, depending upon presenting symptoms and observed musical responses. For example, a disorganized patient suffering from a manic state may have greater periods of focus on the music therapy experience if he or she has an instrument option, such as a pair of bongo drums, to play within a recognizable, predictable song form or musical style that is provided by the therapist in an individual session. However, with that same patient, an experienced music therapist can encourage the use of an instrument with many options, such as a xylophone. Introducing the concept of a tonal center may help to anchor the patient's focus in the improvisation. With sufficient musical structure provided by the therapist in the form of a musical holding environment (externalized ego support), the patient may be able to effectively use the therapist's musical support to maintain a musically meaningful reality focus in the music.

An example of the therapist introducing a high degree of structure in the form of musical grounding is playing a clear bass pattern or repeated melodic or rhythmic motive for predictability. The patient is initially encouraged to respond by creating a rhythmic response on a drum or a prepared (specific tonal arrangement) xylophone. If the patient seems unable to fit in with the music and plays randomly with great discharge and little connection to the beat, the therapist might suggest a reduction in patient options by saying, "Try playing a little slower with one mallet." Once there is a meeting in the time element of the music, then the therapist can assume that the patient is somewhat oriented to the reality of the music experience and can then encourage greater freedom in experimenting with musical options.

Assessment

There are few tests or approaches to assessment that have received adequate research attention to be used clinically in a reliable way, especially in this setting (see assessment section in Chapter 2). In acute settings, there is limited time for the music therapist to formulate observations into a cogent assessment and determine a course of treatment. In some cases, a patient is seen in only one music therapy group. Therefore, assessment and treatment are occurring in the same session while the therapist is observing and attending to treatment issues of several patients. A keen sense of observation and one's honed ability to make quick and educated clinical decisions can make the music therapy group a valued and beneficial component of a patient's overall assessment.

The Interactive Improvisation Assessment model developed by Nolan (Nolan, Vergare, Hays, & Dulicai, 1982) uses structured and nonstructured musical interactions to elicit information related to ego function and interpersonal functioning. Each musical interaction is recorded and played back during the session in order to learn more through verbal discussion about the musical interactions and any symbolic associations from the patient's perspective. Considerations when analyzing musical behavior during the three improvisations include:

- patient's choice of instrument;
- variability of volume;
- ability to synchronize pulse;
- ability to initiate and use motives or musical ideas;
- ability to respond to and provide musical support;
- ability to recognize and fulfill musical roles within the group, such as leading and following.

A wealth of information that is difficult to ascertain in other modalities or simply through patient self-report is provided through the use of this assessment and shared with an interdisciplinary treatment team. This includes preserved strengths, interpersonal style, and coping strategies. Figure 5.1 summarizes the Interactive Improvisation Assessment Model using three improvisational experiences.

EXAMPLE OF THE INTERACTIVE IMPROVISATION ASSESSMENT MODEL			
Description of Improvisational Experience	Adaptability for Group Assessment	Degrees of Structure	Treatment Areas
I. Predictable harmonic/rhythmic style; affectively neutral at first; musical encouragement of interactive and affective responses; xylophone prepared in pentatonic scale. Therapist attempts to elicit affective musical responses.	Readily adaptable; therapist has opportunity to interact with individual and whole-group responses.	Structured experience to create safe and inviting environment; structure may be modified via new musical material, for example, a musical bridge	Awareness of music, self, and others; ability/willingness to interact; variability of affect
II. Patient chooses instruments for self and therapist; patient initiates and ends improvisation; may become referential.	Adaptable for group with structural modifications.	To increase structure: instruments, entrances and endings planned ahead for more predictability. Less structure: Group context: music begins, develops, and ends naturally.	Internal organization: interpersonal skills; expressive capabilities; abstract vs. concrete levels of thinking
III. Familiar musical style initiated by therapist with more choices on xylophone: "breaks," or brief, unaccompanied solos in music, occurs at stylistically appropriate intervals, such as "trading fours."	Readily adaptable and often used for groups.	Structure can be varied according to predictability of breaks, length of breaks, musical complexity.	Adaptation to familiar style of music; ability to internalize musical constants during brief unaccompanied solos; flexibility of expressive responses; investment in, and relationship to, the music.

Figure 5.1. "Example of the Interactive Improvisation Assessment Model."

Goals for Improvisation

Goals for music therapy improvisation in acute psychiatric settings should be similar to the goals used in most clinics: the "amelioration of symptoms and improvements and enhancement of adaptation, self-esteem, and overall functioning" (Winston et al., 2004, p. 61). The goals should generally be determined with the patient and should be realistic. It is incumbent upon the music therapist in such settings to develop goals and objectives that can be addressed through music therapy experiences and are compliant with guidelines set forth by licensing agencies. Such goals must be "translatable" into clinical treatment (nonmusical) language, but must be substantiated through observations of musical behaviors or objectives.

Within the improvisation sessions, the above goals may be addressed, depending on functioning level, by the two types of music therapy experiences described by Nolan (1994) and Stephens (1983): (a) actual (here-and-now), and (b) symbolic. Goals related to the here-and-now deal with orientation to the self, others, and the immediate environment. It is the musical experience that reinforces awareness of self and others, as well as the cause-and-effect relationship of interaction with musical objects and reality-based auditory stimuli. This primary connection of the external world of reality with internal psychic states is fundamental to the acquisition of further treatment gains. The here-and-now musical realm may also include exploration of parallels between the patient's musical interactions and interpersonal patterns in his or her daily life.

One of the overall treatment goals in inpatient psychiatry is to increase reality orientation. Music therapy improvisation specifically addresses reality orientation since it requires awareness of self and others and ability to use objects in the environment in a purposeful and relevant manner. The underlying premise is that enhancements in flexibility of musical responsiveness and interaction are indicative of improved mental health or more successful adaptation, such as greater ego flexibility. Patients who are "high-functioning" or more psychiatrically stabilized may be able to verbally relate their experience in a music therapy group to their ongoing patterns of social behavior, or even to other events, associations, or imagery. In an acute setting, goals for those patients may include improvements in range of affect, coping strategies, and interpersonal functioning.

Methods and Materials

This section contains musical applications based upon the therapist's instrument and whether it is harmonic/melodic (piano, guitar), single-line melodic (xylophone, winds, or string instruments), or rhythmic. Descriptions of interventions, as well as modifications of structure for level of functioning, are identified. Patient's choice of instrument is a clinical decision that is based upon and has implications for

- the patient's presenting ability to make decisions, for example, choosing from multiple instruments or from two presented instruments;
- the patient's previous responses, for example, always choosing the same instrument, thus the therapist suggests an instrument in order to encourage risk-taking or new interactive and expressive responses;
- the patient's verbal responses, for example, a desire to try new avenues of expression and interaction.

The following examples show how the music therapist can use musical form to influence the patient's experience of structure. Patient uses of musical form can reveal significant information about ego functions, especially control of impulses, creative thinking, and cognition. While these examples are open to variation and overlap, it is our experience that use of piano and guitar, which include opportunities for harmony, melody, and rhythm, give the therapist the widest range of possibilities for adjusting the level of musical structure.

Developing Practical Harmonic Skills for Music Therapy Improvisation

When discussing harmony, chords and their function in Western tonal music first come to mind. However, non-Western and unconventional chord constructions provide colors and textures that may be clinically applicable, depending on the individual or group. The music therapist of any professional level will benefit from experimentation and focused listening to intervallic combinations and alternative chord structures at the piano. For written exercises that address this goal, the reader may refer to *Creative Music Therapy* (Nordoff & Robbins, 1977, pp. 214–233) and Improvisation (Wigram, 2004). Both books include written and recorded musical examples and exercises for developing one's own improvisation skills, as well as methods to incorporate when using improvisation in a clinical context.

In an inpatient setting where the group membership changes frequently and the need for structure is constantly assessed, musical styles and harmonies that are familiar to the patient are often helpful in eliciting musical responses in a nonthreatening manner. Basic chord progressions, such as those found in songs and set in familiar styles or rhythmic patterns, may increase the orienting response and comfort level of the participants while encouraging active expression. The following are examples of specific approaches to improvisation experiences.

Structured musical formats when therapist is using a harmonic instrument. The following examples begin with most structured and move toward least structured.

1. Improvisation within a known song.
    -   *Description*: This is the most predictable of musical forms and therefore the most structured. The group or dyad sings a known song and adds improvisation solos, either with or without group accompaniment. The solo is played on a prepared xylophone (see Appendix A) or nonpitched percussion within the song form, such as in instrumental "breaks" between chorus and verse using the chord progression from either the verse or chorus as accompaniment for the solo.
    -   *Modifications*: The level of structure may be modified for groups that require less musical support by lengthening the improvised sections and by inserting rests, or stops, in the harmonic accompaniment during the improvised sections. Lower functioning or anxious patients who require more support will need continued, uninterrupted musical "presence" from the therapist during improvised sections.

2. Improvisation during a pre-existing instrumental piece.
    -   *Description*: A piece such as Pachelbel's *Canon* (ground bass) or Duke Ellington's *C Jam Blues* offers opportunities for the therapist to "assign" parts. One example of this in the *Canon* can be to have a person playing the chord roots with a single mallet on the xylophone or bells using two mallets to play octaves, and/or adding fifths. In the *C Jam Blues* a person can play the two-note melody. Composed words can be used to sing the melody as well in order to help with the timing. The playing of these pieces can alternate with improvised sections. The therapist may use the musical form, such as the chord progression of the piece, as a foundation for improvisation throughout.
    -   *Modifications*: Although assigning parts is a very structured approach, the timing demands and degree of difficulty may make the musical role more challenging. Therefore, higher-functioning individuals may be successful with assigned parts that alternate with improvised sections. Another modification occurs when using pre-existing instrumental pieces of music that contain extended rests in the melody, such as the fourth, eighth, and twelfth measures of *C Jam Blues*.

3. Improvisation within a specific style.
    -   *Description*: A chord progression in a familiar style (pop, ballad, blues) relevant to the preference of group members is used. The therapist cues entrances or invites responses when "ready."
    -   *Modifications*: Individual entrance cues are often helpful when participants are having difficulty synchronizing or "gelling" as a group. This layered approach allows for more focused listening to each other, as well as giving each person a chance to "fit in" before the next person joins the music. For higher-functioning groups and individuals, the therapist may provide more of an accompanying background role, thus allowing patient musical ideas to emerge as the figure. The therapist may vary in his or her musical role depending upon patient response.

4. Patient initiates the improvisation and therapist responds using a familiar musical style.

   - *Description*: Patient initiates a rhythm for the group to follow. Therapist responds with a chord progression in a musical style that both is familiar to the patient and supports the musical idea. In addition, the therapist supports the expressive qualities by responding, for example, with musical reflecting, maintaining a strong musical background, imitating, and/or adding melodic or rhythmic extensions to patient motifs, while others enter into the music.

   - *Modifications*: The therapist may need to help the patient orient attention to the music by maintaining a grounded and predictable musical role such as a rhythm or stylistic invariant(s).

5. Improvisations incorporating unconventional and non-Western harmonies.

   - *Description*: These improvisations may be initiated by the therapist or a patient and may not be based on a familiar musical form. They often begin as referential improvisations, or from the imagery and associations that may have emerged from subsequent verbal processing. They may also be valued in and of themselves as expressive interpersonal experiences. In some cases, a point of reference, such as an image (e.g., thunderstorm), may be suggested as a group task to help structure an introduction to referential improvisation. This can result in a sense of group cohesion.

   - *Modifications*: As the therapist determines decreased need for structure, for example, increased need for risk-taking among group members, the therapist must be prepared to support and/or guide unpredictable musical responses from patients. It is helpful here to be familiar with a variety of musical styles, non-Western modes, and musical experiences that may have asymmetrical or unpredictable meter. It is also helpful to be open to an atonal music aesthetic, which is equally capable of lyricism and emotional expression. Loosening the structural elements of a clinical improvisation may be considered an advanced level of practice in music therapy.

Using a melody instrument to facilitate clinical musical improvisation. In accordance with the assertion that more "structural" elements of harmony, melody, and rhythm translate to more therapeutic structure, an improvisation led with a melodic instrument potentially provides less structure than a harmonically based improvisation. A therapist may decide not to use harmonic interventions if a group is exhibiting greater flexibility of musical responses and is thus ready for more "responsibility" in the music. Textural and timbral elements become more obvious in the context of the group, and the therapist must develop creative musical techniques for grounding and varying structure when necessary. Some examples presented here use musical forms that are certainly possible on harmonic instruments. These ideas are intended to add to the therapist's repertoire of initiating the music using melodic instruments. Examples of single-line melodic interventions include the following.

1. Ostinato

   - *Description*: Typically, when used in music therapy group improvisation, an ostinato pattern is a repeated single line that serves to organize through its predictability and implied harmonies.

   - *Modifications*: The therapist may play the ostinato pattern if a group member is not capable of doing so. While this is a very structured approach, it may not allow the therapist to respond to musical contributions of group members (except in cases where the therapist is playing the ostinato in the bass of the piano and using the treble to interact). The ostinato may also be assigned to one or two group members who may take turns deviating from the repeated pattern in order to have an opportunity to improvise. Note: Although not single-line musical applications, examples of ostinato figures for the piano may be found in *Creative Music Therapy* (Nordoff-Robbins, 1977, p. 232).

2. Basic melodies with thematic development (Theme and Variations, Rondo)

    *   *Description*: Depending on the group, these melodies may be simple or complex. This technique allows the flexibility for the therapist to use a melodic instrument to work with the musical responses from the group while maintaining a grounding presence. It is helpful and even required that one or more group members are able to maintain a steady pulse within their rhythmic contribution. Although this is crucial if a rhythmically grounded improvisation is the goal, the listener (group member) often attunes to the melody (in this case, the therapist) for direction in the music, as observed by the authors.

    *   *Modifications*: A melody in four-measure phrases with predictable, implied harmonies (I – V7 – I …) provides structure and support for an individual or group playing rhythm instruments. Brief variations of the melody allow for musical interaction and the return to the theme or "A" section. The familiarity and repetition add to the structure. This form then resembles a rondo (ABACADA, etc.). Higher functioning groups may be able to tolerate less predictability in the overall form of the improvisation, leaving possibilities for changes of direction in the music based on patient responses. Variations on the original theme without a return to the exact melody may offer possibilities for verbal processing related to the patient's ability to effect change in a group situation.

3. Improvised xylophone duets

    *   *Description*: In individual therapy, Orff-type xylophones provide an excellent opportunity for reciprocal communication and interaction. The xylophones are placed in a number of ways in proximity to each other depending on the therapeutic needs of the situation. Face-to-face interaction offers an increase in communication but may be threatening to some individuals.

    *   *Modifications*: A musical factor to consider is the configuration of pitches for each xylophone. The music therapist may decide to limit the notes available to the patient in order to limit choices and increase possibilities for meaningful use of the musical instrument. Some patients, however, may be able to tolerate higher levels of anxiety and would benefit from increased expressive possibilities. The reader is referred to Appendix A for scale possibilities on these xylophones.

Rhythmic Interventions in Clinical Musical Improvisation

Rhythmic improvisation encompasses many of the same considerations in structuring as harmonic/melodic interventions. It is again imperative to note that fewer elements presented within an interactive musical context will result in a lesser experience of therapeutic structure. Improvisation with nonpitched instruments clearly does not contain melody (in the traditional sense) or harmony, two musical elements that provide an added level of expression and linear organization. In determining the individual/group needs for external support and structure, the therapist may find the patient(s) may be ready to tolerate the level of musical decision-making required for expressive musical interaction without the structural and organizational musical elements of melody and harmony only after considerable music therapy "experience." Within rhythmic improvisation, the therapist is still left with a number of clinical musical decisions regarding structure. Presenting a steady pulse with no accents or gradation in pitch (as might be available on a large drum) will require the participant to make decisions about musical components such as meter, style, phrasing, and form. The result may be increased anxiety and decreased relatedness due to the paucity of musical elements with which to interact. Or the patients may respond to this type of nondescript repetition with perseveration or other unimaginative response. The music therapist must consider expressive possibilities beyond the basic pulse or rhythm pattern when using rhythmic improvisation: tempo, meter, dynamics, timbre, texture, and style. Facility with multiple musical elements affords a level of aesthetic richness and therapeutic depth crucial to clinical competence. The following examples represent varying levels of structure, from most to least, in rhythmic improvisation. Many variations are possible, depending on group needs. Examples of rhythmic interventions include:

1. Improvisation with phrase completion
   - *Description*: The therapist initiates a rhythm and asks the group members to play a pattern that fits. The therapist then outlines clear four-measure phrases, leaving a rest on 2-3-4 of the fourth measure. Patients are invited to fill in the rest, or "break," with any musical material. This structured format contains clear and predictable four-measure phrases, while encouraging risk-taking in the rests.
   - *Modifications*: The spaces can be filled in various ways: by going around the circle, by cues from the therapist each time, by patients cueing each other, or by volunteering. The last option creates variety in texture, since it is the most spontaneous and may result in solos, duos, and trios in the rests. For groups needing more structure, the therapist may signal for each rest and each new phrase. Higher-functioning patients will be able to predict the rests as well as the downbeats of the new phrase. Verbal processing may center on discussion of risk-taking and heightened interaction, in the voluntary option.

2. Rondo
   - *Description*: The therapist or group with the therapist creates a two-, four-, or eight-bar musical style. This allows alternating of group playing and solos of equal length.
   - *Modifications*: The therapist may add structure through the use of visual cues and, if necessary, an auditory cue such as finger snaps, during the solo sections. Longer "A" sections will require longer periods of time (B, C, D sections) without musical support. Here, too, a voluntary option for the "solo" section will allow for varied texture and spontaneous musical interaction between and among patients.

3. Therapist-supported percussion improvisation
   - *Description*: This is likely the most typical use of percussion improvisation. The therapist begins with a clear rhythm and invites the group to play when ready. The therapist uses various music therapy techniques to develop the musical material, such as incorporating rhythms of the group members and embellishing and varying dynamics to encourage expanded expressive range.
   - *Modifications*: The initiated rhythm should provide an appropriate level of structure in order to invite musical interaction. Describing how the piece will end is also a function of structure. For a higher functioning group, the instruction may be to let the music end on its own. Others may need to know what the ending cue from the therapist will be.

4. Musical role-playing improvisation
   - *Description*: The therapist or group with the therapist lists several possible ways of interacting in the music; for example, leading or imitating the music; following—to enter into the music one at a time or as part of a sequence; supporting—to assist in the continuation of some aspect of the music, such as the basic beat; soloing—to play an independent musical figure in relation to the musical background; and imitating—to play back a musical idea in its original form immediately after someone else has played it. The group, with or without the therapist, chooses one or more roles to "play" during the improvisation.
   - *Modifications*: This improvisation is generally applicable to a higher functioning group, capable of defining social roles and discussing their experience during the interactions. Some patients may benefit from the structure of identifying one or two roles to play prior to a brief improvisation. Others will be able to make the decisions during the musical experience.

5. Referential improvisation or program music
   - *Description*: One version of this example may be a percussion improvisation version of songwriting. The therapist or group identifies an image or theme to represent with percussion instruments, such as "relaxing on the beach." The group decides on instruments to be used and how the music will proceed.
   - *Modifications*: Making advance decisions about how the music will sound adds focus for patients needing structure. Others can be spontaneous throughout. Those with more capacity for abstract reasoning may be able to represent visual imagery and even emotions and ideas through sound.

6. Percussion improvisation with song material
   - *Description*: This experience inherently offers structure through the added organization of melody. A short song may be used in call-and-response fashion with percussion accompaniment. The song itself is alternated with rhythmic improvisations.
   - *Modifications*: Higher functioning groups will be able to tolerate longer and less predictable improvisational sections. This format may also be used in a rap style. With stylistic background rhythms, patients may improvise rap lyrics or perform their composed lyrics within a structured framework. For example, a 16-beat or 32-beat section for a rap verse alternating with an equal-length rhythmic improvisation provides predictability and boundaries.

Working With Musical Responses

Once the therapist has elicited musical responses from the individual or group, spontaneous clinical decisions are made about working with the musical material offered by the patient, generally based on one's theoretical orientation and the patient's goals. When the music ends, the therapist then has the option of processing the material verbally.

Clinical Example

In this example, a group of five patients diagnosed with psychotic disorders, in varying levels of acuity, are involved in the improvisation session. These patients require a structured approach to music therapy improvisation. Some or all have been in recent groups with very structured musical experiences, such as group singing of known songs and limited songwriting and improvisation based on the 12-bar blues form. To begin, the therapist gives each patient a choice of two instruments and gives the verbal direction to begin playing when cued individually by the therapist. The therapist initiates a chord progression on the piano in a familiar style, for example, I vi ii V in a clear pop-rock tempo and groove, and proceeds with entrance cues, allowing each person to blend with the music that came before. Once everyone has entered the music, the therapist begins working with individual and group musical expressions. If the group's expressive range is limited, the therapist may continue leading and modeling techniques, for example, directing the patients to follow the therapist's obvious changes in dynamics. Based on the musical responses, the therapist may then choose to reflect and modulate overall group responses or to interact therapeutically with individuals. The latter offers more opportunity for musical flexibility when working with lower functioning patients. It allows each patient to focus on his or her own music as well as the therapist's interventions.

The therapist also has the opportunity to use individualized techniques based on each patient's music. To make this possible, the therapist verbally directs and/or models softer playing with the group and invites an individual to play louder or to play a "solo." If, for example, the "soloist" is playing a steady pulse with no variation on a tambourine, the therapist may begin by *mirroring* the pulse and possibly *reflecting* the timbrel and textural qualities of the tambourine sound. If this patient has previously played in a disorganized fashion and the concrete organization of a basic pulse represents progress, the therapist may decide to support or to assist in the continuation of that musical behavior, without the need for further intervention. If the patient has been able to organize at this level previously, the therapist may again use modeling to encourage variations in rhythm, either through increased complexity or through rests. In this example, such concrete playing is also related to a narrow range of affect, in which case the therapist may encourage changes in expressive musical qualities, such as dynamics. Changes in tempo should be carefully considered, as they may interfere with a person's sense of grounding. An approach for whole-group intervention is to leave spaces in the treble range of the piano while continuing a steady supportive bass. The treble range is then used for reflection, and motives are used to encourage antecedent-response interaction, embellishment, or variation of melodic themes.

The therapist may decide that the musical experience itself is the agent of change, again depending on goals of treatment, functioning level of the group, and clinical orientation. Certain groups may not currently have adequate cognitive functioning for discussing an experience after the fact or for listening to a recording of their music and discussing the interplay of the members. For people with adequate attention and focus, the group members may benefit from discussion of their interaction and connectedness as experienced during the improvisation and as heard on the recording (Nolan, 2005).

References

Alvin, J. (1975). Music therapy. London: John Claire Books.

Boone, P. (1991). Composition, improvisation and poetry in the psychiatric treatment of a forensic patient. In K. E. Bruscia (Ed.), Case studies in music therapy (pp. 433–449). Phoenixville, PA: Barcelona.

Bruscia, K. E. (1987). Improvisational models in music therapy. Springfield, IL: Charles C. Thomas.

Bruscia, K. E. (1989). The practical side of improvisational music therapy. Music Therapy Perspectives, 6, 11–15.

Bruscia, K. E. (1998). The dynamics of music psychotherapy. Gilsum, NH: Barcelona.

Clendenon-Wallen, J. (1991). The use of music therapy to influence the self-confidence of adolescents who are sexually abused. Music Therapy Perspectives, 9, 73–81.

Darnley-Smith, R. (2002). Music therapy with elderly adults. In A. Davies & E. Richards (Eds.), Music therapy and group work: Sound company (pp. 77–89). London: Jessica Kingsley.

DeBacker, J., & Van Camp, J. (2002). The case of Marianne: Repetition and musical form in psychosis. In S. Hadley (Ed.), Psychodynamic music therapy: Case studies (pp. 273–297). Gilsum, NH: Barcelona.

Edgerton, C. D. (1990). Creative group songwriting. Music Therapy Perspectives, 8, 15–19.

Ficken, T. (1976). The use of songwriting in a psychiatric setting. Journal of Music Therapy, 13(4), 163–172.

Freed, B. S. (1989). Songwriting with the chemically dependent. Music Therapy Perspectives, 4, 13–18.

Gardstrom, S. G. (2001). Practical techniques for the development of complementary skills in music improvisation. Music Therapy Perspectives, 19, 82–86.

Goldstein, S. L. (1990). A songwriting assessment for hopelessness in depressed adolescents: A review of literature and a pilot study. The Arts in Psychotherapy, 16(3), 179–192.

John, D. (1995). The therapeutic relationship in music therapy as a tool in the treatment of psychosis. In T. Wigram, B. Saperston, & R. West (Eds.), The art and science of music therapy: A handbook (pp. 157–166). Chur, Switzerland: Harwood Academic.

Justice, R. W. (1994). Music therapy interventions for people with eating disorders in an inpatient setting. Music Therapy Perspectives, 12(2), 104–110.

Kaplan, H. I., & Sadock, B. I. (1998). Synopsis of psychiatry (8th ed.). New York: Lippencott Williams & Wilkins.

Kortegaard, H. M. (1993). Music therapy in the psychodynamic treatment of schizophrenia. In M. Heal & T. Wigram (Eds.), Music therapy in health and education (pp. 55–65). London: Jessica Kingsley.

Langdon, G. S., Pearson, J., Stastny, P., & Thorning, H. (1989). The integration of music therapy into a treatment approach in the transition of adult psychiatric patients from institution to community. Music Therapy, 8(1), 92–107.

Lindberg, K. A. (1995). Songs of healing: Songwriting with an abused adolescent. Music Therapy, 13(1), 93–108.

Loth, H. (2002). There's no getting away from anything in here: A music therapy group within an inpatient programme for adults with eating disorders. In A. Davies & E. Richards (Eds.), Music therapy and group work: Sound company (pp. 90–104). London: Jessica Kingsley.

Metzner, S. (2004). The significance of triadic structures in patients undergoing therapy for psychosis in a psychiatric ward. In S. Hadley (Ed.), Psychodynamic music therapy: Case studies (pp. 257–271). Gilsum, NH: Barcelona.

Murphy, M. E. (1991). Group music therapy in acute psychiatric care: The treatment of a depressed woman following neurological trauma. In K. E. Bruscia (Ed.), Case studies in music therapy (pp. 465–478). Phoenixville, PA: Barcelona.

Nolan, P. (1983). Insight therapy: Guided imagery and music in a forensic psychiatric setting. Music Therapy, 3(1), 43–51.

Nolan, P. (1991). Music therapy with bone marrow patients: Reaching beyond the symptoms. In R. Spintge & R. Droh (Eds.), Music medicine (pp. 209–212). St. Louis, MO: MMB Music.

Nolan, P. (1994). The therapeutic response in improvisational music therapy: What goes on inside? Music Therapy Perspectives, 6, 49–51.

Nolan, P. (1997). Music therapy improvisation in the treatment of a resistant woman. In K. Bruscia (Ed.), Case studies in music therapy (pp. 451–464). Phoenixville, PA: Barcelona.

Nolan, P., Vergare, M., Hays, R., & Dulicai, D. (Producers). (1982). Interdisciplinary assessment of an adult psychiatric patient [Motion picture]. Available from Hahnemann Creative Arts in Therapy Program at Drexel University 245 N. 15th Street, ms 905, Philadelphia, PA.

Nordoff, P., & Robbins, C. (1977). Creative music therapy. New York: John Day.

Odell-Miller, H. (1991). Group improvisation therapy: The experience of one man with schizophrenia. In K. E. Bruscia (Ed.), Case studies in music therapy (pp. 417–431). Phoenixville, PA: Barcelona.

Odell-Miller, H. (1995). Approaches to music therapy in psychiatry with specific emphasis upon a research project with the elderly mentally ill. In T. Wigram, B. Saperston, & R. West (Eds.), The art and science of music therapy: A handbook (pp. 83–111). Chur, Switzerland: Harwood Academic.

Odell-Miller, H. (2002). One man's journey and the importance of time: Music therapy in a NHS mental health centre. In A. Davies & E. Richards (Eds.), Music therapy and group work: Sound company (pp. 63–76). London: Jessica Kingsley.

Pavlicevic, M. (1995). Interpersonal processes in clinical improvisation: Towards a subjectively objective systematic definition. In T. Wigram, B. Saperston, & T. West (Eds.), The art and science of music therapy: A handbook (pp. 167–180). Chur, Switzerland: Harwood Academic.

Pavlicevic, M. (1997). Music therapy in context: Music, meaning and relationships. London: Jessica Kingsley.

Pratt, R. R. (1992). Healing and art. The International Journal of Arts Medicine, 1(2), 3.

Priestley, M. (1975). Music therapy in action. New York: St. Martin's Press.

Schmidt, J. (1983). Songwriting as a therapeutic procedure. Music Therapy Perspectives, 1(2), 4–7.

Stephens, G. (1983). The use of improvisation for the developing of relatedness in the adult client. Music Therapy, 3(1), 29–42.

Stewart, D. (2002). Sound company: Psychodynamic group music therapy as facilitating environment, transformational object and therapeutic playground. In A. Davies & E. Richards (Eds.), Music therapy and sound work: Sound company (pp. 61–83). London: Jessica Kingsley.

Towse, E., & Flower, C. (1993). Levels of interaction in group improvisation. In M. Heal & T. Wigram (Eds.), Music therapy in health and education (pp. 73–81). London: Jessica Kingsley.

Wheeler, B. (1981). The relationship between music therapy and theories of psychotherapy. Music Therapy, 1(1), 9–16.

Wigram, T. (2004). Improvisations: Methods and techniques for music therapy clinicians, educators and students. London: Jessica Kingsley.

Wigram, T., Pederson, I. N., & Bonde, O. (2002). A comprehensive guide to music therapy. London: Jessica Kingsley.

Winston, A., Rosenthal, R. N., & Pinsker, H. (2004). Introduction to supportive therapy. Washington, DC: American Psychiatric.

Yalom, I. (1983). Inpatient group psychotherapy. New York: Basic Books.

Additional Resources

Bruscia, K. E. (1998). The dynamics of music psychotherapy. Gilsum, NH: Barcelona.

DeBacker, J. (1993). Containment in music therapy. In M. Heal & T. Wigram (Eds.), Music therapy in health and education (pp. 32–39). London: Jessica Kingsley.

Hadley, S. (Ed.). (2003). Psychodynamic music therapy. Gilsum, NH: Barcelona.

Izenberg-Grzeda, C. (1988). Music therapy assessment: A reflection of professional identity. Journal of Music Therapy, 25(3), 156–169.

Kanas, N. (1993). Group psychotherapy with schizophrenia. In H. L. Kaplan & B. J. Sadock (Eds.), Comprehensive group psychotherapy (3rd ed.) (pp. 407–418). Baltimore: Williams and Wilkins.

Loewy, J. (2000). Music psychotherapy assessment. Music Therapy Perspectives, 8(1), 47–58.

Nolan, P. (1995). The integration of mental health concepts in the education of the music therapist. In T. Wigram, B. Saperston, & R. West (Eds.), The art and science of music therapy: A handbook (pp. 433–441). Chur, Switzerland: Harwood Academic.

Nolan, P. (2005). Verbal processing in music therapy. Music Therapy Perspectives: Special Issue: The Role of the Music Therapist in the Music Therapy Process, 23, 18–28.

Sears, W. (1967). Processes in music therapy. In E. T. Gaston (Ed.), Music in therapy (pp. 30-46). New York: Macmillan.

Stephens, L. G. (1989). The integration of music therapy into a treatment approach in the transition of adult psychiatric patients from institution to community. Music Therapy, 8(1), 92–106.

Stone, W. N. (1993). Group psychotherapy with the chronically mentally ill. In Comprehensive Group Psychotherapy (3rd ed.; pp. 418–429). Baltimore: Wilkins and Wilkins.

APPENDIX A

Scale Patterns for Orff-Type Xylophones

(with F♯ and B♭ Tone Bars)

For all scales use the chord tone of the tonic key for the lowest and highest tone bars.

I.   *Major Pentatonic Scale Keys* (using pentatonic tones 1 2 3 5 6): C D F G , and B♭

II. *Major Diatonic Scale Keys*: C, F, and G

III. *Natural Minor Diatonic Scale Keys*: d, e, and a

IV. *Blues Scales*

    1. Use Dorian or Mixolydian diatonic scales (see V. below) with blues chordal accompaniment.

    2. Altered Scales:

        G: D E F G A B♭ B C D E F G A B♭ B

        D: D E F F♯ G A B C D E F F♯ G A

        E: E F♯ G A B♭ B D E F♯ G A B♭ B

    3. Minor Pentatonic (using pentatonic tones 1 3 4 5 7): A, C, D, E, G, or simply use the 6th degree of the major pentatonic as the tonal center.

V.   *Additional Modes*

        Dorian Keys: D, G, A

        Mixolydian Keys: C, D, G

        Lydian Keys: C, F, B♭

APPENDIX B

Development of Prerequisite Musical Skills and Knowledge

Theory

- Key signatures, major and minor (Dorian, Mixolydian recommended)
- Time signatures, including ability to identify aurally
- Interpret chord symbols in jazz and popular music
- Construction of major, minor, augmented, and diminished triads with extensions (sixths, sevenths, ninths)
- Form: AABA, Rondo, Blues; familiarity with Classical forms such as Theme and Variations, Sonata Allegro

Harmony

- Play basic progressions in all keys that are usable with Orff xylophones (see Appendix A) e.g., I-IV-V-I; I-vi-ii-V-I; i-iv-V7-i; ideally all keys
- Be able to create a progression for initiating an improvisation, e.g., I-IV-V-I or substitutions in a four-measure phrase
- Create a bridge, or B section in ABA form, using a different progression
- Blues progressions in all keys available on xylophone
- Be able to add all forms of sevenths for color and stylistic authenticity
- Be familiar with other chord extensions, including sixths and ninths
- Be able to play harmonic progressions in rhythmic stylistic context
- Interpret "fake book" material and insert improvisation "interludes"
- Harmonize original melodies/motives

Melody

- Create a melodic motive; extend and develop
- Improvise melodic figures within context of harmonic progressions
- Melodically reflect contour of melodic responses of another person
- Create ostinato pattern as organizing factor for group improvisation
- Create theme on melodic instrument (xylophone, recorder, orchestral instrument) for eliciting group rhythmic and melodic responses
- Create melodic figures using voice, with or without lyrics, to reflect and encourage client expression
- Create melodic motives for vocal turn-taking supported by harmonic or rhythmic ground

Rhythm

- Technical facility with a variety of percussion instruments, especially hand-held drums
- Ability to create and develop rhythmic themes
- Ability to respond to and imitate others' presented rhythms

- Knowledge of rhythmic patterns or "invariants" found in various styles, including world rhythms, rock beat, jazz beat
- Knowledge of role of various percussion instruments in an ensemble context
- Awareness of musical and expressive capabilities of rhythm instruments
- Ability to improvise in commonly heard meters, e.g., 4/4, 3/4, 2/4, 6/8, 12/8

Ensembles

- Arrange familiar songs with improvisation "interludes"
- Assign "invariants" as rhythm section for solo improvisations or Rondo (alternating group and individual playing)

Chapter 6

Insight Music Therapy with Re-Constructive Goals: An Overview

At this level, music therapy experiences are used to uncover, relive, or resolve subconscious conflicts. Interventions use music to elicit that unconscious material. The music is a critical component in bringing up and expressing the repressed material. This is often referred to as music psychotherapy. This approach is generally explored before specific applications are presented.

SPECIFIC TECHNIQUES

Psychodynamic Music Therapy With Nonpsychotic Adults

Teresa Leite

Among the many applications of music therapy, one specifically calls for the use of music at the service of self-expression and the development of interpersonal relationships: music psychotherapy. In music psychotherapy, the music therapist works primarily in the emotional and interpersonal realm with music playing a central role in the development of the therapeutic relationship (John, 1992). In this type of music therapy work, music is utilized mostly in its symbolic and interactive dimension. As a symbol, the musical elements chosen, the sounds produced, and the expressive qualities all can represent a client's emotional state or underlying issues. Because music is an oral art and involves nonverbal communication, it promotes interaction between client and therapist.

The specific area of music psychotherapy draws on the theoretical principles of the main currents of psychotherapy as defined in the field of psychology (Gurman & Messer, 2003). Although the current literature refers to a wide variety of therapy models, the term *psychotherapy* usually refers to a therapy model that is based mostly on psychodynamic theories.

There are therapy models that are now specific to music therapy, which resulted from a combination of the psychodynamic approach to psychotherapy with methodological principles from areas such as musicology, music recreation, music performance, and other healing practices from non-Western cultures (Wigram, Pedersen, & Bonde, 2002).

Some pioneers such as Juliette Alvin and Mary Priestley (Eschen, 2002) brought music into a central place in the therapeutic process and focused on the emotional, intrapsychic, and interpersonal mechanisms that take place in shared music making, with the goal of helping people overcome a wide variety of personal problems (Bruscia, 1987). In the pioneering days, this work was done mostly with institutionalized people with psychotic disorders, but its principles and methodology have since been applied to nonpsychotic adults at various levels of intervention (Bruscia, 1998a). In this section, the focus is on music therapy work that is done with nonpsychotic adults from a psychodynamic theoretical point of reference.

Theoretical Principles

With most other populations, music therapy intervention is suggested when a particular client presents significant difficulties or even complete inability to use verbal means of expression (Bunt & Hoskyns, 2002). In the case of nonpsychotic adults, music therapy is suggested primarily for the rich possibilities of expression and interaction that music provides, above and beyond the use of verbal expression. In such cases, the client is fully able to speak, but either the client or the treatment team has decided that music therapy is indicated for a number of possible reasons. The treatment team may identify one particular aspect that the client needs to work on, such as body language, emotional arousal, body-mind integration, or nonintellectualized information processing. Music provides added opportunities for the client to work on these aspects and often bypasses the blockages and inhibitions that the person may present in the realm of verbal expression. Music therapy may be indicated if the client expresses the wish or need to use a language other than verbal in a therapeutic context and/or if the client is musically trained.

In music therapy work with nonpsychotic adults, it is quite common for a client to engage in music therapy as the primary form of intervention (Smeijsters, 1993), and it may be used instead of other more traditional forms of psychotherapy, thus placing it at what Bruscia (1998b) calls the intensive or even the primary level of practice. This level of practice requires additional training on the part of the therapist and brings upon the therapist the added responsibility of being the sole provider of psychological help for the client.

Principles of Psychodynamic Psychotherapy

The realm of psychodynamic theories has expanded well beyond psychoanalysis and currently encompasses a wide variety of currents, all of them with the following features:

- The assumption that a person's way of thinking, feeling, behaving, and relating to others is determined by a system of dynamic forces (internal and interpersonal), both conscious and unconscious.
- A significant part of the mechanisms that determine our way of being in, and relating to, the world acts beyond the realm of conscious thinking.
- The person of the client is seen from a developmental approach, which means that the problems visible in the present are conceptualized as having been created throughout the process of development of the person as a whole, according to the dynamics mentioned above.
- There are some relationships that take on a specific importance in a person's life, in the formation of his or her personality and in his or her patterns of relating to other people, especially those that began in the early stages of the person's life, and those that involve people that are particularly important to satisfaction of the person's basic needs (Gurman & Messer, 2003; Ruud, 1990).

In the practice of psychotherapy, these theories have originated an equally varied array of therapeutic approaches, all of them presenting with the following main characteristics:

- The principal focus of therapy is the very relationship between the client(s) and the therapist, as well as the relationships between the clients when working in a group context. The problems presented by the client become visible in the therapeutic relationship and the desired changes in the patient's life are triggered by progressively changing the dynamics that occur within the therapeutic relationship itself.

- One of the main general goals of a therapeutic intervention is for the client to achieve insight over his or her own characteristics, which is considered the first step toward personal change.

- In most cases, therapeutic intervention is aimed at a global change in the person of the client and the lowering of the client's suffering in general, rather than limiting the intervention to the modification of a specific aspect or the relief of a particular symptom.

In the field of music therapy, a few principles were established by the humanistic and existential currents of psychotherapy, which have since been incorporated as core principles of music therapy, even for those therapists who work closer with the psychoanalytic paradigm. These include:

- The therapeutic relationship is a person-to-person encounter where both therapist and client must be genuinely present and relating to one another within the realm of musical experiences, working towards positive change in the person of the client.

- The role of the therapist is one of acceptance, support, and feedback based on comprehensive knowledge of the client as a whole person. The therapist takes a nondirective approach and determines the direction of therapeutic work from the client's needs and goals.

- A corollary of the previous principle that is specific to the music therapy setting is that the musical repertoire and music activities that carry the most therapeutic potential are those that correspond to the patient's preference, musical identity, and musical goals for the treatment process.

- The therapeutic relationship is most efficient in producing meaningful and lasting changes in the client's life when an experiential approach is used in the sessions. New experiences with personal and relational meaning to the client are created, and the progression of shared musical experiences becomes the ground for continuous re-creation of oneself in relation to others (Bunt & Hoskyns, 2002; Wigram et al., 2002).

Principles of Psychodynamic Music Therapy

The integration of the principles of psychodynamic psychotherapy stated above with the principles of music therapy as a whole results in an approach that is focused on a number of the main concepts listed below (Bruscia, 1998a).

Intrapsychic dynamics and the unconscious. Music is seen as a multidimensional activity that triggers unconscious dynamics and leads the person to integrate unconscious affect and thought with conscious thinking and behaving in the context of any musical activity—be it listening, playing, or creating. Therefore, the music therapist uses music to access unconscious parts of the client's mind and also relates to the client through the music in a conscious as well as unconscious way (Streeter, 1999).

In a music therapy setting, it is necessary that the unconscious dynamics (those issues that are not in conscious awareness) be enacted in the musical experience, so that the client can gain awareness of such processes (insights) and make the desired changes, with the help of the music therapist, in the development of their musical experiences together. Insight is a central concept in psychodynamic therapy (Gurman & Messer, 2003). It refers to one's ability to think about oneself and understand the internal motives for our behavior. In music therapy, insight is achieved by examining our musical choices, our behaviour, and our way of relating in the music, and the qualities of our musical productions in and of themselves (Amir, 1993).

One important difference between psychotherapy and music therapy is that in the latter, insight does not necessarily imply verbalization, and the concept of consciousness goes beyond the Freudian definition of the conscious processes (Ruud, 2003). In music therapy, one can achieve insight at a physical, an intellectual, an emotional, and even a spiritual level through processing of musical experiences without ever getting to verbalize them (Amir, 1993). The music itself is a way to register information and increase knowledge about our selves.

The symbolic power of music. In psychodynamically oriented music therapy, music is thought of as a symbolic language, a form of meaningful expression that may or may not be translated into words (Pavlicevic, 1997). It is the part of music that cannot be put into words that constitutes a way of widening and enriching the client's expressive repertoire.

Given the symbolism that is contained in the music, the client can identify, in the context of music listening, symbolic meaning to which he or she relates. The client can also actively play music that has personal meaning or create a symbolic message that is communicated to the therapist in the context of their interaction. That message can be verbally ambiguous and yet be full of personal meaning within the musical realm of communication, therefore expanding the possibilities of mutual understanding between the client and other people (Pavlicevic, 1995).

The music that is chosen and/or played by clients is understood by the therapist as a symbolic expression of who they are as a person, the unconscious dynamics of their way of relating, and the characteristics of their internal world at the time (Austin, 1996).

Object relations, transference, and countertransference. The relationship between patient and therapist in psychodynamic psychotherapy is a particularly important one because it tends to re-create the interpersonal dynamics that are characteristic of the patients in relation to their significant others (Bunt & Hoskyns, 2002). In music therapy, the therapeutic relationship plays a double function: (a) it serves as a ground for the re-enactment of the above mentioned dynamics, and (b) it also becomes a musical partnership and/or a collaborative creative project (Ahonen-Eerikainen, 2002).

While therapist and clients actively make or listen to music, the clients assume an emotional position in relation to the therapist that constitutes an enactment of the way they relate to important people in their life. This is called *transference* (Bruscia, 1998b; Streeter, 1999). In this context, the therapist also assumes certain positions in relation to the client that are complementary to the patient in that dynamic interpersonal pattern, a phenomenon that takes the name of *countertransference.*

Given that therapist and client develop their relationship through their participation in musical activities, the music that is listened to, played, or created can take on a symbolic meaning and express the interpersonal dynamics that are occurring between them, or else music can, in and of itself, trigger such dynamics (Montello, 1998). This constitutes a great opportunity for self-exploration and experimentation on the part of clients, allowing them to achieve greater knowledge of themselves and to exercise the desired changes in their interpersonal patterns. If this work can be done in the musical activity itself, the clients' progress will become visible in the music repertoire that fills the sessions and also in the clients' daily life outside the therapeutic setting.

The intermediate area of experience. Music can be conceptualized as a concrete event (sound and action) and a symbolic language at the same time. When therapist and client play or listen to music together, they are both taking concrete action and also charging the music material with personal and relational meaning (Pavlicevic, 1997). Their relationship develops within the realm of what Winnicott (1971) called "the intermediate area of experience," a realm of existence that includes elements of reality and fantasy, inner and outer world, and concrete and metaphoric dimensions. In this way, real experiences are produced in the session while, at the same time, a process of reviewing and symbolically re-enacting other important experiences from the client's life occurs. The music interactions between client and therapist are an integrative process that brings the factual and the symbolic elements of experience together (Stephens, 1983).

Identity and relatedness. For the nonpsychotic adult client, the search for a balance between establishing a personal identity and maintaining satisfactory relationships with the important people in the client's life is one of the main challenges that can be worked through therapy. Music is always a source of identification in our lives. Our musical preferences, familiar repertoire, instruments with which we relate, musical practices, and other elements of our musical profile are symbolic expressions of who we are as unique individuals. Also, new music experiences can produce personal changes and foster development of a richer or even new sense of identity (Johnson, 1981).

However, there is an intrinsic need to be connected to other people and to share the true self with others. In that sense, music is also a relational event. In playing music with others, a bond with those people is developed, which certainly goes beyond the level of connection allowed by verbal interaction. Consequently, the music therapist works to establish a musical activity and a relational setting in which clients can be emotionally connected to another person (therapist or other group members) and yet not lose sense of who they are and how they are represented in the music itself (Stewart, 2002).

The simple act of playing in a band, for example, provides the opportunity to hear the self playing on an instrument and, at the same time, tune to the other instruments, the musicians playing them, and the sound of the whole group. This negotiation, although it constitutes a challenge for every band musician, brings about an enormous potential for change in relating to the world and evaluating the individual's place in it (Ruud, 1998).

Settings for Music Psychotherapy With Nonpsychotic Clients

There are two main settings where psychodynamic music therapy with nonpsychotic adults is practiced: private practice and outpatient facilities in the community (Hadley, 2003).

Private practice music therapy is conducted in an office space of some kind. The music therapy office typically has a spacious room with instruments and a few chairs that can be easily moved. Usually a piano or keyboard is in the room, together with various percussion instruments. Since this is a type of population that can easily switch between verbal, musical, and other modes of expression, items are usually placed in a way that allows for that change to occur within the session without much rearranging. Sometimes, there is even a table and chairs with available art materials such as paper, paint, brushes, pastels, and markers.

In an outpatient setting, psychodynamic therapists also work in a private room with similar characteristics. Depending on the characteristics of the center, this room may be shared with other professionals at separate times, but privacy and sound insulation should be provided as much as possible.

Some music therapists have a private practice where they work mostly with self-referred clients (Austin, 1996). Private practice clients can also be referred by another health professional such as a physician, a psychologist, or a social worker. In this case, the music therapist must gather information about the services that the client is already receiving in order to avoid the existence of two "main" therapeutic relationships. This issue is discussed later, since it is a situation that is more likely to occur in outpatient treatment facilities.

Outpatient facilities or clinics are the second most common type of setting where a music therapist can work with this population. These facilities have multidisciplinary teams and clients may receive an array of services or just have the music therapist as their main care provider. (See section on adults with mental disorders in community settings in Chapter 9.)

Some outpatient facilities provide general mental health services to people in the community, but they can also be geared to serve a specific type of population: eating disorders, drug and alcohol use, abuse victims, trauma survivors, etc. (Wigram et al., 2002). Such cases will be contemplated in other chapters of this book and are not described any further in this section. However, it should be said that these are the settings where music therapy is most likely to function at what Bruscia (1998b) called the augmentative level, that is, as a complementary form of intervention geared to enhance the efforts of other forms of treatment. In such cases, the work is more focused on music projects developed by the client and specific treatment issues that are a priority for that particular type of client.

When the facility is not specifically geared to a particular type of pathology, clients can be referred to music therapy by the assessment team. Referral is based on criteria such as the client's relationship to music or specific characteristics that make such a client more likely to benefit from a music therapy approach. In any case, the music therapist will probably work as a primary therapist, in collaboration with other professionals, according to what other specialized services the client may need.

When working from a psychodynamic perspective, the therapeutic relationship is a crucial aspect of the work, and all efforts should be concentrated in one primary therapeutic relationship. For this reason, one aspect should be clarified from the beginning: Is music therapy going to be the main form of treatment, or is the client working with a psychotherapist? This will determine whether the music therapist will focus the approach on the client-therapist relationship or on specific issues the client may need to work on in the context of music activities.

Music therapy with this population is practiced in either an individual or a group format. Private practice music therapists often work in an individual format and outpatient facilities may offer music therapy services in both formats (Wigram et al., 2002). In both cases, sessions have a once-a-week frequency and tend to last between 45 minutes and 1 hour. Psychodynamic music therapists tend to keep the schedule, duration, and format of sessions as rigorous as possible in order to allow for intra- and interpersonal dynamics to develop in a predictable setting and become "visible" to both client and therapist.

The style of leadership of a psychodynamically oriented music therapist is usually nondirective, especially when working with nonpsychotic adults. Clients are usually free to decide what type of musical activities they want to be involved in and to choose the instrument they want to play. Therapists that have further training in a specialized approach such as the Bonny Method of Guided Imagery and Music

(BMGIM) are an exception, since the approach itself may determine the musical activity that is carried out in the sessions (Clarkson & Geller, 1996).

When working mostly with music-making activities, the music therapist often suggests a specific activity or invites the client to play a particular instrument, depending on the topics they are working on and the dynamics that have been developed until that moment in the symbolic use of music-related material.

Assessment

Assessment is a fundamental component of any music therapy intervention. Most music therapists gather initial information that covers three main axes: the person, the pathology, and the music, or better yet, the relation between each of the previous aspects to the music in the life of the client (Jahn-Langenberg & Schmidt, 2003). In psychodynamic music therapy, the initial assessment is done throughout the two or three first sessions in two complementary ways: the music therapy interview and clinical observation.

The music therapy interview. An initial interview is conducted with the client, given that most nonpsychotic adults have verbal skills and can carry a more or less continuous verbal dialogue. In most cases, this interview has a nonstructured format. The therapist asks clients open questions and invites them to talk freely about the presenting problem(s), the reason for coming to music therapy, their relationship to music, and the clients' own goals for music therapy (Jahn-Langenberg & Schmidt, 2003).

In this nonstructured interview, most music therapists let the conversation evolve in a way that is as spontaneous and comfortable to the client as possible, keeping in mind the need to gather information within the following topics:

- Main presenting problem(s)
- Psychiatric diagnosis, if there is one
- Current living situation, including main relationships
- Brief history of the client: childhood and adolescence review, occupation and activities, primary relationships, significant events and milestones, significant places, etc.
- A musical profile of the client (Bunt, 1994). This should include all aspects of the client's history and current personality that relate to sound and music:
  - familiar sound and musical environments
  - musical preferences
  - music training
  - instrumental practice
  - positive and negative experiences related to music
  - association between musical experiences and certain relationships
  - current relationship to particular musical styles, instruments, and musical practices

Despite the nondirective approach to assessment that is typical of psychodynamically oriented music therapists, there is an ongoing effort to structure and solidify the assessment procedure through the use of more structured tools. Jacqueline Verdeau-Paillés (2004) established the Psychomusical Assessment, which includes a structured interview, a music listening projective test, and a standardized setting observation with the music therapist in the strict role of the observer. The music therapist then reviews the information gathered in these three parts to establish some conclusions and therapeutic goals for each particular client.

Clinical observation. For most psychodynamically oriented music therapists, the assessment phase is also the beginning of the therapeutic process. This means that in the beginning stages of therapy, the therapist assumes the position of a participant-observer. The therapist is gathering information but is also actively working on the establishment of a therapeutic relationship that allows the client to comfortably engage in exploratory work and in any musical experiences that may be available to them (Bunt, 1994). Juliette Alvin, one of the pioneers in music therapy, strongly advocated for the role of the music therapist as an active but nondirective presence in the sessions, always being very attentive to the information arising from the free playing of the client and progressively engaging in an active music-making relationship with the client (Bruscia, 1987).

The participant-observer approach leads the assessment stages to take on a format that is very similar to the later music therapy sessions, because the therapist is already engaged in music activities with the client. The therapist assumes a nondirective approach in both verbal dialogue and music playing or listening portions of the session.

However, in the assessment phase, the therapist asks more questions and uses more exploratory musical activities than in the following phases of the therapeutic process (Bruscia, 1987). The client may be experimenting with some instruments or exploring the available collection of recorded music. The therapist may follow the client's choices or can make tentative activity proposals to the client. After some time, a session format starts emerging that alternates between music listening/playing and verbal conversation periods. Also, the musical product (improvisation, song, etc.) starts taking shape and both client and therapist may bring material to the session that contributes to the development of such projects.

For a psychodynamically oriented music therapist, free observation (not instruction) is a very important part of the initial assessment. The client's choices and musical behaviors are observed as symbolic expressions of the client's personality, emotional status at the moment, and way of relating to other people (Langenberg, Frommer, & Tress, 1995). The therapist takes the observable behavior and the characteristics of the client's musical production as symbolic representations of the client's issues, and the musical interaction between them is seen as an active metaphor for the client's interpersonal dynamics. Therapeutic goals are then planned on the basis of the problems that arise in the context of such musical interactions.

Diagnosing has always been a controversial topic in music therapy. The discipline of music therapy itself was born out of the need to help people with problems beyond the technicalities of diagnostics and treatment (Kenny, 1985). Many music therapists identify with the humanistic philosophy of approaching the client as a person and not as a "labelled patient."

However, the field of music therapy is increasingly aware of the need to gather diagnostic information and work from the already existing classifications of psychiatric disorders and their general characteristics. In that sense, a music therapist always takes into consideration the diagnostic formulations that were already made for a particular client as an important source of information (Smeijsters, 1993).

As can be expected, psychodynamic music therapists find it most useful to gather information about psychodynamic diagnostic formulations. Such formulations focus primarily on the type of personality structure, interpersonal dynamics, typical defense mechanisms, and types of anxiety and emotional states we can expect for that client (Bruscia, 1998a). Nonpsychotic patients usually present with a clearly established system of defense mechanisms. In the music therapy setting, materials and musical activities that provide the client with an opportunity to reveal such dynamics can be provided and, if and when possible, change the less desirable features in these dynamics into more adaptive patterns of relating.

When a diagnosis has not yet been established for a particular patient, psychodynamic music therapists working in private practice may not always focus on that type of classification. Instead, they tend to work on the relational aspects from the very beginning. However, it is always important—and in an outpatient center setting, absolutely necessary—to refer to the widely accepted systems of diagnostic classification such as the *DSM-IV*. The establishment of a psychiatric diagnosis does not have to be taken merely as a labelling procedure or a restrictive influence on the therapist's approach to the patient. It should be used as a point of reference for treatment planning and as a ground for clearer communication among mental health professionals.

Diagnostic formulations always provide us with the following types of information:

- The main areas of functioning that are affected by the client's pathology
- The client's most likely cognitive, behavioral, and interactive style
- The client's most typical state of humor and response to anxiety
- An idea of what to expect for the client's progress throughout the course of therapy

Following is a list of the most typical *DSM-IV-TR* diagnostic categories represented in the practice of a psychodynamically oriented music therapist, among the group of nonpsychotic disorders:

- Mood disorders, in particular, major depressive disorders and dysthymia
- Anxiety disorders, in particular, generalized anxiety, obsessive-compulsive, and posttraumatic stress disorders
- Personality disorders, in particular, borderline, histrionic, schizoid, schizotypal personality disorders
- Adjustment disorders
- Psychosomatic disorders

Other disorders, such as substance abuse disorders and eating disorders, can be found but are discussed further in other sections of this book.

Whether focusing on diagnostic categories or not, a number of issues are prevalent in most nonpsychotic adult patients that can be worked in music therapy with particularly good results, depending on the techniques used by the therapist. The following list illustrates the types of characteristics that are often taken as the main focus of a music therapist's intervention with such clients (Loewy, 2000):

- Rigidity of thinking and acting
- Difficulties with emotional expression
- Difficulties with interpersonal boundaries
- Identity issues—dependence on others versus differentiation of the Self
- Depression, self-criticism, and lack of self-confidence
- Difficulty managing negative emotions and interpersonal conflicts
- Difficulty managing anxiety
- Difficulty managing intimate relationships
- Difficulty coping with external events
- Creative blocks
- Performance anxiety
- Psychological effects of abuse or trauma

Typical Goals and Objectives

Psychodynamically oriented music therapists tend to establish general goals or even focus areas to work on with the client, rather than establishing specific and measurable goals and objectives (Smeijsters & van den Hurk, 1999). Throughout the first two or three sessions, the therapist develops an overall idea of the client in two main dimensions: (a) the client's psychological features and most prevalent problems, and (b) the client's ideas and preferences for musical activities to be developed.

These two dimensions overlap and the information gathered up to that point leads the music therapist to establish treatment goals in a more qualitative approach, rather than a quantitative one. In other words, the main questions to be asked are:

- What is there to work on?
- How does the client relate to me at this point?
- How should we approach these issues in the music?

The goals most typically established by a psychodynamically oriented music therapist working with this population are to

- release blockages of emotional expression;
- create new ways to represent internal states, feelings, and ideas;
- increase knowledge of unconscious dynamics that may be triggering pathological behaviors or negative emotional states;
- review negative events through alternative modes of expression and find creative ways to process them in a way that is acceptable and productive in one's current life;
- practice new ways of interaction that allows the therapist to get his or her needs met and still maintain a connection with important others;
- develop creative thinking and build new projects;
- help the client define and expand his or her own identity;
- decrease feelings of isolation and alienation;
- decrease anxiety and depression;
- decrease self-criticism.

This type of work develops on a long-term basis through the development of somewhat regular musical activities that constitute the ground for the "working through" of long-established patterns of behavior on the part of the client. The client-therapist relationship also evolves within a long-term time frame and both musical and nonmusical interactions between them may eventually show significant changes while the setting's routines are maintained. These changes acquire a symbolic meaning and reflect the client's progress toward the initially established goals (Nolan, 2003).

In summary, music therapists working with nonpsychotic adults are mostly concerned with the development of the client's unique identity; the development of more mature and satisfying patterns of relating to others; and the development of creativity, in and out of the musical realm (Smeijsters, 1993).

Techniques for Working Psychodynamically With Nonpsychotic Clients

A number of issues are related to this form of music therapy when working from a psychodynamic approach.

The session format. In psychodynamic music therapy with nonpsychotic adults, the session format is based on an alternating pattern of verbal dialogue and music-making or music-listening activities. These two parts of the session do not have rigid boundaries and, therefore, verbal exchanges may occur during the musical experiences and vice versa.

Given that nonpsychotic adults often have the capability to speak and make decisions, the therapist adopts a nondirective approach, letting the client decide the content of the conversation and the type of musical activities to be developed. Usually, the session starts with a brief dialogue about ongoing issues or relevant aspects of that particular day. Based on that initial dialogue, a musical activity is "designed." This activity may be decided in three possible ways:

- It is triggered with the intent of "musically processing the verbal experience" (Austin, 1996)?
- Does it constitute a new musical activity that the client chose to do?
- Does it come in the context of other musical experiences that occurred in previous sessions?

Psychodynamic music therapists all have different ways of deciding and processing the musical experiences that take place in the session, according to their specific theoretical orientation or to the music therapy model they follow. However, the session tends to evolve freely from the first musical experience, as both therapist and client reflect verbally upon it, propose modifications to it, or move on to a different experience (Amir, 1999). Each session ends with a verbal exchange that brings closure to the musical experiences of that session and prepares the client for a different mode of functioning outside the music therapy room.

Music making versus music listening. The majority of the psychodynamic music therapists working with this population propose primarily either music-listening or music-making experiences, while some of them combine these two types of activities and may even add movement or visual arts activities. For those who work primarily with either music-listening or music-making activities, the specific music therapy model for which they have been trained determines such choice. For example, Bonny Method of Guided Imagery and Music (BMGIM) therapists tend to work exclusively with music-listening activities (Clarkson & Geller, 1996), while analytical music therapists (the Mary Priestley model) tend to work exclusively with music-making activities (Eschen, 2002).

Since verbal clients are able to make choices and to more or less manage their own behavior within the proposed activities, the therapist does not establish a very concrete structure or decide on the content of the musical experience. The music therapist may or may not initiate the playing and give an open suggestion as a starting point, but for the most part, the therapist takes a more supportive role, letting his or her contributions arise from what the client is doing (Bruscia, 1987).

If the work is mostly focused on the internal world of the client and its representation in the music, therapists mainly act to encourage more participation of the client, to contain the force of the client's emotional release, or to help the client organize the musical ideas (Hadley, 2003). If, on the other hand, therapists work from a more relational approach, then their musical (and verbal) behavior will be a more interactive one. They may deliberately enact the role that is assigned to them by the client's transference mechanisms in the context of what is happening in the therapeutic relationship (Austin, 1999b). These dynamics tend to be processed verbally afterwards, although it is very important that the verbal processing include a mutual contribution of both therapist and client. It is also very important that the verbal conversation that follows be clearly focused on the musical experience that triggered it, generating ideas for further music experiences where the client is invited to make changes in his or her own musical functioning patterns.

The role of improvisation. Improvisation is the most commonly used activity in psychodynamic music therapy. The use of improvisation in a clinical context dates back to the work of the pioneers (Wigram et al., 2002). It is a main feature in core models of music therapy work. Improvisation as a tool in insight music therapy with re-educative goals was addressed earlier in this chapter. Improvisation in psychodynamic music therapy began when Mary Priestley used musical improvisation at a metaphoric level to re-enact internal dynamics and relational processes that were reported or demonstrated by her clients in individual music therapy (Eschen, 2002). In the Priestley model, the therapist works mostly at the piano and the client can choose the instrument that best symbolizes the role he or she is about to enact in the music. In this model, most improvised music is determined by verbal suggestions in the form of titles or the description of particular situations—real or imaginary—that client and therapist enact in the music-making process. For example, clients can be asked to put into music their latest episode of intense fear, or they can propose to play with the therapist and improvise the sound of an imaginary conversation between husband and wife.

Juliette Alvin, another pioneer of music therapy, developed a model of intervention based on free improvisation, enhancing the importance of freeing ourselves from pre-established musical rules in order to maximize the expressive possibilities of the instrument and the notes available to us. She believed that improvised music had the power to blur the boundaries between conscious and unconscious processes, allowing the therapist access to otherwise inaccessible aspects of the client's internal world. In this model, improvisation can start with no verbal induction and is mostly led by the client. The therapist plays only when directly suggested by the patient and fulfills mostly a role of support or encouragement for the expression of musical ideas that seem to be inhibited or even blocked (Bruscia, 1987).

Winnicott (1971), a well-known psychoanalyst, described at length the immense value of free and symbolic play in the psychological development of the child's self and his or her relation to others (at first the maternal figure) at both a symbolic and a concrete level. Improvisation is often referred to as the musical equivalent of the intermediate area of experience described by Winnicott: while improvising, both client and therapist explore sounds and silence in a dynamic process of interaction (Pavlicevic, 1997). In that interaction, music acquires a symbolic meaning while being a concrete sound production. Client and therapist are free to play in whichever way occurs to them. There is a wide array of possibilities for altering the course of action and responding to new elements coming from one another and the music itself. Together, they create a musical product that is neither a direct expression of the unconscious nor an externally determined piece of music, but instead one that acquires here-and-now meaning to the person of the client and to the therapeutic relationship.

When music playing is totally exploratory and not induced by verbal suggestions, the role of the therapist is to support the client's musical ideas and try to capture the emotional quality of what the client is playing. If, at each moment, the therapist's music reflects or matches the qualities of the client's music, an atmosphere of congruency and relatedness is created and the client is likely to take the next step into freer and more authentic forms of expression (Montello, 1999).

Improvisation can be compared to the free association technique that is used in psychoanalytic psychotherapy, where the client is asked to talk freely and let himself spontaneously associate between ideas and topics (Austin, 1999b; Eschen, 2002). The goal of this technique is to make visible to the therapist—and ultimately the client—the unconscious dynamics that are responsible for such associations.

Improvisation not only allows for the free association between musical ideas and the emotional experiences connected to them, but it also has a dynamic quality in the sense that the music itself can change the client's initial experience as it is being created. If the music is played by client and therapist together, the quality of their musical interaction can, in and of itself, bring new experiences of relating to the client and an expanded awareness of who he or she is.

In a group setting, improvisation becomes a particularly powerful way to work, for it serves as the basis for each participant to become part of the group as a whole, despite the differences in personal style and musical skills that may exist within the group (Ahonen-Eerikainen, 2002). Music improvisation is a rich tool for people to build relationships with one another and to negotiate their needs and wants while maintaining a positive connection among them (Langenberg et al., 1995).

Secondly, the musical task of the group is free from the traditional music rules and a previously established musical content leads to the creation of a particular metaphorical space for interaction among the group members and for the group dynamics to emerge. The sound that results from group improvisation can be described throughout the various stages of the group in the same way that the group itself and the relational dynamics among them can evolve in time.

Rolando Benenzon (1997), a music therapist from Argentina, presents a method for working with music therapists in training that relies solely on group musical improvisation. In these groups, unconscious dynamics occur within and in between the group members, allowing each of them to develop their knowledge of themselves while in relation to others and to work on their interaction patterns in a quasi-therapeutic setting.

Song repertoire in psychodynamic music therapy. As explored earlier in this chapter, people relate to songs in individual and unique ways. By actively listening to these songs, one is touched by their words and musical atmosphere. A degree of pleasure is experienced as feelings and experiences are represented in that song, and the author's creation can be owned and appreciated by the listener. When playing that song, the process of identification becomes more alive and sometimes intense, as a certain degree of authorship is embodied, and the performer draws aesthetic, physical, and emotional pleasure from bringing the musical material to life. Some of the personal internal dynamics in the here-and-now are re-experienced in relation to that song.

When working with clients that are particularly vulnerable or not yet ready for a direct verbalization of their musical experiences, the music therapist may choose to play and create songs. Even though the playing of the song itself can become quite an intense experience, the verbal meaning of what was experienced is encapsulated in the song itself and is not always talked about at a separate moment, creating a less intrusive and more supportive way to integrate music and words in the therapy setting.

In the context of a music therapy intervention, improvisation may not be enough to satisfy expression or aesthetic needs. On the other hand, a blockage in the realm of free musical expression may be experienced that goes beyond the limits of how much one can challenge oneself. In that case, a more structured musical form is needed. A composition project or simply a "cover song" project with the help of the therapist may address this need.

The role of the therapist in composition and song writing is to: (a) musically assist the client in the creation and arrangement of the song, (b) share the musical experience with the client and to support the client when powerful or difficult emotions are triggered by the song itself, and (c) help the client understand the meaning of that particular song and how it can contribute to the therapeutic process (Chumacero, 1998).

Songs are also a creative way to integrate the verbal and the nonverbal realm of expression without resorting to a form of verbal processing that is clearly outside of the musical experience. Songs sometimes bring to light certain aspects of the client's experience in the very choice of themes, musical styles, and lyrics (Nolan, 1998).

Case Study 1: Carrie and the Interpersonal Area of Improvisation

The subtitle of this section constitutes a word association to Winnicott's (1971) phrase—the intermediate area of experience—that is widely mentioned in the music therapy literature. In fact, music being a form of art exists in that realm of experience that intersects with fantasy and reality. This is where musical experiences gain meaning (Pavlicevic, 1997).

Based on that idea, it can be said that a music therapist invites the client to be and relates to him or her primarily in the realm of symbolic play through music making. Consciously and unconsciously, the client enacts functioning patterns and ways of relating in the act of making music. The changes that occur in that relationship are the very core of the therapeutic process, and they take place in that factual and symbolic space of action that is the process of making music together.

"Carrie" (not her real name) is a 32-year-old professional woman who has been in therapy for 5 months. She is a human resources manager and studied the piano throughout adolescence. She requested therapy due to significant difficulties managing her romantic relationships and the anxiety associated with them. We are creating sound-related metaphors to work on this issue. By using improvisation, exercises were developed that help us think about her experiences and at the same time create new relational experiences between us.

Since the beginning of therapy, Carrie has explored her numerous romantic relationships and her fear of ending up alone. She talks about there being "too much noise" in her intimate relationships and dissatisfaction with all of them. There seems to be a compulsive need to move into the relationship very fast and confirm a total, unconditional love that is unlikely to happen so quickly. The failure to find this always ends up reinforcing her lack of trust in the other person. Very soon after that, she engages in the next relationship, as if running from herself or the silence and loneliness that come up between relationships.

Carrie associates this pattern to childhood memories of feeling abandoned and betrayed by her parents who always "promised her the world" and then left her alone at key difficult times. She says that in the present, she has difficulty believing even her closest friends when they tell her "they are there for her." Lately, she has accepted the challenge of trying to create a "pause" between relationships, exploring other issues in her life and searching for her own areas of interest, but she finds it very difficult to overcome the feelings of emptiness and fear when she spends time alone.

In a particular session, I invite her to "get into that space" she feels is empty and get to know it, trying to discover herself and with what or who she would like to fill it. She said that every time she tries to get into this space, she feels a knot in her stomach, a kind of discomfort that is lonely and mind-blocking at the same time, causing her to "blank out" when trying to find something she would like to do on her own. I invite her to close her eyes and let an image arise in that space: "What do you see in it?"

Faced with this request, Carrie produces an image with a sound—she says it's like a single beat of a deep and low register sounding drum. The sound from that one beat stays in the air in a mysterious way and then slowly gives way to empty space again in the total silence.

This is a significant moment in the session, for it represents a blockage in the verbal realm of expression and, at the same time, a creation of the possibility for exploration as the imaginary sound is mentioned. I felt Carrie's powerlessness to go further on this issue and her fear that she would not see anything in that space, as requested.

I take a large single-skin Native American drum and its mallet, and I offer it to her, inviting her to experience the feeling of what she had just mentioned. She plays a single beat in the center of the skin. I let it resonate until the sound faded into absolute silence. A few seconds later, I play two tentative soft beats on a similar but smaller drum. I want to acknowledge the enactment of that silent space after a lonesome beat, while at the same time letting her know that I was there with her. The next silence feels more like an anticipating/suspension silence, rather than an empty silence.

She smiles, looking as if she is waiting for my instructions or simply trying to figure out whether she should continue playing. I wait, ready to play. She plays a small phrase. I play a simpler, long-note phrase. She responds with another phrase, and I end up playing a supportive tempo, nonverbally inviting her to continue with my facial expression. We develop an interactive improvisation that goes from hesitant phrases to a sort of accompanied solo on Carrie's part, exploring phrases with the support of my tempo beat. Every once in a while, phrases are separated by brief pauses where she looks at me, as if asking for suggestions. I play a simple variation on her last phrase, acknowledging the basis for our playing together but also letting her know that this is her space to fill. I am just there to accompany on this stroll through a new space that is felt at first as empty and insecure, evolving into a kind of shared sound meditation.

In this clinical example, music making served as an active way to explore the client's personal space, a way to overcome the fear and the void that had been established, and also a way to create a connection with the client, instead of leaving her alone in that verbal blockage.

Most of all, improvisation functioned as an active metaphor that helped establish a relational space between client and therapist. Carrie was invited to explore that space without the demands of verbalization, and I offered my presence in a tentative, nonintrusive way, to reduce the fear of loneliness without making promises that could be felt as hollow by her. At a factual and also a symbolic level, the sound realm was a new space for Carrie to explore, to develop her own ideas. Only time could bring her some reassurance that I would not leave her alone there. My role was to make her feel safe, but I did not want to let her depend on me for ideas. I also did not want to fill that void for her, because that would eventually lead her to feel unacknowledged and lonely, much in the way she was feeling with the men in her life.

Conclusion

In psychodynamic music therapy with nonpsychotic adults, the relational dynamics, the symbolic expression of emotions, and the building of the client's identity are the main aspects to be worked on through the music. Music is used as an active metaphor for being and relating, an alternative field for the development of interaction and the creation of meaning in our lives.

Therapeutic work can be done in individual or group settings. The musical experiences that take place in the sessions are mostly active music making, with the exception of BMGIM and other specific methods that may rely exclusively on music listening. Musical improvisation is widely used, for it offers both therapist and client the opportunity to change the score as they are creating it, opening up a wide range of possibilities for communication and interpersonal dynamics. Such dynamics are mostly worked in the here-and-now, although many times they relate to other relationships and experiences outside of the session.

The connection between what happens in the session and outside of it, as well as the connection between musical and verbal experiences in the session itself, may or may not be verbalized. It is truly in the musical realm that re-enactment of meaningful experiences takes place and therapeutic interventions are made. However, for the most part, a verbal interaction section follows or precedes every musical experience in the session. This verbalization works as a way of processing what happened in the music or to induce and plan the next music-making experience.

Music therapists working with this approach may work with the so-called normal adults, clients with anxiety or depression problems, those with personality disorders, and survivors of traumatic events. In general, the role of the music therapist is to provide the client with an alternative way to process their experiences and to use music as a field of interaction where the client may explore new ways of relating to others.

Vocal Psychotherapy

Diane Austin

Jean was talking rapidly in a high-pitched voice. "I got a letter from my mother and she gave away my grandmother's heirlooms. She never even asked me if I wanted anything. . . This is so typical of her. I'm always excluded. It's like she hates me, like I'm not even a member of my own family."

As she talks, I listen to the music of her speaking voice as well as the content of her words. I watch as she inhales quickly and continues to talk. I notice that she does not exhale and that her voice sounds constricted and disconnected from her body. She does not leave room for me to engage with her. I wait for a pause so that I can interact with her but none comes, so I interrupt and say, "What are you feeling right now?" Jean looks at me. "I don't know—stressed," she replies. I suggest we do some breathing together. "Why?" she asks. I explain what I have noticed about her speaking pattern, that she talks fast and breathes shallowly, often holding her breath.

We talk about the way she unconsciously controls her feelings by controlling her breathing. I think about how often I feel as if she comes in and dumps all this stuff in my lap and resists digesting what's buried in all of her words. I tell her the breathing will help her to slow down so that she can experience her feelings. I suggest that we do a simple breathing exercise together. "Inhale through your mouth as if you are sipping something delicious through a straw, slowly, savoring the taste. When you are completely filled up, exhale very slowly on a 'whew' sound until you have squeezed out all the stale air."

We breathe together like this for several minutes. I then suggest that Jean allow sounds to emerge with each exhalation. The "whew" gradually turns into a "wah" then "waaah." I tone with her, matching her pitch, volume, and vocal quality. As we continue, her voice becomes louder, and she holds the tones longer. Eventually, her one note becomes two as she descends to a minor third. As we tone, I feel waves of longing and sorrow flowing through my body. When her tears begin to fall, they seem like a natural accompaniment to her sounds. "It's so sad . . . I feel so sad." "I know," I reply.

Vocal psychotherapy is defined as the use of the voice, improvisation, song, and dialogue within an analytic orientation to promote intrapsychic and interpersonal change. The example above illustrates the use of breathing techniques and toning. In this article, working with the voice through breathing, toning, vocal improvisation, and songs, and through awareness of the music of the speaking voice is described and illustrated. Although the case examples are from a private practice with adults, many aspects of vocal psychotherapy have been used effectively with other populations.

The Lost Voice

We enter the world and with our first sound announce our arrival. Our first cry proclaims our birth and the life force flowing through us. We begin as vital, spontaneous beings, curious and open, and the sounds we make express this. We laugh, we cry, we scream. We make sounds instinctively and receive pleasure from playing with our lips, tongue, and vocal cords. There is a flow, a freedom to the sounds and movements we make that characterize spontaneity and health.

We are also born listeners. The ear is the first sensory organ to develop and is functional 4-1/2 months before we are born (Minson, 1992). The sounds we hear in the womb, the rhythm of our mother's heartbeat, the flow of her breathing, and the nuances of her voice "stimulate our brain and fire electrical charges into our cortex" (Minson, 1992, p. 92). These electrical charges provide nourishment that is critical to the development of the brain and the central nervous system (Minson, 1992; Storr, 1992; Tomatis, 1991).

Somewhere between the 3rd and 4th month after birth, infants produce sounds that resemble singing. At about 6 months of age, babies enter the lall-ing period and move their lips and tongue rhythmically making sounds like "la-la-la" (Moses, 1954). During this stage, babies are not trying to communicate; they are simply enjoying the pleasurable sensation of repeating simple syllables.

> Voice production in this wordless age leaves solely agreeable memories . . . [and] is practically unlimited. Happiness and displeasure can be expressed over endless periods; no hoarseness will interfere. The breathing capacity does not seem to have limits; it functions ideally. (Moses, 1954, p. 19)

During this same period, babies begin to recognize the sound of their mother's voice. The vocal interaction in speech and song between mother and child and its continuity is crucial in fostering the child's ability to bond with others and critical to the child's developing sense of self. This sound connection reflects the emotional and psychological relationship between the mother and her child (Moses, 1954; Newham, 1998). For example, a mother suffering from postpartum depression may be unable to interact with her child, vocally, somatically, and emotionally. This lack of connection can seriously affect the child's ability to form a secure attachment to the mother and later in life may result in difficulty establishing and maintaining intimate relationships (Minson, 1992; Tomatis, 1991).

As children continue to grow and develop, they are affected by the spoken and unspoken messages they receive from the significant people in their lives. One client I work with was told by her father, "If you cry, I'll hit you even harder." Of course, this client now has a very difficult time not only crying, but also vocally expressing herself in any form. When I began working with her, she spoke in a barely audible voice and sped through her sentences as if someone was chasing her. Someone was.

Emily's mother became very ill when Emily was 8 years old. She had to be quiet in the house and could not have friends over to play because her mother was not to be disturbed. Unconsciously, Emily took in the message that she had to stifle her feelings and sounds of excitement and joy. "Not just because I couldn't make noise; it was more than that . . . how could I allow myself to feel alive when everything around me felt dead?" Emily was a professional singer but stopped singing when her mother died. Through vocal psychotherapy, Emily gradually began to express her grief and anger and allow herself to sing again.

Many of us lose our individual voices, sometimes subtly and gradually without even realizing it is happening and sometimes not so subtly. When our feelings and needs are judged or ignored, we learn to judge or ignore them. We shut down for self-preservation. We silence ourselves. Vital parts of the personality that represent our true voices are hidden away because it is not safe to express what we really think and feel. We fear disapproval, rejection, and abandonment. The saddest part is that when it is finally safe to come out, we no longer have access to these authentic aspects of ourselves. We have hidden them away so well we can no longer find them (Austin, 2002; Miller, 1981).

Our emotions are blocked and censored, and our voices reflect the blockage. "As long as we are emotionally protective our breathing cannot be free . . . the voice will depend on compensating strength in the throat and mouth muscles" (Linklater, 1976, p. 12). When we do feel a spontaneous impulse, it is short-circuited by a secondary, inhibiting one. These secondary impulses become habitual and familiar and what is familiar feels safe. Natural impulses become difficult to trust because they are unfamiliar and unknown. Spontaneity is hard to access because it can become associated with the fear of loss of control and judgment. Additionally, neuromuscular patterns develop into habits that cut us off from our instinctual connection between emotion and breath (Linklater, 1976). Our breathing becomes constricted, our vocal range becomes limited, and our voices become inaudible, tight, and tense or breathy and undefined. We may adopt aspects of our parents' voices or develop a "false voice," perhaps lovely to listen to but not connected to the core of who we are (Austin, 2002, 2004). That child who once was so alive playing in a free flowing stream of sounds, movements, and emotions is lost to us.

Reconnection: The Breath

Before becoming a music therapist, I was a professional singer. I was also a voice teacher and vocal coach. I remember realizing one day that many of the people who came to me for singing instruction were really seeking permission to feel. Some of them associated singing with a time in childhood when they were free to express themselves vocally and take pleasure from it. Others who were emotionally blocked and shut down found singing was a safe way to gain access to their feelings. Because of the safe, nonjudgmental structure of the voice lesson and the containing quality of songs, my students were often able to tap into emotions evoked by the deep breathing necessary to sustain tones as well as the emotional associations triggered by the music and the lyrics. Additionally, singing is more accepted as a form of expression than screaming, crying, or other displays of strong emotion. The majority of the students I worked with were not looking to become singing stars. They were looking for themselves.

Finding one's voice is often used as a metaphor for finding one's self. Finding one's voice in a literal sense facilitates the process of speaking one's truth and claiming one's unique identity. This process takes time, patience, and courage, but the rewards are ample.

Recovering one's true voice requires re-inhabiting the body. The first step in reconnecting to the body-self is learning to breathe deeply. It is interesting to note that the Greek word *opsyche*, which means soul, has the same root as the word *opsychein*, which means to breathe. Breath is the life force that connects the mind, body, and spirit. Cutting off the breath by constricting the throat, chest, or abdomen can sever the connection to feelings and dramatically affect the quality of both the speaking and singing voice (Austin, 1986, 1991, 2001). The ability or inability to deeply inhale and exhale reflects our personality traits and psychological issues. Can we relax enough to fully take in what is occurring in the moment? Can we let go of the feelings we are holding? Can we trust our bodies to sustain the life force, or do we push, force, and constrict our bodies and our breath out of lack of trust or misconceptions of the breathing process? As one client expressed it:

I was surprised by how difficult it was to breathe without forcing it . . . as we continued with the deep breathing, I felt as if a knife were lodged in my lower chest. I began sighing deeply, and as I slowly began to let the air flow in and out of my body, I was filled with grief.

The way we breathe influences how we feel and what we feel has a direct effect on how we breathe. According to Gaynor (1999), "Breathing is much more than a mechanical reflex for oxygen exchange; it is the basis for all of our cellular functions, our energetic well being, even our emotional health" (pp. 56–57). When we breathe deeply, we produce a current of energy that can be channeled to parts of the body that need soothing, tension release, and revitalization. Deep breathing slows the heart rate and calms and nurtures the nervous system. It stills the mind and body, relaxing the musculature and creating an experience of groundedness. The relaxed, centered state that results is beneficial to everyone but especially helpful to anyone in a state of panic or anxiety (Austin, 1999b, 2001; Braddock, 1995; Gardner, 1990; Newham, 1998).

Case Study 2

Karen sat beside me at the piano. I suggested we do some breathing together before singing. Singing was very risky for Karen, but she felt it would benefit her. As a child, she tried to avoid her mother's physical attacks and her father's verbal attacks by making herself as invisible as possible. She was thin and wraithlike and spoke in a quiet, tense voice. Being seen or heard was dangerous while growing up, and even though she yearned to be listened to and acknowledged, the old fears were deeply embedded in her psyche.

We began to breathe together, sipping the air in slowly as if through a straw, then exhaling on an "s-s-s" sound, like a balloon slowly deflating. As we began the second round, she looked at me and said, "I'm flying off," shaking her body as if she had chills. Karen remembered "blanking out a lot" as a child. When her mother hit and kicked her, she would leave her body and go off into her own world. This dissociative defense that initially protected her psyche from annihilation no longer served her, but had become habitual and took over in times of stress and anxiety. I asked her what would help her feel safer and she said, "Close to the ground feels safer . . . to sit on the floor." I grabbed two pillows and we sat on the floor facing each other.

I suggested that for today we stay with the breathing and work on ways to help her stay in her body. We began the breathing exercise again, and I asked her to slow down the process and tell me everything she was experiencing. She started feeling anxious on the exhalation and felt herself starting to "go up." I suggested we use movement to ground her. We raised our arms on the inhalation and on the exhalation we pretended to be pulling a heavy bar down. We kept eye contact throughout. After several attempts, she was able to stay present during the exhalation. She said the movement and the support she experienced through moving together and keeping eye contact was very helpful. "I felt you wouldn't let me go off—I started to. I was very scared but I stayed with you. . . . I felt the breath going down into my lower body—scary, very scary there. That's where the terror lives. I couldn't stay there too long, but I didn't fly off! That's good. I'm getting better."

Breathing exercise. Another breathing exercise that I often use, especially with clients who suffer from anxiety, is one that I learned from my yoga teacher. It is called alternate nostril breathing. I usually do the exercise with a client after I have explained and demonstrated it. We prepare by sitting opposite each other on chairs and keeping the head and spine in a straight, upright position. The feet are planted firmly on the ground. We begin by bringing the right hand to the nose and covering the right nostril with the right thumb and inhaling through the left nostril. We then cover the left nostril with the right index finger and exhale through the right nostril. We keep the index finger covering the left nostril and inhale through the right nostril. Again we cover the right nostril with the right thumb and exhale through the left nostril. We then inhale and switch sides so that we are exhaling and inhaling through one nostril then switching to the opposite nostril and continuing to exhale and inhale on that side. We continue this breathing pattern for several minutes.

When clients become comfortable with this exercise, I may suggest a more advanced version in which the exhalation is prolonged. We count to 5 as we inhale, then count to 10 as we exhale. The idea is to double the time given to the exhalation. Another variation is to count to 5 on the inhalation, hold the breath (both nostrils closed) for a count of 5, and then exhale while counting to 10. Imagery can be useful, such as asking clients to imagine they are inhaling their favorite color or fragrance or something they need to take in and then imagine they are exhaling stress, stale air, or something they want to release.

Exhalation is the most relaxing part of the breath cycle and promotes the release of feelings that are being held onto. Deep exhalation empties the body of all stale air and makes it ready to receive fresh air. The nervous system is quieted and the body begins to relax and come to a state of relative balance.

Natural Sounds

I define natural sounds as sounds the body emits spontaneously, sounds that are instinctive expressions of what we are experiencing at any given moment, such as a gasp of surprise, a sigh of pleasure, a yawn, a sneeze, a groan, a moan, a laugh, a cry, or a scream. As stated previously, just as we restrain our breathing in order to control our feelings, many of us consciously or unconsciously learn to control and repress our instinctive impulses and the sounds that accompany them out of fear of judgment, rejection, or harm.

As we begin to allow our natural sounds to emerge, the result may be primal sounds of emotions long repressed (Rugenstein, 1992). These sounds may cause anxiety because they reflect parts of the self we have abandoned or neglected. This occurs because significant people in our lives judged or abandoned them, leading us to believe these parts and their sounds are not acceptable. It follows that we may have difficulty recognizing and accepting these aspects of ourselves and their accompanying sounds and emotions. Accessing, relating to, and gradually integrating these parts of our personalities enlarges and strengthens our sense of who we are and opens the door to a richer, more fulfilling life. This journey toward wholeness is what Jung referred to as the individuation process (Austin, 1986, 1991, 1993, 1996, 1999a, 2004; Jacobi, 1965).

Breathing exercises can help clients relax and settle deeper into their bodies and are a good way to prepare for working with vocal sounds. For some clients, a playful approach is helpful. A game can provide an activity with a focus that is not on sounding "good" but is geared toward having fun while entering unexplored territories. The emphasis is on vocal exploration and the attitude that we can all make sounds. It requires no training and is different from singing. This kind of focus can create a playful space that facilitates a therapeutic regression in order to promote spontaneity and creativity. The emphasis on playing with sounds can help clients stop thinking about what and how they are doing and allow them to be more fully present to what and how they are experiencing.

I find that singing and making sounds naturally can be even more challenging for vocalists and musicians who have had their spontaneity trained out of them. Music theory and technique can sometimes get in the way of "being with" whatever emerges. As one client experienced:

> *The wild sounds we were making became more melodic. I wasn't thinking at this point, just doing. I wasn't stopping the flow of emotions by reasoning each sound. Then there was a point where I realized you were singing a fifth and I was on a major third. I slid into a minor third and toyed with that, which got me thinking. The situation went away as easily as it had come.*

When I work with groups, I always introduce an exercise by modeling it. I have found that my willingness to explore primitive or silly sounds makes it safer for others to take risks vocally and emotionally.

Name game. The following is one exercise that I use with groups and individuals. I begin by asking everyone to find a comfortable position sitting cross-legged on the floor or in a chair with both feet on the ground. I then suggest the following:

> *Close your eyes and breathe deeply. Remember a time when you were young and enjoyed making sounds. Remember the freedom of yelling, screaming, and laughing out loud. Move your tongue and see what sounds you can make. Use your lips and teeth and allow yourself to sound silly. Allow yourself to be a child again, to enjoy the sensations you can experience by riding on a vowel like "eeeeeeeeeeeeee" or being a percussive instrument with consonants like "t-t-t-t-t-t" or "d-d-d-d-d-d." Indulge yourself. Taste the different vowels and consonants and delight in the sensual pleasure of making sounds. Now think about all the different sounds in your name, all the vowels and consonants, and all the various ways you can play with them. Explore the fun of changing the dynamics, the pitch, and experiment with different vocal qualities.*

I then begin by modeling the exercise. I play with the sounds in my name. I repeat the "d-d-d-d-d-d-d" and draw out and ride on the "I" as if I was riding a wave. We then go around the group and each person takes a turn.

Toning

Natural sounds can lead into or act as an effective warm-up for toning. Toning is the conscious use of sustained vowel sounds for the purpose of restoring the body's balance. Sound vibrations free blocked energy and resonate with specific areas of the body to relieve emotional and/or physical stress and tension (Campbell, 1989; Crowe & Scovel, 1996; Goldman, 1992; Keyes, 1973). Keyes (1973) refers to toning as "an inner sonar massage" (p. 35) and believes toning can heal illness and restore wholeness through toning for oneself or having another person or people tone for you.

Practitioners of toning vary, from those who use it as a tool for meditation and/or release, to those who believe in its mystical healing powers. Goldman (1992) explores toning, using overtone chanting based on a number of ancient healing practices. Gardner (1990), Goldman (1992), and Hamel (1978) use specific toned vowel sounds to vibrate and activate what many believe are the seven chakras in the body. *Chakra* is the term used by many eastern spiritual schools to describe energy centers in the body

(Gaynor, 1999). Gaynor (1999) describes toning using single syllable Sanskrit words that correspond to the chakras. The Sufis assign divine properties to the vowels they use to activate each chakra.

Yoga teachers have suggested specific vowel sounds to open different parts of the body. For example, "Ooooo" vibrates the root, or lowest chakra; "Oh" vibrates the belly chakra; "Aw," the solar plexus; "Ah," the heart; "Eh," the throat; "Ih," the area between the eyebrows; also known as the third eye; and "Eee," vibrates the top of the head or crown chakra.

Although there are various ways to tone and differing beliefs about what toning can achieve, "all involve the use of pure, nonverbal sound to increase the flow of breath, balance energy flow, release emotion . . . and restore harmony to the body-mind system" (Gaynor, 1999, p. 98). Every therapist consulted on this subject by the author believes people benefit from recognizing and going with the natural flow of energy in our bodies and that toning is one way to facilitate this process.

Toning can be a very intimate experience, especially when toning with one other person. The exchange of energy and vibrations can feel similar to being physically touched. As one client described it:

> *Being connected to my feelings and body in this way was a sensual experience. Towards the end of toning I felt very close to you. Your voice was deep, grounded, seeming to resonate from within me. It was like I could "feel" your voice on my body. It was pleasurable and soothing.*

Toning can also be very effective when working with disassociated clients and clients with eating disorders to help them become more aware of and accepting of their bodies. Pam initially got chills whenever we toned together. Once, I asked her to rub her hands together until they got warm and then place them on her jaw. We then toned on an "eee" vowel. She could easily feel the vibrations and was fascinated enough to risk more toning. Again, I asked her to rub her hands together and when they were warm to place them on her heart. We toned together on an "ahhh" sound. Pam was surprised to feel her heart resonating. "I'm not sure if I like it or not . . . I got those chills again. I guess I feel more alive and I feel closer to you and that is a little scary." Pam was anorexic, hated her body, and often reported feeling "dead" or "empty." Toning and singing became pleasurable ways for her to be in her body, if only for a short time. Toning together also created a feeling of closeness with me that she grew to enjoy and seek out more often.

The immediacy of toning can provide clients with a musical encounter in the here-and-now that is physical, emotional, and spiritual. It is possible for clients to be directly involved on sensory and feeling levels with another (the therapist), who is also fully present and available for a relationship. Clients can have their needs for mutuality met and feel safe enough to freely experiment with sound with the possibility of transcending previous creative limitations. This musical encounter can bring about a moment of healing when change and growth can occur (Austin, 1996).

Lori described her toning experience this way: "That was so beautiful it made me cry. It made me realize that there is an expressive being inside all of us, and trusting our bodies and our surroundings is the way to let that part of ourselves emerge."

Toning can also induce an altered state of consciousness and mediate contents from the personal and collective unconscious to the conscious mind. Creating sounds and tones is a way to access the invisible world—the world of image, memory, and association. Different kinds of repetitive chant-like singing or sounding can function as a bridge over which parts of the self, normally not heard from, can cross over into consciousness where they can be experienced, related to, and ultimately integrated into one's self-concept (Austin, 1993, 1996).

These parts of the self are directly related to what Jung (1970) called complexes, psychic fragments that have split off from the self as a result of traumatic influences or incompatibility with parental and societal values and expectations. A complex is an emotionally charged energy center comprising a number of associated ideas and images. At the core of the complex is an archetype—a transpersonal universal pattern of psychic experience and meaning. An archetype is made up of emotion, image, and, I believe, sound (Austin, 1996; Edinger, 1972; Jung, 1969, 1970; Kast, 1992).

The client's healing process involves experiencing the feelings, images, and sounds associated with the complex and bringing them into consciousness. The contents of the complex can then be assimilated by the ego and integrated into the client's self-image, making valuable energy available for conscious use. Jung believed that the energy contained in the complex is precisely the energy the client needs for continued healing and individuation (Jacobi, 1965; Kast, 1992). Any experience with archetypal energies is extremely powerful and transformative. Sounding and toning is one effective way of working with complexes and their archetypal cores.

Case Study 3

Suzy had been working to become more assertive. "It's difficult for me to connect with my masculine side. . . I'm used to being the listener, the one who goes along with what everyone else wants to do . . . anything to avoid conflict." Suzy's survival in a household fraught with tension and fighting depended on her ability to be adaptable. " I was the good child . . . I tried to mediate, to keep the peace between my mother and father and my father and brother."

At this point in her life, she felt everyone took advantage of her "need to please," and she was sick of it and sick of suppressing her own anger and turning it against herself. Vocal work was empowering for her. "I hear myself and I know I'm alive; I exist and then I feel my body tingling and it's empowering, especially recently because I can sing louder and my sounds don't have to be pretty."

When we began working together a year ago, Suzy was anxious about making primal sounds and improvising. She was afraid of losing control and that something ugly or disgusting might come out of her mouth, causing me to reject her. With time she realized she grew up fearing that her feelings and her self were bad, "ugly." She initially transferred her negative father complex (introject) onto me. Eventually, we were able to work through some of her anger and fear of rejection. She no longer saw me as her father but as a positive mothering figure. This development created a feeling of safety that freed up her self-expression. Now we frequently work with sounds and singing.

We began this session by talking about her need to confront a colleague and the challenge that presented. She wanted to work with sounds and maybe toning. We started with deep breathing. I attuned my breathing to hers. Gradually she yawned, then groaned, and soon we were both moaning together. I said, "Allow anything to come out that needs to." Her sounds were low and gruff and then gravelly, mostly "ah" sounds. The "ah" became "rah" and the notes changed and went up a third and then another half step. When we stopped, she said she heard a voice calling to her. At first she thought it was a man but then realized it was a woman with a low voice.

I asked, "What would help her to come out more—movement, other instruments?" She wanted us to play drums while we toned. She played an African drum, and I played the conga drum. This time her tones were clearer and stronger and mostly comprised of minor intervals. I sang unison most of the time and occasionally harmony or dissonant tones. Gradually the tones became words: "Come closer . . . come here . . . don't be afraid." Her eyes were closed as she chanted "down . . . ground" and then she went back to sounds and slowly came to a conclusion.

Afterwards she told me she had felt a tremendous rush of energy surging through her body. She said she saw a tall, dark-haired woman all alone in a forest. The woman looked like a warrior, fearless and strong. She told Suzy to take off her shoes and feel the ground under her feet, to keep her feet on the ground, to hold her ground. We talked about the connection between strength and anger that was grounded in the body, strength that can be used to be direct and effective. Suzy was very moved by the experience and felt she needed to hear those words. We ended the session by drawing so that Suzy could make a picture of her warrior woman to take home with her and remind her to hold her ground.

Vocal Improvisation

Vocal improvisation in music psychotherapy can be viewed in three complementary ways: as a creative experience in the here and now, as a bridge to the unconscious so that repressed or dissociated psychic contents can come to consciousness through playing with sounds and words, and as a symbolic language (Austin, 1996). Improvisation comes from a natural impulse, and when that impulse is not blocked but is allowed free expression through vocal and musical play, spontaneity is released (Spolin, 1963).

Spontaneity plays a dynamic role in most forms of psychotherapy. When clients are able to be spontaneous, they can allow their natural flow of impulses and can express themselves from an authentic center of being. Healing can occur because clients can connect with their true voices. They can experience themselves freed from the tyranny of "should's" and "ought to's" and access and release genuine feelings, thereby opening a channel to the self. In Winnicotts' (1971) words, "It is in playing and only playing that the individual child or adult is able to be creative and to use the whole personality, and it is only in being creative that the individual discovers the self" (p. 54).

Free improvisation as used by music therapists has direct parallels to Freud's technique of free association. When clients improvise vocally and/or instrumentally, with or without words, they are free-associating and creating a musical portrait of themselves. These musical improvisations can reveal much about a client's strengths, vulnerabilities, conflicts, and feelings. Much can also be learned about the therapeutic relationship and the transference and countertransference dynamics when client and therapist vocally improvise together (Austin 1998, 2001, 2002, 2004; Darnley-Smith & Patey, 2003; Streeter, 1999; Turry, 1998).

I regard the whole vocal psychotherapy session as an improvisation, whether client and/or therapist are singing, improvising, or speaking (Austin, 2004). I never know what the client will bring into the room each session, and where we go and how we get there often surprises me. An improvisational attitude frees the client and the therapist from old frames of reference and ready-made responses and allows for the unexpected and the instantaneous. Improvisation makes room for the creation of new behaviors, ways of relating, and concepts of the self to emerge. An improvisational attitude encourages deep listening and immersion in the unique "music" of each client at each encounter.

When I vocally improvise with clients, I give them choices. Sometimes we sing a cappella and, at other times, with varied instrumental accompaniment. Depending on the clients and their needs in the moment, we may sing with a drum, xylophone, singing bowl, guitar, or piano. At times the client and I play the same instrument. Sometimes clients might play their primary instrument (for example, piano or cello), and

I might accompany them on a different instrument or use only my voice. At other times I might play the piano while the two of us improvise vocally.

The "blues" for vocal improvisation. Sometimes a familiar chord structure like a 12-bar blues is an effective way to begin improvising with the voice, especially for someone who has little or no experience. There are many forms of the blues, but the 12-bar blues is the most common.

The term *12 bar* refers to the number of measures or musical bars. Nearly all blues music is played to a 4/4 time signature, which means that there are 4 beats in every measure and a quarter note is equal to one beat. A 12-bar blues is divided into three 4-bar segments. A standard blues progression typically features three chords, the I, IV, and V chords, usually with the dominant seventh added. The lyrics of a 12-bar blues often follow what is called an AAB pattern. "A" refers to the first and second 4-bar verse, and "B" is the third 4-bar verse. In a 12-bar blues, the first and second lines are repeated, and the third line is a response to them, usually ending in a rhyme (Bagdanov, Woodstra, & Erlewine, 2003).

$$\text{I \quad IV \quad I \quad I}$$
$$\text{IV \quad IV \quad I \quad I}$$
$$\text{V}^7 \text{ \quad IV \quad I \quad I}$$

The repetitive structure of the 12-bar blues is familiar to most people and easy to learn. The melody often has the same rhythmic pattern within each phrase. The musical phrases are short, and the simplicity and predictability of the I, IV, V chord progression make the blues ideal for vocal improvisation. The basic form is internalized quickly and can then be used to experiment by varying the melody, tempo, and rhythm. Improvising music or music and lyrics to a blues song is often a safe, enjoyable experience, especially for the novice.

Vocal holding techniques. Vocal holding techniques is the name ascribed to a method of vocal improvisation I have been developing and refining since 1994 (Austin, 1996, 1998, 1999b, 2001, 2004). Vocal holding techniques involve the intentional use of two chords (I have on occasion used one chord as a "drone" or three chords) in combination with the therapist's voice in order to create a consistent and stable musical environment that facilitates improvised singing within the client-therapist relationship. This method provides a reliable, safe structure for the client who is afraid or unused to improvising. It supports a connection to self and other and promotes a therapeutic regression in which unconscious feelings, sensations, memories, and associations can be accessed, processed, and integrated. These unconscious experiences are directly related to parts of the self that have been split off and suspended in time due to traumatic occurrences. When contacted and communicated with, these younger parts can be reunited with the ego, and the vital energy they contain can be made available to the present-day personality. Developmental arrests can be repaired and a more complete sense of self can be attained.

This improvisational structure is usually limited to two chords in order to establish a predictable, secure musical and psychological container that will enable clients to relinquish some of the mind's control, sink down into their bodies, and allow their spontaneous selves to emerge. The simplicity of the music and the hypnotic repetition of the two chords, combined with the rocking rhythmic motion and the singing of single syllables (sound, not words initially) can produce a trance-like altered state and provides easy access to the world of the unconscious. The steady, consistent harmonic underpinning, the rhythmic grounding, and the therapist's singing encourage and support the client's vocalization. Within this strong yet flexible musical container, the client can explore new ways of being, experience the freedom of play and creative self-expression, and allow feelings and images to emerge (Austin, 1996, 1998, 1999b). The client's voice, feelings, and emerging aspects of the self are all held within this musical matrix.

This method is especially useful in working through developmental injuries and arrests due to traumatic ruptures in the mother-child relationship and/or empathic failures at crucial developmental junctures (Austin, 2001). "Vocal holding" facilitates a therapeutic regression that helps in healing attachment trauma, abandonment issues, and other forms of preverbal trauma. Babies begin to vocalize at about 5 weeks of age and the attachment between the infant and mother develops gradually over the baby's first year of life through physical contact and an ongoing dialogue of cooing, babbling, gazing, and smiling that promotes emotional closeness. Vocal interactions in sounds, song, and, later, speech are critical in providing adequate relational bonding. The important of the voice and vocal holding in building and repairing the connection between self and other has significant implications when working in depth with clients suffering from the consequences of emotional, sexual, or physical abuse. Interpretation and illumination of psychic conflict is of minimal value in working with adults traumatized as children until the link between self and other is rebuilt, and the client's capacity for relationship is restored (Herman, 1992; Kalshed, 1996). Cindy felt she could not hide in the simplicity of the music.

> *I felt you really saw me; I was shy at first but then it felt so reassuring. I wasn't alone*
> *and you felt safe . . . I could hear and feel you singing—you were really there with me*
> *and for me, just for me.*

Vocal holding techniques are not meant to be a prescription or recipe and are not necessarily used in the order that follows. For the sake of clarity, the process is described, as it appears to complement the developmental stages. As with any therapeutic intervention, however, the client's history, diagnosis, transference reactions, and unique personality and needs should determine the approach taken to accomplish therapeutic goals. For example, when improvising, Ann initially felt more comfortable using words and may have experienced vocal sounds as more regressive and associated with loss of control. Marie felt more comfortable in the open realm of nonverbal singing in our earlier sessions, perhaps because she had difficulty finding words to express herself and because she often regressed to a preverbal place. At other times, she seemed to need more structure, so precomposed songs were more effective.

Vocal Holding Stages
– unison
– harmonizing
– mirroring
– grounding

In the initial "vocal holding" phase, the client and I sing in unison. Singing together on the same notes promotes the emergence of a symbiosis-like transference and countertransference. This was important for Marie, who never had a satisfactory experience of merging with an emotionally present, attuned mother. In our initial vocal holding experiences, Marie preferred singing in unison with me. When I moved to another note to harmonize with her, she followed me. Over time, she allowed me to leave her note and sing in harmony with her. Gradually she began to explore more of her vocal range and create more expressive melodies. The second stage, harmonizing, creates the opportunity for the client to experience a sense of being separate yet in relationship.

Mirroring occurs when the client sings his or her own melodic line, and I respond by repeating the melody back to the client. I often used mirroring with Cindy to support her in finding, strengthening, and staying grounded in her authentic voice. Mirroring also helped her to hear and accept new parts of her personality, like the happy child, when they emerged. This musical reflection provides encouragement and validation. *Grounding*, when I sing the tone or root of the chords, often provided a base for Cindy's vocalizations later in the process. She would improvise freely and return to "home base" whenever she wanted to check in. This musical intervention is reminiscent of a typical pattern of interaction between the child and the maternal figure that occurs when the child begins to move away from the mother to explore the environment. In the ideal situation, the mother stays in contact with the child and supports and encourages the child's increased effort to individuate (Mahler, Pine, & Bergman, 1975).

Vocal holding techniques are introduced into the music psychotherapy session in various ways. With a client who is especially anxious about improvising vocally but wants to try, I usually explain this method in detail, emphasizing the many choices that are available. Usually, however, I give a minimal description and explain this method as one way of exploring the voice that is effective and does not require previous experience with vocal improvisation. When clients have a musical background, I ask them what two chords they would like me to play or if they would prefer major, minor, or a combination of chords.

With clients who have little or no knowledge of chord structure, I might play examples of different chord combinations (major, minor, suspended, etc.) and ask for their preference. Sometimes clients describe a mood or feeling they would like to create and together we search for and find the fitting chords (Austin, 1999b). Clients may also suggest a rhythm and a piano setting (I use a Clavinova that has various settings such as strings, organ, etc.). Giving choices and working collaboratively empowers the client and contributes to the creation of a safe therapeutic environment. (For an audio example of this technique, see *Music Therapy Perspectives 19*(1), 2001, "In Search of the Self: The Use of Vocal Holding Techniques With Adults Traumatized as Children.")

Free Associative Singing

Free associative singing is the term used to describe a technique that can be implemented when words enter the vocal holding process. It is similar to Freud's technique of free association (1913, 1938) in that clients are encouraged to verbalize whatever comes into their head with the expectation that by doing so, they will come into contact with unconscious images, memories, and associated feelings. It differs from Freud's technique in that the client is singing instead of speaking, but more significantly, the therapist is also singing and contributing to the musical stream of consciousness by making active *verbal* and musical interventions. The accompaniment (two-chord holding pattern or repetitive riff) and my singing continue to contain the client's process, but the emphasis now is not only on "holding" the client's emerging self and psychic contents, but on creating momentum through the music and the lyrics that will propel the improvisation and the therapeutic process forward. The progression to words and the more active role I take on generally promote a greater differentiation between the client and myself. When I begin questioning, reframing, and adding my own words to the improvisational dyad, the transference and countertransference can become much more complex. The client may experience me not only as the "good-enough" mother, but in other roles as well (figures from the client's interpersonal and intrapsychic world).

In its simplest form, free associative singing involves the client singing a word or phrase, with the therapist mirroring or repeating the words and melody back to the client. The vocal holding techniques of singing in unison, harmonizing, and grounding add additional support and variation. With the movement to words, there is often a need for more variations in the music. The two chords remain the basis for the musical improvisation, but changes in the client's feeling states and emotional intensity often require a broader musical palette. Variations in dynamics, tempo, voicing, arpeggiation, rhythm, accents, rests, alternate chord substitutions, and chord extensions (adding 7ths, 9ths, 11ths, 13ths) enable me to reflect and support the client's experience. In this way, I use not only my voice and the lyrics, but also the music to deepen the vocal improvisation and the therapeutic process.

Throughout the improvisation I am making critical decisions about when, how, and what to sing with the client. This is especially true when I move beyond simply mirroring the client's lyrics and music and begin to vocally provide empathic reflection, ask questions, use repetition to emphasize important words, and musically role play significant people in the client's life as well as parts of the self as they emerge in the therapy. By taking a more active role in musically facilitating the therapeutic process and with the singing of words, I can help clients understand and make meaning out of what they are experiencing in the present and what they experienced in the past and how these events affected their sense of self. Old, unhealthy self-concepts can be replaced by new, realistic ones, resulting in self-acceptance and increased self-esteem.

Vocal holding is often an effective way to lead into free associative singing and similarly to provide closure at the conclusion. When clients have experienced an intensely emotional session, nonverbal vocalizations can provide them with lullaby-like comfort and time to digest and begin to integrate what has occurred. Therapist and client can sing together, or the client may prefer to be sung to.

Case Study 4

The first thing I noticed about Michelle was her voice. It was very soft and airy and seemed to be coming from far away. Like her voice, Michelle seemed more spirit than flesh. She appeared to be disembodied, had low energy, and looked younger than her age. Although she said she had "a happy childhood," over time I learned that she was extremely neglected as a child and spent a lot of time alone in her own world. She could not remember many concrete details of her early life, except that the family moved frequently. One move from her grandparents' home in Italy back to Canada was very traumatic for her. She remembered being happy in Italy but returning to Canada after a year and continuing her isolated existence. "I had a glimpse of life, then lost it again."

As our work progressed, Michelle began to connect with dissociated aspects of herself, primarily through songs and free associative singing. During the following session she was able to contact an isolated young part of herself, begin to accept the truth about her childhood, and feel compassion for the sad and lonely girl she was.

We begin with vocal holding. Michelle prefers minor chords. Today she chooses B minor to E minor. We sing in unison on "Ah" for several moments and then move in and out of harmonizing. She closes her eyes and seems to enter an altered trance-like state. She begins singing words, and I begin echoing her words and melody.

Michelle:	*I see the trees*
Therapist:	*I see the trees*
Michelle:	*and the river*
Therapist:	*and the river*
Michelle:	*and I'm looking*

Therapist:	and I'm looking
Michelle:	in the woods
Therapist:	in the woods
Michelle:	alone
Therapist:	alone
Michelle:	but there never seems to be anything to do
Therapist:	anything to do
Together:	anything to do

I notice that her vocal range is limited and that her melodies contain a lot of descending thirds and fourths and have a childlike quality to them. After several minutes, I begin introducing other words and phrases that might be true for her instead of simply mirroring back (repeating) her lyrics.

Michelle:	I'm wandering
Therapist:	all alone
Michelle:	just the trees and the water
Therapist:	I'm alone
Michelle:	I'm alone
Therapist:	it is peaceful
Michelle:	all alone
Therapist:	and I'm sad
Michelle:	and I'm sad

I use my induced countertransference to make the musical intervention "and I'm sad." I feel sadness pass through me before singing these words. When Michelle repeats them, I feel she is acknowledging the sadness as her own. She now has words and validation for this feeling. I continue to make more active interventions lyrically and musically to move the process forward. I pick up the tempo slightly and sing a little louder.

Therapist:	Where is everybody?
Michelle:	Where is everybody?
Michelle:	I know they're not there
Therapist:	all alone—where is everybody?
Michelle:	I am here but alone and I know they won't come here
Therapist:	and I know they can't see me
Michelle:	they can't see me
Therapist:	they can't see me
Together:	they can't see me!
	they can't see me!

I think this last phrase is connected to Michelle's early childhood experience of feeling invisible. I doubt she ever felt really seen, heard, or understood as a child, so now she struggles with identity issues and an inability to know and act from her authentic feelings and needs. We continue to sing. We sing about whether she is ready to leave or not and that she does not have to hide anymore. She has a choice.

Michelle:	I wish I could go back, back to school
Therapist:	back to school
Michelle:	and learn again, how not to be alone
Therapist:	I wish my mother had taught me

Michelle:	*had been there*
Therapist:	*to help me*
Michelle:	*to give me what I needed to grow*
Therapist:	*no one really was there*
Michelle:	*no one really was there*
Therapist:	*to understand what I felt*
Michelle:	*that's the truth*
Together:	*that's the truth*
Michelle:	*no one helped me*
Therapist:	*no one helped me*
Michelle:	*no one listened*
Therapist:	*no one knew*
Michelle:	*how sad and lonely I was*
Therapist:	*no one helped me*
Michelle:	*to feel*
Therapist:	*to feel*
Michelle:	*that's the truth!*
Therapist:	*that's the truth!*
Together:	*that's the truth!*
Together:	*that's the truth!*

Psychodramatic Singing

Psychodrama has interested me for years. I have a background in theatre that led me to take courses in drama therapy and psychodrama during my graduate studies at New York University. I returned to it 6 years ago after attending a workshop and learning that many psychodrama therapists are working effectively with trauma survivors (Bannister, 2000; Dayton, 1994, 1997; Hudgins & Keisler, 1987; Kellerman, 2000).

There is a relationship between free associative singing and psychodrama. I recently realized that a technique I use frequently and find invaluable that I had referred to as an "alter-ego" (Austin, 1998, 1999b) was actually a musical version of the psychodramatic "double" (Moreno, 1994). The "double" is the inner voice of the client. The director or someone the client chooses to play the "double" speaks in the first person using "I" and expresses feelings and thoughts the client might be having but either has no words for or is unaware of experiencing. The words can be protested or confirmed by the client. Hearing the words spoken aloud supports the client and enables him or her to name the feelings, express them, and process and integrate previously repressed or dissociated emotions (Dayton, 1994, 1997).

Free associative singing could be thought of as a form of musical psychodrama. When I "double," I sing as the inner voice of the client and use the first person ("I"). Drawing on induced countertransference, empathy, and intuition as well as knowledge of the client's history, I give voice to feelings and thoughts the client may be experiencing but is not yet singing, perhaps because the feelings and thoughts are uncomfortable, unconscious, or the client has no words for, or ability to conceptualize, the experience. When the doubling is not accurate, it still moves the process along as clients can change the words to fit their truth. When it is accurate, it provides clients with an experience of being truly seen and understood.

It also encourages a bond between client and therapist and over time strengthens the client's sense of self.

This intervention is especially useful for clients working to integrate thinking and feeling or a mind/body split. Doubling offers an effective way to breathe feelings into words and supply words for feelings. In addition, the naming or labeling of unprocessed trauma material can aid in preventing uncontrolled regression and retraumatization (Hudgins & Keisler, 1987).

Besides singing as a double, I may take on (sing) roles from the client's story as it unfolds in the improvisation. Following is part of an excerpt taken from an audiotaped transcription of a vocal psychotherapy session. It illustrates psychodramatic singing and the interventions I now refer to as "doubling" and "role-playing." It also gives an example of "resourcing"—helping clients connect to their inner and outer resources (the supports and strengths they have).

Case Study 5

Cindy is a jazz singer. She has fears of success tied up with separation anxiety and abandonment issues. Last year she had nodes on her vocal chords which made it impossible for her to sing for almost a year. She was sexually abused as a child. To succeed is equated with leaving behind her emotionally disturbed mother and her rejecting father and being alone without support. Even though she knew rationally they never protected her from the abuse or supported her growth, emotionally the child in her still felt dependent on them and feared losing them.

I ask Cindy, "Was there anyone you could talk to (as a child) that you felt safe with?" She shakes her head and says "no." "Did you have a pet or a favorite stuffed animal?" Again she says "no." I am feeling sad for her and trying to think of what might have helped her to survive when she says, "There was a tree." I ask her to tell me more about it, and she says, "It was huge and beautiful and right outside my bedroom window. . . . I guess the tree was my friend growing up." I ask Cindy if she would like to sing as the tree, to the tree, or about the tree. My intention is to put her in touch with a resource she has—an image she can return to when she feels unsafe. I also want to give her choices. Giving choices is empowering and is especially important when working with traumatized clients. She wants to sing as the tree and asks me to play something "soft and warm." I try a few chords and she chooses C, F/C, G/C. She likes the pedal tone sustaining throughout. I suggest we begin by breathing together several times. My intention is to help her relax and ground her in her body. She starts by singing "ah-h-h." I join her briefly in unison and then in harmony. She begins to cry softly and sings:

Cindy:	Sweet little girl I hear your tears
Therapist:	I hear your tears
Cindy:	I see you crying
Therapist:	I see you crying
Cindy:	and I wish my arms could hold you—reach around and hold you close
Therapist:	and hold you close—reach around and hold you close
Cindy:	but my arms can't move that way and my arms can't give you touch
Therapist:	but I'd like them to—reach around, reach around, reach around you
Cindy:	maybe you can look at me and see you're not alone
Therapist:	maybe you can look at me and see you're not alone

I repeat her words and melodies—echoing them back to her, but when I sing, "I'd like them to," I am offering a reparative experience as a mother-tree. At the end of "you're not alone," my melody resolves the phrase and feels comforting to me, and I hope to her.

Cindy: Maybe you can see my arms reaching up, reaching out, maybe you can see my strength, maybe you can see me connecting to the earth (her singing becomes stronger, her melody soars up, building, and she sustains the last note for two measures).

Therapist: The earth (I join her in unison).

Cindy: Can you see me?

Therapist: Can you see me? See my arms?

Cindy: I'm just staring at the bedspread (she's now singing as her little girl).

Therapist: staring at the bedspread.

Cindy: The spread turns into different patterns, what a bore, what a bore staring at my bedspread.

Therapist: Wouldn't you like to play says the tree, wouldn't you like to play with me, climb up in my branches, put your arms around me? (I decide to sing as the tree, the nurturing, positive mother figure that offers her support. I also sing an entirely different melody. Her melody consists of three repeated notes, the sound of boredom. I sing of play and my melody reflects that by jumping up to a fourth, then to a sixth and creating a singsong effect.)

Cindy: I'm afraid (she cries).

Therapist: We could just sit then, it's okay to be afraid, it's okay, it's okay, it's okay (she cries and blows her nose).

Therapist: I will stay here outside your window and you can cry if that's what you need to do. (My singing has a lullaby quality to it, both my voice and the melody. Again, I am offering a reparative experience—an empathic mother-tree who is accepting and empathic.)

Cindy: But what if lighting strikes you down?

Therapist: (I pause here—stuck for a moment, how do I answer that? I wasn't expecting it, but she needs to know I won't be destroyed by the lightning or the intensity of her needs.) My spirit will always be here with you.

Cindy: You'll be here with me?

Therapist: I'll be here with you. (I feel relieved that I came up with an acceptable answer. I feel very close to her—very moved by her.)

Conclusion

Music and words can do the same things in the therapeutic process—build trust, offer support, clarify issues, stimulate insights, access feelings, uncover unconscious material, contain and hold the client's psychological process, and help the client integrate new experiences. The effectiveness of either depends on when, how, and with whom they are used. The clients' strengths, vulnerabilities, defenses, and needs have to be considered as well as the part of the client that is being worked with and the emotional age of that part of the personality.

Vocal psychotherapy integrates music and words within a depth psychology approach. There is music in the speaking voice that can reveal much about the clients' physical, emotional, and psychological state. There are "words"—images, associations, and meanings communicated in the clients' music. When singing lyrics in precomposed songs, improvised songs, or engaging in free associative singing, the words and music are one. The combination of music and words and having the comfort and flexibility to move and flow from one "language" to another gives therapists more avenues of access to clients so they can be reached at whatever developmental stage they are working through. The verbal and musical interventions overlap and support each other. Over time, the words and music within the context of the therapeutic relationship help clients connect with, relate to, and gradually begin to integrate encapsulated parts of the self that have been rejected, lost, or hidden away. The stream of images, sensations, feelings, and energy exchanged between the client and the therapist in the sounds, music, lyrics, speaking voice, and silence provides clients with an opportunity to have corrective emotional experiences and to renegotiate crucial junctures when the relationship with the primary caretaker was ruptured.

The music and words work together to help clients access and contain strong emotions while also providing them with safe outlets for self-expression. Clients gain self-esteem by realizing that, whatever their illness, they are still creative human beings. Singing helps the isolated connect with themselves, other people, and the community. Singing songs helps the elderly remember significant events, people, and places and sing words they cannot speak. Singing relieves and helps manage physical and emotional pain. Sounding and singing are empowering. One feels the life force flowing through the body to produce strong prolonged tones and create something that did not exist until that moment, something surprising, something beautiful, something filled with raw feeling, something authentic. Finding one's voice is finding one's self.

Music and Imagery

Anne B. Parker

Imagery is a natural human cognitive process, recognized as having therapeutic and healing potential for centuries. Indigenous cultures used imagery in healing practices for as long as shamanic practice has existed. In Western culture, the ancient Greeks integrated imagery into medical practices of the day and systematized its use. Historic physicians such as Asclepius and Paracelsus wrote about the curative powers of imagery. In our culture, the last 15 years has seen an explosion of imagery techniques provided by teachers, facilitators, and therapists of many kinds, with applications as diverse as cancer treatment, sports performance enhancement, and spiritual growth. With the widespread acceptance of guided imagery as a music therapy technique and other uses of imagery in music therapy practice, an exploration of imagery and music is important to consider in work with individuals with mental disorders.

What Is Imagery?

The Oxford Dictionary (Abate, 1997) defines imagery as "images collectively" and "mental images collectively" (p. 387). Image is defined as a "representation of an object," "semblance or likeness," and "mental representation, idea or conception" (p. 387). Imagination is defined as the "mental faculty forming images or concepts of external objects not present to the senses," "ability of the mind to be creative or resourceful," and "process of imagining" (p. 388). The verb *imagine* is defined as to "form a mental image or concept of," "picture to oneself," and "think or conceive" (p. 388).

The word *image* probably entered the English language in the 16th century, derived from the Latin *imago* meaning "likeness of something" (Ayto, 1990, p. 294). The verb *imaginari* was derived from the Latin noun meaning to "form an image of in one's mind, picture to oneself," which became the English word *imagine*.

A major misconception about imagery is that the word refers only to the inner sense of vision, the mind's eye, when referring to mental images. The word visualization is often used instead of the word *imagery*. Even the above definitions reference visualization when they use the word *picture*. Imagery is more fully defined as "the thought process that invokes and uses the senses: vision, audition, smell, taste, the senses of movement, position, and touch. It is the communication between perception, emotion, and bodily change" (Achterberg, 1985, p. 3). As Achterberg's definition indicates, imagery may be, and actually is best experienced, in any and all of the internal senses. It is commonly referred to as our mind's eye but can also be thought of as a mind's ear, mind's nose, mind's tongue, and mind's skin! In addition to the five primary senses—visual, auditory, olfactory, gustatory, and tactile—imagery may also be experienced in our kinesthetic sense, our sense of movement in space, as well as in our intuitive sense, our sense of knowing without the usual cognitive reasoning.

Just as individuals learn dominantly through one or two senses, they tend to image dominantly in one or two senses. This awareness becomes critical for the therapist when using imagery techniques that verbally guide a client through an imagery experience. For example, if the therapist says to a client, "Picture yourself at the beach," or "See yourself at the beach," the client is being asked to use his or her inner vision sense, the mind's eye. However, if the therapist says "Imagine yourself at the beach," the client has the opportunity to use one or more inner senses. Some clients may indeed see the colors of the sand, water, and sky. Others may predominantly hear the sound of the waves on the shore and the calls of the sea birds, while still other clients may primarily feel the heat of the sun on their shoulders and the texture of the sand beneath their feet as they walks. Yet others may immediately remember a particular time at a particular beach with a particular person.

Another misconception about imagery is that it is not useful because "we just make it up." Some critics say that, because it comes from our imagination, it is not real. However, look again at the definitions above. They do not say anything about images being unreal. They do confirm that images are internally formed and perceived in the mind, as mental processes. Just because images are produced and brought to awareness through internal processes as opposed to internal sensory stimulation does not mean they are not real. In fact, some would say that makes them more a reality.

Guided by the work of well-known Jungian analyst, Robert Johnson (1986), when clients express concern that their images are not valid because they are "making them up," I say, "Great! That is the way it should be done!" In his book, *Inner Work* (1986), Johnson discusses images as reflections of the unconscious, "a marvelous universe of unseen energies, forces, forms of intelligence . . . that live within us" (p. 3). Johnson states, "When you begin to see your imagination for what it really is, you will realize that it reflects the inner world of your unconscious as faithfully as a highly polished mirror" (p. 151). In that reflection is the power, surprise, and therapeutic potential of imagery.

Another aspect of imagery that is important to recognize is the occurrence of synesthesia. *Synesthesia* is defined as "a phenomenon in which one type of stimulation evokes the sensation of another" (Morris, 1973), or the simultaneous perception of more than one sense through a single sense. For example, synesthesia is experienced when a sound is perceived as having color or smell, or when a texture has a taste or a sound. It is an intersensory integration experience. Music stimulates synesthesia, as the perception of music is multisensory and facilitates intersensory experiences.

It is also useful to identify the types of imagery that may be experienced. Receptive imagery includes "those images that flow through or 'bubble up' into the conscious mind—one doesn't deliberately create these images" (Achterberg, Dossey, & Kolkmeier, 1994, p. 38). Active imagery is imagery that is "consciously and deliberately" constructed (Achterberg et al., 1994, p. 39). Process imagery involves imaging in a step-by-step manner "toward the goal that one wishes to achieve" (Achterberg et al., 1994, p. 41). End state imagery images the final state one wants to achieve (Achterberg et al., 1994). All of these types of imagery have their place in therapy with persons with psychiatric disabilities and may be used and enhanced with music.

Guided Imagery

The term *guided imagery* generically refers to any number of imagery techniques in which the therapist/ teacher verbally guides the client through an imagery experience. Progressive Relaxation, developed by Edmund Jacobson (1962), whose work was first published in the 1920s, and Autogenics, developed by J. H. Schultz and Wolfgang Luthe (1969) in the 1940s and 50s, were the first formal systems of guided imagery to be developed within Western medicine. Dr. Carl Simonton (Simonton, Simonton, & Creighton, 1978) was one of the pioneers in developing guided imagery for use with people with medical diagnoses, particularly forms of cancer. Other forms of guided imagery were formulated and became popular, including techniques developed by Ira Progoff (1992), Steven Levine (1991), Jean Achterberg, Barbara Dossey, and Leslie Kolkmeier (1994), and Bellaruth Naparstek (1994). Today it seems that there are imagery programs available for almost every kind of physical, emotional, mental, or spiritual problem one has. Some of the claims made by the developers of these programs are reasonable, and others are quite sensational.

In general, guided imagery is imagery that is stimulated or evoked by a verbal stimulus. There are thousands of books, audiotapes, and CDs published in the past 10–15 years that provide scripts for assisting with all types of self-healing and wellness, including stress management, preparation for surgery and childbirth, and meditation and spiritual practices. Almost every meditation, yoga, and relaxation class offered at the local gym includes some component of guided imagery. Even popular exercise classes, such as Spinning™, include imagery as a way of motivating participants and enhancing the overall experience. It is now quite common, particularly in cancer treatment centers, to see patients being instructed in various forms of imagery techniques and being given tapes, CDs, or scripts to use in their own imagery practice to support their healing.

This plethora of material has made guided imagery accessible and acceptable to many. It can also be a wonderful place for those new to the intentional practice of guided imagery to start. This material helps people understand the purpose of imagery and assists in focusing and structuring a practice. Music therapists may find these resources helpful as they learn how to guide clients in imagery experiences and discover how to match music to an imagery experience and the client.

However, there are drawbacks and limitations to this kind of guided imagery. The biggest one, whether experienced live, directly from a therapist or teacher, or from a recording, is that the client is being asked to image someone else's imagery. It cannot be assumed, as many do, that a particular image, color, symbol, or place has a universal interpretation. For example, in the 1970s the Pac Man video game was the newest thing and quite ubiquitous. It became common for cancer patients to receive the suggestion that they image their tumors being gobbled by Pac Man. But for those patients who had never played the Pac Man game or who disliked the little figure and sounds that went with it, the image was not helpful. As another example, a client who had experienced a near drowning experience in the ocean would not find a beach image relaxing or the sounds of the ocean conducive to relaxation. In fact, ocean and beach images could easily have the opposite effect and induce anxiety for that person.

On a physiological level, prepackaged guided imagery may also have unintended and potentially harmful effects. For example, a common and effective image in autogenic training is to imagine parts of the body being warm to facilitate increased blood flow and relaxation. However, someone with gastritis, a form of stomach inflammation, already has increased blood flow to that area. Imagining warmth in that region would be contraindicated. A menopausal woman suffering from hot flashes would also be someone who would benefit from a different image than warmth.

Another drawback to guided imagery recordings is that the client may not like the voice of the guide, finding it irritating or distracting. The music that accompanies the verbal guiding may also be irritating or distracting. The words and music that support the intention of the guided imagery for one person may not at all be supportive to another, no matter what the tape or CD claims.

In my own practice, I have found it beneficial to use published or recorded scripts as a foundation to assist clients in adapting them to their particular intentions and sensibilities. I have also found it helpful to assist clients in making a recording of the adapted script in their own voices. Practicing the guided imagery exercises guided by their own voices seems to amplify the effectiveness of the process, as if self is speaking to self. Achterberg et al. (1994) gives guidance on making your own imagery tapes.

Guided Imagery and Music

The most well established clinical application of music and imagery is Guided Imagery and Music (GIM) developed by Helen Bonny (Bonny & Savary, 1990). This particular approach to music and imagery "refers to all forms of music-imaging in an expanded state of consciousness" (Bruscia, 2002, p. 38). GIM is the general term encompassing a variety of individual and group structures where music is given the role of the imagery-evoker. In other words, the client's imagery is stimulated and evoked by the music itself, rather than the music playing a supportive or background role to verbal suggestion. As Bruscia (2002) discusses quite thoroughly, this general umbrella title of GIM encompasses music-evoked imagery techniques that have their foundation in and were evolved from the Bonny Method of Guided Imagery and Music (BMGIM), developed by music therapy pioneer Helen Bonny in the late 1960s and 1970s. This technique is discussed at length later in this section.

Effects of Imagery

The emotional and physiological effects of imagery have been actively researched since Jacobson's pioneering work in the late 1920s and 1930s. He demonstrated that if a person thinks about a particular body movement in an intense and focused manner, the motor neurons appropriate to that movement are activated (Jacobson, 1962). The firing rate of the neurons is low but measurable. This discovery led to using imagery in a variety of ways to effect muscle activity, including focused relaxation of muscle tension and mental rehearsal of physical activities such as athletics and sports.

By the 1940s, effects of imagery on blood pressure were documented as well as effects on "common psychoneurosis" and "nervous breakdowns" (Jacobson, 1962). In later decades, research showed the effects of imagery on heart rate, respiration, eye movement, galvanic skin response, skin resistance levels, production of the salivary glands, blood glucose, gastrointestinal activity, blister formation, and immune function (Achterberg, 1985). Desensitization techniques, developed for and used successfully in the treatment of phobias and anxiety disorders, rely on imagery to help patients unlearn the association between stimulus triggers and the physiological arousal that accompanies them. Other researchers investigated the effects of imagery on emotion and found that imagery of painful childhood memories or typical emotions of sadness, anger, and fear could be differentiated by changes in behavior and attitude as well as physiology (Achterberg, 1985). Achterberg summarizes the research findings on imagery as follows:

- Images relate to physiological states.
- Images may either precede or follow physiological changes, indicating both a causative and reactive role.
- Images can be induced by conscious, deliberate behaviors, as well as by subconscious acts (electrical stimulation of the brain, reverie, dreaming, etc.).
- Images can be considered as the hypothetical bridge between conscious processing of information and physiological change.
- Images can exhibit influence over the voluntary (peripheral) nervous system, as well as the involuntary (autonomic) nervous system. (pp. 115–116)

Two other areas of research on the effects of imagery are particularly worth noting because of their relationship to music. Recent research published in the journal *Psychology and Aging* (Liu & Park, 2004), showed that imagery helped patients between 60 and 81 years of age with diabetes to remember to take their medication and monitor their blood glucose levels. Because music has been shown to help people remember needed information, the pairing of music and imagery for memory training and improved recall can be quite powerful.

Another area of recent research focus is on imagery and biochemistry, including hormones, neurotransmitters, and endorphins. Endorphins are those feel-good chemicals, endogenous opioids, associated with joy and a natural high (Achterberg, 1985). Music also creates changes in endorphins (Goldstein, 1980). Other studies show that music affects

- S-IgA, an immunoglobulin (McCraty, Atkinson, Rein, & Watkins, 1996; Rider, Mickey, Weldin, & Hawkinson, 1991; Tsao, Gordon, Maranto, Lerman, & Murasko, 1991);
- interleukin-1, a mediator in immune system response, and cortisol, a stress hormone (Bartlett, Kaufman, & Smeltekop, 1993);
- adrenocorticotropic hormone (ACTH), cortisol, and beta-endorphins (Spintge, 1991);
- beta-endorphins (McKinney, Tims, Kumar, & Kumar, 1997);
- cortisol (McKinney, Antoni, Kumar, Tims, & McCabe, 1997).

These and other studies demonstrate that the therapeutic aspects of music are biochemical as well as behavioral and emotional. Because imagery and music affect the same elements of biochemistry, the pairing is and can be quite powerful when appropriately applied to a therapeutic situation. "Imagery seems to occur not as an independent mental faculty, but as an extension of the anticipations required for any cognitive act" (Jourdain, 1997, p. 227). Brain scans show that imagery emanates from the same areas of the brain as perception. In other words, visual imagery activates the visual cortex, auditory imagery, the auditory cortex, kinesthetic imagery, the somatosensory cortex, and so on (Jourdain, 1997). As with all cognitive function, however, images cannot emanate from a single area of the brain (Crowe, 2004). Multiple areas of the brain are involved in the production of imagery.

Hunt (1995) proposes two types of images: sensory and autonomous. Sensory imagery reflects sensory experience and memory and is similar to the sensation as originally experienced, arising from the corresponding perceptual cortex in the brain. "This kind of imagery can only express what the brain already knows and can never produce novel knowledge" (Crowe, 2004, p. 160).

Autonomous imagery evokes new insights and knowledge. "In this type of imagery, individuals can learn new things from the actual images, which leads to new insights beyond previous learning" (Crowe, 2004, p. 160). Autonomous imagery is the language of inner self, a natural and true expression of the individual psyche. "It established a bridge between body, mind, and spirit as well as forming a vital link with the inner self" (Bush, 1995, p. 48). Music can be paired with, support, and enhance both of these imagery types.

Music and Imagery

Music is commonly paired with imagery. Most practitioners give little thought to what role the music plays when paired with imagery, nor even what specific music is used. Because of their unique training, music therapists should be able to make the best choices about what music to pair with imagery. However, the music therapy literature gives little concrete guidance for these choices (Parker, 1998). What follows is my endeavor (a) to classify what role the music is to play in a particular imagery experience, and (b) to identify what elements in the music support that role.

This is not a *prescriptive* music approach, but instead a way to determine what the music is meant to do, what the therapeutic intention is, and then how to make the best choice of music to accomplish desired results based on the music itself, the client, and the objective of the imagery experience. To this end, I propose three general classifications for music and imagery: (a) music-supported imagery, (b) music-enhanced imagery, and (c) music-evoked imagery.

Music-supported imagery is a descriptor of how music is most commonly paired with imagery. In this pairing, the imagery is verbally guided and the music serves primarily as a safe support for the client. The music provides an energetic and sonic *container* for the imagery experience. Music used in this manner is emotionally neutral and not particularly evocative. The music may also serve as a *focuser*, enabling the client to use the music as a productive distraction from typical mental activity and supporting mental focus on the imagery itself. Music used as a support for imagery is typically unfamiliar to the client so as not to evoke specific memories associated with that music. The music is usually not very complex but is intended to create an ambiance that is comfortable to the client. It may contain elements to assist in the client's relaxation.

In *music-enhanced imagery,* the music takes on an expanded role to assist in moving the imagery experience along. Again, it is usually paired with verbally guided imagery and still provides that supportive role of *container* and *focuser*. However, with music-enhanced imagery, the music is chosen to match the energy and mood of the imagery script and is slightly evocative or suggestive of the imagery being verbally indicated to assist the client in moving along in the imagery experience. In this way the music serves as a *connector*, connecting the client more acutely and personally to the imagery experience. The music is more complex, may be familiar to the client, and is particularly suited to match the objective of the imagery experience.

In *music-evoked imagery*, the music takes on the primary role of guide for the client's imagery experience. The music still supports the client and serves as *container, focuser,* and *connector*. However, the music now also takes on the role of *catalyst* for the imagery and is specifically chosen to match the objective of the imagery experience. The music itself becomes the imagery guide instead of the therapist/facilitator. The music is complex and there may be little to no verbal guidance from the therapist. The Bonny Method of Guided Imagery and Music is the most developed form of music-evoked imagery.

Container ⇨ *Focuser* ⇨ *Connector* ⇨ *Catalyst*

Sierra Stokes-Stearns, music therapist, educator, and trainer in the Bonny Method of Guided Imagery and Music, invites therapists to think of the music accompanying imagery as the *soundscape* and *soundtrack* of the imagery experience (Stokes-Stearns, Bush, & Borling, 1995). The *soundscape* is the auditory field or environment that the music creates. A soundscape can be thought of in the same way you think of a landscape. Is it even and smooth, hilly with gradual rises and falls or sharp changes in elevation? Is the view clear and far-reaching to the horizon, or is it encumbered by trees, buildings, clouds, etc.? Does it feel open, engaging, and inviting, or is it closed, dark, mysterious, and even scary? The soundscape can also be thought of as the ambiance or surrounding atmosphere that the music creates for the imager.

The *soundtrack* is just like the soundtrack of a movie—it animates the story. If we think of imagery as a story evolving from our imagination, the music provides the soundtrack for that particular story. A good movie soundtrack both reflects and intensifies the action, emotion, or interchange taking place on the screen. An imagery soundtrack does the same for the client's imagery (Stokes-Stearns et al., 1995).

The first step, then, in choosing music for imagery is to be clear about the kind of soundscape and soundtrack you want to create for the imagery experience. These concepts form the foundation for the next level of thinking about your music choices.

Role of the Music

So what does it mean to have music serve as *container, focuser, connector,* and *catalyst*? How do these terms describe music, and how do they apply to pairing music and imagery (Stokes-Stearns et al., 1995)?

After you have a feeling for the kind of soundscape you want to create for the client's imagery experience, that awareness will guide you to think about the *container* you want the music to provide. The simplest way to relate to the concept of container is the size of the auditory field the music creates. The size of container has to do with both the length of the music in time and the affective size of the music, usually perceived through its structure. Stated simply, 5 minutes of music creates a smaller container than 20 minutes. The length of the music selection greatly depends on the client's ability to attend to the imagery experience. Typically, shorter lengths of time are used with any client new to therapeutic imagery and may continue to be used with clients whose ability to attend or tolerate longer periods may be compromised.

The musical structure has much to do with how the container is perceived. For example, baroque orchestral music typically has a moderate, steady tempo that provides a predictable rhythmic foundation that is perceived as safe and comfortable by many clients. Impressionistic orchestral music is often expansive and open in its form with less predictable tempos and a more free-flowing energetic feeling (Stokes-Stearns et al., 1995). The Native American flute music of Carlos Nakai, while only one instrument, often gives clients the feeling of vastness, images of a big, open sky, mountains, or canyons.

Music as *focuser* is a basic concept in many music therapy techniques. It is that characteristic of music that affects brain function to assist the client in concentrating on the music or musical task, productively diverting typical mental activity. Achterberg (1985) states:

> *Repeated monotonous stimulation of any sense changes the focus of awareness. For the shaman, the usual choice of sound stimulus comes from drums, rattles, sticks, or other percussion instruments. . . . Chants and songs, of course, are important to healing ceremonies of all cultures. . . .They may serve the purpose of bypassing the logical, language part of our brains, and touching the intuitive. (pp. 41–42)*

When music is paired with imagery, the music serves as the sensory input that assists the client in shifting out of normal cognitive patterns to concentrate more fully on the imagery experience. The client's ability to focus is enhanced because of music's ability to involve both hemispheres of the brain. Simply stated, rhythm is processed in the left hemisphere and melody is processed in the right hemisphere. If the music used has both rhythmic and melodic elements, perception of that music becomes a whole brain activity (Crowe, 2004).

The *connector* aspects of music are particularly powerful when paired with imagery. Johnson (1986) speaks of "the image-forming capacity called imagination" as the part of us that "receives meanings from the spiritual and aesthetic worlds and forms them into an inner image that can be held in memory and made the object of thought and reasoning" (p. 23). Music connects conscious mind with unconscious mind, imagination with analytical thinking, sensation with feeling, inner perceptions with outer perceptions, body to mind. As stated previously in this chapter, research in the last 25 years demonstrates that music, and specifically music and imagery, has a direct effect on the biochemicals in our bodies such as endogenous opiods, neurotransmitters, and stress hormones. Because of the auditory nerve's effect on structures in the midbrain, particularly the amygdala, music is also a powerful connector to memory (Crowe, 2004). Band, Quilter, and Miller (2002) report that people who are imaging with music experience higher percentages of visual details, bright colors, and sensations of movement, as well as experiencing more emotions and images of the past than individuals imagining in a no-music condition. All of these interactions and results support music's role as a connector within an imagery experience.

Music's role in imagery as a *catalyst* is unique to music and includes all of the above concepts. However, in this discussion, I am particularly referring to music as an energetic catalyst, how it may evoke emotional response and creativity through its stimulation of imagination. Verbal guidance of imagery does not come close to touching the deep levels of Self that music can. Stephanie Merritt (1996) refers to music as "the magnet that reaches into the silent world where images live, and pulls them to the surface" (p. 187). As Robert Johnson states:

> *Both music and imagery speak the language of the unconscious, allowing us to make contact with the inner world. As a gateway to the images and symbols of the inner Self, music can bridge the gap between the conscious and the unconscious. It is a natural way to stimulate waking dreams and active imagination so that we can communicate with the unexplored or disowned parts of ourselves. (quoted in Merritt, 1996, p. 7)*

In psychological language, music helps the client get underneath his or her persona and outside of the usual ego functions, complexes, and defense mechanisms. Imagery gives us a form by which to relate to and understand complex emotions. Music's close relationship to emotional response heightens that expression and understanding.

Musical Elements

Now that the roles music plays in an imagery experience have been discussed, it is important to review the musical elements that support those roles as the choices of music to pair with imagery are developed. The musical elements considered below include rhythm, melody, harmony, pattern, timbre, genre, preference, and familiarity.

Rossi (1993) presents a neuropsychological foundation for the following discussion of musical elements. He discusses the role of the reticular activating system in the brain stem receiving sensory information from all of the neural pathways in the body, particularly the auditory nerve, and then acting as a filter, passing on to the higher levels of brain function only that information which is either novel or persistent. Rossi (1986) states:

> It is the brain's ability to wake up, to become alert and attentive to novel patterns of sensory stimuli and information, that enables it to focus its activity on new learning and creativity. . . . When novel stimuli are received . . . neural connections stimulate the onset of brief states of heightened responsiveness in the higher cortical areas of the brain . . . Novel stimuli (create) a heightened psychobiological state. Dull, repetitive situations, on the other hand, decrease activity . . . and lead to relaxation, drowsiness, and sleep. The fact that what is novel and fascinating actually heightens brain activity is a very important, though still generally unappreciated, pre-condition for all forms of creatively-oriented psychotherapy and mind-body healing experiences. (p. 31)

This information gives clear direction for characteristics of musical elements to consider when choosing music to pair with imagery.

Rhythm. Some theorists believe that rhythm is the most fundamental element of the music to consider, as our responses to rhythm begin at the subcortical level in the brain. With any kind of imagery intervention or technique, the client is best engaged when in a relaxed state. Repetitive rhythm is particularly effective in promoting the relaxation response. Entrainment is a concept that naturally goes along with rhythmicity in music. Entrainment occurs when one frequency or rhythm synchronizes with another. It is an active process that involves changing the natural oscillatory patterns of an object and replacing them with another (Koepchen, Droh, Spintge, Abel, Klussendorf, & Koralewski, 1992). Usually one rhythm is the leading rhythm, in this case, the rhythm of the music, and the other is the dependent rhythm, for example, the heart or respiration rate of the imaging client.

In considering the element of rhythm in music for imagery, the following questions must be identified. Is there a rhythmic pulse? Is it steady and constant, or irregular and unpredictable? Does it have strong accents or syncopation? What is the tempo of the rhythmic pulse? Is it fast or slow, driving or gentle, how many beats per minute? Is the meter duple or triple?

In general, for music-supported imagery, the therapist chooses music that has a steady, even pulse at a pace just at or under a relaxed heart rate to facilitate entrainment with the pulse and physiological relaxation in the client. A steady, even pulse can provide a foundation or psychological ground that is easy to relax into for an imaging client. If the objective of the music is just to create a comfortable, holding soundscape, the music may not have a pulse at all but have long, sustained sounds or drones, like those found in some kinds of chant or Native American and East Indian music. In either case, the rhythmic elements are simple and predictable so as to provide a safe, supportive, and secure sonic environment for the imaging to occur.

For music-enhanced imagery, the rhythmic elements may be a little stronger, more suggestive. For example, a gentle triple meter can be suggestive of the rocking of a lullaby for some clients. If the imagery script has energizing focus, the rhythmic elements may be a bit more driving, faster, or with accented beats. Syncopated rhythms disrupt the expected pattern or create a new one and may be appropriate if the imagery is oriented towards creativity or new learning.

With music-evoked imagery, rhythmic elements may run the gamut of characteristics. Since the music used in music-evoked imagery tends to be more complex, the rhythmic elements must be evaluated in the context of the entire role of music as guide.

Melody. Melody and melodic line give a sense of direction and provide musical shape to the imager (Stokes-Stearns et al., 1995). Consider these elements of melody in music for imagery: Does the melody present itself in repetitive phrases, or is there no particular pattern? Is the sense of direction linear, circular, or ambiguous? Does the melody ascend, descend, or jump around? Does it move in progressive tonal steps or intervals, or are there large leaps between tones? Is the overall pitch range of the melody high or low? Does the melody reflect a major or minor key or particular mode? Is there tension and release in the melody? How do sustained or suspended pitches or intervals contribute to that feeling of tension and release?

For music-supported imagery, the melody is simple, progressing by tonal steps without large intervals and with a small to medium range of pitches. The melody is also predictable, following a pattern consonant to the ear, contributing to the feeling of support and safety being created. The melody would not evoke a particular mood or emotion but rather be neutral.

In music-enhanced imagery, the melody may be a bit more suggestive of mood or emotion to match the mood or emotion in the imagery script. The energetic movement of the melody also matches the energy of the imagery script. There may be portions of the melody that are less predictable or contain a bit of surprise if the objective of the imagery is to create some open space for new or unexpected images to occur. A melody might be used that is familiar to the client if that familiarity is consistent with the intention of the imagery. A familiar melody used or orchestrated in a different way is sometimes suggestive enough to shift the client's perception of the familiar.

With music-evoked imagery, melody provides the overall shape of the imagery experience. When the music serves as the guide, the melody must be complex enough to provide that sense of direction throughout the imagery experience.

Harmony. Like melody, perception of harmony greatly depends upon our anticipation of patterns and whether those expectations are met. Is the harmony consonant or dissonant to the client's ear? Does the harmony support the melody or provide another dynamic? What is the interplay between and among harmonic elements? Is the harmony simple or complex? Or, if the music is played by a solo instrument, what is the feeling associated with no harmony? Harmony also determines major or minor key and our associations with mood. Do keys shift back and forth or stay consistent? What mood or moods are conveyed? Does the harmonic structure and interplay provide a feeling of openness and expansion, or a feeling of smallness or tightness? Does the harmony intensify the mood or drama to a climax, does it provide tension and release, or is it more subtle and gentle in its energy? Does the music end in a way that grounds the client, such as ending on the tonic?

Like melody, with music-supported imagery, the harmony is simple, consonant, and predictable, following a pattern consonant to the ear and contributing to the feeling of support and safety being created. Again, the harmony would not evoke a particular mood or emotion but be rather neutral.

Also similar to melody in music-enhanced imagery, the harmony may be a bit more suggestive of mood or emotion to match the mood or emotion in the imagery script. The harmony may shift between keys to support a shift of mood or energy. The interplay of the harmony is more complex, often providing some tension and release to match the energetic intention of the imagery script and may be more open to create a larger container for the client's imagery.

With music-evoked imagery, harmony provides the overall mood and sequences the imagery experience. When the music serves as the guide, the harmonic structure and interplay must be complex enough to support the complexity of the unconscious and the imaginal experience that is being brought to consciousness. The drama in the music, as exemplified by building to climax and releasing, sustaining tension and then letting it go, shifting moods and energies, and changing textures and harmonic structures, contributes greatly to the evocative aspects of music. These elements must be used carefully and only by music therapists specially trained to guide this kind of imagery work.

Pattern. To some theorists such as Jourdain (1997), pattern is the key element in how the emotionality of music is perceived. He states that

> it's easy to see how music generates emotion. Music sets up anticipations and then satisfies them. It can withhold resolutions, and heighten anticipation by doing so, then to satisfy the anticipation in a great gush of resolution. When music goes out of its way to violate the very expectations that it sets up, we call it "expressive." (p. 312)

According to Thaut (1990), "Listeners develop expectancy schemes when following music patterns. A carefully crafted interruption of the expectation—followed by a period of suspension and resolution in the composition—will evoke an affective experience in the recipient" (p. 4). These ideas, and others like them, emphasize the importance of perceived pattern in musical elements as a primary component in explaining the connection between music and emotion. Pattern as musical form, e.g., ABA, canon, concerto, etc., is also an element to note (Stokes-Stearns et al., 1995).

In Goldberg's (1992) theory of emotion and imagery, emotion gives rise to image, whether the emotion is conscious or unconscious. This concurs with Aristotle's belief that "the emotional system does not function in the absence of images" (Achterberg, 1985, p. 56). Goldberg elaborates by stating, "If the emotion is unconscious, the image will appear to emerge first; however, the image emerges as a manifestation of emotion and a sign or symbol of the issue it represents for the listener" (p. 10). These ideas give the music therapist pause as even the most *unemotional* or seemingly *nonevocative* music may elicit strong or unexpected emotion in the client. The images themselves may make the client conscious of emotion that has been repressed, suppressed, or blocked, compelling the client to acknowledge feelings that he or she heretofore successfully avoided. While this may, in the right setting and with the right client, be therapeutic, care must be taken not to unintentionally force clients into an emotional situation for which they are not ready. Therefore, even when using music that is predictable with pleasing, repetitive rhythmic and melodic patterns that seem emotionally neutral and comfortable, one must be aware of the potential emotional connections the music and imagery may arouse.

Timbre. Timbre, also referred to as instrumental color, is the characteristic sound of a particular instrument or voice. Timbre is created by the size and shape of the resonance chamber of the instrument (including the human body), the material from which it is made, and how the vibration is created, such as blowing, striking, plucking, or bowing. It is the quality of sound that distinguishes tones played or sung on different instruments, even if the pitch and loudness are the same. Timbre is determined by the distribution of harmonic energy of a particular tone and "the composition of the overtone series (how many overtones are heard, how loud they are, and how they are distributed)" (Crowe, 2004, p. 54). Physiologically, perception of timbre is one of the most complex aspects of audition as the effects of harmonics are multiple and occur in various places in the ear and brain, as well as other parts of the body. I believe that timbre is the most under-acknowledged element in research on the effects of music on humans.

For the purposes of this chapter and the pairing of music and imagery, timbre must be considered for its associative and energetic properties. Most clients have a subjective preference for particular timbres based on familiarity or association, i.e., "the guitar sounds relaxing," "the flute is so soothing," or "the trumpet energizes me." The instrument, or combination of instruments, that performs the music plays a major part in how the music is perceived. For example, the ubiquitous "Canon in D" by Pachelbel is often touted and used as music for relaxation and/or imagery. However, I have recordings of that composition played by string ensemble, brass ensemble, woodwind ensemble, synthesizer emphasizing space sounds, sung with vocables and with lyrics, even with barking dogs! Clearly, the different timbres represented by these combinations have an impact on how the music is perceived and, therefore, what kind of imagery is supported, enhanced, or evoked.

I propose that how the instrument is played and the manner in which its particular timbre is produced also have an effect on perception. For example, a violin that is bowed is likely to be perceived as a more relaxing sound than a violin that is plucked. Piano is used in many different ways in music, but it is important to note that it is a percussion instrument. Fingers hitting keys and hammers hitting strings create the sound. In my experience, some clients, particularly those who are physically weak or frail or emotionally reactive, are sensitive to the energetics of that percussiveness and find the timbre of the piano intrusive, distracting, or even painful. If I am conducting a music and imagery session with an objective of relaxation and use piano music with one of those clients, the piano often works at cross-purposes to the imagery.

It is important to take particular note of the use of voice in music paired with imagery. Sung lyrics can interfere with the creation of imagery as lyrics in a language the client understands stimulate the language centers in the brain. This has the effect of keeping the client in a more cognitively oriented process and interferes with the music's power to stimulate imagination from a noncognitive or intuitive perspective. Sung lyrics in a language the client does not understand are usually perceived as vocables and, like songs or chants without lyrics, do not stimulate the language centers in the brain in the same manner. The use of voice in music can be a wonderful connector for imagery as it is the sound the body naturally makes, the way we create music without need of an instrument external to the body. This makes the perception of voice very personal and can sometimes add meaning to the imagery stimulated by it.

Though not timbre in the musical sense, recorded environmental sounds must also be considered as they are often used alone or paired with music for use with imagery. For most people, environmental sounds quickly evoke concrete images and memories. If the intention of the imagery is to move the client into new awareness, the use of familiar environmental sounds interferes with that process. Care must also be taken not to assume that particular environmental sounds will evoke certain feelings or images. For example, the sound of ocean waves that may be perceived as relaxing to one client and foster images of a pleasant day at the beach may remind another of a near-drowning experience. Sounds of a tropical rainforest may evoke tranquil, comforting images to one client but stimulate feelings of darkness and claustrophobia in another. Individual variation in response to environmental sounds make them particularly difficult to use with groups or those imaging that are unknown to the music therapist.

Musical genre. One of the biggest mistakes made by music therapy practitioners and researchers, as well as nonmusic therapy-trained imagery facilitators, is to classify music by genre. For example, many research studies describe the music used only or primarily by genre, i.e., classical versus New Age (Parker, 1998). In 1948, just as music therapy was becoming an organized profession, a book called *Music and Medicine* was published that reviewed the prevailing status of the use of music in medicine. Elston (1948), a musician, stated, "It is an astonishing fact that the music itself has been the least investigated of all the factors involved" (p. 283). "Often the music used is not specified beyond the general description that is 'popular,' or 'classical,' or 'folk song'" (Elston, 1948, p. 282). Though acknowledging the complications of doing research on musical elements that cannot be studied as isolated factors, over 50 years of research shows that very few researchers have even tried to isolate those musical elements and, instead, still describe the music used by genre.

Though generalizations can be made, every genre of music contains a wide range of tempos, rhythms, melodic contours, harmonic structure, timbral combinations, etc. Musical genres contain so much variation within them that genre alone is a weak way to classify music for imagery. For example, within the classical genre, music may be found that is slow and melodic with simple harmonies and regular rhythms, as well as music that is fast, dissonant, and changeable with complex harmonies and irregular rhythms. There are great differences among a baroque concerto, a classical symphony, an impressionistic etude, and a contemporary 20th century classical form. The genre identified as "New Age" is often paired with imagery. However, this is such a broad and loosely defined genre that the variations of musical elements within it are as extensive as within the classical genre.

Preference and familiarity. Musical preference and familiarity are related. Clients usually prefer music with which they are familiar or prefer a genre in which they like certain pieces of music. Preference is an important consideration when pairing music and imagery, because the music needs to be easily accessible to the client, particularly in music-supported imagery or music-enhanced imagery. Cultural context and experience must also be considered. If the music is too strange or foreign-sounding, it becomes a novel stimulus and keeps the client in a state of arousal, which may or may not be conducive to the intention of the imagery experience.

Familiarity is also important to consider, primarily because of music's direct link to memory and emotion. If the client has strong associations and memories with a particular music, those associations and memories may interfere with the therapeutic intention of the imagery experience. On the other hand, if a particular music stimulates specific responses or feelings that are supportive of the therapeutic intent, familiar music may be useful.

Clinical Applications of Imagery and Music

In work with clients with psychiatric disorders, there are varied clinical objectives that imagery and music may support. Two of the most common are for relaxation and/or stress reduction with clients with a variety of diagnoses and as systematic desensitization in treatment of phobias. Other appropriate objectives could include the following:

- Meaningful and appropriate acknowledgment and expression of emotion
- Insight awareness and development
- Conflict clarification and resolution
- Mental rehearsal of upcoming events or interactions
- Shift of locus of control and reduction of powerlessness
- Values clarification
- Modulation of mood
- Processing of grief and loss issues
- Increased problem-solving skills and enhanced creativity
- Positive suggestion and affirmation
- Development and/or enrichment of connection to the spiritual

Because of imagery's ability to tap into a client's imaginative aptitudes and create the possibility of a different perspective, as well as music's ability to enhance and amplify those processes, music and imagery may be used with a diversity of clients to support a variety of treatment goals. Once learned, imagery is also a tool that a client may effectively use independently of a therapist.

Imagery is most appropriately used with clients with nonpsychotic diagnoses such as anxiety disorders (including panic disorders, phobias, and obsessive-compulsive disorder); mood disorders (including depression and bipolar disorder); addictions; eating disorders; and sleep disorders. Imagery may be very helpful in dealing with troubling, uncomfortable, or difficult-to-express emotions such as anger, fear, sadness, grief, hopelessness, and helplessness.

Imagery is contraindicated in clients with active psychotic disorders, particularly psychosis that involves hallucinations. These clients already have difficulty distinguishing between inner and outer realities. Introducing an imaginal technique at a time when the treatment focus is on grounding the client in outer reality makes imagery contraindicated. There are other music therapy techniques that are better suited to this population and its treatment goals. Imagery is also usually contraindicated in clients with dementia, except in memory and recall tasks.

Imagery may be carefully used with clients with personality disorders but should be used only by therapists who are particularly skilled with both treatments of these population and imagery techniques. Imagery may be effective with children and adolescents but, again, should be used only by therapists skilled in treatment of these populations and adaptations of imagery and music techniques appropriate to the developmental level of the client(s).

The music therapy literature does not contain a large amount of research in the area of imagery and music with psychiatric disorders, except for research and case studies that specifically use the Bonny Method of Guided Imagery and Music (BMGIM). The *Journal of the Association for Music and Imagery* is an excellent resource for these articles. There are also articles on the use of BMGIM with psychiatric populations in the *Journal of Music Therapy, Music Therapy,* and *Music Therapy Perspectives.* Most of the research with music and imagery has been done with medical populations and is reported in journals and publications in the fields of music medicine, nursing, cancer care, and psychology, as well as music therapy. This literature, though not directly dealing with clients with psychiatric disorders, may give the music therapist insights into the effective uses of music and imagery that are transferable to a population with psychiatric disorders.

In general, when introducing an imagery and music intervention with any client, it is important to start slowly, allowing the client to become comfortable with entering and exploring the imaginal realm by using short, structured imagery exercises and supportive music. The *container* should be kept small and the music used to help the client focus on the imagery suggested. Starting treatment with *active* imagery (Achterberg et al., 1994) paired with supportive music assists the client in becoming comfortable and familiar with using imagery in an objective, oriented manner. With some clients, starting with structured recall of pleasant or at least nontraumatic memories is a good place to begin. The principles of *music-supported imagery* are best used in this stage of treatment and, with some clients, may be where the process remains.

Receptive imagery, as described by Achterberg et al. (1994), allows the client to begin to more freely explore images that spontaneously arise. The principles of *music-enhanced imagery* may be effectively applied in this process as the music can also serve as *connector* to personal evolving imagery. Emotional expression in and with the imagery is more likely to occur with receptive imagery, so the music selected must be able to support the client's emotional experience. At the end of a receptive imagery session that is enhanced with music, it is particularly important to assure that the client is *re-grounded*, or fully reconnected with present time and place, and fully in his or her body. Often, the imagery and music takes the client into a deep state of relaxation or into a transpersonal space or experience. Making sure the client is fully alert, present, and grounded is essential to the success of the imagery experience.

When using recorded music with imagery, ensure that good quality stereo equipment is available for use. Make sure the stereo player and its speakers produce a full range of frequencies and give a good quality musical sound. Bad sound quality can, at best, not assist with and, at worst, distract and distort the imagery experience.

Whether the client is in a seated, reclining, or prone posture, the speakers should be positioned behind the head of client, equidistant from the ears, if possible. This equalizes mechanical and neurological perception as much as possible and allows the same amount of sound to be heard by each ear and, therefore, each hemisphere of the brain (Parker, 1998). Be aware of the client's perception of loudness and adjust the volume to a comfortable level. When pairing music and verbally guided imagery, be careful of the balance of music and voice so the client may attend to both in a complementary fashion and not feel that the sounds compete against one another.

Headphones or earphones are sometimes used with verbally guided imagery or for music listening. However, in a clinical treatment setting, I recommend that speakers be used so that the therapist and client may verbally communicate as necessary and so that the music therapist may hear the music the client is hearing. This is critical to tracking the client's response to the music and the connection between the music and the imagery being experienced.

When using recorded music, make sure that you have listened thoroughly to the piece or pieces of music being played. The music therapist *must* be very familiar with the music used to most effectively analyze its characteristics and musical elements to match the client and the objective of the imagery session. This also assures that surprises in the music that disrupt or distract the client's imagery do not occur, such as bird calls in the middle of music that suggests the natural world, or unexpected dynamic changes in the composition or the specific performance. When using the classical music genre, be particularly attentive to the specific performance used, as interpretations of classical composition range widely by artist and conductor. Again, using the ubiquitous "Canon in D" by Pachelbel as an example, I have recordings of that piece of music that range in playing time from 3 to 8 minutes. The tempo variations alone suggested by the disparity in playing time prompt me to listen carefully to the selections and choose the one best suited to the client and imagery objective.

Improvised, live music is also an option for an imagery session. This is particularly suited to music-supported imagery if the music therapist is proficient with the instrument and able to play the music and track the client's imagery process simultaneously. I have seen a simple melodic instrument, such as a Native American flute, used successfully in this manner in the hands of a skilled music therapist.

Music-evoked imagery is a powerful, transformative process that must be carefully used with clear therapeutic intent and only by music therapists who have received appropriate advanced training. Clients must be carefully screened for their readiness for this kind of therapy, and therapists must be able to adapt this treatment to a client's specific needs.

As indicated earlier, the Bonny Method of Guided Imagery and Music is the best-developed method of music-evoked imagery. It has also been successfully used with a variety of clinical populations over the last 30 years. In 1990, the Association for Music and Imagery defined the method this way:

> The Bonny Method of GIM is a music-centered, transformational therapy, which uses specifically programmed classical music to stimulate and support a dynamic unfolding of inner experiences in service of physical, psychological and spiritual wholeness. The GIM therapist/guide maintains an active dialogue with the listener throughout the session, providing encouragement and focus for the emotions, images, physical sensations, memories and thoughts that occur. (Clark, 2002, p. 22)

Helen Bonny was the first to develop a method of using music to evoke imagery *and* change consciousness. She discovered that guiding a person into an expanded state of consciousness enhances the person's responsiveness to music and gives the person greater access to his or her own imaginal world. She used specifically designed classical music programs to guide the person's imagery experience and formulated a means of verbal interaction with the person listening to the music, while supporting and maintaining the expanded state of consciousness. "Bonny's strategy for working simultaneously with consciousness, music, and imagery is uniquely and originally her own" (Bruscia, 2002, p. 41). BMGIM is characterized by the experience of spontaneous imagery in response to specifically selected music while interacting with a specially trained guide.

GIM is practiced within a variety of treatment settings and philosophical approaches and is applied in psychotherapy, counseling, medicine, nursing, education, spiritual direction, and other healing traditions. The successors to Helen Bonny have further developed both the method and its application. Though GIM is now recognized as a modality or method within the field of music therapy, some GIM practitioners are not music therapists. Postgraduate training and supervision is required to become a qualified GIM therapist. Information on BMGIM and training requirements and resources may be found by contacting:

The Association for Music and Imagery
P.O. Box 4286
Blaine, WA 98231-4286
(360) 756-8096
ami@nas.com or www.bonnymethod.com/ami

Conclusion

Imagery and music, individually, are each natural yet powerful therapeutic processes. When paired, the therapeutic potential is greatly enhanced and amplified. When used appropriately in a treatment process, imagery and music can bring clients to a whole new set of inner resources they may not have known they had or did not know how to constructively use. Music therapists are in a unique position to most effectively pair music with imagery to support therapeutic objectives. The professional music therapist can use the knowledge of music repertoire, musical elements, and human perception of and response to music to make the best choices possible in pairing music and imagery in a clinical setting. The work of the music therapist can also model for other professionals the most effective use of music with imagery to assist our clients' growth, development, and healing.

Transpersonal Approach to Music Therapy With Individuals With Mental Disorders

Laurie Rugenstein and Barbara J. Crowe

What is transpersonal music therapy, and how is it similar to or different from other music therapy approaches? In order to address this question, it is necessary to briefly define *transpersonal psychology*, which serves as the ground for transpersonal music therapy.

Transpersonal Psychology

Transpersonal psychology is based on two assumptions: (a) human development beyond "normal" is possible, and (b) a transegoic (beyond ego) stage of life is possible (Crowe, 2004). It is based on a model that views human consciousness as being connected to something larger than the individual personality. It acknowledges the existence of the spiritual dimension and its impact on the individual psyche. Issues arising from dream states, paranormal experiences, spiritual experiences, and other nonordinary states of consciousness are explored as part of the therapeutic process. Working from a transpersonal context, clients are often able to transform limiting core beliefs and patterns that manifest as physical, emotional, mental, or spiritual difficulties (Maslow, 1968; Walsh & Vaughan, 1993).

Although it is difficult to formulate a single, all-inclusive definition of transpersonal psychology, the following description conveys its essence: "Transpersonal psychology is concerned with the study of humanity's highest potential, and with the recognition, understanding, and realization of unitive, spiritual, and transcendent states of consciousness" (Lajoie & Shapiro, 1992, p. 91).

Transpersonal Music Therapy

When discussing transpersonal psychology and transpersonal music therapy, three dimensions must be considered: (a) transpersonal content, (b) transpersonal process, and (c) transpersonal context (Vaughn, 1979). Each are addressed as it relates to music therapy practice.

Transpersonal content pertains to the subject matter dealt with in therapy. This includes experiences that can be considered transcendent, mystical, paranormal, cosmic, archetypal, or spiritual. A true transcendent experience grabs your whole attention and envelops you in an indescribable experience. It is unmistakably beyond the ordinary. A transcendent experience involves an altered state of consciousness and has a number of qualities:

- Ineffability—an experience that cannot be described in words
- Noetic quality—heightened sense of clarity and understanding
- Altered perception of time and space
- Intense, positive emotion, experience of the holistic, unitive nature of the universe and one's unity with it (Crowe, 2004)

However, transpersonal content does not necessarily need to be present in transpersonal processes and approaches to music therapy.

Transpersonal process refers to the techniques used by the music therapist. Transpersonal psychology processes could include meditation, altered states work, ritual, imagery, dream work, shamanic journeying, bodywork/movement, and various art expressions. Since music can be considered an inherently transpersonal process, any therapeutic approach that involves music has the potential to be transpersonal.

Since ancient times, human beings have understood that music has the power to induce altered states of consciousness and to evoke mystical, transpersonal, and peak experiences (Berendt, 1987; Reck, 1977; Tame, 1984).

> *Music is a special energy. It is of this world, but it also acts as a bridge to the spirit world. Music is our connection to the world of the soul, the subconscious that lies beneath waking states. It becomes a universal language, a spirit language, with the power to change consciousness. (Hart & Lieberman, 1999, p. 131)*

Engaging in music can lead one into a transpersonal state without the intention to do so.

A number of music therapy techniques can serve as transpersonal processes, including the following:

- General aesthetic response to music as an intense, attention grabbing experience
- Improvisation as "flow"—that is, "a psychic state where incidences follow each other in a united, organic way without our conscious participation" (Ruud, 1995, p. 97)
- Music-evoked imagery and specific techniques like the Bonny Method of Guided Imagery and Music (Bonny & Savary, 1990)
- Music as a ritual experience creating a symbolic statement of cultural values, a sense of community, a symbolic form, and a relationship within the community (Crowe, 2004; Kenny, 1982). Ritual links experience, feeling, intuition, and reason to provide a new interpretation of one's place in the world (Winkelman, 2000)
- Music to produce an altered state of consciousness through repetitive drumming, chanting, singing, and movement to music (Crowe, 2004)

These processes allow clients to experience transcendence in a safer, more acceptable form. Music both evokes and contains or structures these experiences, making them therapeutically more relevant and useful (Crowe, 2004).

There is a temptation to define transpersonal music therapy based on such processes or techniques, because they are the most easily observable aspects of a music therapy session. However, technique is actually the least important aspect of transpersonal music therapy. Any technique can be transpersonal when it is used in a *transpersonal context*. Since transpersonal context relates to the orientation of the music therapist, any music therapy intervention could be considered transpersonal if the music therapist is relating to the music therapy session from a transpersonal context.

Context is what truly defines a transpersonal approach to music therapy, and transpersonal techniques that are not grounded in transpersonal context are, essentially, meaningless. Transpersonal context is the consciousness of the therapist, his or her intention for the session. Transpersonal context may not be evident to the observer, since it does not refer to "what the therapist says or does, but [to] the silent frame that operates behind the therapist's actions" (Cortwright, 1997, pp. 15–16). The attitudes a music therapist holds concerning healing, suffering, consciousness, and spiritual growth and development are what create a transpersonal context. *It is the consciousness of the therapist that brings the transpersonal context into being.* Therefore, it is important for music therapists who wish to work within a transpersonal framework to develop themselves, becoming familiar with the depths and heights of their own consciousness.

In order to hold a transpersonal context for music therapy work, the therapist must have experiential knowledge of the transpersonal realm. This is gained through various spiritual/ religious practices, spontaneous peak experience, experiences as a client in the Bonny Method of Guided Imagery and Music (BMGIM), improvisation, dream work, and other forms of transpersonal psychotherapy.

Jordan (1990) speaks of a musician's need to connect with his or her spiritual center. The same could be said of a music therapist:

> *One's innermost spiritual seat, the place from which all musical impulse grows and is nourished, can only be accessed through time spent with one's self. (p. 21)*

> *One can only access that place through quietness and calm. It can be said that music is created out of the quiet, centered self. For most of us, accessing center through quietness will be our most formidable challenge. (p. 31)*

Most of the World Wisdom traditions incorporate some form of meditation or prayer as a means of quieting the mind and connecting with the transpersonal realm. The reader is encouraged to seek out a form that resonates with his or her own spiritual path. (See Additional Resources at the end of this chapter.)

Assessment in Transpersonal Music Therapy

Several general assessments for transpersonal psychology can be useful in music therapy, which include

- MARI (Mandala Assessment Research Instrument) by Joan Kellogg (1984);
- Myers-Briggs Type Indicator, based on Carl Jung's theory of psychological types; and
- other transpersonal assessment tools, such as the Enneagram and astrology, must be used by a practitioner who is well-trained in their use and should be used only by a music therapist with that specific training.

There are some music therapy-specific assessments for a transpersonal approach, including the following:

- Pavlicevic's (2003) intuitive process of "tuning in" to the music space before beginning a session. To "tune in" is to listen to the "feel" of the room before beginning the session and also listen to your listening. If the room feels flat and devoid of energy, beginning singing and playing in a way that reflects those very qualities may be needed.

- Priestley's (1994) concept of E-countertransference could be considered to be a type of ongoing transpersonal assessment. It is based on the music therapist's intuition and the bodily sensations experienced while working with a client. Priestley describes this as an "'echo effect' in which the pain of the patient can be echoed in the healer's own body" (p. 99). She finds that this effect is especially strong when the therapist and client are improvising together. An image of E-countertransference would be of a plucked string instrument (the patient) whose music resonates on its sympathetic strings (the therapist), and the very word concordant, which literally means "with string," affirms this image.

Populations Who Can Benefit From Transpersonal Technique/Approach

Individuals with nonpsychotic mental disorders can certainly benefit from a transpersonal music therapy approach. In particular, clients dealing with substance abuse, repressed memories and emotions, and depression can utilize this approach. There are music therapists operating from a transpersonal context whose work may not initially appear to include transpersonal processes/techniques. The following statement shows that the pioneering music therapy team of Paul Nordoff and Clive Robbins held a transpersonal context in their work with children with developmental disabilities: "Our clinical experience has provided us with knowledge of other experiential realms—of time, music, and human capacity. . . . This experience has expanded our world view and consciousness" (Aigen, 1996, p. 30). Clarkson's experience of working from a transpersonal context with individuals with autism is documented in her book, *I Dreamed I Was Normal* (1998). Some music therapy techniques are intentionally based on transpersonal process. Probably the best known of these is the Bonny Method of Guided Imagery and Music. (See section on imagery and music in this chapter.) Kenny's (1982) work with ritual is also rooted in the transpersonal process. Music therapists should note that many of the transpersonal processes and techniques are rooted in the religion and mythology of non-Western cultures. Caution should be exercised in inappropriately appropriating sacred techniques and rituals for use outside their traditional cultures and in violating clients' beliefs in this area.

References

Abate, F. R. (Ed.). (1997). The Oxford dictionary and thesaurus: American edition. *New York: Oxford University Press.*

Achterberg, J. (1985). Imagery in healing. *Boston: Shambhala.*

Achterberg, J., Dossey, B., & Kolkmeier, L. (1994). Rituals of healing: Using imagery for health and wellness. *New York: Bantam Books.*

Ahonen-Eerikainen, H. (2002). *Group-analytic music therapy: Using dreams and musical images as a pathway to the unconscious levels of the group matrix.* Nordic Journal of Music Therapy, 11*(1)*, 48–53.

Aigen, K. (1996). Being in music: Foundations of Nordoff-Robbins music therapy. *St. Louis, MO: MMB Music.*

Amir, D. (1993). *Moments of insight in the music therapy experience.* Music Therapy, 12*(1)*, 85–100.

Amir, D. (1999). *Musical and verbal interventions in music therapy: A qualitative study.* Journal of Music Therapy, 36*(2)*, 144–175.

Austin, D. (1986). The healing symbol: Sound, song and psychotherapy. *Unpublished master's thesis, New York University.*

Austin, D. (1991). *The musical mirror: Music therapy for the narcissistically injured. In K. E. Bruscia (Ed.),* Case studies in music therapy *(pp. 291–307). Phoenixville, PA: Barcelona.*

Austin, D. (1993). *Projection of parts of the self onto music and musical instruments. In G. M. Rolla (Ed.),* Your inner music *(pp. 93–99). Wilmette, IL: Chiron.*

Austin, D. (1996). *The role of improvised music in psychodynamic music therapy with adults.* Music Therapy, 14*(1)*, 29–43.

Austin, D. (1998). When the psyche sings: Transference and countertransference in improvised singing with individual adults. In K. E. Bruscia (Ed.), The dynamics of music psychotherapy (pp. 315–333). Gilsum, NH: Barcelona.

Austin, D. (1999a). Many stories, many songs. In J. Hibben (Ed.), Inside music therapy: Client experience (pp. 119–128). Gilsum, NH: Barcelona.

Austin, D. (1999b). Vocal improvisation in analytically oriented music therapy with adults. In T. Wigram & J. DeBacker (Eds.), Clinical applications of music therapy in psychiatry (pp. 141–157). London: Jessica Kingsley.

Austin, D. (2001). In search of the self: The use of vocal holding techniques with adults traumatized as children. Music Therapy Perspectives, 19(1), 22–30.

Austin, D. (2002). The voice of trauma. A wounded healer's perspective. In J. Sutton (Ed.), Music, music therapy and trauma: International perspectives (pp. 231–259). London: Jessica Kingsley.

Austin, D. (2004). When words sing and music speaks: A qualitative study of in-depth music psychotherapy with adults. Dissertation Abstracts International, 3110989. Proquest Information and Learning.

Ayto, J. (1990). Dictionary of word origins. New York: Arcade.

Bagdanov, V., Woodstra, C., & Erlewine, S. T. (2003). All music guide to the blues (3rd ed.). San Francisco: Backbeat Books.

Band, J. P., Quilter, S. M., & Miller, G. M. (2002). The influence of selected music and inductions on mental imagery: Implications for practitioners of guided imagery and music. Journal of the Association for Music and Imagery, 8, 13–33.

Bannister, A. (2000). Prisoners of the family: Psychodrama with abused children. In F. Kellermann & M. K. Hudgins (Eds.), Psychodrama with trauma survivors (pp. 97–113). London: Jessica Kingsley.

Bartlett, D., Kaufman, D., & Smeltekop, R. (1993). The effects of music listening and perceived sensory experiences on the immune system as measured by interleukin-1 and cortisol. Journal of Music Therapy, 30, 194–209.

Benenzon, R. (1997). Music therapy theory and manual: Contributions to the knowledge of nonverbal contex (2nd ed.). Springfield, IL: Charles C. Thomas.

Berendt, J. (1987). Nada brahma: The world is sound. Rochester, VT: Destiny Books.

Bonny, H. L., & Savary, L. M. (1990). Music and your mind (2nd ed.). Barrytown, NY: Station Hill Press.

Braddock, C. J. (1995). Body voices. Berkeley, CA: Pagemill Press.

Bruscia, K. (1987). Improvisational models of music therapy. Springfield, IL: Charles C. Thomas.

Bruscia, K. (1998a). Defining music therapy. Gilsum, NH: Barcelona.

Bruscia, K. (1998b). The dynamics of music therapy. Gilsum, NH: Barcelona.

Bruscia, K. E. (2002). The boundaries of guided imagery and music (GIM) and the Bonny method. In K. E. Bruscia & D. E. Grocke (Eds.), Guided imagery and music: The Bonny method and beyond (pp. 38–61). Gilsum, NH: Barcelona.

Bunt, L. (1994). Music therapy: An art beyond words. London: Routledge.

Bunt, L., & Hoskyns, S. (2002). The handbook of music therapy. East Sussex, UK: Brunner-Routledge.

Bush, C. A. (1995). Healing imagery and music: Pathways to the inner self. Portland, OR: Rudra Press.

Campbell, D. (1989). The roar of silence. Wheaton, IL: The Theosophical Publishing House.

Chumacero, C. L. D. (1998). Consciously induced song recall: Transference and countertransference implications. In K. Bruscia (Ed.), The dynamics of music therapy (pp. 364–385). Gilsum, NH: Barcelona.

Clark, M. F. (2002). Evolution of the Bonny method of guided imagery and music (BMGIM). In K. E. Bruscia & D. E. Grocke (Eds.), Guided imagery and music: The Bonny method and beyond (pp. 5–27). Gilsum, NH: Barcelona.

Clarkson, G. (1998). I dreamed I was normal. St. Louis, MO: MMB Books.

Clarkson, G., & Geller, J. (1996). The Bonny Method from a psychoanalytic perspective: Insights from working with a psychoanalytic psychotherapist in a guided imagery and music series. The Arts in Psychotherapy, 23(4), 311–319.

Cortright, B. (1997). Psychotherapy and spirit. Albany, NY: SUNY Press.

Crowe, B. J. (2004). Music and soulmaking: Toward a new theory of music therapy. Lanham, MD: Scarecrow Press.

Crowe, B. J., & Scovel, M. (1996). An overview of sound healing practices: Implications for the profession of music therapy. Music Therapy Perspectives, 14(1), 21–29.

Darnley-Smith, R., & Patey, H. M. (2003). Music therapy. London: Sage.

Dayton, T. (1994). The drama within: Psychodrama and experiential therapy. Deerfield Beach, FL: Health Communications.

Dayton, T. (1997). Heartwounds: The impact of unresolved trauma and grief on relationships. Deerfield Beach, FL: Health Communications.

Edinger, E. (1972). Ego and archetype. New York: Penguin Books.

Elston, A. (1948). The musician's approach to musical therapy. In D. M. Schullian & M. Schoen (Eds.), Music and medicine (pp. 282–292). New York: Henry Schuman.

Eschen, J. T. (2002). Analytical music therapy. London: Jessica Kingsley.

Freud, S. (1913). On beginning the treatment. London: The Hogarth Press.

Freud, S. (1938). An outline of psychoanalysis. New York: W.W. Norton.

Gardner, K. (1990). Sounding the inner landscape. Stonington, MA: Caduceus.

Gaynor, M. L. (1999). Sounds of healing: A physician reveals the therapeutic power of sound, voice, and music. New York: Broadway Books.

Goldberg, F. S. (1992). Images of emotion: The role of emotion in guided imagery and music. Journal of the Association for Music and Imagery, 1, 5–17.

Goldman, J. (1992). Healing sounds. Rockport, MA: Element Books.

Goldstein, A. (1980). Thrills in response to music and other stimuli. Physiological Psychology, 8, 126–129.

Gurman, A., & Messer, S. (2003). Essential psychotherapies (2nd ed.). New York: The Guilford Press.

Hadley, S. (2003). Psychodynamic music therapy: Case studies. Gilsum, NH: Barcelona.

Hamel, P. M. (1978). Through music to the self. Boulder, CO: Shambhala.

Hart, M., & Lieberman, F. (1999). Spirit into sound: The magic of music. Petaluma, CA: Grateful Dead Books.

Herman, J. (1992). Trauma and recovery: The aftermath of violence from domestic abuse to political terror. New York: Basic Books.

Hudgins, M. K., & Kiesler D. J. (1987). Individual experiential psychotherapy: An analogue validation of the intervention model of psychodramatic doubling. Psychotherapy, 24, 245–255.

Hunt, H. T. (1995). On the nature of consciousness: Cognitive, phenomenological, and transpersonal perspectives. New Haven, CT: Yale University Press.

Jacobi, J. (1965). The way of individuation. New York: New American Library.

Jacobson, E. (1962). You must relax. New York: McGraw-Hill.

Jahn-Langenberg, M., & Schmidt, H. U. (2003). A comparison of first encounters: Diagnostic impressions of a music therapy session and the analytic first interview. Nordic Journal of Music Therapy, 12(1), 91–99.

John, D. (1992). Towards music psychotherapy. British Journal of Music Therapy, 6(1), 10–12.

Johnson, E. R. (1981). The role of objective and concrete feedback in self-concept treatment of juvenile delinquents in music therapy. Journal of Music Therapy, 18(3), 137–147.

Johnson, R. A. (1986). Inner work. San Francisco: Harper.

Jordan, J. (1990). The musician's soul. Chicago: GIA.

Jourdain, R. (1997). Music, the brain, and ecstasy. New York: William Morrow.

Jung, C. G. (1969). The archetypes and the collective unconscious. The collected works of C. G. Jung, volume 9. Bollingen Series. Princeton, NJ: Princeton University Press.

Jung, C. G. (1970). The structure and dynamics of the psyche. The collected works of C. G. Jung, volume 8. Bollingen Series. Princeton, NJ: Princeton University Press.

Kalshed, D. (1996). The inner world of trauma. London: Routledge.

Kast, V. (1992). The dynamics of symbols. New York: Fromm International.

Kellerman, P. F. (2000). The therapeutic aspects of psychodrama with traumatized people. In P. F. Kellerman & M. K. Hudgins (Eds.), Psychodrama with trauma survivors (pp. 23–38). London: Jessica Kingsley.

Kellogg, J. (1984). Mandala: Path of beauty. Clearwater, FL: MARI.

Kenny, C. (1982). The mythic artery. Atascadero, CA: Ridgeview.

Kenny, C. (1985). Music: A whole systems approach. Music Therapy, 5(1), 3–11.

Keyes, L. (1973). Toning: The creative power of the voice. Marina del Ray, CA: DeVorss.

Knoblauch, S. H. (2000). The musical edge of therapeutic dialogue. Hillsdale, NJ: The Analytic Press.

Koepchen, H. P., Droh, R., Spintge, R., Abel, H.-H., Klussendorf, D., & Koralewski, E. (1992). Physiological rhythmicity and music in medicine. In R. Spintge & R. Droh (Eds.), MusicMedicine (pp. 39–70). St. Louis, MO: MMB Music.

Lajoie, D., & Shapiro, S. (1992). Definitions of transpersonal psychology: The first twenty-three years. Journal of Transpersonal Psychology, 24(1), 83–98.

Langenberg, M., Frommer, J., & Tress, W. (1995). From isolation to bonding: A music therapy study with a patient with chronic migraines. The Arts in Psychotherapy, 22(2), 87–101.

Levine, S. (1991). Guided meditations, explorations and healings. New York: Doubleday.

Linklater, K. (1976). Freeing the natural voice. New York: Drama Book Specialists.

Liu, L. L., & Park, D. C. (2004). Aging and medical adherence: The use of automatic processes to achieve effortful things. Psychology & Aging, 19, 318–325.

Loewy, J. (2000). Music psychotherapy assessment. Music Therapy Perspectives, 18(1), 47–58.

Mahler, M. S., Pine, F., & Bergman, A. (1975). The psychological birth of the human infant. New York: Basic Books.

Maslow, A. (1968). Toward a psychology of being. New York: Van Nostrand.

McCraty, R., Atkinson, M., Rein, G., & Watkins, A. D. (1996). Music enhances the effect of positive emotional states on salivary IgA. Stress Medicine, 12, 167–175.

McKinney, C. H., Antoni, M. H., Kumar, A. M., Tims, F. C., & McCabe, P. M. (1997). Effects of guided imagery and music (GIM) therapy on mood and cortisol in healthy adults. Health Psychology, 16, 390–400.

McKinney, C. H., Tims, F. C., Kumar, A. M., & Kumar, M. (1997). The effects of selected classical music and spontaneous imagery on plasma beta-endorphin. Journal of Behavioral Medicine, 20, 85–99.

Miller, A. (1981). The drama of the gifted child. New York: Basic Books.

Minson, R. (1992). A sonic birth. In D. Campbell (Ed.), Music and miracles (pp. 89–97). Wheaton, IL: Quest Books.

Montello, L. (1998). Relational issues in psychoanalytic music therapy with traumatized individuals. In K. Bruscia (Ed.), The dynamics of music therapy (pp. 299–313). Gilsum, NH: Barcelona.

Montello, L. (1999). A psychoanalytic music therapy approach to treating adults traumatized as children. Music Therapy Perspectives, 17(2), 74–81.

Moreno, L. (1994). Psychodrama. McLean, VA: American Society for Group Psychotherapy and Psychodrama.

Morris, W. (Ed.). (1973). The American heritage dictionary of the English language. New York: American Heritage.

Moses, P. J. (1954). The voice of neurosis. New York: Grune & Stratton.

Naparstek, B. (1994). Staying well with guided imagery: How to harness the power of your imagination for health and healing. New York: Warner Books.

Newham, P. (1998). Therapeutic voicework: Principles and practice for the use of singing as a therapy. London: Jessica Kingsley.

Nolan, P. (1998). Countertransference in clinical song writing. In K. Bruscia (Ed.), The dynamics of music therapy (pp. 387–406). Gilsum, NH: Barcelona.

Nolan, P. (2003). Through music to therapeutic attachment: Psychodynamic music psychotherapy with a musician with dysthymic disorder. In S. Hadley (Ed.), Psychodynamic music therapy: Case studies (pp. 319–338). Gilsum, NH: Barcelona.

Parker, A. B. (1998). How to choose music to support physiological and emotional processes: A neuropsychological approach. Unpublished master's thesis, Prescott College, Prescott, AZ.

Pavlicevic, M. (1995). Interpersonal processes in clinical improvisation: Towards a subjectively objective systematic definition. In T. Wigram, B. Saperston, & R. West (Eds.), The art and science of music therapy (pp. 167–178). Chur, Switzerland: Harwood Academic.

Pavlicevic, M. (1997). Music therapy in context: Music, meaning and relationship. London: Jessica Kingsley.

Pavlicevic, M. (2003). Groups in music: Strategies from music therapy. London: Jessica Kingsley.

Priestly, M. (1994). Essays on analytical music therapy. Phoenixville, PA: Barcelona.

Progoff, I. (1992). At a journal workshop: Writing to access the power of the unconscious and evoke creative ability. Los Angeles: Jeremy Tarcher.

Reck, D. (1977). Music of the whole earth. New York: Charles Scribner's Sons.

Rider, M. S., Mickey, C., Weldin, C., & Hawkinson, R. (1991). The effects of toning, listening, and singing on psychophysiological responses. In C. D. Maranto (Ed.), Applications of music in medicine (pp. 72–84). Washington, DC: National Association for Music Therapy.

Rossi, E. L. (1986). The psychology of mind-body healing. New York: W. W. Norton.

Rossi, E. L. (1993). The psychobiology of mind-body healing (2nd ed.). New York: W. W. Norton.

Rugenstein, L. (1992). Becoming a sound woman by reclaiming the power within. In D. Campbell (Ed.), Music and miracles (pp. 208–215). Wheaton, IL: Quest Books.

Ruud, E. (1990). Music therapy and its relationship to current treatment theories. St. Louis, MO: Magnamusic.

Ruud, E. (1995). Improvisation as a liminal experience: Jazz and music therapy as modern "Rites de Passage." In C. Kenny (Ed.), Listening, playing, creating: Essays on the power of sound (pp. 91–117). Albany, NY: State University of New York Press.

Ruud, E. (1998). Music therapy: Improvisation, communication and culture. Gilsum, NH: Barcelona.

Ruud, E. (2003). "Burning scripts": Self psychology, affect consciousness, script theory and the BMGIM. Nordic Journal of Music Therapy, 12(3), 115–123.

Schultz, J. H., & Luthe, W. (1969). Autogenic training: A physiological approach to psychotherapy. New York: Grune & Stratton.

Simonton, C., Simonton, S., & Creighton, J. (1978). Getting well again. Los Angeles: Jeremy Tarcher.

Smeijsters, H. (1993). Music therapy and psychotherapy. The Arts in Psychotherapy, 20(3), 223–229.

Smeijsters, H., & van den Hurk, J. (1999). Music therapy helping to work through grief and finding a personal identity. Journal of Music Therapy, 36(3), 222–252.

Spintge, R. (1991). The neurophysiology of emotion and its therapeutic applications in music therapy and music medicine. In C. D. Maranto (Ed.), Applications of music in medicine (pp. 59–72). Washington, DC: National Association for Music Therapy.

Spolin, V. (1963). Improvisation for the theater. Evanston, IL: Northwestern University Press.

Stephens, G. (1983). The use of improvisation for developing relatedness in the adult client. Music Therapy, 3(1), 29–42.

Stewart, D. (2002). Sound company: Psychodynamic group music therapy as facilitating environment, transformational object and therapeutic playground. In A. Davies & E. Richards (Eds.), Music therapy and group work (pp. 27–42). London: Jessica Kingsley.

Stokes-Stearns, S., Bush, C. A., & Borling, J. (1995). Level II guided imagery and music training. Annapolis, MD: Mid-Atlantic Training Institute.

Storr, A. (1992). Music and the mind. New York: The Free Press.

Streeter, E. (1999). Definition and use of the musical transference relationship. In T. Wigram & J. DeBacker (Eds.), Clinical applications of music therapy in psychiatry (pp. 84–101). London: Jessica Kingsley.

Tame, D. (1984). The secret power of music. Rochester, VT: Destiny Books.

Thaut, M. (1990). Neuropsychological processes in music perception and their relevance in music therapy. In R. Unkefer (Ed.), Music therapy in the treatment of adults with mental disorders (pp. 3–32). New York: Schirmer Books.

Tomatis, A. (1991). The conscious ear: My life of transformation through listening. New York: Station Hill Press.

Tsao, C. C., Gordon, T. F., Maranto, C. D., Lerman, C., & Murasko, D. (1991). *The effects of music and biological imagery on immune response.* In C. D. Maranto (Ed.), Applications of music in medicine *(pp. 85–121). Washington, DC: National Association for Music Therapy.*

Turry, A. (1998). *Transference and countertransference in Nordoff-Robbins music therapy.* In K. E. Bruscia (Ed.), The dynamics of music psychotherapy *(pp. 161–212). Gilsum, NH: Barcelona.*

Vaughan, F. (1979). *Transpersonal psychotherapy: Context, content, and process.* Journal of Transpersonal Psychology, 11, *25–30.*

Verdeau-Paillés, J. (2004). Le bilan psychomusicale et la personalité *(3rd ed., revised). Paris: Fuzeau Éditions.*

Walsh, R., & Vaughan, F. (Eds.). (1993). Paths beyond ego. *New York: G. P. Putnam's Sons.*

Wigram, T., Pedersen, I. N., & Bonde, L. O. (2002). A comprehensive guide to music therapy. *London: Jessica Kingsley.*

Winkelman, M. (2000). Shamanism: The neural ecology of consciousness. *Westport, CT: Bergin 7.*

Winnicott, D. W. (1971). Playing and reality. *London: Routledge.*

Additional Resources

Austin, D. (1999). *Vocal improvisation in analytically oriented music therapy with adults.* In T. Wigram & J. DeBacker (Eds.), Clinical applications of music therapy in psychiatry *(pp. 141–157). London: Jessica Kingsley.*

Austin, D. & Dvorkin, J. (1993). *Resistance in individual music therapy.* The Arts in Psychotherapy, 20, *423–429.*

Csikszentmihalyi, M. (1991). Flow: The psychology of optimal experience. *New York: HarperCollins.*

Davies, A., & Richards, E. (2002). Music therapy and group work. *London: Jessica Kingsley.*

Gunaratana, H. (1991). Mindfulness in plain English. *Boston: Wisdom.*

Jordan, J. (1990). The musician's soul. *Chicago: GIA.*

Kabat-Zinn, J. (1994). Wherever you go there you are. *New York: Hyperion.*

Keating, T. (1994). Intimacy with God. *New York: Crossroad.*

Merritt, S. (1996). Mind, music and imagery: Unlocking the treasures of your mind. *Santa Rosa, CA: Aslan.*

Montello, L. (2002). Essential musical intelligence. *Wheaton, IL: Quest Books.*

Nachmanovitch, S. (1990). Free play: Improvisation in life and art. *New York: Jeremy P. Tarcher/Putnam.*

Section 3:

Treatment Delivery Formats for Adults With Mental Disorders

Chapter 7

Clinical Practices in Music Therapy With the Chronic Adult Psychiatric Inpatient Population
Gary Johnson

The President's New Freedom Commission on Mental Health stated that a major mental illness, including schizophrenia, bipolar disorder, clinical depression, and obsessive-compulsive disorder, when compared with all other diseases (such as cancer and heart disease), is the most common cause of disability in the United States (Free-Definition, 2004). According to the National Alliance for the Mentally Ill, 23% of North American adults will suffer from a clinically diagnosable mental illness in a given year (NAMI, 2005).

Music therapy in the treatment of persons with a mental illness became a hospital-developed practice, which originated in psychiatric hospitals (Tyson, 1981). In these settings, music therapy became a viable intervention providing quality care for persons who had psychosocial, affective, cognitive, and communication needs, even when other approaches failed (AMTA, 2004). Currently found in psychiatric treatment facilities, community mental health centers, drug and alcohol programs, half-way houses, and rehabilitation facilities, music therapy is a viable and efficacious treatment for adults with various chronic psychiatric diagnoses as reported in research and in clinical, evidenced-based outcomes. This chapter focuses on inpatient treatment for clients with severe forms of mental illness.

The purpose of this chapter is to present topics essential to music therapy practice. The chapter content is derived from years of experience and clinical observations as a practitioner and as a music therapy internship director. This information serves to guide students, professionals, and others who are interested in developing and facilitating a music therapy program for adults with chronic psychiatric conditions. These clinical practice topics, or points to consider, include developing good politics in the workplace, initiating a music therapy program, knowing the patient, recognizing agitation, identifying signs of agitation, assuring safety for patients and staff, and designing and facilitating successful music applications.

Developing the Politics of the Workplace

Establishing a professional rapport with the patient's doctor, nurse, social worker, and other members of the multidisciplinary treatment team is essential to productive working relationships. This can be difficult because not all staff accept the use of music therapy to treat psychiatric conditions. Some may feel threatened or may feel their professional boundaries are in question. They may also have misconceptions about music therapy, may have never heard about it, or may just not want the intrusion. Some solutions for breaking through difficulties resulting from such attitudes and misunderstandings include giving in-service trainings; providing documented research; inviting staff to observe music therapy sessions; or asking staff, especially nursing, what in particular would help them perform their job more effectively. Then, the articulated need can be developed into a music therapy application. Problems solved through consideration of staff needs may then result in cooperative efforts for improved patient care and treatment. Through demonstrated competence and without becoming defensive and arrogant, the practitioner can articulate the benefits of music therapy for both patients and treatment staff.

Initiating a Music Therapy Program

When planning and initiating a music therapy program for persons with chronic psychiatric disorders, there are four basic steps to consider. The program should first focus on the treatment needs or problem behaviors of the patient. Examples of treatment needs could include difficulties with attention span and focus, staying on task, impulse control, and socialization. Once the needs are determined, goals and objectives are established. The second step to consider when initiating a music therapy program is consultation with nursing staff and other members of the patient's treatment team. Each member of the treatment team has the professional expertise to provide valuable information regarding treatment issues, which will provide tips concerning how music therapy can be included. Since nursing staff sees the patient on a regular basis, additional information provided by nurses, such as behaviors, moods, and mental stability, assists in determining if the patient is an appropriate candidate for music therapy. The third step to initiating a music therapy program is to predetermine the essential music equipment needed, a planned budget, and a suitable space in which to conduct a music therapy session. Essential music equipment such as rhythm or percussion instruments, drums, guitars, keyboards, and cassette and CD players/recorders needs to be reliable, durable, easy to operate, relatively easy to repair, and age appropriate. The budget determines what financial resources are available to support a music therapy program. It is important to prioritize what necessary equipment and materials are needed. The treatment area or room used to conduct music therapy sessions should have adequate space, good lighting, easily located electrical outlets, and comfortable chairs. The fourth step is to determine what type of clinical setting is best for the patient. After assessing the patient and determining specific problems and needs, one-to-one and small and large group treatment settings should be provided accordingly.

Know the Patient

In order to provide effective treatment for a person with a chronic psychiatric condition, it is important to know the patient. Having a clear understanding of the patient's psychiatric diagnosis is necessary. Online and internet resources give detailed definitions and descriptions of mental illnesses and psychiatric disorders. (See section on definition of mental disorders in Chapter 1.) Once the diagnosis is comprehended, indicators of the patient's personality, including any inappropriate behaviors, can be easily identified. Some examples include resistive and manipulative behaviors, agitation, verbal and physical outbursts, and poor impulse control. Some recommended ways to learn more about how the patient manifests the diagnosis include consulting the patient's medical records, physician, nursing staff, social worker, other treatment team members, and possibly the patient's family. The patient's physical, social, emotional, and cognitive needs are also considered to determine which music therapy interventions to implement.

Recognizing Agitation

Persons with psychiatric disorders commonly exhibit delusions, hallucinations, anger, depression, anxiety, and manic states. Agitation, a possible manifestation of these characteristics, can be an unpleasant state of extreme arousal that includes increased muscle tension, increased physical activity, and irritability. It can also be associated with a wide range of psychiatric diagnoses such as bipolar disorder, schizophrenia, schizoaffective disorder, and posttraumatic stress disorder. It can last for a few minutes, weeks, or months. Agitation can come on suddenly or gradually. When agitation becomes extreme, the patient is often confused, hyperactive, very negative, and potentially abusive and hostile.

Identifying Signs of Agitation

It is important for any clinician who provides treatment for patients with chronic psychiatric disorders to recognize the signs of agitation.

- The patient may be more talkative than usual with progressively accelerated speech.
- The patient may show signs of increased pacing and restlessness evidenced by repetitive moving from one position to another within a room or hallway.
- The patient's hands may tremble and the overall body may shake and twitch.
- If the patient drinks alcohol, uses illegal drugs, or does not take prescribed medication, agitation may likely occur.
- In addition, a specific event that is too overwhelming for the patient to cope with may trigger agitation.

Assuring Safety for Patients and Staff

Assuring safety for staff and patients is always a concern for any psychiatric treatment situation. Knowing basic safety precautions provides a better therapeutic environment.

- Become aware of entrances and exits from treatment areas such as clinics and dayrooms.
- Know what surrounds these areas and avoid situations where you may be alone in an area with little opportunity to obtain assistance. Most facilities have a code or system for calling staff to help. It is very important to know what the specific code or system for staff assistance is and how to use it.
- Always maintain a comfortable distance from the patient and know his or her personal boundaries. When a patient appears agitated or verbally threatening, maintain eye contact, never turn away, and obtain support from other staff.
- Since a person with a chronic psychiatric disorder may exhibit bizarre behaviors and can be argumentative, it is important that the clinician remains calm and redirects the patient instead of arguing. Such reflective statements as "it appears that" or "you seem" are best in efforts to de-escalate and diffuse a potentially volatile situation.

Successful Music Therapy Applications

The music therapy applications provided here for the chronic psychiatric population are defined as passive and active music-making applications. Passive music making includes music listening, song analysis, and songwriting. Active music making includes individual instrument playing, rhythm instrument/percussion playing, and singing.

Music Listening

Music listening is a useful application to help manage stress, develop relaxation skills, and improve social interaction. The person should prefer the music selected. If there is a music listening group, the members can learn to share and cooperate by taking turns (choosing the music or using the CD player), solving problems (reaching group consensus about what they will listen to), and making decisions (deciding upon the order of song selections).

Song Analysis

Song analysis is a music application that provides the patient the opportunity to recognize specific characteristics and elements of a song. It can be used to help patients express themselves, improve concentration, and explore personal feelings. Song analysis involves interpreting the lyrics, describing instrumentation, and recognizing melodic directions. The patient can also be encouraged to rate the song and express how the song relates to his or her life situation. (See section on use of songs in Chapter 5.)

Songwriting

Songwriting is implemented to encourage verbal and nonverbal expression, improve self-esteem and self-worth, and improve decision-making skills. This application can be facilitated in different ways, but the simplest approach is to encourage the patient to substitute a word for a lyric found in an existing song. A blues structure, for example, is a simple way to encourage engagement in a songwriting application, as shown in the example below:

Sometimes I feel _____,

And sometimes I look _____,

Sometimes I feel _____,

And sometimes I look_____,
Well, I have the feelin' _____ and lookin' _____ blues today,
But I know tomorrow is comin' and I'll really feel somethin'
Cause I have the feelin' blues today.

(See section on songwriting in Chapter 5.)

Individual Music Instrument Playing

Individual music instrument playing is defined here as the learning of an instrument for the first time or continuing an interest in playing an instrument once learned. Treatment goals can include improving attention span and focus, improving self-esteem, improving constructive use of leisure time, and developing coping and relaxation skills. Common instruments include, but are not limited to, guitar, piano, voice, woodwinds, brass, strings, and drums/percussion. Instrument learning is actually secondary to the overall functional treatment goal. For example, a person who shows the ability to play all the notes on the piano or a song using one or both hands can reach the music goal but can also show the ability to focus attention, sequence stimuli, and follow through to achievement, which increases confidence and improves self-esteem. (See section on musical instruction in Chapter 4.)

Percussion Instrument Playing

Rhythm/percussion instrument playing, which also includes drumming, is an application used frequently in music therapy practice. Goals addressed include improving concentration (i.e., learning a new part), attention span (i.e., waiting to be cued), memory (i.e., echoing rhythm patterns), decision making (i.e., composition elements), self-expression (i.e., improvisation), and socialization (i.e., ensemble playing). (See section on drumming in Chapter 4.)

Singing

Singing addresses functional goals, including increased attention span and focus, relaxation, self-esteem, and social skills. Applications of singing include voice lessons, choral ensembles, sing-a-longs, and even use of a karaoke machine. An evaluation of the patient's skill level, music preferences, and interests allows the music therapist to design a singing program that suits their individual strengths and needs. A patient's outcome may range from delusions of grandeur about their abilities to a fear of singing, all of which indicate careful planning on the music therapist's part. One of the most important results of singing as a music therapy application is the personal joy and accomplishment experienced by the person. (See section on group singing in Chapter 4.)

Conclusion

The information provided here points out some important concepts in the planning and implementation of music therapy programming for persons with a chronic mental disability. It is not intended as a procedural manual, but as a practical guide to assist the reader with some basic tools that can be developed over subsequent years of service.

References

American Music Therapy Association. *(2004).* Music therapy and mental health. *Retrieved September 15, 2005, from http://www.musictherapy. org*

Free-Definition. *(2004).* Mental illness. *Retrieved February 15, 2005, from http://www.free-definition.com/Mental-illness.html*

NAMI. *(2005).* The nation's voice on mental illness. *Retrieved February 15, 2005, from http://www.nami.org*

Tyson, F. *(1981). Music therapy in hospitals. In F. Tyson (Ed.),* Psychiatric music therapy: Origins and development *(pp. 7-12). New York: Fred Weidner & Sons.*

Chapter 8

Music Therapy and Acute Care Psychiatric Treatment
Carylbeth Thomas

The economic revolution in healthcare and the resulting changes in the practice of psychiatry have clearly had a major effect on the delivery of services by music therapists as well as all other treatment providers. One of these changes is a shift from long-term to short-term or acute care. Acute care psychiatry essentially provides an accurate diagnosis and formulation of the symptoms, signs, and problematic experiences that a patient may present, along with the provision of the most worthwhile treatments in the least restrictive, cost-effective sites of service. Treatment programs also seek to provide care that brings clinical improvement in a manner that meets the patients' definition of satisfaction, and that, in turn, promotes a higher level of treatment compliance and successful return to their lives in the community. Key therapeutic functions to be considered in this type of treatment are containment, support, structure, involvement, and validation for the client.

The evolution of managed care in American health care has had a serious impact on the role of music therapy and the available jobs in the field of psychiatric care. The current length of stay in most inpatient hospital settings for acute psychiatric care has been reduced to an average of 7–10 days or less. Acute care and short-term treatment is not limited to the actual inpatient hospital unit anymore but is frequently found in day programs or other outpatient settings that patients may be referred to initially or discharged to after a brief stay in a hospital. Many day programs have become a kind of "hospital without walls" where the client's level of acuity may be very high. Because of this, major concerns occur as to whether adequate supervision and safety can be provided for many of its consumers (clients). Whereas music therapy continues to be a valuable and effective treatment modality in acute care, the profession is being challenged to rethink and redevelop our conceptual models of treatment. In this section, some of the issues and challenges of acute care treatment are presented, as well as a discussion of ideas, principles, approaches, and rationales for the effective use of music therapy in these settings.

Acute Care Settings

In 1997, the American Academy of Child and Adolescent Psychiatry and the American Psychiatric Association jointly published *Criteria for Short-Term Treatment of Acute Psychiatric Illness* to provide criteria leading to more effective communication between managed care companies and clinicians and to improved treatment planning. This document specifically addresses levels of care under health plans that currently provide for short-term treatment of acute psychiatric illness. The most frequently utilized settings include acute inpatient hospitalization, medically supervised psychiatric residential treatment, acute partial hospitalization, intensive outpatient treatment, and general outpatient treatment. There are various factors in the level-of-care decision-making process. A patient may need to be admitted to a more intensive level of care, even when he or she does not meet the criteria, if the most appropriate treatment setting is not immediately or logistically available. Clearly, the choice of setting would be that which is most clinically indicated for each client but often is affected by other issues such as location and proximity, availability of programs, or openings in the programs.

Music therapists may be found working in any of these settings and most often as group therapists. Some amount of individual work may occur, but therapists in general focus on group work, because there is often simply not enough time with such brief lengths of stay in inpatient and residential programs for individual sessions. Individual music therapy treatment tends to occur more frequently on an outpatient basis and in less intensive phases of treatment.

Levels of Treatment

Wheeler (1983) refers to three classifications of psychiatric music therapy —music activity therapy, re-educative music therapy, and re-constructive music therapy—as discussed in Chapter 3. In most acute care treatment, music therapy is conducted primarily on a supportive or activity-oriented level, with *active* being the key word. Given the severe level of symptoms in acute care (i.e., psychosis, mania, depression), clients may initially gain the most from the direct benefits of music (emotional, physiological, and spiritual) and the here-and-now experience of active music making. The goal is to restore patients to an emotional balance so that they can function as closely as possible to their premorbid levels. Re-educative levels of work are also feasible in acute care, if the client's condition allows for some amount of insight or ability to process material from the sessions directly and on a more conscious level. Due to the dynamic, flexible, and communal nature of music, it can afford patients the opportunity to recognize interpersonal problems and reinforce interpersonal strengths, whether on a conscious level or more spontaneously and in the moment. In acute care, clients are in a crisis, survival mode. The immediate goal for therapy is alleviation of distress. Therefore, the here-and-now focus and structure of music provides a grounded, secure, and reality-based experience for patients, and the sense of being able to better manage their current situation.

Active or supportive use of music therapy refers to a variety of activities that may assist a patient in connecting or reconnecting with the skills needed to attain the control necessary to function in life. Having insight into one's behavior or illness is not necessary. Rather, the patient must be actively involved and have greater awareness of the here-and-now through music experiences, especially those with a clear structure provided by the therapist. The therapy takes place through participation in the music, not necessarily through insight achieved through the musical events. Active music making fosters participation, improves socialization, and increases self-awareness and awareness of others. Structure, concrete directions, and nonverbal "modeling" of musical response from the therapist may be needed to encourage and support sound production (vocal and instrumental) and to reduce anxiety via tension release through musical expression. Active music making can also serve as a diversion from obsessions, auditory hallucinations, and current stressors and can be helpful in controlling impulsive behaviors and increasing attention span and concentration. This level of work tends to be used when acute or short-term treatment is all that is necessary or available with clients who have not responded well to more intensive therapies, or with more seriously ill, disorganized, or compromised clients.

Re-educative or more insight and process-oriented therapy is generally used to help clients achieve some insight into therapeutic material that comes up during the music experience on a relatively conscious level. It is still focused primarily on the here-and-now but with greater emphasis on verbal reflection or some kind of processing in conjunction with the music experience. When individuals are able to make the connection from the abstract musical response to specific behavior patterns, there may also be more freedom for expression both in and out of the music. The focus is directed towards feelings, the exposition and discussion of which leads to insight and can, in turn, result in improved functioning. This type of processing promotes goals in the identification and expression of feelings, problem solving, enhanced awareness, and insight of one's own behaviors and others. With higher functioning clients, it may be utilized in exploring and dealing with maladaptive attitudes and behaviors, sharing feelings with others, facilitating change, and reorganizing values. This level of work tends to be used with patients whose psychotic symptoms may have lessened or with patients with less severe symptoms such as in substance abuse issues, affective disorders, neuroses and anxiety disorders, or personality disorders.

Music Therapy Treatment in Acute Inpatient Care

In the current state of managed care in America's health care system, inpatient mental health treatment represents the most intensive level of psychiatric care. Multidisciplinary and multimodal interventions are provided in a 24-hour, secure, and protected treatment environment that is medically staffed and psychiatrically supervised. Music therapy often takes place as part of the structured treatment milieu required in addition to nursing and medical care. The goal of acute inpatient care is to stabilize individuals who display acute psychiatric conditions associated with a relatively sudden onset and a short, severe course, or a marked exacerbation of symptoms associated with a more persistent, recurring disorder. Typically, the individual poses a significant danger to self or others or displays severe psychosocial dysfunction. These inpatient units are most often locked units, and special treatments may include physical and mechanical restraint and seclusion.

Due to the increasingly diminished length of stay in acute care and the primary focus of treatment being stabilization and discharge, the strongest emphasis is frequently on psychopharmacological treatment. This has created a decrease in the focus on rehabilitative treatment, with admission assessment and discharge planning occurring simultaneously, and a predominance of group rather than individual treatment. Some of the additional challenges that short-term acute care presents to the treatment and assessment process for music therapists include: (a) a consistently high level of acuity and symptomatology in patients; (b) a wide range of psychopathology; (c) frequently limited access to information/history; and (d) rapid turnover, inconsistency and ever-changing group dynamics.

Music Therapy Assessment

Given that assessment is a vital and necessary component of any music therapy treatment process, acute care presents obvious challenges and issues to consider. If the overall focus of acute care is primarily accurate diagnosis, stabilization, and discharge to the next level of care, how are we as music therapists to contribute? Assessment is an ongoing process in acute care, with the determination of goals and choices of treatment interventions often occurring as one is accumulating and assimilating new information about the client. Bruscia (1988) determines that there are four possible objectives in clinical assessments: diagnostic, interpretive, descriptive, and prescriptive. Due to the limitations of time and contact in acute care, diagnosis and description are the primary focal points. Efforts are made to understand the client and detect, explain, and classify his or her pathology in terms of severity and prognosis. Prescriptive aspects may be considered in terms of recommendations for follow-up treatment. Of the six possible areas Wilson (2002) suggests that the assessment process might address, an acute care music therapy assessment seems most likely to assist in determining or supporting (a) the client's current strengths and weaknesses, (b) goals and objectives of the treatment program, and (c) differential diagnosis. Since music is such a unique form of human behavior, the opportunity to observe clients in musical situations provides a particularly different and distinct perspective on the client's presentation and behavior that might not be seen in other areas of the treatment team's assessment. Even though clients may not typically be accustomed to spending time with others in a musical experience, it often affords them the opportunity to engage with others in a somewhat normalized setting. These observations and interactions may reveal new or varying considerations for a client's treatment or may confirm an already suspected concern or diagnosis.

Since acute care essentially demands assessment and treatment of the client simultaneously, there is often little time for individual interviews, testing, or ability to review existing information prior to actual treatment. The music therapist must rely mostly on observation and intervention concurrently in order to work efficiently and successfully in acute care settings. In these kinds of settings, each session needs to be considered in its own right as a one-time experience. The music therapist is often expected to assess several new individuals during this process. An overall objective for music therapy is to find a musical means of meeting as many needs of the people in the group as possible in that particular moment in time while compiling impressions and information. Using a loose overall framework of an opening, middle, and closing section allows therapists to be open to whatever needs may present themselves. Some musical structures are obviously needed, but within these structures, there also needs to be freedom to improvise and explore. It is vitally important to be prepared to change direction to accommodate the needs of these clients. The medium of music allows one to do this with more flexibility and adaptability than many other forms of treatment.

Since there is generally limited time for gathering of information in acute care, a conceptual model can be useful as a guideline for therapists as they engage clients in this process of assessment and treatment. Loewy (2000) presents a useful model for assessment that identifies 13 areas of inquiry that are then grouped together into 4 central areas that she considers essential to a music psychotherapy assessment. Loewy's 4 areas of observation are:

- Relationship (awareness of self, others, and of the moment; listening; collaboration; independence);
- Dynamics (thematic expression, range of affect, performance, use of structure);
- Achievement (investment/motivation, self-esteem, risk-taking); and
- Cognition (concentration, integration).

These areas of investigation might be used as a format for introductory themes that could serve as a baseline for future courses of therapy. They can also be utilized more quickly and directly in short-term treatment. Keeping these four major themes in mind while engaging with clients in a music experience, one can observe how clients respond to either structured or improvised music and develop a fuller understanding of their relationship to themselves, others, and their current situation. Each of these areas can be observed in both musical and nonmusical interactions with clients. However, it only stands to reason that in the short period of time allotted in acute care, the music experience is principally where both data are gathered and therapeutic relationships are formed with the clients.

When working in acute care, assessing the individual clients' needs is obviously important but is often an in-the-moment kind of process and may not be as thorough or formalized as in longer-term treatment. The unique ability of music to bring people together and to provide a sense of "immediacy" (Bonny, 1987) and community makes it an even more important and significant modality in settings with these types of challenges. In particular, the use of live music making and direct involvement with music can yield a forum for both staff and clients to be engaged and relational in ways that often nothing else can achieve in these kinds of settings. In these interactions provided by music, music therapists as well as other staff may glean important and unique information germane to the client's total level of functioning.

Goals for Music Therapy

Whereas the primary goals for the hospitalized patient in acute care may be to resolve a psychotic depression, slow down a manic patient, or diminish hallucinations or delusions, the music therapist may have other important goals to address. More generalized goals such as behavioral containment, emotional support, structure of experiences, involvement with others, and validation of the individual are always to be considered with all clients. Irwin Yalom (1995) suggests the following guidelines for achievable goals in acute inpatient therapy groups:

- Engage the patient in the therapeutic process.
- Demonstrate that talking [expressing] helps.
- Problem spot.
- Decrease isolation.
- Be helpful to others.
- Alleviate hospital-related anxiety.

Music therapy has the potential to directly address all of these goals, even in a single session or "one-off group" (Pavlicevic, 2003), which is most often the case in acute care treatment. Acute care inpatient groups rarely have the same membership more than one time as someone is always coming or going from the unit. It is imperative that the therapist considers the life of the group to be only a single session. But if clear about their role and the purpose of the session, therapists can successfully structure and develop the music therapy group to achieve these generalized goals each time. The use of music can bring about a sense of community as well as individualism, containment as well as freedom, listening and being heard, unity and diversity, challenge and nurturance, excitement and relaxation. These kinds of shared experiences in music clearly support the overall treatment goals of stabilization, symptom relief, and symptom management in acute care.

Clients in acute inpatient care are generally confused, distressed, and unhappy with being in the hospital. Therefore, one of the main aims of any treatment is to provide a secure base for the client where recovery, safety, and quality of life are paramount while delivering the most effective treatment options.

Yalom (1995) refers to the installation of hope and cohesion as being two significant therapeutic factors in any form of treatment. Clients provided with music therapy are often more motivated and inspired with the expectations of recovery heightened, because they are able to view their therapy in a more positive light. For many patients, having a music therapy experience that is an alternative means of self-expression and communication provides the spontaneous release of anxiety accompanied by pleasurable response. Music therapy as part of an acute care treatment program helps to provide a balance of structure and spontaneity through engaging, dynamic therapeutic approaches.

Approaches to Treatment

The importance of both structure and spontaneity when working in a concentrated and abbreviated time frame has been previously mentioned. Sometimes the more traditional methods and theories of psychiatric treatment or group psychotherapy simply cannot be applied in acute care. There is no time for working through interpersonal issues. Instead, the treatment team must help clients deal with interpersonal problems and reinforce interpersonal strengths, while encouraging them to attend aftercare therapy where they can continue to work on the issues that may have been identified in acute care. The music therapist must deal with what is presented at the time and be prepared for abrupt changes in the program environment. Clients' consistency in groups is not available for myriad reasons—admissions and discharges are a daily occurrence and consistency in group composition is nonexistent. The idea of a closed group is rare, due to both the level of acuity and the length of stay. So, in order to conduct effective treatment, the clinical conditions of acute care demand modifications in technique. For this reason, it may be useful to consider seeing clients in several different formats. As mentioned before, the majority of music therapy in acute care tends to be group work. Having an open ward group as well as smaller more focused groups can be useful.

Open groups are an excellent means to introduce clients to music therapy in a general way. Many clients feel more comfortable being able to come and go from the group, as they are able to tolerate it. For example, a client with severe paranoia might be able to observe and take part in a group structured to allow the client to maintain a safe distance and the ability to leave as needed. Such a group makes it more possible for some to attend at all. Smaller groups help the therapist to better concentrate on a constant influx of new faces and issues, but the smaller group may not fit the needs of the unit as well as a larger group might. Ideally, there should be a balance of both open and closed groups in order to provide opportunities for clients to become involved based on their needs and conditions. Whether the groups are open or closed, the format and structure of the sessions are important considerations.

A session should begin with a clear introduction or beginning by the therapist to immediately create a sense of structure and clarity of what the group is there to do. This might involve a brief discussion of the use of music as a mode of recovery or rehabilitation, or it may be an opening piece of music that welcomes and invites the clients to a musical environment. A song that creates a sense of coming together or honoring this particular group of people may be used. A more spontaneous call-and-response song set to drumming may create the scene for this gathering. This period of warm-up is vitally important, as it is when the therapist sets up the session and assesses where each member is emotionally, cognitively, and physically. This is often a significant moment where choices of direction and decisions as to what plan is utilized are made. It is especially important for music therapists in acute care to have many types of activities and interventions available, with the ability to implement them into the session quickly. Having some type of music as part of their initial experience is not only welcoming to group members but helps to inform and prepare them for what is to come. This may be followed or accompanied by introductions and a brief conversation that allows a sense of rapport to begin, as well as gives the therapist a moment to pick up on what the client may be bringing into the session.

After the group has been established, the session moves into the middle or working section, where clients are involved in musical activity. These activities may include:

- singing and/or playing instruments;
- playing both composed and improvised music;
- using lyric substitution or creating song lyrics;
- moving to music;
- using art with music;
- listening actively to music as a form of participation or to facilitate imagery and learn relaxation skills.

The session may take many directions at this point and, again, it is not only an opportunity to engage clients in the many benefits of music but also continued opportunity to ascertain how they deal with the situation at hand and the people around them. Borczon (1997) emphasizes the importance of understanding that any response a client may have in these sessions is a valid response and that it can and will vary widely.

> This response is what the client offers you as an indicator of where they are. . . . It is
> important to understand that what the group offers to you, is offered. Take what they
> give you, learn from it, and work with it. (p. 27)

This again is how the therapist gains important information about not only how the clients are interacting with the therapist and their peers, but also their responses and interactions with the music on an individual basis. The focus of the work is to address states of anxiety; to make contact with reality and organize thinking; and to improve the ability to identify and communicate needs, thoughts, and feelings in a productive manner. The blending of the assessment, evaluation, and treatment process continues.

As the session begins to move towards closure, it is important for the therapist to keep in mind that the entire experience and treatment process with some of these clients has taken place in this one meeting. For others, there may be a few more opportunities to engage in music therapy, but especially within group work, that particular group has come full circle in one hour. Borczon (1997) refers to the

> dynamic action that flows from the moment the clients enter the room until they leave.
> The action is set up by that which they bring into the session and is completed with that
> which they remember after they leave the room. (p. 24)

Giving some type of indication that it is time for the session to come to a close is important to allow clients time to prepare for its ending. Having a few moments to help them reflect on their experience as part of the closing is just as important as creating a welcoming environment, especially in these "one-off" experiences. Each person may be offered the opportunity to make a closing statement, verbally or in the context of the music. A song created specifically for ending that leaves a space for each person to give his or her own response might serve this purpose well. The intent would be for clients in some way to take their internal response and make it audible and conscious as an integrative response to the shared experience of the music therapy session. The opportunity for clients to share something meaningful about their experience provides a sense of completion for that session. For the music therapist, concluding activities provide a final glimpse of the client's level of ability to develop and manage relationships, as well as his or her dynamics, achievements, and level of cognition.

Conclusion

The practice of acute care essentially addresses crisis intervention, assessment, and stabilization. The task for the treatment team is to identify short- and long-term goals that promote wellness and optimal level of functioning for the client and to help prepare the client to work towards these goals. Even though there has been a radical shift in the way that treatment is managed in recent years, one could argue that the modality of music therapy is needed even more and is essential to the arduous task of providing adequate acute care treatment. The benefits of music can be utilized in many ways and can promote a more vibrant community of patients and staff committed to creativity and change to overcome disability, illness, and stigma. Music therapy naturally fits the needs of the acute care unit and aids in reduction of symptoms and anxiety. It can be utilized for psychoeducational purposes, to develop healthy coping skills and improve abilities, and to increase client self-efficacy through the development of self-image, increased self-esteem, self-concept, and self-awareness.

References

American Academy of Child and Adolescent Psychiatry and American Psychiatric Association. (1997). Criteria for short-term treatment of acute psychiatric illness. Washington, DC: American Psychiatric.

Bonny, H. (1987). Music: The language of immediacy. The Arts in Psychotherapy, 14, 255–261.

Borczon, R. M. (1997). Music therapy: Group vignettes. Gilsum, NH: Barcelona.

Bruscia, K. E. (1988). Standards for clinical assessment in the arts therapies (Special issue). The Arts in Psychotherapy, 15(1), 5–10.

Loewy, J. (2000). Music psychotherapy assessment. Music Therapy Perspectives, 18(1), 47–58.

Pavlicevic, M. (2003). Groups in music. London: Jessica Kingsley.

Wheeler, B. L. (1983). A psychotherapeutic classification of music therapy practices: A continuum of procedures. Music Therapy Perspectives, 1, 8–16.

Wilson, B. L. (2002). Assessment of psychiatric clients: The role of music therapy. In R. F. Unkefer & M. Thaut (Eds.), Music therapy in the treatment of adults with mental disorders (pp. 155–180). St. Louis, MO: MMB Music.

Yalom, I. D. (1995). The theory and practice of group psychotherapy (4th ed.). New York: Basic Books.

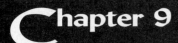

Chapter 9

Adults with Mental Disorders in Community Settings
Roberta Wigle Justice

Forms of treatment for people with a variety of mental health diagnoses have undergone, and continue to undergo, changes since the middle of the 20th century. In Western countries, including the United States, there has been a shift from long-term inpatient stays and institutionalization to shorter inpatient stays and more outpatient forms of treatment (Nieminen, Isohanni, & Winblad, 1994). State and private psychiatric hospitals continue to be closed or downsized. This is, in part, a reaction to the belief that human beings should be able to function at their highest potential in the least restrictive environment, and a reaction to financial concerns and pressures. Since managed care has become the primary mode of health care payment, the emphasis on cost effectiveness has increased and continues to do so. Inpatient stays focus on specific, immediate symptoms or life-threatening issues. Long-term (greater than 3 weeks) hospital treatments are becoming increasingly rare. As this trend continues, therapists and researchers are searching for effective and cost-efficient treatments that can be provided in outpatient or community settings.

In the search for more effective and cost-efficient treatments in mental health, a variety of different formats exists. These formats include intermittent inpatient treatment and community-based programs, such as day treatment programs, intensive outpatient programs, clubhouse models, and services taken to clients directly in their supported apartments and group homes. These programs can, but do not always, include specific treatment approaches like cognitive behavioral therapy, supported employment programs, and/or recreational/social activities.

Also in the search for effective and cost-efficient treatments, therapeutic approaches that are not limited to strictly verbal techniques are gaining more attention. These "holistic," "complementary," or "alternative" therapies include a wide range of approaches like yoga, massage, biofeedback, and creative arts therapies, including music therapy. Music therapy has been part of psychiatric inpatient programs for over 50 years and part of psychiatric day treatment programs for over 20 years in some instances (Kenny, 1982; Priestly, 1994). Most recently, music therapy is being provided within group homes and supported living environments.

Intermittent Inpatient Admissions

A recent partial solution to crisis admissions is the concept of intermittent inpatient admissions. Intermittent inpatient treatment programs admit people with chronic mental illness or emotional illness at regularly scheduled time periods for short-term inpatient stays. One of the purposes of these programs is to intervene before a client's struggle reaches a crisis stage and to maintain the person outside the hospital as much as possible. Short-term inpatient settings follow guidelines for structured treatment goals that are developed in the outpatient setting with the patient (Nehls, 1994; Silk et al., 1994). The goals are based on a variety of cognitive/behavioral and psychodynamic approaches and are individualized to the needs of the patient.

Community-Based Programs

In the community, people find themselves with a range of available support. Partial and day treatment programs provide structure and support during the day. Outpatient groups and individual therapy can provide support and continued growth and progress on therapy goals. These interventions are often provided weekly. For many people in mental health systems, a case manager is the closest thing to an individual therapist they will have available. Psychiatrists are often relegated to managing medications. Psychologists and master's-level social workers are supervisors and/or run the therapy groups. Visiting nurses provide medical support. Many people reside in supported living programs with medical support and clubhouses available, or group homes with nutritional support, medicine management, and activities available. The primary issues of people with mental illnesses are often not addressed in any form. They are basically maintained in the community.

Music Therapy With Mental Health Clients in the Community

Clients served in various community settings represent a wide spectrum of clinical diagnoses and problem areas. Clients with schizophrenia or mania have severe disabilities, often experiencing bothersome internal stimuli, problems with short attention span, delusional thoughts, social isolation, and agitation and intrusive behavior. Clients with depression and Axis II disorders (American Psychiatric Association, 1994) experience uncomfortable feelings and thoughts and generally have problems with interpersonal relationships and the ability to connect with others or express their thoughts or feelings. They often have developed coping skills for dealing with stresses in life that have become detrimental to their health, such as the use of chemicals, drugs, or food; dissociation; or self-destructive behaviors, such as cutting or burning themselves.

Choosing interventions and approaches for the diverse clients served in these settings can be challenging. Wheeler's (1983) continuum of music therapy interventions with its three levels of music therapy experiences enable the music therapist to adjust the amount of activity structure in any given situation to meet the needs of the patients at the moment. (See section on levels of structure in Chapter 3.) Then, the therapy experience of "best fit" can be provided to promote the maximum amount of client growth and change in a safe environment. Interventions from the levels of supportive, activity-oriented and insight music therapy with re-educative goals are most useful in these settings. For example, a basic receptive experience in music therapy is listening. These music therapy interventions include relaxation, writing, drawing, or moving to music. Basic expressive interventions include singing, playing instruments, and composing.

Community Settings for Music Therapy With Clients With Mental Disorders

Music therapy services can be provided in a variety of community-based clinical settings, including group homes, community mental health centers, day treatment programs, clubhouses, or supported living programs.

Group Homes

Group homes are houses and apartments in the community where from four to eight individuals live with 24-hour staff support. Generally, those individuals are not able to care for themselves in an independent living situation due to problems of money management, poor judgment related to personal safety and/or health, and the potential to become homeless. In mental health clients, these problems are generally related to psychotic disorders or forms of dementia. However, individuals with developmental disabilities may be housed together with psychiatric clients. People with dual diagnoses of chronic mental illness and substance abuse may also be housed in group homes, either as a separate program or with people of other diagnoses.

Music therapy in the group home. Such practice usually occurs in the general living area with either all house members invited to attend or a subset of the house members being the focal point for services. Problems faced by the music therapist in group homes include the inconsistency of attention and interest demonstrated by clients with chronic mental illnesses (most observable by their wandering in and out of sessions), lack of understanding of the staff about music therapy and its goals, and addressing a potentially wide range in age and musical interests of house residents in a 1-hour session. A broad musical repertoire, interesting and adult-appropriate instruments, and the ability to involve individuals at their own level of function and interest serve the music therapist well. The music therapy approach in this setting generally falls within Wheeler's first level of experience. Additionally, music therapy can help facilitate positive and more appropriate relationships among house members.

The music therapy sessions typically have high levels of external structure and are multidimensional. A consistent sequence of experiences and types of activity interventions helps the clients with self-organization and time management. A variety in pieces of music or themes for sessions helps with cognitive stimulation and emotional expression. A typical session might have the following structure:

1. Consistent opening of a verbal greeting, an opening theme song when verbalizations are too difficult for the clients, or an opening greeting song using names for seniors or others with severe memory problems

2. Music and movement experience that includes gentle stretching and breathing exercises to warm up the body and voice, followed by a more vigorous music and movement exercise, vocal warm-ups, or a nontuned percussion playing experience

3. Instrumental part playing, possibly including choir chimes, instruments such as guitar, keyboard, drums, autoharp, etc., for ensemble playing of one or two songs, or ethnic instruments for holidays or cultural observances used to accompany related songs

4. Song listening or singing of songs chosen by clients for the group to sing from a songbook (compiled by the music therapist) or from CDs. (Cautionary note: When working with people who have internal processes such as delusional thoughts or hallucinations, it is wise to remain as highly structured as possible. Song listening does not demand the external attention that singing does, unless the therapist focuses the listening experience on the words or specific musical components of the song.)

5. Brief verbal recognition by the therapist or the group of the contributions that clients have made to the session.

6. Consistent closing song chosen by the group. This does not have to be a "good-bye" song but should reflect group members' input. Later the song selection may change or become the group's choice of several songs identified as good for closing.

Music therapy equipment for use in group homes. Equipment useful in this setting includes:

- personal accompaniment instrument;
- small portable CD player (unless one is available in the home) and CDs;
- hand percussion instruments, such as maracas, tambourine, claves, afuche, castanets;
- songbooks;
- music stands for books (to free hands for playing);
- snare drum, high-hat cymbals, other drums;
- choir chimes for any choir chime experiences.

Additional instruments may come from the clients themselves or be based on their interests (autoharp, banjo, etc.). A large rolling suitcase or duffel bag is essential for this type of work. When negotiating fees, make sure the prospective organization understands that the fee includes all equipment and subsequent repair.

On the following page are two examples of documentation forms suitable for use with adults with mental disorders in community settings, created by Roberta Justice and used by permission in this monograph. The intent of these two forms is to take data on behaviors that are occurring during sessions and for subsequent treatment planning for clients.

Form 1								
Key: 1: Not seen 2: Did sometimes 3: Did 50% 4: Did most of the time 5: Did consistently								
Name ↕ Date ↪								
Observed ability for client to do the following:								
Participate in singing								
Playing								
Make choices of songs								
Find songs in books/booklets								
Follow structured music sheets								
Be aware of self/own behavior								
Listen to others								
Interact socially								
Accept choices of others								
Concentrate for duration of songs								
Affect								
Comments								

Plan: Client will be scheduled for structured music therapy x 1 q wk.
Objective:
   1. Patient will demonstrate externally focused behaviors, indicating an interruption of internal processes.
   2. Patient will demonstrate behaviors consistent with increased self-organization (as measured by the behaviors listed in Form 1).

Form 2

Structured Music Therapy Time within group _____

Observed ability for patient to do the following:

Participate in music experience of _____   0%   25%   50%   75%   100%

Make choices of songs _____   Accept choices of others _____

Follow structured music sheets _____   Find songs in books/booklets _____

Be aware of self/own behavior _____   Listen to others _____

Interact socially _____

Concentrate for duration of songs _____   Affect _____

Comments _____

_____

_____

Figure 9.1 Examples of Documentation Forms (Justice, 2005)

Community Mental Health Centers and Day Treatment Programs— Clubhouses or Supported Living Programs

The function of community mental health centers varies from state to state. In some areas, these centers provide case management only. In other areas, therapy and support groups may be available (or required) for the clients based on their need. These are usually not full day programs. Partial Hospital Programs (PHP) provide daytime treatment programs often from 9:00 a.m. to 3:00 p.m., which clients are required to attend for a prescribed number of days per week and length of time. Decisions for partial hospitalization lengths and intensity are often made in conjunction with the client. Day Treatment Programs can be similar to Partial Hospital Programs, but Day Treatment Programs can also be specifically for geriatric or developmentally disabled clients, in which cases they are not time-limited. Partial Hospital Programs most closely approximate the support and treatment of an inpatient program, without the 24-hour care, although some Partial Hospital Programs also have beds available for those in transition from inpatient to home care. Clients do not usually need as much close supervision as on an inpatient unit. For example, they may be recovering from a depressive episode and beginning to respond to medications and are not suicidal, but they may not be ready to handle the stresses of being in the community.

Clubhouses are voluntary or drop-in programs where informal socialization and support can occur as well as organized activities. In many clubhouses, the consumers (clients) are responsible for certain aspects of the house management, such as cooking lunch, selling meal tickets, cleaning, or organizing activities. In some clubhouse models, consumers are required to be a member and be involved in these responsibilities. In others, requirements are more flexible and more drop-in oriented, with some consumers having responsibilities and others participating based on ability. Educational classes and social activities are available for those who are interested. Clients from independent living, supported living, and group homes all have access to the clubhouse programs.

Supported living programs provide minimal staff support for clients living in the community in independent apartments or nonstaffed group homes. The staff support is often limited to passing medications for those who need monitoring; transportation and assistance with shopping and laundry for those with problems in these areas; assistance with problems of daily living, like dealing with utility companies or neighbors; and social events, such as picnics and holiday parties. Even though the majority of clients live independently with minimal or no assistance, each program is often a small subcommunity of people who know each other.

Music Therapy in Community Mental Health Centers and Day Programs

Music therapy groups for these settings range from informal social music groups to more organized and specific music therapy groups (even though many of these clients balk at the word "therapy"). Assessment for appropriateness of client placement in a particular group is based mostly on self-organization skills and cognitive functioning as described by Wheeler (1983).

Social Music Group

Social music groups can be part of any voluntary or drop-in setting. This group is the least demanding cognitively, socially, and emotionally. It meets the needs of those who fit in Wheeler's first level of music therapy experiences. It also matches Sears' (1968) basic level of music therapy experiences, where any person can be part of the group simply by being present. Participation in this group is based on the interest of the clients. A typical session could have the following structure:

1. Consistent verbal or musical opening as determined by the needs of the group, which could include the following:
   - Welcome to new people, hello and what's been happening to people who have not attended in a while
   - Hello to everyone
   - Announcement of birthdays, etc.
   - Improvisatory warm-up with instruments, or a consistent song chosen by the group members as a good opener. The membership of the group will determine the best "ritual" for themselves over a few sessions (if you listen to them and let it happen)
2. Singing/playing of instruments:

- Songbooks should be developed by the therapist in conjunction with the members (over time) of favorite styles of music. There should be enough books for every person with only occasional sharing. Instruments, as determined by the interests and abilities of the group, are available with occasional suggestions from the therapist about the suitability of certain sounds for certain songs.

- The types of instruments and songs are determined by the members of the group and will probably change over time. A mini-drum set or tubanos can be a great addition. Clients with specific musical skills, including singing and playing saxophone, keyboard, drums, xylophone, guitar, bass, flute, and fiddle, can be in the group from time to time. Other clients may thrive on the hand drums, congas, tubanos, and djembes.

- At this point, the group members take turns choosing songs from the songbook for the group to sing or play. Sometimes a trend develops, such as seasonal songs, Beatles' songs, songs from the '50s, etc. This can become an informal theme; whether to stay with the theme can be a "game" allowing for all people's choices and abilities. People develop favorites, which can be recognized verbally. Instrumentalists may choose songs in which there is a solo for them. This needs to be supported musically. Solos performed by individuals on whole songs may be requested by the soloist or by the group membership. The therapist needs to keep the needs of all clients in mind, supporting these at times, but also supporting the opportunity for everyone to be part of the song on occasion.

3. Consistent closing

- Closing musically makes sense after participating in music for 1 to 1½ hours. Just prior to the final song, the therapist or a group member (a) states that time is running out, (b) thanks everyone for coming or comments on how good it was to see everyone, (c) reminds them of the next time and place for the group, and (d) leads them in the final song. This can be a consistent song, a choice of several that the group likes to use for closing, or one that the group determines to be the closing song that day. This should be a consistent procedure, like a ceremony, again providing for structure and self-organization.

A protocol for a sample session with a social music group is presented in Figure 9.2.

Title:	*Social Music Group*
Definition:	*Social music is a medium that elicits attention, gives immediate auditory feedback, and promotes active listening. The intervention is designed to interrupt the processes of disturbing thoughts and auditory hallucinations and promote cooperative participation.*
Purpose:	*Increase attention span, improve reality orientation, improve awareness and interaction with others on a basic functional level.*
Description:	*Intervention occurs 1 day per week for 90-minute sessions. Group size: 2–15 clients. The structured music group focuses on nonverbal skills necessary for communication, i.e., awareness of others, active listening and cooperative participation with group members utilizing handbells, singing, and musical instruments.*
Target Population:	*Adult patients with identified problems in verbal communication, thought disorder, poverty in content of speech, impaired social functioning, and/or disturbances in psychomotor behaviors.*
Mode of Delivery:	*Within a group environment.*
Outcomes Information:	*Assessment of reality orientation, concentration, responsiveness, and social interactions.*
Clinical:	*1.* *Increase ability to connect with and remain in reality.* *2.* *Increase ability to listen and interact appropriately with others.* *3.* *Increase range of affect and awareness of self.* *4.* *Improve cognitive functioning.*

Figure 9.2. Sample Session Protocol for a Social Music Group

Music Improvisation Group

Music improvisation groups can be varied to fit all of Wheeler's levels of experiences, depending on the needs of the clients and the training of the therapist. First-level groups should have a high level of external structure, focusing on developing a sense of beat and rhythm, learning to listen to each other and play together, and developing harmonic structures and melodic lines and layering these. (See the section on improvisation in Chapter 5.) Discussion of the improvisations is limited and focused on the musical components. Examples of activities used with this type of group include the following:

- *Basic beat.* The therapist sets a simple steady beat (the "heartbeat"), and others join the beat. In this technique, each person takes a turn playing his or her own style of heartbeat, with the group joining.
- *Playing in the spaces.* The therapist sets a heartbeat, and each individual takes a turn playing in between the beats (soloing around the group). In this technique, the therapist sets a heartbeat, and each individual plays a rhythm accompanying the beat (on the beat and in between the beat), adding rhythms one at a time, either around the group consecutively or by name when called on by the leader. A focused discussion about simple rhythms and everyone having a space may be needed.
- A variation of the above techniques uses a harmonic instrument playing open fifths, an ostinato, or simple chord progressions to replace the heartbeat on drum. Rhythms or melodies may be added, depending on the instrumentation available.

Second level groups can add representational foci: emotions, situations, colors, or words. Improvisation is focused by drawing word cards (angel cards, universal cards, or 3 ×5 cards), with each individual then leading the group in an improvisation on the word drawn. The improvisation can also be based on the personal feelings of the group members, in the moment or related to a situation. Verbal processing of these takes place in a cognitive-behavioral format, in the here-and-now, asking the question, "What can you learn from this?"

Music Reinforced Relaxation Group

The focus of a music reinforced relaxation group is generally to teach people stress management techniques for coping with anxiety, anger, and other difficult emotions. Awareness of oneself and one's bodily reactions to stress are part of the educational component, as well as techniques for relaxing the body and mind. (See Chapter 4 for specifics of relaxation techniques to music.)

Expressive Music and Creative Arts Therapy Group

Expressive music and creative arts therapy groups best meet the needs of those who fit in Wheeler's second and third categories. These are usually people who are not actively psychotic and who can cognitively understand and process feelings and thoughts. Often people with mental health issues have difficulty developing and maintaining interpersonal relationships and are socially isolated. This type of group can help develop interpersonal skills and decrease the isolation. Because following through with commitments can be difficult for people with emotional and mental illnesses, this group functions best when meeting in modules of 6–8 weeks. The group meets at a neutral place, such as the therapist's studio or a community space, and is limited to no more than eight members. Each person must agree to attend the full number of scheduled sessions, and each person must be at the first session of each module to be included in the group. Absences due to illness or other appointments must be reported to the therapist and other group members. Each module focuses on a theme or topic determined by the group members and uses music and other creative arts media in the sessions to explore the theme or topic. Initially, all members must agree to maintain confidentiality of each other's material, although they are free to discuss their own material with others. Issues about the group or between group members are to be dealt with only in the group. A sample group protocol is presented in Figure 9.3.

Title:	Expressive music and creative arts therapy group
Definition:	People living with mental disorders often experience mood swings, difficulty establishing and maintaining relationships, and problems understanding themselves.
Purpose:	Use of music and other expressive arts to develop the ability to use healthy coping mechanisms for dealing with uncomfortable emotions, self-awareness, problem-solving skills, the ability to work in group therapy settings, and the use of social support networks.
Description:	Intervention occurs 1 time per week for 90–120 minute sessions. Experiences include music making and listening, movement, drawing, painting, and clay work.
Target Population:	Adults who have difficulty maintaining stable relationships or expressing their thoughts, ideas, or feelings; have low self-confidence, poor self- or body image, or high narcissistic needs; and experience social withdrawal or fears.
Approach:	Instructions are given verbally, explaining the purpose and focus of each group. A focus will be selected by the therapist with direct consideration of the treatment needs of the group members, or may be chosen by the group itself. Each session revolves around the use of music, either playing, singing, or writing music; or listening to music in conjunction with creative writing, drawing, painting, sculpture, or movement. The experience is worked within the group through group therapy processes, developing insights into one's issues and life.
Objectives:	A. Ability to follow relaxing and centering directions B. Ability to use music-stimulated imagination as a medium for symbolic imagery C. Ability to work in a group therapy setting D. Ability to connect one's symbols with one's own issues (develop insight) E. Develop improved self-esteem and belief in skills F. Develop awareness of individual uniqueness as positive G. Develop awareness of self and others as separate
Expected Outcomes:	Increased belief in self and skills (self-esteem) Increased ability to see self as differentiated from others Decreased fear of others Increased relatedness to others Increased ability to use group process

Figure 9.3. Sample Session Protocol for an Expressive Music and Creative Arts Therapy Group.

Figure 9.4 provides an example of a pregroup flyer circulated among people in a supported living program for an expressive music and creative arts therapy group.

New Series
Music and Creative Arts
Personal Growth Group
Meeting Place:
Tuesdays 2:00-3:30 p.m.
May 13–June 24, 2003

This group is for any member of _____ who is interested in using music and other creative arts for personal growth. Anyone may attend the first meeting, and you <u>must</u> attend the first meeting on May 13 to attend the rest of the sessions in the series. After the first meeting, the group will be closed to new members until the next series begins. You do not need to have any background or specific talent in either music or art to participate in these sessions.

The focus of this series will depend on the interests of the people who are at the first meeting. Suggestions so far have been: developing a positive sense of self, continued work in personal relationships, or developing personal creativity and problem solving.

Music and Creative Arts therapy serves all that have an interest and willingness to engage in the experiences.

Presented by: _____ *MM, MT-BC*
in conjunction with _____
For more information please call _____ *and leave a number*

Figure 9.4. Sample Pregroup Flyer for an Expressive Music and Creative Arts Therapy Group.

Music Combined With Other Creative Arts in Therapy

When choosing music to use with other creative arts, the following musical elements should be considered:

1. *Rhythm.* Inherent in the concept of rhythm in music is tempo and beat. People respond to beat with movement and respond to tempo with the speed of those movements. Strongly structured, repetitive beats stimulate people to exercise-like movements, and they work to match themselves to that tempo. This is true in movement artwork, in instrumental playing, in singing, and in imagery. Less strongly beated music can still stimulate movement but allows for more awareness of and response to the other aspects of music.

2. *Melody.* Melody is the carrier of the song. Melody tells the story and moves the listener through time on a journey of up and down and of leaping and stepping. The twists and turns of melody act on the listener through expectation. If the melody is predictable, it can carry a sense of surety and comfort or one of boredom. If the melody is unknown, the response of the listener is either a stimulated imagination or a sense of fear and insecurity, depending on the psychological state of the listener. Complex melodies, such as counterpoint or fugue, offer a wide choice of responses to the listener, stimulate imagination, and overstimulate a person who needs more predictable structure.

3. *Harmony.* Harmony supports the melody and sets the emotional tone of the music. Simple, repetitive harmonies act like known melodies, providing support and structure. Complex, changing harmonies act like complex melodies and provide greater levels of ambiguity in the music. This allows the listener to respond to any number of combinations of sounds and aspects of the music.

4. *Timbre.* The sounds of different instruments have different effects on people. The greater the number of timbres interplaying, the higher the level of ambiguity in the music. The same piece of music played on piano, by string quartet, or by an orchestra has different effects.

Generally speaking, the greater the complexity of the music, the greater the ambiguity and the greater the range of responses elicited from the clients in a group or from an individual at different times. It is important to consider all the qualities of the music chosen for the experience being provided for the clients.

For music and creative arts experiences like drawing, writing, or sculpting, the music can be considered a holding device. Therefore, this music is not extremely complex and not as repetitive as music for relaxation. Examples include *Cristofore's Dream* by David Lanz, *Magical Child* by Michael Jones, and *Piano Reflections* by Kelly Yost. In some instances (like for the emotion series), the art work is completed in silence and music is improvised by the group to reflect the emotional content of the drawings.

Figure 9.5 presents examples of various series of groups using music and creative arts experiences.

Initial Series: Beginning Self-Exploration
　　1. Introductions: Picking songs to listen to, choosing areas of interest and goals for self
　　2. Personal mandala
　　3. Mandala and improvisation on "Power"
　　4. Mandala and improvisation on "Peace"
　　5. Mandala and improvisation on difficult emotion
　　6. Review and celebration
Series: Identifying Personal Strengths
　　1. Introductions: Picking songs to listen to, choosing areas of interest and goals for self
　　2. Bag collage
　　3. Percussion improvisation, identifying personal strength songs
　　4. Personal strength mandala
　　5. Improvisations on mandalas
　　6. Clay symbol of personal strength
　　7. Song writing (cloze)
　　8. Review and celebration
Series: Exploring Emotions
　　1. Drawing on Love
　　2. Drawing on Peace
　　3. Drawing on Joy
　　4. Drawing on Guilt
　　5. Drawing on Anger
　　6. Drawing on Sadness
　　7. Drawing on Fear
　　8. Pie drawing and celebration
Series: Self-Affirmations
　　1. Overview or affirmations
　　2. Focusing on parts of life/behaviors you'd like to change
　　3. Developing self affirming mantra, with chant/drums reinforcement
　　4. Developing personal symbol for mantra
　　5. Creating solid (Sculpey) representation of symbol
　　6. Continued
　　7. Using symbol, mantra, and chant to reinforce affirmation
　　8. Celebration
Series: Self-Esteem/Value/Worth CD (two consecutive series)
　　1. Deciding on focus
　　2. Discussion about what is self-esteem/value/worth
　　3. Beginning to explore songs and related topics
　　4. Beginning to bring in personal songs
　　5. Sharing thoughts about songs, singing them
　　6. Sharing thoughts about songs, singing them
　　7. Sharing thoughts about songs, singing them
　　8. Celebration

　　NEW SERIES
　　9. Continuation of singing songs
　　10. Choosing songs for the CD that reflect all group members
　　11. Making decisions about recording arrangements/parts
　　12. Continued
　　13. Recording
　　14. Continued
　　15. Continued
　　16. Hearing completed CD and celebration
Foci of other Series:
　　Self-expression song writing
　　Self-expression of emotions in a variety of media
　　Past/present/future
　　Things about self you'd like to change
　　Dreams for self
　　Self-control techniques (mantra/chant/clay symbol/situations and how to use)
　　Relationships (marriage/family)
　　Songs for inspiration

Figure 9.5. Various Series of Groups Using Music and Creative Arts Experiences.

Figure 9.6 provides examples of two documentation forms that can be used with expressive music/ creative arts groups.

Form 1						
Key: *1: Not seen 2: Did sometimes 3: Did 50% 4: Did most of the time 5: Did consistently*						
Name:	intro	first mandala	"power"	"peace"	diff. emotion	review
Observed ability for client to do the following:						
Participate in group discussions						
Express self clearly						
Identify and express feelings						
Reflect on self/own behavior						
Listen to others						
Give suggestions to others						
Take suggestion from others						
Willingness to try nonverbal approach of session						
Able to produce personal symbol(s)						
Able to explain personal symbol to group						
Able to reflect on connection of symbol and therapeutic issues (gain weight)						
Affect						
Comments						

Form 2

Date _____   CAT group   Time in group _____

Observed ability for patient to do the following:

Participate in experiences of centering   0%   25%   50%   75%   100%   NA

Participate in experiences of creating symbols 0%   25%   50%   75%   100%   NA

Symbol created _____

Connect symbol to personal issues _____

Participate in group discussions: 0%   25%   50%   75%   100%   NA

Expressive self clearly _____   *Identify and express feelings* _____

Reflect on self/own behavior _____   *Listen to others* _____

Give suggestions to others _____   *Take suggestion from others* _____

Affect _____

Figure 9.6 Examples of Documentation Forms for Expressive Music/Creative Arts Groups

Community Music Therapy Model

Barbara J. Crowe

A new model of music therapy, community music therapy, has emerged in recent years (Pavlicevic & Ansdell, 2004). According to Ansdell (2002), community music therapy reflects the communal reality of music making and is a response to both individualized treatment models and to the isolation experienced within society leading to issues of mental health. "It involves extending the role, aims, and possible sites of work for music therapists" (Ansdell, 2002, p. 121). Community music therapy constitutes an approach to working musically with people in a cultural and social context. It involves shifting the emphasis and approaches utilized in music therapy and the venues where it is practiced.

Ruud (1998) summarizes this approach as involving not only the direct therapeutic effort for the individual needs of clients but also the larger structural barriers in society that impede the client's sense of personal agency. In community music therapy, the broader sociological and cultural needs of the clients are also addressed. Group music making, including improvisation, performance groups, and group drumming experiences, is used in social and cultural settings embedded in a given community. These venues could include community centers, parks and recreation programs, neighborhood groups, and storefront centers. The community music therapist is both a musician and music-making facilitator and therapist. It is profoundly a music-centered approach used in a broader social and cultural context (Aigen, 1999).

Specific examples of community music therapy include Boxill's (n.d.) Music Therapists for Peace and Students Against Violence Everywhere (SAVE), Aasgaard's (1999) work in palliative care in community settings, Crowe's (2004) work in gang prevention in an inner-city school setting, and Turrey's (2005) work in moving music therapy psychotherapy practice into the community through performance.

References

Aasgaard, T. (1999). Music therapy as milieu in the hospice and paediatric oncology ward. In D. Aldridge (Ed.), Music therapy in palliative care. London: Jessica Kingsley.

Aigen, K. (1999). The true nature of music-centered therapy theory. British Journal of Music Therapy, 13(2), 77-82.

American Psychiatric Association. (1994). Diagnostic and statistical manual of mental disorders (4th ed.). Washington DC: Author.

Ansdell, G. (2002). Community music therapy and the winds of change. Voices: A World Forum for Music Therapy. Retrieved October 21, 2005, from http://www.voices.no/mainissues/Voices2(2)ansdell.html

Boxill, E. (n.d.). Students against violence experiences through music therapy. New York: Music Therapists for Peace.

Crowe, B. J. (2004). Music and soulmaking: Toward a new theory of music therapy. Lanham, MD: Scarecrow Press.

Kenny, C. (1982). The mythic artery. Atascadero, CA: Ridgeview.

Nehls, N. (1994). Brief hospital treatment plans for persons with borderline personality disorder: Perspectives of inpatient psychiatric nurses and community mental health center clinicians. Archives of Psychiatric Nursing, 8(5), 303–311.

Nieminen, P., Isohanni, M., & Winblad, I. (1994). Length of hospitalization in an acute patients' therapeutic community ward. Acta Psychiatrica Scandinavia, 90, 466–472.

Pavlicevic, M., & Ansdell, G. (Eds.). (2004). Community music therapy. London: Jessica Kingsley.

Priestley, M. (1994). Essays on analytical music therapy. Phoenixville, PA: Barcelona.

Ruud, E. (1998). Music therapy: Improvisation, communication, and culture. Gilsum, NH: Barcelona.

Sears, W. W. (1968). Processes in music therapy. In E. T. Gaston (Ed.), Music in therapy (pp. 30–44). New York: Macmillan.

Silk, K. R., Eisner, W., Allport, C., DeMars, C., Miller, C., Justice, R. W., & Lewis, M. (1994). Focused time limited treatment of borderline personality disorder. Journal of Personality Disorders, 8(4), 268–278.

Turry, A. (2005). Music psychotherapy and community music therapy: Questions and considerations. Voices: A World Forum for Music Therapy. Retrieved October 21, 2005, from http://www.voices.no/mainissues/mie0005000171.html

Wheeler, B. (1983). A psychotherapeutic classification of music therapy practices: A continuum of procedures. Music Therapy Perspectives, 1(2), 8–16.

Additional Resources

Aigen, K. (2005). Music-centered music therapy. Gilsum, NH: Barcelona.

Allen, M .G. (1990). Using extended sessions in ongoing group therapy. Psychiatric Annals, 20(7), 368–371.

Ansdell, G. (1997). Musical elaborations: What has the new musicology to say to music therapy? British Journal of Music Therapy, 11(2), 36-44.

Bunt, L. (1997). Clinical and therapeutic uses of music. In D. Hargreaves & A. North (Eds.), The social psychology of music. London: Oxford University Press.

Gfeller, K., & Thaut, M. (1999). Music therapy in the treatment of mental disorders. In W. Davis, K. Gfeller, & M. Thaut (Eds.), An introduction to music therapy, theory and practice *(2nd ed) (pp. 89–117).* Dubuque, IA Wm. C. Brown.

Gouk, P. (2000). Musical healing in cultural contexts. *Aldershot, England: Ashgate.*

Hodges, D. A. (Ed.). (1996). Handbook of music psychology *(2nd ed.). San Antonio, TX: IMR Press: The University of Texas at San Antonio.*

Horden, P. (2000). Music as medicine: The history of music therapy since antiquity. *Aldershot, England: Ashgate.*

Priestley, M. (1975). Music therapy in action. *St. Louis, MO: MMB Music.*

Procter, S. (2001). Empowering and enabling: Improvisational music therapy in non-medical mental health provision. Voices: A World Forum for Music Therapy, 2(2). Retrieved October 21, 2005, from http://www.voices.no/mainissues/Procter.html

Smith, G. B. (1995). Case management for psychiatric nursing: Strategies for success. *Paper presented at a psychiatric nursing conference, Orlando, FL.*

Solomon, D. A., Keitner, I .G., Miller, I .W., Shea, M. T., & Keller, M. B. (1995). Course of illness and maintenance treatments for patients with bipolar disorder. Journal of Clinical Psychiatry, 56(1), 5–13.

Stige, B. (2002). Culture-centered music therapy. *Gilsum, NH: Barcelona.*

Streeter, E. (1999). Finding a balance between psychological thinking and musical awareness in music therapy theory: A psychoanalytic perspective. British Journal of Music Therapy, 13(1), 5–10.

Scovel, M., & Gardstrom, S. (2002). Music therapy within the context of psychotherapeutic models. In R. F. Unkefer & M. H. Thaut (Eds.), Music therapy in the treatment of adults with mental disorders: Theoretical bases and clinical interventions *(2nd ed.) (pp. 117–132).* St. Louis, MO: MMB Music.

Yalom, I. D. (1975). The theory and practice of group psychotherapy *(2nd ed.). New York: Basic Books.*

Section 4:

Music Therapy Practice for Specific Disabilities

Chapter 10

Music Therapy for Clients with Substance Abuse Disorders
Rick Soshensky

Addiction is a complex and progressive disorder, which, unless arrested, eventually disrupts virtually every aspect of one's life—family, work, social, physical, and mental health. The *DSM-IV* (American Psychiatric Association, 1994) has divided the substance use disorders into two general diagnoses. *Substance Dependence* primarily identifies features related to compulsiveness such as withdrawal symptoms, the need for increasingly greater amounts of the substance, and frequent, unsuccessful efforts to control or cut down use. *Substance Abuse* refers to the pattern of persistent use despite severe adverse consequences. The main text of Alcoholics Anonymous (1976) sums up addiction's engulfing effects as "the utter inability to leave it alone, no matter how great the necessity or wish" (p. 34).

Because of the complexity of the problem, a broad variation of treatment programs exists within the field. No single model has been widely accepted as the most effective intervention or proven to be appropriate for all individuals. Currently, the two most prevalent orientations are based on the *12-step model* and the *biopsychosocial model*. The 12-step model, originating with Alcoholics Anonymous and its offshoots (Narcotics Anonymous, Gamblers Anonymous, etc.), holds that addiction is a disease for which one is not responsible and recovery is based on admitting powerlessness over one's compulsion. Since the addict's personal decision-making ability, particularly as it relates to substance use, has become so unreliable, this approach advocates adopting group norms and suggestions for recovery. The heart of the 12-step value system traditionally entails a *spiritual element* involving the choice to turn one's will over to the God of one's understanding. For individuals seeking a more conventional therapeutic approach, the biopsychosocial model views addiction primarily as a *medical condition*. As with the 12-step model, the biopsychosocial model stresses that those suffering from addiction need treatment, not judgment or condemnation. But, in contrast to the 12-step model, this perspective encourages the client to accept full responsibility for his or her addiction and is likely to integrate medication, psychotherapy, and behavioral approaches into a recovery process.

Although some fundamental differences exist between the two approaches, they are not mutually exclusive and many programs combine both, to various degrees. A person in search of recovery, according to his or her financial resources and inclinations, must sort through a multitude of treatment models, as well as deciding between outpatient programs, long-term residential (therapeutic communities), short-term residential programs, private therapy, or 12-step meetings. A detoxification program to reduce the medical complications of withdrawal may be a precursor to any of these options. Statistics regarding the viability of various approaches are conflicting and further obscured by inconsistencies in the way outcomes and follow-ups are reported by the diverse programs. According to the National Institute on Drug Abuse (1999), engaging in some form of treatment reduces drug use by 40 to 60% and is about as successful as treatment of other chronic diseases such as asthma, diabetes, and hypertension.

As with those medical conditions, the patient's willingness to take an active role in treatment plays a major part in achieving remission. It must also be noted that a sizable group of active substance users who are not ready to stop may be clients in treatment settings such as homeless shelters, HIV/AIDS programs, and inpatient and outpatient psychiatric programs. In these cases, a clinician may need to consider a "harm reduction" orientation. In addition to offering information and options in an effort to reduce the most injurious behaviors, a harm reduction approach "recognizes that there are active substance users who want help and are able to actively and effectively involve themselves in helping relationships despite the fact that they intend to continue using" (Tatarsky, 1998, p. 33).

Even for motivated clients, long-term recovery from substance abuse can be a difficult process encompassing multiple relapses. According to Alan Leshner, director of the National Institute on Drug Abuse (National Institute on Drug Addiction, 1999):

> Many people equate addiction with simply using drugs and therefore expect that addiction should be cured quickly, and if not, treatment is a failure. In reality, because addiction is a chronic disorder, the ultimate goal of long-term abstinence often requires sustained and repeated treatment episodes. (p. 9)

Jacobs (1997) noted that clinical studies suggest that once the course of an addiction has reached an advanced stage, the likelihood of effective reversal diminishes until such time that an individual reaches a stage of exhaustion, also expressed in 12-step terminology as "bottoming out." This insight, when and if it arrives, marks the end of ambivalence and denial regarding the devastating effects an addiction has had on one's life. The circumstances of this turning point are different for each person and, unfortunately, as Jacobs reported, are typically preceded by years of personal and interpersonal hardship, illness, and devastating economic and social ramifications.

Assessment of Substance Use Clients

The American Music Therapy Association (2003) *Standards of Clinical Practice* defines music therapy with clientele who have addictive disorders as "the specialized use of music to restore, maintain, and improve mental, physical, and social-emotional functioning" (p. 21).

The National Institute on Drug Abuse (1999) has also advised that treatment attend to the diverse issues of the addict beyond the drug use. In order to be effective, treatment must target medical, psychological, social, vocational, and legal problems. Most programs include comprehensive evaluation/ screening in these areas, as well as areas related to treatment history, including relationship, sexual and social history, leisure interests, and spirituality profile. Music therapy literature reflects several assessments for adults, notably as delineated by Bruscia (1987). However, no standardized assessment form is universally employed. (See Assessment section in Chapter 2.)

The Prochaska/DiClemente "Stages of Change" Model

One of the more widely utilized models to assess a client's level of readiness to respond to treatment is the Prochaska and DiClemente (1986) model, which identifies six stages in the process of change.

Stage 1: Precontemplation—there is no conscious awareness of a problem.

Stage 2: Contemplation—a problem is admitted and consideration is being given to the matter, but there is still ambivalence regarding change.

Stage 3: Preparation—there is a readiness to change and preliminary steps are being taken, such as reading a book or inquiring about a program.

Stage 4: Action—concrete steps are taken to correct the problem, although this is a volatile period and relapses often occur.

Stage 5: Maintenance—change has begun and new coping strategies are being established.

Stage 6: Termination—change has become well integrated into self-image and behavior.

The model assists the therapist in identifying clients' current perception regarding their substance use and in determining realistic goals to help clients in gradually shifting their experience so they can move to the next stage. Resistance to treatment and the therapeutic relationship is reduced if client and therapist are working together on the same stage of change. Even if a client has voluntarily entered a treatment program, there may still be great psychological ambivalence and vulnerability toward regression to an earlier stage. Persons with addictions often attend numerous treatment facilities before achieving long-term remission. Therefore, a client may be in a stage 4 "action" stage while still maintaining numerous attitudes related to earlier stages. If a therapist is too adamant in furthering stage 4 or 5 work and discounting client tendencies related to earlier stages, it will be difficult to form an authentic therapeutic alliance.

As with any developmental model, the stages need to be negotiated in successive order. The therapist must support the client's natural rate of change even if the client does not seem to be progressing or, in many cases, may seem to regress. Relapse can be a normal part of healing as the client attempts new ways of being and then retreats to the familiar. This understanding will alleviate discouragement and judgment as the therapist accepts both the client's movement forward to a new stage as well as movement back to an earlier stage as a predictable pattern in a therapeutic process.

Issues in Treatment

A number of issues should be considered when working with clients dealing with substance abuse.

Countertransference

Due to the seemingly willful self-destruction involved in addiction, clinicians who work with individuals with substance abuse problems must remain aware of their *countertransference* issues. It is normal for a therapist to have personal feelings and reactions during the course of therapy. However, Imhof (1995) found widespread negative attitudes toward substance users in those who treat them. Rothschild (1995) reported that many therapists in private practice decline to work with active addicts entirely, viewing their inability to achieve abstinence as indicative of a lack of readiness to engage in meaningful treatment. Rothschild pointed out that this paradoxical refusal to treat a patient seeking help until there is an amelioration of symptoms is seen only in the treatment of addiction. For example, it would be inconceivable (and unethical) for a therapist to deny treatment to a patient with depression until suicidal ideation ceased.

A therapeutic environment that fosters subliminal disapproval may lead to a dogmatic course of treatment, within which every intervention or interaction deals with relapse prevention, the negative consequences of addiction, or the "joy of recovery." In coming to understand the effects of such countertransference, music therapist Paul Nolan (1998) described a possibility that

> *the therapist may become aware that he responded to the group as if he had become a domineering authority in order to help the clients meet their treatment objective, designated by the treatment team . . . and that his structuring and preaching behaviors served to defend him from intense feelings and associations. (p. 394)*

A therapist who is uncomfortable with a client's expression of ambivalence, defensiveness, hopelessness, or rage is denying the fundamental nature of addiction.

Individual Versus Group Therapy

Individual and group therapy approaches offer differing assets and liabilities. Individual sessions are important in developing a sense of intimacy and trust between client and therapist, allowing the client to explore issues that he or she may not feel ready to bring out in a group. This can be extremely helpful for individuals who tend to feel unworthy of anyone's genuine concern. However, this undivided attention can also feed into a sense of entitlement and self-involvement that can impair effective functioning in those with substance abuse histories.

Flores (1997) found that most professionals working with people with substance abuse problems agree that the specific issues that arise in addiction—depression, anxiety, isolation, denial, shame, transient cognitive impairment, and character pathology—respond better to group treatment than individual therapy. The opportunity to work together in cooperative, creative endeavors can be a challenge for individuals who have become volatile loners. Tempers can flare, but as long as they do not sever relationships permanently, such episodes can be valuable. With an understanding of the nature of transference involved in groups, the therapist is in a better position to guide interpersonal friction productively. Flores (1997) and Yalom (1995) have described the therapist's role as helping group members begin to recognize counterproductive patterns.

However, rather than simply identifying dysfunctional styles of relating, the music therapist is able to create conditions where, as Aigen (1996) put it:

> *Both therapist and client are living as completely as is possible in the music. When this occurs, one's entire physical, emotional and spiritual being is becoming manifest in the music and the music functions as an extension of the person. (p. 12)*

In this way, Kenny (1982) suggested, music becomes "not so much a connector as a vehicle of inspiration which reminds us that we are already connected. And this connected feeling forms the basis of whole health" (p. 32). Feeling safe and taking part with others in music without the use of drugs can be a powerful experience for many clients in addiction treatment, since their primary associations with music and socialization may have been drug-related (going to clubs "high," drinking while "hanging-out," and listening to music with friends, etc.). As such, some have considered music to be a *relapse-trigger*.

However, as Turry (1989) described, when one's private music begins to connect to the outside world in music therapy, there is a sense of belonging and relating to the word. This connection redirects the energy from self-focus toward the world. This can lead to improvements in self-awareness, healthier relationships, self-esteem, and hope for the future, all of which form the foundation for letting go of an addictive pattern.

Goals for Music Therapy With Substance Use Clients

Some experts have described addiction as a *motivational problem* (Cox & Klinger, 1988; Heather, 1992). According to Donovan and Rosengren (1999), resistance to treatment is equated with defense mechanisms such as minimalization, denial, and rationalization, which are considered to be nearly universal traits among people who abuse substances. While we can agree that the central and defining goals of treatment may be arresting substance use and preventing relapses, the nature of addiction is not effectively understood simply as a condition to be eliminated. Glover's (1956) pioneering work on the psychology of substance abuse saw addiction as an attempt at mastering, rather than avoiding, anxiety. This important distinction emphasizes a progressive, as opposed to regressive, intent and function of substance use. The reason addiction can be so tenacious is because changing an addictive pattern entails a fundamental restructuring of one's primary coping strategies. The task, then, of the therapist is not to convince clients what they need to give up, but rather in helping them to discover with what to replace the loss.

Frankl (1984) pointed to studies indicating that 90 to 100% of addicts and alcoholics have intense feelings of meaningless. Without hope for a better future, the client will not have the motivation to confront his or her defenses or deal with any of the challenges inherent in a process of recovery. Without a sense of purpose, the client cannot commit to therapy. Although many researchers have focused on actual or feared negative events or losses as motivators for seeking help, Varney et al. (1995) found that an individual is likely to seek treatment only if the anticipated positive consequences of treatment are perceived as more beneficial than continuing to use drugs. Although this may seem like a foregone conclusion to many treatment professionals, it may not be such a clear-cut choice to chronic substance users who have found a way to subsist and, according to Jacobs (1997), tend to be resigned to their lifelong inner experience as "unpleasant, different from other people and essentially immutable. Many express feelings of being victims of nature in this regard" (p. 172). I have even heard clients express the fear that they have seen friends and acquaintances die of a serious medical condition only after they "got clean."

Utilizing music's capacity to safely contain and express opposing, ambivalent feelings can help facilitate a process of awareness, acceptance, and transformation. Through musical expression and interaction, the client's strengths and resistances are revealed in dynamic, tangible form. Neumann (1959) claimed the principal function of the artistic experience was "to bring the individual himself to transcendence" (p. 106). The idea of transcendence need not represent anything mysterious or mystical. It can refer to a loosening of attachments to fixed thoughts and outdated, nonfunctional self-concepts. Jung (1997) described the transcendent function as arising from the union of conscious and unconscious material, with the therapist mediating in this process to help the client develop a new attitude. As fresh possibilities are revealed, the client can see things from a different perspective. The therapist works to validate and bring increased attention to any new insights. As the client experiences alternatives to habitual and counterproductive thought/response patterns by tapping into formerly unknown inner resources, goals reflecting shifting attitudes can be realized. Examples of such goals might be:

- increasing proactive, hopeful attitudes;
- developing alternative coping-skills/response patterns for strong feeling states (anger, anxiety/panic, self-loathing, loneliness, depression, despair, even happiness);
- improving frustration tolerance;
- improving ability to manage impulsivity;
- improving ability to trust;
- addressing ambivalence;
- improving perception and differentiation of feelings;
- improving social/collaboration skills;
- exploring identity as a "clean and sober" person;
- acknowledging a sense of loss—of long-standing identity and social connections, of pride in admitting the need for help;
- enhancing ability to envision a meaningful postrecovery lifestyle;
- acknowledging fear—of failure, of the physical and emotional pain involved in recovery.

Music Therapy Interventions for Substance Use Clients

There are several music therapy interventions that are especially useful for work with clients who have substance abuse problems.

The Improvisational Psychotherapy Approach

If music therapist and client can become partners in seeking the willingness to expand into the unknown—to be open, to explore and face whatever the creative process may reveal—each session may be considered an improvisation. Ruud (1995) defined improvisation as creating or arranging something here and now, to put something together on the way, out of available resources. It is connected to the present—a fluid, moment-to-moment experience. The authority of the therapist is reduced with the therapist and client in, more or less, the same predicament, that is, not knowing exactly what to do or what might happen next. Aigen (1996) has stated, "If the hope is for clients to overcome the growth-inhibiting forces within them, then the therapists must embody and offer forth the fruits of the same struggle within themselves" (p. 282).

Improvisation may be a less comfortable position for a music therapist than coming into a session with a specific goal-related activity in mind. It may bring up anxiety for the client, as well. But according to Flores (1997), many clients with drug or alcohol addition truly believe that they are not worthy or are damaged individuals. Therefore, within a highly structured agenda, emphasizing the hierarchy implicit in the client/therapist relationship, it is possible that clients will do, say, or play what they think is "right" or "what the therapist wants to hear" (if they do not reject the situation altogether). In any case, such an approach may engender the defensiveness, grandiosity, manipulation, and duplicity of the false-self formation (Flores, 1997) characteristic in addiction pathology. Consequently, Flores concluded that diverse views of addiction all have the same common goals of cure and treatment. "Addicts and alcoholics must become *real and authentic*" (p. 186). Ruud (1995) wrote:

Improvisation may be understood to create a situation where change, transformation and process come into focus. In this sense, improvisation not only means to get from one place to another, but from one state to another. In this sense, improvisation means to change a relation to other human beings, phenomena, situations—maybe the very relation to oneself. In this sense, improvisation is a transitional ritual, a way of changing position, frames, status, or states of consciousness. (p. 93)

As well as offering a definition of improvisation, this passage seems to describe the underlying fundamentally healthy intent of substance use. (Try reading the passage while substituting the words "getting high" for the word "improvisation.") Most substance abuse patterns begin during adolescence. Without appropriate role modeling, information, or ego-strengths at that time, the attempt to satisfy these needs may go badly awry. Thus, by increasing the ability to access personal creative power, it becomes possible to experience the addictive craving for transformation and change without the use of substances. This may be a completely revelatory experience for clients suffering from chronic addiction. Helen Bonny (Bonny & Tansill, 1977) referred to music therapy as a "legal high" that brings "insight and awareness from deeper levels of the psyche to the normal conscious state for the purpose of effecting behavior change and for living a more holistic and satisfactory life" (p. 114). If such a shift in awareness is accomplished, clients often spontaneously transcend longstanding pathological tendencies in music therapy. A process of reintegration and generalization is set in motion.

Getting into the Groove—Drumming and Rhythm

Many clients may relate to drumming/percussion as a familiar, pleasurable, and nonthreatening means of engaging in music. Drumming and other rhythmic music can address multiple needs of people with addictions. On a physiological level, drumming may positively impact brain chemistry (Winkelman, 1993). The National Institute on Drug Abuse (1999) has determined that long-term drug use results in changes in brain functioning that persist long after an individual has stopped using drugs, making relapses virtually unavoidable. Winkelman (2003) presented evidence to suggest that drumming restores balance to some brain functions damaged by substance use, such as the opiate and serotonergic neurotransmitter systems, as well as restoring the relaxation response. Drumming may also help people dealing with addictions to establish a desperately needed sense of collective consciousness (Winkelman, 2003). Additionally, the repetition of rhythmic drum patterns can produce an altered state of consciousness, bringing participants into a state of "flow." As Csikszentmihalyi (1990) described it, "Flow helps to integrate the self because in that state of deep concentration, consciousness is unusually well ordered. Thoughts, intentions, feelings, and all the senses are focused on the same goal. Experience is in harmony" (p. 41). Consequently, drumming and rhythmic music can offer a means of experiencing a sense of well-being and release from the pain of psychic fragmentation and conflict that the client formerly could not achieve without substance use.

Case Study 1

Rodney was a 49-year-old man, a former heroin addict who had been on a methadone program for 8 years and was also abusively using Elavil, a potent and highly addictive psychiatric antidepressant available on the street. Rod presented as thin and unkempt with a low, gravely, lethargic voice. On first impression, he appeared concerned with little else than his day-to-day existence and the procurement of his drugs.

Over time, however, his love of music became evident, and offered the opportunity, he eventually became a consistent music therapy participant, although he never said much.

One day, in an individual session, approximately one year into the treatment process, Rod played a conga (the instrument he typically chose for almost every session) while I played guitar. As we began to improvise, Rod played with a commitment, passion, and technical mastery that I had not heard before, executing complicated syncopations with a level of energy that seemed beyond him. The music established a driving urgency that took on a life of its own. What happened when we came to a conclusion could not have been predicted. After some exclamatory "whew's" and "whoa's," and a short transition period, Rod began to freely discuss his history. He told me of his hatred for his father who had abused and abandoned him. He discussed his feelings of guilt and shame regarding being sexually abused as a child by an older man from his neighborhood. He talked of his drug addiction, criminal past, the breakdown of his marriage, and of his greatest horror and torment—how he had physically abused his own children whom he had not seen in 12 years.

Rod informed me that he had never spoken of these things to anyone. This outpouring of a lifetime of pent-up anguish occurred all in this one session. Ruud (1995) wrote, "Music may express what is feared or hidden by the language and intellect" (p. 105). As such, the drumming provided a nonverbal and nonthreatening means of disclosure for Rod, allowing him to invest and project himself into his playing, accessing memories and feelings. Once the pathways for this outgoing energy and healing potential had been opened, Rod was inspired and courageous enough to reveal himself verbally. Skaggs (1997) wrote:

> It is essential that the recovering addict become fully awake to the rhythms of body, to thoughts, feelings, and the dynamics of relationships. It is important to be awake to the influences of the unconscious, to memories and feelings that were stored there when too painful to face. Then the feelings and memories that have been awakened must be experienced in a moving through, rather than around, them. Recovery that is fully conscious then becomes possible, and the addict begins to know what it means to be whole. (p. 21)

I was awestruck by the trust Rod had placed in me and cognizant of my responsibility for being a nonjudgmental and safe container for his pain. In subsequent sessions, the process continued along similar lines. Any discussion of personal material always followed our drumming. According to Winkelman (2003), drumming enhances awareness of preconscious dynamics, a release of emotional trauma, and reintegration of self. Rod eventually became trusting enough of other members, so that he began to open up in groups, as well. This newfound beginning of self-acceptance strengthened Rod's resolve to "get clean." He made several attempts and continually relapsed, but his periods of "clean time" progressively increased. He also began to take steps in reuniting with his children, writing them letters of apology and making phone calls. His intelligence and dry sense of humor became more apparent, and his general presence and force of personality was clearly intensified as he made strides in becoming a healthier personality who felt more comfortable with himself.

Singing Popular Songs

When a popular song connects with the deep needs of an individual or group, the effects can be profound. Rolla (1993) found that "lyric content of unconscious musical impulses may infer, reflect, or reveal areas of psychic conflict or concern, as well as a desire for resolution" (p. 25). Lyric or thematic discussion can assist in this process. Heimlich (1983) suggested that the metaphoric use of song lyrics could aid in identifying and communicating feelings. However, just the simple act of singing songs, particularly with a group, can flood one with feelings, memories, a sense of sharing with others, and connection with oneself. Gurumayi Chidvilasananda (1999) suggested, "Singing removes barriers and invites you into a greater world" (p. 93).

Case Study 2

One day, while looking through a songbook, a group member came across the classic song from the 1950s, "I Believe." He felt attracted to this song with its lyrics of spiritual comfort, although he said it held no other association for him. Originally, the session included only myself and two other group members, but as we began to sing and the sound of our music wafted through the music room door into the hall, we were joined by two other program members. As the group sang the beautiful melody with lyrics reflecting a promise of hope for the hopeless, the energy and enthusiasm began to rise.

> *I believe for every drop of rain that falls, a flower grows*
> *And I believe that somewhere in the darkest night, a candle glows*
> *I believe for everyone who's gone astray*
> *Someone will come to show the way*
> *Yes, I believe, oh, I believe*
>
> *I believe that above the storm the smallest prayer can still be heard*
> *I believe that someone in the great somewhere hears every word*
> *Every time I hear a newborn baby cry or touch a leaf or see the sky*
> *Then I know why I believe.*
>
> *(I Believe. Retrieved September 1, 2006, from http://www.lyrics.astraweb.com)*

As we continued work on the song, several more program members joined in and then more, so that, eventually, there were eight members interweaving parts and harmonies. None of the participants were trained singers or experienced in choral harmony, yet the voices complemented each other, generating rich, complex chords. Another six members looked on, seemingly transfixed by this big and beautiful sound. It was rare to have such a large group working on a piece of music and even more atypical to have people watching. Normally, I would not think of a music therapy session as a quasi-performance, but in this instance, the communal feeling took on a life and intent of its own. Unlike with drugs, which once administered can only cause one to succumb to the effects, music allows clients to be conscious participants entirely by choice through each step of the process.

Here were 14 individuals, all chronic addicts, many of whom were usually too preoccupied with their own survival issues, general malaise, and drug-related concerns to take part or show interest in a music session. They were drawn together and inspired by the message of faith in the lyrics and the harmony in the music that was being created. Kenny and Faunce (2004) found that singing increased active coping responses, not only for the singer, but for the listener, as well. If, as Woodman (1993) proposed, addiction is a response to a sense of despair and alienation, these clients had found the way out, without drugs, at least for the moment.

Songwriting

Ritholz and Robbins (1999) have described composing or improvising songs as

> *an inevitable part of the practice of music therapy. To the extent that an individual or group identifies positively with a particular song or instrumental activity, these pieces have the potential to play unique roles in courses of therapy, and so in the development of clients' lives generally. (p. 6)*

Clinical songwriting involves several important principles relevant to addiction treatment. Songs can:

- give form to and enhance emotional expression;
- safely contain disturbing or opposing emotions and ambivalence;
- validate clients' inner experience and ability to communicate with the outside world;
- stimulate emotional identification and self-awareness;
- facilitate group cohesion.

There are three general approaches to clinical songwriting. The clinician can write a song outside of the session, then present it to the client with the idea that the client might, in some way, relate to it or adapt it in the session. This may be a viable intervention with children, but, in general, adults dealing with substance issues are capable of far greater responsibility and involvement in the composition process. Client and therapist can also conceive a relatively long-term project, collaboratively composing a song that holds personal meaning and relevance to the client. This can be an extremely powerful process but may take quite a few hours to complete and, as such, might require multiple sessions and a consistent and committed client. I have been disappointed, having started a promising song with a client and then, for various reasons, not seeing the client for several weeks. By the time we are ready to resume the project, the original impetus has seemingly diminished. This can be a purely logistical issue, or it may represent resistance on the part of the client. Also, clinicians in short-term programs or detox programs may see a client only for one or two sessions in total.

For these reasons, I prefer to achieve a sense of realization in one session. Further honing or processing can occur in subsequent sessions if warranted but, hopefully, the main body of the work is completed. Whether originating out of an improvisation or a more structured initiative, this is not a process that can be forced. It usually arises of its own accord. When it does, I try to seize the moment and push it through to completion. The therapist needs to be ready, remaining alert and prepared to support a client's process as it emerges. The effort may not always yield a cohesive, finished piece of work, but when it does, the rewards can be significant. (See section on songwriting in Chapter 5.)

Case Study 3

Given the addict's wounded self-image, Zoja (1989) has suggested a Jungian view of the drug addict's search for identity, resulting in a personification of the "negative hero" archetype. Zinberg (1997) offers a similar perspective in his reference to Erikson's idea of a negative identity providing a measure of self-esteem and self-definition. This process was given voice by Karl, a 35-year-old man struggling with an addiction to cocaine that forced him to leave his career as an elementary school teacher. Karl attended Narcotics Anonymous meetings, toward which he had deeply ambivalent feelings. His pattern was to go for a week or so without using drugs, relapse/binge for a few days, and begin the process again.

Karl was a talented singer/songwriter/guitarist and had written a number of songs prior to our association through music therapy. One day we were planning to sing one of his previously composed songs in a group session. It was a gentle ballad and there were four other members in the room prepared to assist with percussion and background vocals. We set up the music room with Karl in front of a microphone and the others in their places. We also planned to use a drum-machine. As we were ready to begin, I must have hit a wrong button because instead of the mellow rhythmic feel we were expecting, an up-tempo tango beat filled the room. Everyone laughed, and I was about to start again when I noticed that Karl was singing to the driving beat. He was chanting, "If you want to do it, do it right. Do it for me." The group began supporting Karl as he improvised the following lyrics in a rap idiom.

I'm Bad
I come around to the city looking at all the dark faces
I come around to the city. I've seen many dark places
So I'm bad. Yes, I'm bad. Yes I'm bad. Yes, I'm bad
My mother told me that I would grow up to be nothing
People always getting down on my case
Yes, I'm bad, yes, I'm bad . . .
I run in and out of many institutions
People always telling me that I'm a loser
Yes, I'm bad, yes, I'm bad . . .
Some day, I will get out of here. Some day, I will get out of here.
AAARRRGGGGG! AAARRRRGGGGG! (he is screaming at this point)
Some people think I do commercials. Some people think I don't know her
Yes, I'm bad, yes, I'm bad . . .
I never drive my car at the speed limit
I always want a God to solve my problems
I'm always getting down and this and that
Yes, I'm bad, yes, I'm bad . . .
My dad was a f------ alcoholic
My brother was a junkie, too
And I am trying to change the pattern
I've got to get away from you
Yes! Yes! Yes! I'm bad, yes, I, I'm bad . . .!
I've done a lot of things in my days
I walk around sometimes and I'm in a haze
I don't know which direction I'm going
I've got to get somewhere now!
Yes, I'm bad, yes, I'm bad . . .

As the song gained momentum, Karl began screaming in parts. The driving beat propelled him onward as other members danced around the room playing hand percussion and echoing his "I'm bad" refrain. The rhythm and the repetitive intensity of the music created an energy that served to safely contain Karl's painful, potentially depressing emotions. It was an amazing display of spontaneity and honesty, illustrating music's capacity to release intensely painful and private emotions, transforming them into a joyous catharsis. The opposite of depression is not happiness. The opposite of depression is expression.

At first, Karl recounts the negative influences in his life, evaluating himself and his life harshly. As these elements are creatively expressed and given form in his song, the authenticity and power of his spontaneous lyrics stimulate the support and empathy of his peers. With their support, the piece comes to a dynamic climax then moves to a surprising psychological transformation with the lines: "And I am trying to change the pattern," and "I've got to get away from you . . . I've got to get somewhere now!" Karl's passionate, exclamatory singing seemed to simultaneously communicate resolve, determination, desperation, and hope for the future. In acknowledging and reframing his self-image of being the "bad," ill-fated drug addict in the context of this shared and joyful creative process, Karl experienced a process of letting go of the shame and depression that chained him to the past. His song showed him his potential to take matters into his own hands in his life. He was not trapped. He had the ability to change and was not simply a victim of his past or (as he sees it) his flawed personality. This constituted a significant attitudinal shift with which an addict must come to terms in order to begin recovery.

Performance

Performance in music therapy is controversial. Some may feel it confuses the roles and boundaries of the therapeutic relationship or that it places the client in a potentially exploitative and vulnerable position. However, handled in an appropriate, supportive, and sensitive manner, it can be an extremely potent intervention. Ansdell (2002) described a movement in the music therapy field known as community music therapy that

> reflects the essentially communal reality of musicing. The aim is to help clients access
> a variety of musical situations, and to accompany them as they move between therapy
> and wider social contexts of musicing. . . . It involves extending the role, aim and
> possible sites of work for music therapists. (p. 120)

Nurturing a client's journey into the communal world of sharing and visibility involved in performance can address and counteract the isolation, shame, and guilt involved in addiction. Inherent components of performance—preparation, risk-taking, the need to "show-up," and the potential for acknowledgment/ recognition—can also provide an opportunity to address some of the core character pathologies of addiction such as narcissism, grandiosity, and unreliability. However, ill-advised or poorly handled performance situations can also aggravate these problems. Therefore, a therapist must consider the decision carefully. Austin (2003) described a situation in which a client of hers who wanted to perform later thanked her for refusing the request. For this client, a feeling of being safely contained from her impulsivity was a more important therapeutic concern. Austin and Dvorkin (1998) also advised that a therapist must remain aware of his or her own "narcissistic need for recognition and validation that has not been worked through" (p. 132). However, utilized discerningly and with awareness, the performance can feed back into the therapy process. Turry (2004) regarded the experience of being valued and attended-to after the performance by the therapist to be more powerful than the public response in helping clients to feel an internal sense of validation.

Case Study 4

Alan was a 41-year-old man whose addiction to crack cocaine spanned over 10 years. He was formerly addicted to heroin and was also currently on a methadone maintenance program. He was not an educated man but was highly intelligent and enjoyed reading a wide range of material, most often of a spiritual or mystical nature. He seemed to possess deep feelings of morality, although he had engaged in nonviolent criminal activities such as burglary to support his addiction. Wurmser has theorized that splitting of the super-ego is an inevitable development of addiction as trustworthiness, reliability, honesty, and commitments to others are neglected. As Wurmser put it, "The drowning man has commonly little regard for questions of integrity" (cited in Flores, 1997, p. 244).

Alan seemed to fancy himself a philosopher and teacher of sorts and was constantly attempting to engage other program members in serious discussion, although they generally paid little attention to him. Through our association in music therapy, Alan came up with a rap song that addressed the ravages of addiction. Clearly the voice of experience, Alan worked in an extremely earnest fashion for several sessions on his apparently heartfelt antidrug statement. It dealt with the downward spiral of addiction's pattern of compulsion, futility, deterioration of health, degenerating quality of life, isolation, loss of morality, descent into crime, and, ultimately, prison or death. All the while, Alan continued using crack. Wurmser also identified a split between observation and action that occurs with addiction. Thus, Alan's song portrayed his situation with a clear eye, even though he could not actively respond to his own warning. Obviously, he could not be totally unaware of the contradiction, and we discussed it. His rationale (some might say, rationalization) was that, although he was still active in his substance abuse, he was counseling others through his art not to do as he has done.

Alan's explanation was given some credence when he accepted an opportunity to publicly perform his work during a "talent show" at another program. This was the first time he had ever done such a thing or even considered it. He was extremely nervous, but he fulfilled his intention and commitment. While I drummed out a beat on a conga, Alan rapped his poem. He was well received and expressed such a deep satisfaction and enthusiasm that he could not wait to do it again. I was able to arrange a number of additional performances, including one at a major health exposition before a large crowd. The performances afforded Alan an opportunity to live in the solution—to experience his higher self, the part of him that knew his addiction was not in his interest. Turry (2004) described a case in which a performance with his client

> made a powerful statement. She no longer felt she had to hide her struggles, doubts and fears, and this was extremely liberating. It gave [her] an opportunity to participate and share with others more deeply what she was going through and that helped her to feel less isolated. As she connected with members of the audience, they, in return, felt moved and wanted to connect with her. (p. 4)

The fact that Alan had not become drug-free in his everyday behavior did not invalidate his accomplishment. Songs often represent ideals. Who would deny the fundamental truth yet equal inability to fully live up to a song such as The Beatles' "All You Need is Love"?

However, the essence of Alan's problem was not simply related to an ambivalent relationship with his substance abuse. It was about a greater sense of identity. Who was Alan without drugs in his life? He was dealing with a multitude of issues but had not been forced into a confrontation. His health problems were, thus far, not too troublesome. He received some money and housing through various welfare and disability entitlements. He had not "bottomed-out." But with no family, no intimate or even particularly friendly relationships, no career, and no sense of progress, he was merely surviving. This was enormously painful to a man of his intelligence and energy, but he was clearly not able to fully confront it.

Through his performances, Alan brought out qualities in himself that he could not otherwise manifest. He always showed up on time. He was never "high," as far as could be determined. He exhibited great courage in managing his anxiety and taking risks. Perhaps most importantly, he became the respected teacher that he longed to be, someone with something valuable to contribute, someone worthy of respect and attention. Would it be enough to inspire a comprehensive life evaluation and change? Only time would tell. According to Boesky (1990), modern psychoanalytic theory has long recognized that the concept of resistance is much broader than simply a defense against insight or change. Even in the most fruitful course of therapy, gaining insight into one form of resistance necessarily leads to the construction of another. Discouraging as this might sound, it is actually the best for which a therapist can hope. The most serious problems occur when the process becomes arrested and stuck with just one resistance. Alan's work raised him out of his previously stagnant position into an active process of self-discovery.

Conclusion

The optimism, energy, and honesty shared in the artistry of the clients with whom I have worked represent enormous achievements in the face of their monumental struggles. Some have achieved abstinence. Some have sustained it. Others have not. Some have gone to jail. Some have died. This raises an important question. If the clients do not go on to a productive, drug-free lifestyle, was the treatment useful? The degree to which potentially valuable experiences are accepted or integrated by the client is not in the control of the therapist, who can only do everything possible to offer conditions that encourage it. Addiction ruins lives, obliterates personal potential, and is often a fatal condition. It seems like such a senseless tragedy since all the person has to do is "just stop." Some do not. The treatment issues are too deeply entrenched.

Many who work with the chronically and terminally ill recognize a distinction between curing and healing. The word curing can represent a reductionist view, fragmenting the disease from the whole person. It is a biomedical model of a person as a machine with a breakdown that needs to be diagnosed and "fixed." If the problem seems to be eliminated, the patient is considered to be cured or in remission. Healing has a broader connotation encompassing the enhancement of emotional and spiritual well-being, as well. Moments of insight, acceptance, faith, connection, hope, and courage—these do not fade away. They might be considered peak experiences (Maslow, 1968), and they have a cumulative effect. Thus, a person who may be "incurable" can still heal. Cases of an unexpected reversal of an "incurable" condition, when conventional medicine has nothing left to offer, are generally ascribed to attributes related to healing. Even if a patient's death becomes inevitable, healing is valuable in and of itself. Frankl (1988) wrote:

> If there is meaning [in life], it is unconditional meaning, and neither suffering nor dying can detract from it. And what our patients need is unconditional faith in unconditional meaning. Remember what I have said of life's transitoriness. In the past, nothing is irrevocably lost but everything is irrevocably stored. People only see the stubble field of

transitoriness but overlook the full granaries of the past in which they have delivered and deposited, in which they have saved their harvest. (p. 156)

As Pavlicevic (1999) cautioned, we cannot insist on

anyone feeling what they are not ready to feel, or on them being part of music that they do not experience as being related to them. At the same time, though, as music therapists, we have a responsibility not to avoid darkness and pain, perhaps because of our own discomfort with it. (p. 52)

So the real challenge is this: Do we have the courage, as Priestly (1994) colorfully put it, to "discover the hidden treasures in the heart of the client and oneself as a therapist, even though they are guarded by the symbolic monsters of fairy tales" (p. 124)? Or, to paraphrase Jung, are we willing to put aside our theories and preconceptions when we touch the miracle of the living soul (Corsini & Wedding, 1989, p. 132)? If the music therapist can rise to this calling, fearlessly remaining present and being willing to enter the creative worlds into which our clients lead, healing will occur.

References

Aigen, K. (1996). *Being in music:* Foundations of Nordoff-Robbins music therapy. *St. Louis, MO: MMB Music.*

Alcoholics Anonymous. (1976). *Alcoholics anonymous (3rd ed.). New York: Works.*

American Music Therapy Association (AMTA). (2003). Standards of clinical practice. AMTA Member Sourcebook. *Silver Spring, MD: Author.*

American Psychiatric Association (APA). (1994). Diagnostic and statistical manual of mental disorders *(4th ed.). Washington, DC: Author.*

Ansdell, G. (2002). *Community music therapy and the winds of change—A discussion paper. In C. Kenny & B. Stige (Eds.),* Contemporary voices in music therapy: communication, culture and community *(pp. 109–143). Oslo, Norway: Unipub Forlag.*

Austin, D. (2003). When words sing and music speaks: A qualitative study of in-depth music psychotherapy with adults. *Unpublished doctoral dissertation, New York University.*

Austin, D., & Dvorkin, J. (1998). *Resistance in individual music therapy. In K. Bruscia (Ed.),* The dynamics of music psychotherapy *(pp. 121–136). Gilsum, NH: Barcelona.*

Boesky, D. (1990). *The psychoanalytic process and its components.* Psychoanalytic Quarterly, 59, *550–584.*

Bonny, H., & Tansill, R. (1977). *Music therapy: A legal high. In G. Waldorf (Ed.),* Counseling therapies and the addictive client *(pp. 113–130). Baltimore, MD: The University of Maryland School of Social Work and Community Planning.*

Bruscia, K. (1987). Improvisational models of music therapy. *Springfield, IL: Charles C. Thomas.*

Chidvilasananda, G. (1999). Courage and contentment. *New York: SYDA Foundation.*

Corsini, R., & Wedding, D. (1989). Current psychotherapies. *Itasca, IL: Peacock.*

Cox, W. M., & Klinger, E. (1988). A motivational model for alcohol use. *Journal of Abnormal Psychology, 97, 168–180.*

Csikszentmihalyi, M. (1990). *Flow: The psychology of optimal experience. New York: Harper & Row.*

Donovan, D., & Rosengren, D. (1999). *Motivation for behavior change and treatment among substance abusers. In D. Donovan, G. Marlatt, & J. Tucker (Eds.),* Changing addictive behavior *(pp. 127–159). New York: Guilford Press.*

Flores, P. (1997). Group psychotherapy with addicted populations. *Binghamton, NY: The Haworth Press.*

Frankl, V. (1984). Man's search for meaning. *New York: Simon & Schuster.*

Frankl, V. (1988). The will to meaning. *New York: Meridian.*

Glover, E. (1956). On the etiology of drug addiction. On the early development of the mind. *New York: International Universities Press.*

Heather, N. (1992). Addictive disorders are essentially motivational problems. British Journal of Addiction, 87, *828–830.*

Heimlich, E. P. (1983). The metaphoric use of song lyrics as paraverbal communication. Child Psychiatry and Human Development, 14(2), *67–75.*

Imhof, J. (1995). *Overcoming countertransference and other attitudinal barriers in the treatment of substance abuse. In A. Washton (Ed.),* Psychotherapy and substance abuse *(pp. 3–22). New York: Guilford Press.*

Jacobs, D. F. (1997). *A general theory of addictions: A new theoretical model. In D. Yalisove (Ed.),* Essential papers on addiction *(pp. 166–183). New York: New York University Press.*

Jung, C. G. (1997). *The transcendant function. In J. Chodorow (Ed.),* Jung on active imagination *(pp. 42–60). Princeton, NJ: Princeton University Press.*

Kenny, C. (1982). The mythic artery. *Atascadero, CA: Ridgeview.*

Kenny, D., & Faunce, G. (2004). *The impact of group singing on mood, coping, and perceived pain in chronic pain patients attending a multidisciplinary pain clinic.* Journal of Music Therapy, 41*(3), 241–258.*

Maslow, A. (1968). Toward a psychology of being. *New York: Van Nostrand Reinhold.*

National Institute on Drug Abuse. (1999). Principles of drug addiction treatment: A research-based guide. *National Institute of Health Publication No. 99-4180.*

Neumann, E. (1959). Art and the creative unconscious. *Princeton, NJ: Princeton University Press.*

Nolan, P. (1998). *Countertransference in clinical songwriting. In K. Bruscia (Ed.),* The dynamics of music psychotherapy *(pp. 387–406). Gilsum, NH: Barcelona.*

Pavlicevic, M. (1999). Music therapy—intimate notes. *London: Jessica Kingsley.*

Priestly, M. (1994). Essays on analytical music therapy. *Gilsum, NH: Barcelona.*

Prochaska, J., & DiClemente, C. (1986). *Towards a comprehensive model of change. In W. Miller & N. Heather (Eds.),* Treating addictive behaviors: Processes of change *(pp. 3–27). New York: Plenum.*

Ritholz, M., & Robbins, C. (1999). Themes for therapy. *New York: Carl Fischer.*

Rolla, G. (1993). Your inner music. *Wilmette, IL. Chiron.*

Rothschild, D. (1995). *Working with addicts in private practice: Overcoming initial resistance. In A. Washton (Ed.),* Psychotherapy and substance abuse *(pp. 192–203). New York: Guilford Press.*

Ruud, E. (1995). *Improvisation as a liminal experience: Jazz and music therapy as modern "rites of passage." In C. Kenny (Ed.),* Listening, playing, creating *(pp. 91–110). Albany, NY: State University of New York Press.*

Skaggs, R. (1997). Finishing strong: Treating chemical addictions with music and imagery. *St Louis, MO: MMB Music.*

Tatarsky, A. (1998). Harm reduction psychotherapy with active substance users. *Harm Reduction Communication, 6 (Online newsletter).*

Turry, A. (1989). An approach to using the music in music therapy. *Unpublished master's thesis, New York University.*

Turry, A. (2004). Music psychotherapy and community music therapy: Questions and considerations. *Unpublished manuscript.*

Varney, S., Rohsenow, D., Dey, A., Meyers, M., Zwick, W., & Monti, P. (1995). *Factors associated with help seeking and perceived dependence among cocaine users.* American Journal of Drug and Alcohol Abuse, 21, *81–91.*

Winkelman, M. (2003). Drumming out drugs. *American Journal of Public Health, 93(4), 674–679.*

Woodman, M. (1993, Winter). *Stepping over the threshold.* Noetic Sciences Review.

Yalom, I. (1995). The theory and practice of group psychotherapy. *New York: Harper Collins.*

Zinberg, N. (1997). *Addiction and ego function. In D. Yalisove (Ed.),* Essential papers on addiction. *New York: New York University Press.*

Zoja, L. (1989). Drugs, addiction and intuition: The modern search for ritual. *Boston: Sigo Press.*

Additional Resources

Rogers, C. (1961). On becoming a person. *New York: Houghton Mifflin.*

Turry, A. (1998). *Transference and countertransference in Nordoff-Robbins music therapy. In K. Bruscia (Ed.),* The dynamics of music psychotherapy *(pp. 161–212). Gilsum, NH: Barcelona.*

Chapter 11

Music Therapy Practice for Clients with Eating Disorders
Sammi Siegel

Overview of Eating Disorders

Eating disorders, such as bulimia nervosa, anorexia nervosa, and binge-eating disorder are complex disorders that are caused and maintained by various social, psychological, and biological factors. These disorders represent potentially life-threatening, incapacitating conditions that can seriously affect physical, emotional, and behavioral development. When diagnosed and treated in childhood or adolescents, eating disorders have a relatively good prognosis (Lask & Bryant-Waugh, 1993). However, if not treated, these individuals develop chronic conditions by adulthood. The devastating consequences can include irreversible medical, behavioral, and emotional outcomes.

Diagnostic Criteria

The *Diagnostic and Statistical Manual of Mental Disorders* (4th ed.) (American Psychiatric Association, 1994) describes the criteria for diagnosing anorexia nervosa, bulimia nervosa, and eating disorder not otherwise specified (NOS). According to the *DSM-IV*, diagnostic criteria for *anorexia nervosa* include:

- refusal to maintain body weight at or above a minimally normal weight for age and height;
- intense fear of gaining weight or becoming fat, even though underweight;
- disturbance in the way in which one's body weight or shape is experienced, undue influence of body weight or shape on self-evaluation, or denial of the seriousness of the current low body weight;
- in postmenarcheal females, amenorrhea, i.e., the absence of at least three consecutive menstrual cycles (pp. 544–545).

The diagnostic criteria for *bulimia nervosa* include:

- recurrent episodes of binge eating; an episode of binge eating is characterized by eating, in a discreet period of time, an amount of food that is definitely larger than most people would eat during a similar period of time and under similar circumstances, and a sense of lack of control over eating during the episode;

- recurrent inappropriate compensatory behavior in order to prevent weight gain, such as self-induced vomiting; misuse of laxatives, diuretics, enemas, or other medications; fasting; or excessive exercise;
- binge eating and inappropriate compensatory that behaviors both occur, on average, at least twice a week for 3 months;
- self-evaluation that is unduly influenced by body shape and weight;
- the disturbance not occurring exclusively during episodes of anorexia nervosa (pp. 549–550).

The diagnostic criteria for eating disorder not otherwise specified includes:

- for females, all of the criteria for anorexia nervosa except that the individual has regular menses;
- all of the criteria for anorexia nervosa except that, despite significant weight loss, the individual's current weight is in the normal range;
- all of the criteria for bulimia nervosa except that the binge eating and inappropriate compensatory mechanisms occur at a frequency of less than twice a week or for a duration of less than 3 months;
- the regular use of inappropriate compensatory behaviors by an individual of normal body weight after eating small amounts of food, such as repeatedly chewing and spitting out but not swallowing large amounts of food.

In addition to anorexia nervosa, bulimia nervosa, and eating disorder NOS, the *DSM-IV* identifies *binge eating disorder* (BED) as a proposed category warranting further investigation for inclusion in the next version of the *DSM*. The research diagnostic criteria for BED include the same diagnostic criteria for bulimia nervosa regarding recurrent episodes of binge eating. However, in addition to recurrent episodes of binge eating, three or more of the following criteria must also occur: (a) eating much more rapidly than normal; (b) eating until feeling uncomfortably full; (c) eating large amounts of food when not feeling physically hungry; (d) eating alone because of being embarrassed by how much one is eating; and (e) feeling disgusted with oneself, depressed, or very guilty after overeating. For a diagnosis of BED, the binge eating is not associated with the regular use of inappropriate compensatory behaviors (p. 731).

Because more favorable outcomes occur when treatment begins soon after the onset of the disorder, it is important for clinicians to identify and treat these individuals as soon as possible, often before they meet full *DSM-IV* diagnostic criteria. Several authors have identified warning signs of potential eating disorders in children and adolescents. Woodside (1995) identifies warning signs of a possible emerging eating disorder to help distinguish between the "normal" dieter and pathological dieting:

- Dieting that is associated with decreased weight goals, setting lower weight goals after previous goal has been met
- Dieting that is associated with increased criticism of the body—dieting does not lead to increased satisfaction with body image following successful weight loss
- Dieting that is associated with increased social isolation—isolating themselves more, often restricting their activities to dieting and compulsive exercise

Atkins and Silber (1993) identify three major precipitants for dieting during preadolescence:

- Early physical maturation

- Entry into junior high/middle school
- Object loss, i.e., death of a relative, best friend moving away

Other possible precipitants for dieting leading toward childhood anorexia include an illness associated with weight loss, peer teasing, or a summer camp experience.

Lask and Bryant-Waugh (1993) further identify three additional points to consider when diagnosing eating disorders:

- Food avoidance for any reason
- Weight loss or failure to gain weight during preadolescent growth
- Any two or more of the following: (a) preoccupation with body weight; (b) preoccupation with counting calories, fat grams, etc.; (c) distortion of body image; (d) fear of fatness; (e) self-induced vomiting; (f) extensive exercising; (g) purging or laxative abuse

When working with children who have been diagnosed with an eating disorder, it is important to keep in mind possible differential diagnoses. Closely related disorders that look like eating disorders but are not include: (a) food refusal—maybe consider oppositional defiant disorder; (b) pervasive refusal to eat, drink, walk, talk, or engage in self-care—maybe consider posttraumatic stress disorder; (c) selective eating—maybe consider behavioral problem; (d) appetite loss secondary to depression; (e) food avoidance—maybe consider feeding/swallowing disorder.

Clinical Features of Eating Disorders

The major clinical features of anorexia nervosa and bulimia nervosa include extreme concerns regarding body weight, shape, and size. An individual's assessment of self-worth is almost exclusively in terms of body shape and weight. These individuals adopt strict and inflexible dietary rules, including extreme restricting of nutrition, self-induced vomiting, misuse of purgatives and diuretics, as well as rigorous exercise. A minor transgression of these behaviors is interpreted as evidence of poor self-control and self-worth. Often, individuals suffering with bulimia nervosa consider themselves to be a "failed anorexic." Clinical features of binge eating disorder resemble those of obesity. Individuals with BED are often overweight because they maintain a high calorie diet without expending comparable energy. The overeating that occurs in BED is often accompanied by feeling out of control, leading to feelings of despair or hopelessness.

Other clinical features seen in individuals with eating disorders encompass a general range of psychopathology, including such symptoms as depression, anxiety, obsession features, poor concentration, and impaired social functioning. Although many of the symptoms of eating disorders can be reversed simply by weight restoration, proper nutrition, and gaining control over eating, many treatment protocols, as well as psychopharmacology, show more lasting effects.

Medical Complications of Eating Disorders

Individuals with eating disorders present unusual challenges to the mental health professional in that these individuals often develop significant medical complications that require treatment. These complications can be very serious and fatal, if not addressed (Mitchell, Pomeroy, & Adson, 1997). Many of the physical symptoms of anorexia are secondary to the starvation and malnutrition. However, bulimic behaviors, such as purging, laxative abuse, and diuretic abuse also cause similar symptoms. Electrolyte abnormalities are most common with these individuals. Decreased fluid intake and increased loss of potassium due to purging, laxative abuse, and diuretic abuse is linked to hypokalemia (low potassium). Hypokalemia can be associated with cardiac arrhythmias and cardiac arrest. The dehydration that results from these chronic bulimic behaviors also causes the body to retain fluid and sodium in its attempt to maintain homeostasis. This edema is often distressing to the individual, triggering increased purging, laxative abuse, and diuretic abuse.

The endocrine system is profoundly affected in individuals with anorexia nervosa. Inadequate body fat content causes low levels of hormones involved in menstruation and ovulation. Because these hormones are necessary to maintain bone density, these individuals are at increased risk of developing osteoporosis.

Several areas of the gastrointestinal system are affected by eating disorders. Swelling of the parotid glands can be seen in individuals with anorexia and bulimia. Delayed gastric emptying is common in anorexia, causing the individual to feel bloated and full. Malnutrition and purging can result in gastrointestinal bleeding, which can develop into esophagitis and tears in the esophagus. Abuse of laxatives can cause complications of the large intestine. These problems include severe constipation wherein the colon ceases to function. Chronic laxative abuse is associated with steatorrhea, malabsorption, and protein-losing gastroenteropathy. Although rare, pancreatitis is also seen in individuals with anorexia, bulimia, and BED.

Many individuals with anorexia nervosa will develop lanugo, soft body hair on the face, forearms, and other parts of the body. In addition, these individuals report loss of scalp hair as well as the presence of dry skin and brittle nails.

Chronic, self-induced vomiting exposes the teeth to highly acidic gastric contents. This acid causes erosion of the enamel on the teeth. Frequent vomiting can also cause an increase in dental cavities, inflammation of the gums, and other periodontal diseases.

Assessment for Music Therapy

The evaluation of eating disorders requires a comprehensive, multidimensional assessment. At the very outset, building trust and establishing mutual respect serves as a basis for on-going exploration. The assessment is viewed as a process that may occur over several sessions and serve several purposes, such as establishing a diagnosis and gathering information relevant to treatment planning. Crowther and Sherwood (1997) outline three methods of assessment.

First, the initial interview obtains information regarding current weight and height as well as a detailed weight history, particularly any relationships between significant life events and weight fluctuations. In addition, information is gathered regarding weight during childhood and adolescence. The weight history also includes information about parents with an eating disorder as well as parental perception of their child's body weight, shape, and size. Information regarding the individual's own perception of his or her body and any disturbances in cognitive abilities, affect, or abnormal behaviors are also assessed. Specifically, the meaning attached to achieving and/or maintaining the ideal weight and the impact that this weight has on individuals' thoughts and feelings about themselves is gleaned. During the initial interview, the clinician gathers information about the individual's family and social history, educational and occupational history, and motivation for treatment. Unstructured interviews have been shown to offer more flexibility with regard to establishing a therapeutic relationship than structured interviews. Also, attention should be paid to concurrent psychiatric disturbances, especially affective and anxiety disorders, obsessive-compulsive disorders, substance abuse, suicidal tendencies, and personality disturbances.

Second, the use of self-report questionnaires has multiple purposes in assessing eating-related symptomatology. Self-report questionnaires can serve as a screening tool for the presence and/or severity of these abnormal behaviors. By identifying and clarifying these issues, self-reports can help guide treatment planning. Garner and Garfinkel (1979) devised measures for evaluating eating-related behaviors. The Eating Attitudes Test (EAT) and the EAT-26 have been used in both clinical and research contexts and show adequate reliability and validity. Garner (1991) also created the Eating Disorder Inventory (EDI) Symptom Checklist and the EDI-2. These tools provide a comprehensive assessment of the behavioral and psychological dimensions that are characteristic of eating disorders. The major advantage of these tools is that they generate a psychological profile that can be used to target treatment goals.

Lastly, self-monitoring is also used to help identify eating behaviors. Specifically, the individual records frequency and timing of meals and snacks, as well as binge behaviors and/or compensatory behaviors. In addition, these self-monitoring assessments include awareness of emotions before and after eating. Self-monitoring as an assessment tool serves several functions. Recording events that create stress and discomfort around eating can help clarify the relationship between events and abnormal eating patterns. Assessment in the treatment of eating disorders is seen as an on-going process that continues throughout the course of treatment, guiding treatment planning, goals, and objectives.

Specific Music Therapy Assessments

To date, there is not a specific music therapy assessment tool used specifically with individuals with eating disorders. However, much of the literature citing clinical improvisation as treatment for eating disorders has identified commonalities among these individuals in their music making. Sound qualities representative of an individual's psychological or emotional state are noted to be similar. For instance, personality characteristics of an individual with anorexia nervosa include being introverted, controlled, ritualistic, perfectionistic, demanding, and paranoid. During the initial music therapy assessment, especially in improvisation where the therapist is most likely establishing a trusting relationship, the music exchanges reflects the individual's psychological way of being. Personality characteristics of an individual with bulimia nervosa include being extroverted, accomplished, obsessive-compulsive, moody, impulsive, and indecisive. Most likely, the music qualities also reflect these characteristics. This author believes that it is important for the individuals to be able to express themselves nonverbally in a safe, containing environment at the beginning of treatment, in order to not feel judged or criticized by the therapist's words. It is through this music-making relationship that continued treatment and assessment go hand in hand.

Loewy (2000) describes a model for a music psychotherapy assessment that may be appropriate for working with individuals with eating disorders. Hermeneutics, a qualitative research method for gleaning meaning from an experience, may be an appropriate method of assessment. When individuals with an eating disorder seek the meaning that their relationship with food holds for them, their understanding comes through in their relationship with their music, as well. For example, if the meaning of their relationship with food is around issues of control, their experience of improvisational music making may be that of a controlled nature. The music therapist can reflect back to the individual the parallels that are drawn between one's relationship with music and one's relationship with food. It is the skilled therapist that can guide the individual to this understanding.

Treatment Goals

Treatment goals for clients with eating disorders vary depending on the specific diagnosis:

Anorexia Nervosa

- Restore healthy weight
- Regain menses
- Instill a regular healthy eating pattern and eliminate dieting restraint
- Develop an understand of the adaptive function of the eating disorder
- Establish healthy interpersonal relationships
- Increase body awareness
- Increase self-esteem
- Learn appropriate coping skills
- Learn relapse prevention skills
- Learn more adaptive means of managing dysfunctional thought patterns, unpleasant mood states, and interpersonal distress

Bulimia Nervosa

- Eliminate binge-purge behaviors by instilling a regular healthy eating pattern
- Decrease anxiety
- Decease impulsivity
- Develop an understanding of the adaptive function of the eating disorder
- Establish healthy interpersonal relationships
- Increase body awareness
- Increase self-esteem
- Learn appropriate coping skills
- Learn relapse prevention skills
- Learn more adaptive means of managing dysfunctional thought patterns, unpleasant mood states, and interpersonal distress

Binge Eating Disorder

- Eliminate binge eating by instilling a regular healthy eating pattern
- Eliminate the chaotic eating and lack of control associated with binging
- Develop a realistic weight standard and body acceptance
- Develop the capacity to delay gratification
- Develop an understanding of the adaptive function of the eating disorder
- Learn relapse prevention skills
- Learn more adaptive means of managing dysfunctional thought patterns, unpleasant mood states, and interpersonal distress

Major Approaches to Music Therapy Treatment

This section presents a brief overview of several approaches to music therapy treatment interventions and their corresponding psychological theoretical orientation for work with clients with eating disorders. Treatment goals are addressed within each philosophical domain.

Behavioral Music Therapy

Behavioral music therapy is the use of music to shape maladaptive behaviors. Individuals with an eating disorder have developed several inappropriate behaviors surrounding their relationship with food. Various music rewards can be applied when the individual begins to establish a normal relationship with food. For example, a music therapist may structure a contract with the individual that allows a predetermined period of music listening after eating a healthy meal without exhibiting any restricting or binging and purging behaviors. Another example of behavioral music therapy with individuals with eating disorders is teaching the individual relaxation techniques paired with a musical stimulus to manage and decrease impulsive behaviors, such as binge eating. In addition, relaxation training (Justice, 1994) has been shown to foster self-regulation and decrease anxiety states. Listening to soothing music after mealtime has been shown to decrease anxiety and aid digestion (Hilliard, 2001).

Cognitive Music Therapy

Cognitive music therapy is the use of music to modify and shift faulty cognitions. Individuals with eating disorders possess extreme irrational beliefs about their body weight, shape, and size. These dysfunctional thought patterns create unpleasant mood states and interpersonal distress. Music therapy interventions can be structured to encourage and support rational thinking, which promotes more pleasant feelings about oneself and relationships to others. For example, simply singing songs about self-acceptance, gratitude, and serenity can reinforce positive thinking about oneself. When one can change his or her dysfunctional thinking, thoughts of self-worth and self-esteem increase. In addition to singing songs that promote self-awareness, group improvisational music therapy fosters healthy interpersonal relationships in a nonthreatening, focused, and playful manner. These music experiences help maintain healthy cognitive patterns.

Psychodynamic Music Therapy

Psychodynamic music therapy aligns itself with several psychological theories of practice. The developmental theorists Winnicott, Klein, and Mahler are addressed in the music therapy and eating disorders literature. Nolan (1989) describes the use of music improvisation as a transitional object that can support an individual during moments of intense internal conflict. Working through the music-making process leads to the development of more adaptive means of managing times of internal distress. By engaging in the music experience, the individual can move through the process of musical dissonance or conflict leading to musical consonance or resolution. This positive experience of being able to work through distress can be empowering for the person experiencing the internal conflict. Robarts and Sloboda (1994) address issues of attachment in the individual with an eating disorder. They draw a parallel between the healthy mother-infant development and the musical improvisatory nature of that relationship. The reciprocal nature of the musical play between mother and infant encourages the development of that healthy relationship. Loth (2002) is influenced by the work of Klein and the early mother-infant relationship. She maintains that family re-enactment can be addressed through the group music therapy experience, leading to a greater awareness of family dynamics.

Developing an understanding of the adaptive function of the eating disorder is paramount to the success of treatment. Sloboda (1993) explored various instrumental sounds to represent family members of an individual with an eating disorder. This awareness of feelings associated with the sound qualities of the family led to an understanding of the ways in which this individual used food in detrimental ways to cope.

Sloboda (1995) draws upon Jungian psychotherapy to work through the goals of body awareness. Using dreams, fantasies, and myths can help women develop a more accepting relationship with their bodies.

When physical or sexual abuse precipitates an eating disorder, individuals may dissociate from their body that betrayed them, or they may regress to a time when they were smaller, prior to the abuse, when they were safe. Rogers (1995) explains how the process of clinical improvisation offers the individual the experience of deep emotional expression while being heard and musically supported. This humanistic approach to music therapy allows for unconditional, positive regard for the individual. The degree to which the music conveys the nonverbal message of "I hear you and understand you" directly relates to the amount of therapeutic change the individual can achieve.

Frederiksen (1999) draws upon the work of humanistic thought when exploring the resistance of the individual with an eating disorder. She maintained that resistance is essential in that it protects the person from feelings of emptiness and chaos. The goal in music therapy is not to eliminate the resistance but to understand it and incorporate it into the individual's understanding of the adaptive function of the eating disorder.

Medical Music Therapy

Medical music therapy focuses on helping individuals to improve, restore, or maintain physical well-being and focuses on the emotional concerns that accompany medical treatments. Medical music therapy provides a nonpharmacological intervention for decreasing stress, anxiety, and/or pain for the individual. Taylor (1997) provides a neurobiological basis for anorexia and explains how individuals can take control of their stress response through music activities by influencing cortisol output. When individuals learn to develop an "internal locus of control," they are able to develop healthy coping skills as well as develop strategies to prevent relapse.

Theoretical Considerations in Music Therapy Practice

Wheeler (1983) identifies a psychotherapeutic classification of music therapy practice, as explored earlier, that also complements treatment goals for individuals with eating disorders. She identifies three levels of music therapy practice: music therapy as an activity therapy, insight music therapy with re-educative goals, and insight music therapy with re-constructive goals.

Supportive, Activity-Oriented Music Therapy

There is little in the music therapy literature to suggest that activity-based music therapy is beneficial to the individual with an eating disorder. Parente (1989) provides the only reference to using the activity of stage production to meet the treatment goals for those with eating disorders. By actively working together, these women were able to bring about changes in their behavior surrounding their issues of increasing self-worth, maintaining commitments to others, and improving their situations. Another example of an activity-based music therapy intervention with individuals with eating disorders is learning to play an instrument to increase self-esteem and confidence. At this level of treatment, goals are achieved through activities that require little insight and cognitive abilities.

Insight Music Therapy With Re-Educative Goals

At this level of treatment, the music itself takes on a more prominent function in achieving treatment goals. The music alone elicits certain emotional and cognitive reactions necessary for therapeutic change. In the eating disorder literature, cognitive-behavioral therapy is the most researched and first line of treatment with good success rates. In cognitive-behavior therapy, the individual with an eating disorder learns to challenge faulty assumptions and dysfunctional beliefs about body weight, shape, and size. Hilliard (2001) provides examples of music therapy interventions at this level by analyzing song lyrics and writing and composing music. It is at this level that awareness of feelings in the here and now is close to consciousness. Although the music is present to elicit deeper emotions, it is the verbal dialogue and cognitive restructuring that help individuals reach their targeted goals. For instance, through music therapy, Sloboda (1993) aims to help individuals understand what function their eating disorder serves in their lives. She achieves this goal by dialoguing with her patients about the qualities of their improvisations and how this connects to their internal struggles.

Insight Music Therapy with Re-Constructive Goals

Much of the music therapy literature addressing individuals with eating disorders takes place at this level of treatment. The very nature of clinical improvisation tends to elicit unconscious material that is then worked through to help reorganize the personality. When working at this level, the therapist must be thoroughly trained in models of psychotherapy as well as psychopathology. The works of Frederiksen (1999), Robarts (1995), and Sloboda (1995) most aptly fit this category. Taking their foundation from developmental theorists, they analyze and interpret the musical improvisations as core structures in the individual's personality. Robarts maintains that a music therapy model that accesses musical dynamic form in the relationship acts as a transformer of self-organization and personality integration.

Another music therapy intervention appropriate with individuals with eating disorders is the use of the Bonny Method of Guided Imagery and Music (BMGIM). BMGIM is a process whereby the individual listens to serious, classical music in a relaxed state, allowing images, symbols, feelings, and memories to become manifest. It is through spontaneous verbalizations, movements, or art that unconscious awareness is accessed and healing occurs. (See the section on Music and Imagery in Chapter 6.)

References

American Psychiatric Association. (1994). Diagnostic and statistical manual of mental disorders *(4th ed.). Washington, DC: Author.*

Atkins, D., & Silber, T. (1993). Clinical spectrum of anorexia nervosa in children. Journal of Developmental and Behavioral Pediatrics, 14, 211–216.

Crowther, J., & Sherwood, N. (1997). Assessment. In D. Garner & P. Garfinkel (Eds.), Handbook of treatment for eating disorders (pp. 34–49). New York: Guilford Press.

Frederiksen, B. (1999). Analysis of musical improvisations to understand and work with elements of resistance in a client with anorexia nervosa. In T. Wigram & J. DeBacker (Eds.), Applications of music therapy in psychiatry (pp. 211–230). London: Jessica Kingsley.

Garner, D. M. (1991). Eating Disorder Inventory 2. Odessa, FL: Psychological Assessment Resources.

Garner, D. M., & Garfinkel, P. E. (1979). The eating attitudes test: An index of the symptoms of anorexia nervosa. Psychological Medicine, 9, 273–279.

Hilliard, R. (2001). The use of cognitive-behavioral music therapy in the treatment of women with eating disorders. Music Therapy Perspectives, 19(2), 109–113.

Justice, R. W. (1994). Music therapy interventions for people with eating disorders in an inpatient setting. Music Therapy Perspectives, 12(2), 104–110.

Lask, B., & Bryant-Waugh, R. (Eds.). (1993). Childhood onset anorexia and related eating disorders. Hillsdale, NJ: Lawrence Erlbaum Associates.

Loewy, J. (2000). Music psychotherapy assessment. Music Therapy Perspectives, 18(1), 47–58.

Loth, H. (2002). "There's no getting away from anything in here": A music therapy group within an inpatient programme for adults with eating disorders. In A. Davies & E. Richards (Eds.), Music therapy and group work (pp. 90–104). London: Jessica Kingsley.

Mitchell, J., Pomeroy, C., & Adson, D. (1997). Managing medical complications. In D. Garner & P., Garfinkel (Eds.), Handbook of treatment for eating disorders. (pp. 383–393). New York: Guilford Press.

Nolan, P. (1989). Music as a transitional object in the treatment of bulimia. Music Therapy Perspectives, 6, 49–51.

Parente, A. (1989). Feeding the hungry soul: Music as a therapeutic modality in the treatment of anorexia nervosa. Music Therapy Perspectives, 6, 44–48.

Robarts, J. (1995). Towards autonomy and a sense of self. Music therapy and the individuation process in relation to children and adolescents with early onset anorexia nervosa. In D. Dokter (Ed.), Arts therapies and clients with eating disorders (pp. 229–246). London: Jessica Kingsley.

Robarts J., & Sloboda A. (1994). Perspectives on music therapy with people suffering from anorexia nervosa. Journal of British Music Therapy, 8(1), 7–14.

Rogers, P. (1995). Sexual abuse and eating disorders: A possible connection indicated through music therapy? In D. Dokter (Ed.), Arts therapies and clients with eating disorders (pp. 262–278). London: Jessica Kingsley.

Sloboda, A. (1993). Individual therapy with a man who has an eating disorder. In M. Heal & T. Wigram (Eds.), Music therapy in health and education (pp. 103–111). London: Jessica Kingsley.

Sloboda, A. (1995). Individual music therapy with anorexia and bulimic patients. In D. Dokter (Ed.), Arts therapies and clients with eating disorders. (pp. 247–261). London: Jessica Kingsley.

Taylor, D. (1997). Biomedical determinants of control reversal therapy. In D. Taylor, Biomedical foundations of music as therapy (pp. 76–83). St Louis, MO: MMB Music.

Wheeler, B. (1983). A psychotherapeutic classification of music therapy practices: A continuum of procedures. Music Therapy Perspectives, 1(2), 8–12.

Woodside, D. (1995). A review of anorexia nervosa and bulimia nervosa. Current Problems in Pediatrics, 25, 67–89.

Additional Resources

Heal, M., & O'Hara, J. (1993). The music therapy of an anorectic mentally handicapped adult. British Journal of Medical Psychology, 66, 33–41.

Daily, L. (2004). I wanna live. On I Wanna Live [CD]. California: The House.

[Note: Laurie Daily composed a CD to help in her eating disorder recovery. She writes, "This CD (I Wanna Live) is dedicated to eating disorder recovery. I struggled with my own eating disorder and low self-esteem for many years. No matter how wounded I felt, I learned that it was my responsibility to keep facing it so that I could heal. With the help of treatment, specialized professionals, and peer support I started to enjoy life again. As time went by, I wanted to sing. I saw a vision of myself singing and telling my story of recovery. I wanted to share my gift with you, so that you can heal too . . ."]

www.edreferral.com — This International Eating Disorder and Information Center has the most comprehensive and easiest-to-search database of eating disorder treatment professionals in the world.

Chapter 12

The Forensic Mental Health Institution
Vaughn Kaser and Erin Bullard

Forensic mental health often involves a locked, secure hospital facility where patients with mental illness are placed by the courts after having committed some type of crime. This setting is different from a mental health program housed in a correctional facility, though there may be many similarities in terms of the type of treatment the patients might receive. Treatment in a forensic facility addresses the patient's legal status in addition to his or her mental health issues. The patient's legal status has an impact upon the length of stay in the facility, since state laws may specify any other agencies involved in determining when a patient is able to return to the community or wherever else he or she might be sent when released from the forensic setting.

The Legal Process

Most of the penal codes related to serious crimes committed by an individual with a mental illness are put into law by state legislatures. How the courts and the forensic mental health care system operate and work together vary by state. Even within a state there may be differences related to the mental health services available in each county. In most cases, after an adult commits a serious crime, forensic jurisdiction begins in the county jail system.

Despite the differences that occur in how laws are written within the United States, at least two similar legal statutes take into account the individual's mental condition. The first statute refers to those who are "Incompetent to Stand Trial." In most states, if the defendant is too mentally ill to understand what is happening, cannot cooperate with the attorney, and cannot prepare and conduct his or her own defense, the defendant is considered "Incompetent to Stand Trial." Most states have laws that prevent incompetent persons from being tried without full understanding of the charges being brought against them. The defendant is then sent to a facility to receive treatment for his or her mental illness and to restore competency so that the individual can return to court.

The second statute refers to those persons deemed as "Not Guilty by Reason of Insanity" (NGI), also referred to as the Insanity Defense or "Guilty but Insane." This means that the court determines that the individual was greatly impaired by his or her mental illness at the time the crime was committed. This type of commitment has very strict criteria. The NGI plea usually carries an indeterminate sentence and may require the judge to give the maximum sentence for the crime. Convicted individuals are sent to a forensic mental health facility for treatment of their mental illness. This may also prevent those with severe mental illness from being sent to a regular correctional facility where treatment is often not available. The American Bar Association (n.d.) offers general criminal justice standards to define mentally ill and mentally retarded prisoners (Standard 7-10.1)

Courts rely on mental health professionals to provide a mental health evaluation of clients and an opinion on their condition for the judge or the jury to determine the outcome of each case. The defendant with a mental illness deals with both the legal criminal court system and the mental health system. Some states have passed legislation that extends the sentence time a criminal with a mental illness is held by the state to provide further treatment if necessary. This law is specifically written to keep violent criminals out of the community if they are still considered dangerous due to mental illness. Some states have been using a similar statute to keep repeat sex offenders incarcerated for treatment of their sexually deviant behavior beyond the parole date.

The Forensic Treatment Setting

The facility described in this section is a maximum-security state hospital for adult male felons diagnosed with Axis I or Axis II mental illness (American Psychiatric Association [APA], 2000). Most of the patients in this facility have also spent time serving criminal convictions in the state correctional facilities. Forensic patients who have spent time in either juvenile facilities or prison often have more criminal-type behaviors acquired from living in this type of environment. The hospital is divided into seven different programs according to the patient's criminal code commitment type. Each program is then divided into four to five separate units. One treatment team, including the music therapist, is responsible for 35–50 patients on the unit. Some groups, such as a music therapy group, are available to patients within the same program.

Patients are initially interviewed on the unit and available groups are discussed. They are encouraged to get involved in as many groups as they would like. The only criterion for entrance to the music therapy treatment group is patient consent, though a patient's inappropriate behavior, such as being in restraints, could prevent participation. Some patients are more reluctant to get involved when they are first admitted to the unit. Encouragement from other members of the treatment team is often helpful. Patients often become more motivated to get involved when the treatment team is successful in explaining the relationship between a well-rounded therapy program and a successful conclusion to their stay in a locked facility.

Music therapy sessions are usually held in a centrally located music area within the hospital, which has several treatment rooms and a wide selection of musical instruments and sound equipment. The patients either meet together on the unit and walk to the music area together or, if permitted, go to the area on their own. Groups are usually held once a week for one hour.

The Interdisciplinary Treatment Team

The comprehensive treatment team includes a psychiatrist, psychologist, social worker, rehabilitation therapist, and a registered nurse. Disciplines that fall under rehabilitation in forensic settings might include those in the creative arts group: art therapist, dance/movement therapist, and music therapist. Creative arts therapists may also be grouped with the recreation therapist and the occupational therapist. In addition, the team may receive input from teachers, multicultural advisors or counselors, dietitians, and vocational placement advisors.

Each discipline has a specific role in the team and contributes to the overall treatment of each patient. The psychiatrist is responsible for evaluating and approving the overall treatment of the patient and is usually the head of the treatment team. The psychiatrist also prescribes and adjusts medication as needed and may provide counseling in this area. The psychologist provides various tests and evaluations for proper diagnosis of the patient and provides counseling and information for the patient regarding his mental illness. The social worker gathers patient history, medical records, and legal reports and is in contact with the family and the patient's attorney. The social worker may also provide group or individual counseling through verbal discussion.

The rehabilitation therapist, encompassing all creative arts therapists, provides information regarding social, recreational, interpersonal, and leisure time-management skills. Rehabilitation therapists provide specialized groups for the patients and assist in the overall treatment process. The nursing staff, including registered nurses, aides, or psychiatric technicians, usually spend the most time with the patients. They can provide valuable information related to a patient's personality, interpersonal skills, and general behaviors related to following directions and rules. The registered nurse provides nursing care plans, informs the patient why he is taking certain medications, and teaches medication management to the patients. Teachers often provide information related to a patient's learning disabilities and overall academic/cognitive skills.

Assessment

A patient's mental illness can be difficult to accurately diagnose and treat. External factors and psychological history affecting behavior and cognitive function may be unknown initially. Patients in a forensic setting may have additional problems related to their dangerous criminal behavior that can further add to an already complicated list of psychiatric disorders. Assessing and properly diagnosing a violent patient is not only a mental health issue; it is also a safety issue. A team of mental health professionals best completes a proper and thorough assessment. Assessing and predicting a patient's risk for dangerous or violent behavior in the future is very important in order for the team to develop the patient's treatment program.

Assessment Tests and Tools

Valuable data are gained from standardized psychological testing, live interviews with the patient, historical data, behavioral observation on the unit, and, upon permission, discussions with family members. Another useful method of assessment is the data based on observations of the patient in a variety of creative arts and recreational therapeutic group activity experiences.

In a survey of music therapists practicing in correctional psychiatry, Codding (2002) reports that 91% of the respondents did not use standardized assessment measures of any kind. Very few standardized assessments are used in forensic psychiatry, and it appears most are adapted for use by the music therapist depending on the facility. One type of assessment commonly used by recreation therapists is the Comprehensive Evaluation for Recreational Therapy, or CERT (Parker, Ellison, Kirby, & Short, 1988).

This standardized assessment tool is designed primarily for short-term psychiatric facilities as a method for assessing a patient's overall behaviors based on their participation in any therapeutic recreational activity, which could include a music therapy group. This assessment can be used to help evaluate and document changes in a patient's overall functional skills throughout the treatment process.

A similar tool developed and used at a large forensic state hospital is the Functional Skills Assessment-Rehabilitation (FSA-R). The purpose of the FSA-R is to measure behaviors associated with successful participation in rehabilitation therapy activities, as well as the level of compensatory functioning in relation to common underlying problems in the patient population. This measurement of general interpersonal and cognitive skills, required for an individual to interact successfully in any type of therapeutic group setting, can be very helpful in generalizing findings to other types of therapeutic group settings.

Creative arts and therapeutic activity observational assessments are conducted within social interactive groups where the patients are asked to spontaneously interact, cooperate, and work together as a team with other patients and staff. Whether it is playing softball, improvising music, or painting a mural, each patient responds differently depending upon his or her own set of interpersonal characteristics. Consequently, each patient's individual set of mental health problems creates dysfunctional characteristics or has impact upon these characteristics, which trained therapists can then assess from their observations of the group.

In addition to observing and identifying dysfunctional interpersonal skills, the creative arts therapists are able to provide further assessment of the patient's mental health problems based upon the manner in which the individual expresses himself through the arts medium. Expression of any kind usually reflects the individual's personality, emotional state, and other internal factors not otherwise readily apparent or observable. Knowing how mental illness and dysfunctional behavior affects movement, creating visual art, and playing music is an important and useful facet of all the creative arts therapies.

Music Therapy Assessment

At this time, there are no standardized, written music therapy assessment tools developed specifically for the forensic mental health patient population. However, it is possible to observe and collect important data related to patients' forensic mental health problems from the way they play in a music therapy improvisation group. A study by Boone (1991) found that improvisation was the most effective assessment technique in working with an incarcerated male diagnosed with paranoid schizophrenia. Observation of how the patient plays an instrument provides data on instrument use and ability to be expressive, while an observation of how the patient interacts musically with the group provides further social and interpersonal data (Bruscia, 1987). Reed (2002) explains that mental illness can affect musical behavior and notes that music improvisation was significant in revealing how mental illness affected a patient's playing. The music therapy assessment needs to measure not just musical skills and aptitude, but the skills necessary to make progress in treatment (Loewy, 2000). This information is extremely useful for developing an effective treatment plan for both the music therapist and the treatment team.

The music therapist can assess various symptoms of the patient's illness by learning how musical behavior is affected by a mental illness. For example, a psychotic patient may have difficulty feeling the pulse and playing on the beat. Cohen (1987) describes the musical behavior of an incarcerated male recovering from a psychotic episode. Limited expressive and physical range on the xylophone is compared with his behavior outside of music. A sex offender with a narcissistic personality is self-focused, ignores the rest of the group, and plays louder than everyone else (Kaser, 1991). Both situations can be viewed as an impairment that affects the coordination of individuals' mental processes and functioning within their environment.

Assessing musical interactive behaviors in a music therapy improvisation group can be done over a period of time. The therapist should take careful notes after each group to document the behaviors observed. The patient may need several sessions to play in a group to develop some coordination and skill. Proficiency of playing an instrument may affect how the patient actually expresses himself musically in the group. Certain playing behaviors, style, and patterns begin to emerge that can be identified in relation to the patient's diagnosis. A patient may have difficulty with control, impulsiveness, listening to and respecting others, and responding spontaneously to others. The lack of flexibility in personality becomes even more apparent when an Axis II diagnosis is involved (APA, 2000).

It is recommended that the therapist provide a wide range of percussion instruments, including xylophones, and encourage the patients to play a variety of instruments. In a structured music improvisation assessment format, the therapist can quickly observe and collect data related to how patients' mental illness affects their behavior. The structured format emphasizes the use of order to structure movement through the experience (Bruscia, 1987).

The structured improvisation assessment may be designed as follows:

- The therapist sets out a variety of percussion instruments such as drums, hand-held instruments, and xylophones in the room.
- The patient selects any instrument of his or her choice in the room.
- The therapist plays a blues progression or song on the guitar or piano and encourages the patient to improvise to the structured set of chord changes. If the patient is given a xylophone, further assessment data can be collected. This method encourages the patient to try to organize musical thoughts by playing a melody. Having the patient begin offers data related to the patient's ability to establish a steady pulse when playing alone.
- The therapist should improvise along with the patient on any instrument as well. It will be possible to observe how the patient is able to interact spontaneously with one person.
- After the improvisation ends, the therapist may want to ask the patient a few questions about the experience related to how the patient felt about the experience.

To illustrate this process, the patient may not feel it is necessary to play the xylophone in an organized melodic manner. When playing a chord progression, the therapist can ask any patient in the group to play a solo during the song in order to encourage melodic expression. Problems in free melodic expression on the xylophone may indicate problems that are affecting the patient's ability to organize and express his or her feelings (Bruscia, 1987).

This music improvisation playing experience takes less than 30 minutes. When it is over, the therapist has a considerable amount of data related to how patients' mental illness affects their musical behaviors, which, in turn, relates to their ability to express themselves rhythmically and melodically and to their interactive ability—how well they listen to and respond spontaneously to another person. Observations of patients' playing behaviors should be documented objectively and can be interpreted by the music therapist.

Typical Music Therapy Goals and Treatment Objectives

Music therapy can be a valuable treatment approach in a forensic mental health setting. Music therapy groups are usually offered to any patient who is deemed appropriate by the treatment team and interested in participating in this type of treatment. Groups often include clients with a wide variety of diagnoses, issues, levels of functioning, or reasons for commitment. The musical sounds and the interactive musical expressive experience within the group provides unique therapeutic benefits to the patients in a forensic mental health setting as with most patient populations.

Music therapy has the potential for addressing several of the problems a patient might have that may contribute to behaviors associated with criminal and destructive behavior. The goals and objectives presented in this section address the types of problematic behaviors these patients often exhibit. Patients diagnosed with personality disorders often have a negative attitude toward any type of therapeutic group. Personality disorders, especially antisocial personality disorders, are generally considered nonamenable to any treatment (Cellini, Hinze, Speaker, & Wood, 2000). Many of their problems relate to lack of interpersonal skills and inability to get along with others.

The primary therapeutic goals and treatment objectives with a forensic mental health population addressed in this chapter include the following:

- To reduce resistance and help to develop a more positive attitude toward the therapeutic experience
- To improve reality testing and integration
- To reduce stress, frustration, and anger through positive physiological effects
- To develop awareness of and the ability to express feelings
- To develop interpersonal skills

Reducing Resistance

Reducing a patient's negative defensive attitude toward the therapeutic process is often a necessary objective in the forensic mental health setting. Resistance is a common characteristic of many patients in treatment (Elliott, 2002). Psychological defenses such as denial, rationalization, or intellectualization can work to prevent patients from having insight into their own problems (APA, 2000). The process of change begins when patients are willing to admit that they have a problem (Cellini, 2002). Patients who are resistant to treatment cannot begin the process needed to effectively treat the problems related to the mental illness or criminal behavior.

Many patients in a forensic mental health treatment setting have "criminal" personality traits from being incarcerated for long periods of time or from problems stemming from juvenile incarceration. These individuals can be especially resistant and oppositional toward any type of treatment. The basic "tough guy" from a prison environment has learned the importance of not revealing anything about himself to others that might be used against him (Allen & Bosta, 1981).

Trust is particularly important in a forensic setting where patients often have to discuss their criminal behavior. Being able to trust others is a personality trait that develops at a very early age between the child and the parents. The lack of trust first developed with the parent leads to problems with other authoritative figures encountered in life, such as teachers, counselor/

therapists, coaches, bosses, and law enforcement officials. Defenses may rise over issues of being told what to do, following directions and rules, and losing a sense of personal control. In addition to trust, issues related to control can lead to poor self-image or low self-esteem. This becomes more apparent with individuals who experienced difficulty during important developmental periods in their early years.

In addition to developmental issues, Cellini et al. (2000) identify common behaviors such as "verbal aggression, negative comparisons, defensiveness, manipulation, threat making, exaggeration and lying" (p. 83) among offenders diagnosed with antisocial personality disorder that work against the therapeutic process. There may be little direct psychotherapeutic treatment provided for helping a patient work through issues related to traumatic childhood events and serious mental illness. Therapeutic approaches such as the creative arts therapies can indirectly address some of the issues related to patients' resistance to involvement in treatment.

Resistance can be lowered when fewer demands are placed on the patient by the therapist during the group. Resistant and defensive patients have problems following rules, being told what to do, and having to conform. Most locked institutions run a very structured schedule, which leaves the patient with little control over any aspect of his daily life. They are often required to wear a certain type of clothing, and personal possessions are restricted for security reasons. Unlike some psychiatric patients, they are not able to refuse treatment and sign themselves out of the institution.

Music therapy work with resistance. Kaser (1991) found that music therapy contributed to reducing resistance in the treatment of sex offenders. When appropriate, the treatment team or the therapist should provide a variety of groups and allow patients to choose the type of group to attend and how they will participate in the group. This can be easily achieved through choice of song, instrument, and improvisational activity. Loth (1996) explains the benefit of using music therapy is in the patient's ability to express his anger about having to attend treatment while participating in the group. This makes it possible for the patients to have a sense of control over their own treatment. When a patient refuses every type of group, the therapist may assign the patient to a group initially and provide positive reinforcements for attending.

An effective way to reduce resistance is to engage the patient in a meaningful experience. Musical instruments can be something patients are motivated to try and can lead to the enthusiasm and spontaneity that counters resistance (Loth, 1996). Music also provides a safe ground for developing trust with resistive patients through techniques such as musically synchronizing (to musically coincide in time), syncopating (to accent beats that are normally unaccented while maintaining musical cohesion), and imitating (to copy the musical presentation) (Cohen, 1987). The immediate and initial connections made with the fundamental issues (trust, control, self-esteem) at the root of the patient's problems is accomplished by the therapist sharing in the interactive experience with the patient.

Music therapy can be a nonthreatening supportive experience for a resistant patient. As a treatment team member, the music therapist can provide interesting and often enjoyable experiences for patients. A case study by Boone (1991) illustrates a mentally ill offender who was able to increase appropriate verbal interactions through decreased resistance in music therapy. The trust and rapport developed through music therapy can then be transferred to the treatment team.

Reality Testing and Integration

Reality testing is defined as "the ability to distinguish one's thoughts, feelings, and perceptions (internal reality) as separate from external reality" (Nolan, 1991, p. 464). When dealing with disorders such as schizophrenia, psychosis, mood disorders, or personality disorders, the objective to improve reality testing is a necessary part of treatment. The positive effects, related to continuing improvements in the patient's overall internal integration and the interactions with others then continues with involvement in many treatment modalities, including music therapy.

Medication is the most frequent treatment for the symptoms of mental illness with an organic etiology. Antidepressants and antipsychotic medications are commonly prescribed. However, psychotropic drugs do not completely cure chronic mental illnesses such as schizophrenia. Negative symptoms such as lethargy, social withdrawal, and thought disorders persist, in addition to side effects from the medication. A number of authors (Reed, 2000; Smeltekop & Houghton, 1990) provide an overview of how medications affect individuals with mental illness and how music therapy is used to bring patients into balance.

The function of music and music therapy in reality testing. Playing musical instruments such as drums, hand percussion instruments, and xylophones in a freely improvised manner with others calls upon the coordination and integration of the individual's neuropsychological processes. Musical stimulation of multiple areas of the individual's brain, coupled with the active physical/musical expression, creates a multilevel stimulation feedback system, which, in effect, helps the individual become more integrated with the world of others, in this case the music therapy group. There is a powerful, grounding integrative experience in group drumming that involves (a) playing a drum, (b) feeling the vibration of the sounds inside the body, (c) simultaneously hearing the sounds of the individual's drum and the group's playing, (d) feeling the motion of the body and the hand striking the drum surface, and (e) watching the movements of others in the group playing their instruments.

When using a structured improvisation, additional reinforcement is potentially provided through the use of familiar songs, singing the lyrics, and the use of a predetermined tempo played by the therapist for the group to follow. Playing the xylophone also involves both sides of the brain, since playing a melodic musical statement involves a linear thought process similar to putting words together when speaking. Patients with schizophrenia often strike random notes when playing the xylophone. They have difficulty playing meaningful or organized melodic linear statements, as Boone (1991) describes in a case study with a patient diagnosed as paranoid schizophrenic.

The task of maintaining present awareness for the duration of the music experience is also one of reality testing. Hallucinations, grandiose delusions, and short attention spans often impose on the patient's ability to focus. Playing a musical instrument in a group helps a patient feel more whole and individually connected, while also creating positive connections with others through the mutual musical experience. Any music therapy group such as a performance group, sing along, or improvisation can address the objective of improving a patient's reality testing, grounding, ability to focus, and awareness of the psychosocial connection with others (Reed, 2002).

Reducing Stress, Frustration, and Anger

Patients who have a low frustration tolerance or consistent negative attitudes can benefit from stress-reducing activities. Patients are not always aware of appropriate ways to reduce stress and tension. Instead, they may turn to alcohol, drugs, abusive relationships, or other forms of self-destructive behavior as stress-releasing activities.

Playing instruments can help reduce stress directly through a physical release of muscular stress by moving and through striking instruments, particularly the drums (Kaser, 1991). When songs are used during a structured improvisation experience, the patients are encouraged to sing. The physiological effect of singing is similar to an aerobic workout, in part due to the deep breathing that is employed when a person sings.

An uplifting physiological effect occurs when the improvisation group is playing and interacting rhythmically together. The combination of the physical action involved in playing the instruments, the effect of feeling and hearing the sound vibrations, and the exhilarating effect of the group experience all seem to contribute to the stress reduction and relaxation response. Group music improvisation may help to reduce the negative symptoms of their illness at least while they are playing. The objective is to attempt to distance or disconnect oneself from the stress and frustration of the physical world through the music. An enjoyable spontaneous musical improvisation can create this feeling of being so involved in the music that there is a feeling of being taken away. Listening to music or guided relaxation to music can create this same experience (Kaser, 1993; Nolan, 1983).

Stress-reducing effects from music experiences may be temporary. Some patients still have difficulty controlling their behavior or emotions when they get angry. The more opportunities a patient has to experience a sense of self-control and remain relaxed, the more likely the effects generalize to other aspects of their lives. With repetition of this type of therapy, the positive effects of such a relaxation experience can help reduce anger or allow for more control (Hakvoort, 2002). This type of treatment can allow the patient to experience increased self-esteem by way of controlling and contributing to his own treatment.

The most serious problems the treatment team encounters in a forensic mental health setting are related to the patients' difficulty controlling their anger and acting out in some type of destructive manner. Anger is an emotional response that often leads to aggressive and violent behavior (Davis & Boster, 1988). Anger can trigger crimes such as assault, murder, rape, armed robbery, kidnapping, and arson.

Music therapy can address goals related to the reduction of anger. An anger management program described by Hakvoort (2002) utilizes music to experience and recognize symptoms of anger while playing or listening to music. By practicing control techniques in a safe, controlled environment, the patients are able to develop coping skills (Hakvoort, 2002). Patients' criminal behavior is often directly related to their anger management problems. Fulford (2002) recognized that drumming and singing are effective for relaxation and anger management with this population. Playing musical instruments can help patients relax, reduce anger, develop a more positive attitude, and improve mood.

Expressing Feelings and the Cathartic Effect

Many forensic patients defend against experiencing their feelings. As previously mentioned, they are often in denial of their feelings and tend to intellectualize and rationalize their frustration and anger. These defense mechanisms operate to prevent the individual from experiencing any unwanted feelings. This process begins at an early age, particularly when the individual experiences his or her psychological or abusive trauma. The lack of awareness of feelings reduces the offender's interest in resolving problems in a rational and controlled manner. When too much stress and frustration builds up, these individuals become overwhelmed by their feelings and act out in irrational, aggressive, or violent ways. The tough-guy prison persona and attitude supports the macho male suppression of displays of emotional expression that might be perceived by others as weakness.

Mental illness also creates a difficulty with verbal expression and inappropriate nonverbal expression. Thought disorders may accompany schizophrenia and some affective disorders (APA, 2000). Difficulty in expressing thoughts creates problems when patients attempt to verbally process any frustration and anger they feel. As a result, stress and anger continue to build until they can no longer control their urge to release these feelings through violence.

This type of patient may be able to express his or her feelings in a music therapy group. Loth (1996) describes the value of music therapy for self-expression with forensic patients as "a context in which patients can admit to problems and begin to get in touch with their feelings through externalizing them in the music" (p. 564). It can be very rewarding for patients with a mental illness to verbally express themselve after struggling to do so in other treatment settings. Priestley (1994) suggests, "Sometimes intense emotion may be expressed in a patient's music but the verbalization of this emotion may be blocked" (p. 171). Experiences such as a music therapy improvisation group allow the patients to develop an awareness of their feelings and to express and process these feelings. The cathartic process is particularly important for forensic mental health patients who have problems controlling their violent behavior. Patients often indicate that catharsis is the most valuable aspect of the group (Loth, 1996).

The group dynamics involved in the interactive experience between the patients and the music therapist recreate factors that often trigger anger and frustration. The process of transference is another important psychological concept for the music therapist to understand when discussing the expression of subconscious feelings during a music therapy group. The cathartic release of suppressed subconscious feelings often occurs during interactions resembling the original traumatic events that caused the defense mechanisms to develop in the first place (Nolan, 1983).

For example, a patient who had angry feelings toward his abusive father may feel the therapist (as the father figure in the group) is trying to control him (much like the father did in the past) by playing the drum louder during the musical improvisation. In this case, the patient may suddenly begin to play his instrument even louder in a very aggressive manner. The music therapist needs advanced training in counseling skills to fully observe and understand this interaction. The music therapist can then process this interaction with the patient and connect the patient's conscious cognitive awareness of the memory with the bodily sensation of his angry feelings expressed in the musical interaction.

Interpersonal Skill Development

The term *interpersonal* is often used in mental health facilities to identify a wide range of personality traits and behaviors. Interpersonal problems with this population are often directly related to criminal behavior. The difficulties patients have communicating effectively, problem solving, cooperating, and empathizing with others are often the reason they might turn to violence when dealing with other people. The lack of social problem-solving skills characteristic of mentally ill offenders contributes to interpersonal problems, including criminal activities (McMurran, Egan, Blair, & Richardson, 2001).

Interpersonal problems are often present in the Axis II personality disorders (i.e., antisocial, narcissistic, and borderline). The criteria for the diagnosis of these disorders include behaviors such as lying, cheating, disregard for the safety of others, manipulation, aggressiveness, and impulsivity, as well as having been diagnosed with a childhood conduct disorder (APA, 2000). Individuals with personality disorders often have a history of physical or sexual abuse, neglect, separation from parents, or dysfunctional relationships with significant others beginning in childhood. Difficulty in relationships continue through the course of development, causing the patient to be resistant to change and, thus, challenging to treat successfully (APA, 2000).

Though a mental illness and illicit substance use may alter one's personality to some degree, it should be noted that the great majority of mentally ill patients do not act violently when their illness is in an acute phase. In many cases of criminal behavior committed by violent patients against another person, there is a lack of the fundamental respect and caring for the victim of their aggressive act. This fundamental respect and caring for others is empathy. A lack of empathy for others, combined with a lack of awareness of one's own aggressive actions, is a common symptom of the most dangerous forensic patient with a mental illness (Fernandez, Anderson, & Marshall, 1999).

Cognitive behavioral techniques are commonly utilized in forensic mental health facilities to address violent behavior and inappropriate interpersonal relations. Structured step-by-step problem-solving methods can be taught to patients to help develop more positive interpersonal behaviors. However, a cognitive behavioral treatment group setting does not allow opportunity for the patients to experience how to use these new skills in situations where they are emotionally involved in conflict with another person. Patients in forensic facilities often have limited imagination and concrete cognitive processes, making this form of treatment ineffective. Davis and Boster (1988) suggest creative arts therapy as an effective alternative for learning appropriate social skills. Experiences that allow patients to be involved in an interactive group can automatically provide the opportunity for them to become emotionally engaged. Through this level of personal investment in the experience, the patients may develop the appropriate interpersonal skills for working with others.

Treatment success in many forensic facilities, where the most dangerous patients are often placed, should be measured on a continuum. The lower end of the scale represents patients who are chronically assaultive and mentally ill who may never return to the community. In this case, the number of weeks or even days between assaultive incidents might measure success. Higher functioning patients may actually develop insight into their violent patterns of behavior and emotion. Music therapy can address the objective at any point on this continuum by providing the opportunity for the direct spontaneous expression of feelings.

Music Therapy Interventions and Techniques

A number of music therapy interventions are useful for work with patients in forensic facilities.

Music Therapy Group Logistics

It is important for the music therapist to consider the following components of a music therapy group when planning a session for these clients:

- number of patients in the group
- length of time allotted for the group
- how often the group will meet
- specific entry criteria
- method for selecting which patients will be in the group
- structure of the group; primarily supportive or more psychodynamic
- specific treatment issues: sex offenders, substance abuse issues, etc.
- size and location of the room
- overall treatment style of the team

Consideration should be given to the overall disabling effect the patient's problems have on group and musical behaviors. Assessing the patient's musical behaviors prior to the group helps the therapist determine what type and size of group is best for the patient. A smaller group includes between two to four patients; a larger group may have six to eight patients. Depending on the institution, group size will vary. A survey by Codding (2002) reveals that the average group size with this population is 7–15 patients. The larger the group size and the more severe the disabilities, the more challenging it may be for the group to play together musically.

Supportive and Psychotherapeutic Groups

Two general ways to structure the interventions implemented with this population include supportive and psychodynamic types of groups. Supportive groups focus on the music and the interactions and behaviors between the patients. Psychodynamic or psychotherapeutic groups focus on developing patients' insight into their treatment issues through the music. The music experience may be structured in similar ways for both types of groups. The difference is in how the experience is verbally processed.

A *supportive group* focuses on the present actions. Discussion pertains primarily to the music and the musical interactions between the group members. Redirection is favored over confrontation (Fulford, 2002). The patients in the *psychodynamic group* utilize the music as a means to go deeper into the interpersonal interactions and their feelings related to the experience (Boone, 1991; Nolan, 1983). The therapist might provide the opportunity for discussion and interpretation of how the music experience allows for certain social and emotional behaviors to occur. There is the possibility for confrontation and sharing of patients' more personal information about themselves in the psychotherapeutic group (Bruscia, 1998).

Thaut (1987) explains the function of verbal processing and states the therapist's role is to "facilitate, support, and clarify verbalizations made by the group" (p. 49). Psychotherapeutic music experiences require the music therapist to have advanced training in this area or to co-lead the group with another mental health professional who has advanced training and experience working with this population.

Specific Music Therapy Interventions

The interventions presented here reflect the goals and objectives discussed in this chapter. Though other music therapy interventions not discussed here may address the same objectives, slight variations in method and structure are not likely to change the innate therapeutic benefits derived from the music or the expressive musical experience. Each intervention can be structured as a supportive or psychodynamic group. The categories of music therapy interventions that are discussed include the following:

- Music listening to reduce resistance and help reduce stress
- Music therapy improvisation groups, including free and structured improvisation methods
- Music therapy performance groups, including bands, choirs, etc.
- Bonny Method of Guided Imagery and Music (BMGIM)
- Therapeutic listening
- Lyric analysis groups

Many patients with low self-esteem in a forensic facility are initially reluctant to try new things for fear of losing control, making a commitment, or being overwhelmed by their feelings in this type of group. It is important to allow the patients to have the space and time they need to move at their own pace. One of the therapeutic objectives of the group is for the patients to exercise some control of themselves and their treatment program. If a patient insists on leaving or attempts the activity but decides not to stay in the group, the therapist should support that decision.

Music listening to reduce resistance. A simple music listening group may be the least threatening and the most therapeutic type of group for a resistant patient. Once the group is oriented to the structure of the group, such as rules and responsibilities of the patients, the process of music selection can begin. Each patient selects at least one song for listening. A music listening group presented by Reed (2002) "stressed tolerance of individual differences" (p. 100). When developing this tolerance in resistant patients, it is recommended that no other demands be placed on the patient.

The music listening group can be expanded to the next level of patient involvement. "The music offers a comfortable and reality-based starting point which also motivates the individual to speak up" (Thaut, 1987, p. 49). Some patients may enjoy making comments while their music is being played and appreciate hearing positive comments about the music they selected. The therapist can allow time between recordings for comments. Discussion and comments about the music selected in this group must be carefully structured to create a safe and enjoyable environment.

The patients have some type of emotional investment in the songs they choose to play in the group. The song can be their way of expressing to others how they are feeling (Kaser, 1993). The patient who selected the song being discussed may take comments made by others in the group very personally. Comments made by the therapist can have an impact upon the group and should be supportive or reflective of feelings expressed by the recording. The therapist should refrain from asking "therapeutic" questions, such as "How did that song make you feel?" during this type of supportive listening experience. The therapist might make a statement such as, "What a powerful message. Kid Rock makes me feel very energized," then turn the attention back to others in the group by asking what they think.

The supportive music therapy listening group is much less demanding than other types of verbal psychotherapy groups. Resistant patients can also develop the behaviors needed to be successful in other treatment settings through the music listening group. Patients must learn when the group is held and to be on time for each session. They learn that all groups have rules and routines to which everyone must conform. If a conflict comes up in the group, they learn how to communicate and solve problems with others in the group (Reed, 2002).

Music listening to help reduce stress. Stress associated with the patients' inability to communicate effectively may be reduced through the selection of songs that express feelings to which the patients relate (Kaser, 1993). A music listening group in which the patients choose music can provide this outlet. It is just as important for the therapist to listen to the songs and share the experience with the patients as it is to encourage verbal comments. It is through the sharing of and expressing of feelings through the music that the relationship to others can begin.

Patients who have difficulty controlling their anger and aggressive behavior can greatly benefit from stress-reducing activities. They need to identify feelings of stress and tension in order to learn coping mechanisms (Hakvoort, 2002). Once this is accomplished, application of stress-reducing techniques may then be taught (Thaut, 1999). A popular relaxation technique is progressive muscle relaxation with background music (Jacobson, 1974). This involves contracting and relaxing isolated muscle groups while listening to relaxing music. These types of music therapy groups also provide the patients with skills they can utilize independently.

When referring a patient to a music relaxation group, the music therapist needs to consider the subjective effect music has on the individual. Patients may not experience relaxation when listening to music with which they are not familiar. Others may feel more relaxed when listening to music they enjoy, regardless of style, because of the personal effect it has on them. The music therapist should assess each individual response to the music. Patients who experience active psychosis are not appropriate for this technique (Summer, 1988).

Personal music listening devices are popular with many patients. They allow patients to listen to music they like and simultaneously reduce the stimulation of the environment. Schizophrenic patients who hear voices comment that listening to music through headphones helps reduce the negative impact of voices in their heads. These devices provide the patients with a personal relaxing music activity any time they need it.

The music therapy improvisation group. The use of improvisation as an intervention is the most frequently reported form of music therapy in all the articles reviewed for this chapter. Drumming and improvisation was utilized in a treatment program for adult male sexual offenders to increase self-expression and awareness of feelings, cooperation, and coping skills (Watson, 2002). Thaut (1999) presents the musical semantics model that consists of a hierarchy of three levels in the therapeutic process primarily related to continuous development of the individuals' ability to express themselves in a more organized manner. This organized expression leads to clients' ability to engage in interactive play and ability to transition into more meaningful musical expressions. Improvisation on melodic instruments such as piano and xylophone allowed for the development of insight with a violent patient through interaction with the music therapist (Sloboda, 1997). This section provides an additional approach to music therapy improvisation with the forensic patient. Free and structured improvisations have been utilized by this author to address the goal areas presented in this chapter for several years of practice in a large state hospital.

A number of issues in structure should be considered in improvisation groups. The treatment room where the improvisation group takes place has a piano, full drum set, LP congas, mounted bongos, temple blocks, large gong, and speakers for the sound system in the room. The patients in the group help set up the rest of the instruments used, which include a bass xylophone, alto/soprano xylophone, slit drum, a box containing a variety of nontuned percussion instruments, and microphones. When a drum set is used, the patient should be encouraged to play it as if several different percussion instruments were arranged close together and to start out playing one part at a time. Patients who have little experience with the drum set tend to play a full set in a very disorganized and disruptive manner. It is not necessary to use a full drum set; instead, a single snare drum and a cymbal can be used to create a rock beat. The instruments are set up in a circle. Instruments must also be put away when the group is over.

As a more structured experience, improvising to a familiar song or chord progression has been successful in this facility. Using songs or chord progressions, such as the 12-bar blues form, also makes the group more appealing for resistant patients. Both methods provide additional structure and grounding for the more mentally ill or impaired patients (Reed, 2002).

When using songs in a structured improvisation, the group is provided with a songbook that contains the lyrics to a variety of songs. Music stands are used so the patients are able to sing the lyrics and play an instrument at the same time. The lead singer or xylophone solo may need to be amplified with a microphone. Patients who enjoy singing in the group should take turns at the microphone. Pitches on the xylophone should be arranged in a scale that matches the key signature and style. For example, a blues song in the key of C will sound more like the blues if a B is added to the pitches on the xylophone.

Structured improvisations are approached differently than free improvisation. Depending on the musical functioning level of the group, it may be best for the therapist to start on piano or guitar or have an experienced patient establish a simple steady beat. The patients improvise on various instruments to the basic beat and tempo and continue on while the lyrics are sung. Xylophone solos should be encouraged during designated instrumental sections in the song or chord progression. The rest of the group continues to play, supporting the solo. The group should be encouraged to listen and follow the soloist on the other instruments. When the solos are completed, the rest of the lyrics are sung or part of the song should be repeated over again.

The end of the song is the time when the group and the therapist can be more spontaneous and free with their playing by repeating the chord structure. Different song forms and chord progressions offer a slightly different quality and challenge to the improvisation experience. Simple musical parts or riffs can be taught to the group to provide the patient with an additional cognitive challenge and reward once it is mastered (Reed, 2002).

A structured improvisation experience is designed to resemble a musical performance group. Musical talent is not necessary, and patients with an interest in expressing themselves musically are able to get involved. On the outside, this musical experience does not appear "therapeutic" to the resistant forensic patient who is avoiding getting involved in treatment. Combining free and structured improvisation methods in one group may be effective in encouraging the patients to try both ways of expressing themselves musically.

A more spontaneous type of improvisation is free improvisation. In this type of improvisation, the beginning of the session is used to introduce and orient new patients, make announcements, or briefly discuss anything the group might need to talk about before playing. The patients choose an instrument and can play and move around at the same time if they would like as long as they do not interfere with anyone else in the group. There are only a few rules during a free improvisation: no talking, and do not abuse the instruments. Improvised vocal sounds or spontaneous lyrical comments are encouraged.

In this improvisation, the therapist should first consider how the group might start and end the improvisation. Depending on the functioning level of the patients, the therapist may want to provide several options the group can choose from or simply ask the group how they would like to start. Some options the therapist can suggest are:

- ask the group who wants to start the improvisation;
- use a rotation system that gives each patient a chance to begin;
- try a spontaneous beginning after a brief moment of silence.

The group often suggests that the therapist take the lead. When confronted with this option, the now-reluctant therapist can remind the group that they are rejecting an opportunity to have control over what happens to them in a setting where this is rarely the case.

The therapist may employ one of two ways for the group to end an improvisation. The first suggestion is to select a member of the group before playing begins to be responsible for initiating the ending. The second method is to allow the group to find its own way to end spontaneously. In both situations, the therapist should instruct the group to avoid using verbal comments or movements such as hand gestures to end the playing. A spontaneous ending may take several sessions to accomplish as a group. Within groups where the patients are having difficulty following and listening to each other, a change in the music towards the end may cause the patients to begin paying more attention to each other.

Time should be given for some amount of verbal discussion or processing of the musical experience. The therapist should decide in advance and discuss with the group what will be expected of them during this part of the music therapy improvisation group. There is often a need for many patients to make comments after the music has ended. The therapist should allow the group to talk without interfering as long as their discussion is related to the playing experience.

In a supportive group where there is less emphasis on verbal processing, the therapist may still want to encourage some discussion related to how the group thought they sounded, what they liked or disliked about the experience, how to improve their playing, etc. The basic idea would be to focus the discussion on the music and the patients' musical experience in a positive and less intimidating fashion.

After the discussion phase is complete, the group should then prepare to play again. This would be the time for the patients to switch instruments they are playing. The therapist may want to change the notes on the xylophones to help create a contrasting feeling to the next improvisation. The group can play another free improvisation as just discussed, or the therapist may want to include a structured improvisation method of some type.

Music therapy performance group. This type of music therapy group is structured with the primary goal of rehearsing music to be performed for an audience in the future. The performance group can be a rock band, jazz band, choir, bell choir, or classical ensemble, to name a few. In forensic mental health facilities, the concert must be scheduled somewhere within the secured area. Most facilities have an auditorium or stage area that can hold a performance. In many prisons, these musicians also often provide musical ensembles for religious services.

Performance groups allow the patients to display what they learned and express themselves in a socially appropriate manner (Reed, 2002). This helps support positive self-esteem and self-image. Rehearsing and working toward the goal of performing and receiving the appreciation of the audience is a very uplifting experience. The length of stay is often much longer than other psychiatric settings, allowing enough time to learn the music and performance skills. When the patients are able to achieve a certain level of success in the quality of their effort, they often feel a sense of accomplishment. This can motivate them to practice independently and exercise constructive use of unstructured leisure time, especially those who were musicians prior to being arrested.

A music therapy performance group is an excellent opportunity for the patients to develop their interpersonal skills. Problems with interpersonal skills, such as problem solving, listening and responding to others, cooperation, and empathy can be addressed in this type of group. Issues the patients have with listening and being able to work together successfully directly impact the quality of the music performed. This type of group offers the patients incentive for developing and improving themselves through the music. They must cooperate in order to create the desired sound. The patients also receive immediate feedback of their skill level through the musical product. This also allows the therapist to provide minimal feedback.

To combat resistance, patients who are interested in playing music or singing may be willing to get involved in the music therapy group. The music therapist should put emphasis on playing music and developing personal musical skills as opposed to addressing personal problems and issues the patients in the group are struggling to deal with in treatment. The verbal processing used in the improvisation group might be minimized or omitted from the group process in a performance group.

The basic concept behind creating an environment that is less threatening than typical therapy groups for the resistive patient is to place emphasis on playing instruments and making music so the patients do not feel they are involved in more of a "psychotherapy" type of group. Once the patient is willing to attend this type of group, he can then begin to develop a more positive attitude toward other treatment groups.

A music therapy performance group can be structured to allow the patients opportunities to have more control over what happens in the group. The patients can help decide what type of music the group is going to play. Patients who have musical skills may be able to lead the group in playing a song. They might have to teach others in the group how to play it as well. All patients in the group should be encouraged to offer their feedback and suggestions related to how the song should be played. When playing familiar songs, the therapist may want to encourage the group to create their own arrangements.

When the group performs, the live concert experience offers the patients an excellent opportunity to utilize their life skills. Playing in front of a live audience can be an exciting and stressful experience for the patients in the group. It is a real opportunity to test their ability to perform under pressure (Reed, 2002). It is something most musicians enjoy doing and can be a very positive therapeutic experience for the patients in a forensic facility.

Bonny Method of Guided Imagery and Music. The use of the Bonny Method Guided Imagery and Music (BMGIM) in forensic psychiatric settings is not widely reported on or published in the music therapy literature. Caution should be taken when referring a patient for GIM or even a simple imagery to music activity. Music-assisted imagery of any kind is contraindicated for individuals with active psychosis, such as the hallucinations that can be present in schizophrenia (Summer, 1988). BMGIM can be successful with certain patients under the guidance of a properly trained and experienced therapist. Nolan (1983) found that the use of GIM with a forensic psychiatric patient temporarily lifted defenses to allow the patient to deal with his feelings. It is possible that insight therapy and treatment for past events can be of some benefit.

Therapeutic listening and lyric analysis groups. Music listening groups can be structured as psychodynamic treatment experiences as well as supportive experiences. The effect music has on one's ability to express a range of moods and feelings is the fundamental characteristic that makes it possible to construct a therapeutic listening experience. Songs selected by the therapist in a guided lyric analysis group can be helpful by encouraging patients to address important issues they may be avoiding. There are several ways groups or individual music therapy sessions can be structured to address treatment issues using music as a therapeutic tool.

Small music listening groups can be structured to give the patients an opportunity to select and play music they enjoy for the group. This technique is different than the listening group previously described. When songs are played, the focus is on the lyrics and the music together. This choice reveals how the patient is feeling to the therapist and the rest of the group. Songs can be used as a springboard for patients to use their own words to elaborate further on how they relate to the lyrics. The therapist and the group can offer feedback related to a song to help a patient gain insight into why he or she might have chosen that particular song. In a therapeutic setting, a patient might choose song lyrics that reflect significant subconscious repressed feelings unknown to the patient (Kaser, 1993).

In another type of lyric analysis group, the therapist selects specific songs to help the patients become more aware of feelings relating to an issue important to all patients in the group. The songs selected for this type of group contain lyrics that express universal feelings to which almost everyone can relate. For example, patients involved in substance abuse programs often have troubling experiences that contributed to their substance abuse problem or were the result of those problems. Songs that express the songwriter's feelings related to a certain experience often become popular as a result of others being able to relate and have their feelings validated through the song. Patients can also learn to identify certain aggressive or abusive behaviors through lyric analysis (Gallagher & Steele, 2002).

Music therapists should be aware of various genres of songs, both old and new, that express the types of feelings their patients may be experiencing. A large collection of music makes it more likely for all the patients to find something to which they can relate. The patients will always be a good resource of new or useful songs as well.

Case Studies in Forensic Music Therapy

Case Study 1: Reducing Resistance With Individual Music Listening

Frank was a mentally disordered sex offender with an Axis I diagnosis of schizoaffective disorder and a substance abuse disorder. He was committed to the forensic state hospital for sexually molesting his young niece. Frank had a very low frustration tolerance and was often irritable and angry. He could become loud, verbally abusive, and very intimidating when he was angry, but he was not usually assaultive. His sexually inappropriate behavior was controlled somewhat as he was attracted to young girls under age 14. His sexual arousal was very high, and he spent a considerable amount of time masturbating in his room.

Frank was very resistant to attending any type of therapy group held on the unit. He could not tolerate attending the unit therapeutic community meetings held twice a week and would usually sit outside the group or stay in his room. Frank tried some therapeutic recreation groups but stopped attending after a while due to not being able to tolerate the group rules and routine, not getting along with others, or not attending regularly due to lack of motivation. He had a severe addiction to nicotine, which also prevented him from staying in a group for the entire duration. Frank's negative mental illness symptoms included withdrawn behavior and sleeping for long periods of time during the day, lack of motivation, and poor leisure skills. Frank's primary activities during his free time were sleeping, smoking in the courtyard, and occasionally bothering other patients with provocative abusive verbal comments. He also listened to music with earphones with his portable radio/cassette player.

Frank had a collection of about 20 of his favorite records on the unit sent by his family. He was encouraged to attend the music therapy listening group where he could listen to his records on a professional sound system with the rest of the group. Frank attended one group. He was unable to tolerate a small listening group if he had to listen to music chosen by other group members that he did not like.

Frank was referred for individual music therapy and agreed to come to the treatment room on the unit to listen exclusively to his collection of records. The objective was to develop a positive relationship with a member of the treatment team and to reduce resistance toward group activity through developing a more positive general attitude toward the therapeutic process.

The individual session was designed to increase Frank's willingness to attend the sessions consistently for 30 to 45 minutes a week. He was given the opportunity to select the records to which he wanted to listen. If he needed a cigarette, he was given time to leave the room to go smoke outside and return. Frank was not asked to do anything else during the session. The therapist primarily responded only to comments initiated by Frank and rarely asked personal questions.

Some of the music he enjoyed was not available in the hospital and was not popular with many of the other patients. Included in his small collection of records were several of the early recordings of Frank Zappa, Yes, and Led Zeppelin. Frank was very knowledgeable about the artists and the various bands he enjoyed listening to. He also enjoyed talking about his favorite recordings. He was motivated to attend regularly and rarely became irritable or angry during the listening sessions. Despite his addiction to cigarettes, he rarely asked to leave the room to smoke.

After a few months of individual sessions, Frank was asked if he would like to invite another patient to attend the sessions. He chose to invite a resistant patient who also attended very few groups and was not making much progress on the unit. This patient was very passive, rarely said or did anything to bother his peers on the unit, and did not show preference for any type of music. Since Frank was the only patient in the group with records, they got along well.

Frank began to show progress in attending his other groups and was able to stay for longer periods of time without getting angry. He increased his level of participation in some groups, including the monthly family therapy groups. During the team conference, the psychiatrist noted that Frank's overall behavior seemed to be improving, and others noticed a reduction in his abusive angry behavior on the unit during this time.

The individual music therapy sessions offered therapeutic benefits including developing a positive therapeutic alliance with a member of the treatment team, the opportunity to enjoy listening to music without interruption once a week with the music therapist, listening to his preferred music to improve his mood during each session, and intellectual stimulation from the music and the increase in his ability to express himself verbally. The individual music therapy listening sessions may have contributed to reducing his resistance to attending other therapy groups by helping to provide Frank with more confidence in his ability to tolerate the group experiences.

Case Study 2: Reducing Stress and Anger With Individual Music Therapy

Lewis was a chronically assaultive psychotic patient. He had a long history of fighting since the age of 4. At the age of 16 he was sent to the California Youth Authority for assault, destroying property, making threats, and bizarre behavior. He was diagnosed with schizophrenia–paranoid type with psychotic delusions of grandeur. Reports showed he was not responding to medications and was described as "stark, raving, off-the-wall crazy." He continued to receive numerous assault charges, including attempted rape, assault with a deadly weapon, battery, battery on a police officer, and battery on a prisoner.

Lewis was admitted to the forensic state hospital where he was seen for music therapy at the age of 21. Reports indicated that he was involved in 14 special incident reports (SIRs) over a period of 13 days on the admissions unit. He was frequently placed in restraints to help control his behavior. Later that year, he made an unprovoked attack on a social worker. In November 1983, a psychiatrist described Lewis in his notes as "untreatable, murderous, impulsive, dangerous" and recommended a lobotomy. Between 1984 and 1985, while still incarcerated, Lewis injured three more employees and was involved in 56 SIRs. The treatment team initiated a special behavior modification program in which he was placed in leather wrist restraints and escorted by two staff members. He received heavy doses of psychotropic medications to help reduce his delusional thoughts and aggressiveness.

The treatment team's psychology intern was assigned to meet regularly with Lewis to discuss personal issues and help him develop anger management skills. His initial list of problems included undersocialization, disorganized thinking with loose associations, grandiose delusions, sexually assaultive behavior, assaultive behavior, poor concentration, poor impulse control, and obesity.

Lewis told the recreation therapist that he liked to listen to music and to play the guitar and drum set. Some of his delusional thoughts were identified in his belief that he was George Harrison, his best friend was Ringo Starr, and that the therapist was John Lennon. The treatment team contacted the music therapist, and the first meeting was held on the unit with the recreation therapist and the psychologist. His guitar playing was very disorganized, and he could not remember how to finger the chords. He was able to establish a steady pulse on the desk with drumsticks. His singing was very soft with mumbled lyrics, and he sang slowly.

Music therapy sessions were held on the unit once a week for 30 minutes with at least two staff members in the same room. Lewis had free movement of his arms during the sessions, though the leather straps always remained around his waist. During the sessions, Lewis sang songs, drummed with his hands or the sticks on the desk, or played xylophone solos while the therapist played the guitar. Lewis was allowed to play the guitar and talk about whatever came to his mind. He also tried to play and sing songs he had written and improvise guitar solos.

Some of the songs Lewis enjoyed singing over the next 6 months included "Take It Easy," "Strawberry Fields," "Little Help from My Friends," "Raindrops Keep Fallin' on My Head," and "Eight Days a Week." He slowly learned a few standard guitar chords. Eventually, with the help of the therapist, Lewis was able to write a fairly coherent song loosely based on his incarceration history from juvenile hall to the present. His drumming on the desk continued to be organized, and he was able to sing and keep a beat at the same time.

After meeting on the unit for 6 months, Lewis demonstrated better control of his aggressive behavior and earned permission to go to the music area off the unit. The impact of the music therapy treatment became more apparent during this session. He wanted to play the drum set and took the sticks and began to play in a furious rapid manner all over the set. After settling down he learned a basic rock beat with his hands on the snare and cymbal. When the therapist played songs on the piano, Lewis created his own way of organizing his beat on the various parts of the set. After playing a few songs this way, Lewis looked very pleased with himself as evidenced by a big smile. He moved out from behind the drum set and appeared to be getting ready to give the therapist a hug, but ended up shaking hands.

It seemed his success on the drum set and the energy he had released had a very emotional, cathartic, and uplifting effect on him. What appeared to be a considerable release of anxiety and muscle tension resulted in Lewis becoming so relaxed, yet energized and overjoyed that he wanted to hug somebody. In this moment he appeared aware of the connection he made with another person and how it made him feel.

It was noted a year after the music therapy session had begun that Lewis was able to spend longer periods of time out of his restrains. During the 15 months of individual music therapy, Lewis had no assaults or SIRs. Music therapy was only one of several special treatment interventions used. The impact of one therapeutic intervention is not always evident when a patient is simultaneously involved in several treatments. It did appear that spontaneous creative drumming had a direct and immediate positive physiological effect.

The following case studies are based on individuals involved in the sex offender commitment program within the state hospital. This program is primarily a cognitive behavioral relapse prevention program divided into four separate phases. It is designed for the treatment of Sexually Violent Predators (SVP).

The SVP law keeps repeat offenders locked up for treatment after the completion of the sentence in a state correctional facility. Patients must complete all four phases of treatment before they can be released back into the community.

Case Study 3: Expression of Repressed Feelings

Scott was a 60-year-old pedophile who was active in the sex offender commitment program. While Scott was involved in the music therapy improvisation group, he was active in the Phase II cognitive behavioral relapse prevention group. In this phase, patients are expected to prepare and present the chronological history of their pedophilia behavior to the group. Each patient is also expected to present what is called a "behavior chain" of the actions he would take before and during the commitment of a child molest offense. Scott had made his career as an officer in the military for most of his life. He was an intelligent, soft spoken, well-groomed professional man with no other criminal history or mental illness problems other than having an uncontrollable attraction to girls under the age of 14.

Scott enjoyed playing the drum set and singing. He was able to play in his own creative manner on the beat, though he had no formal training. Scott was in the music therapy improvisation group for several months and played the drum set just about every week. He often requested popular rock and roll songs from the 1960s and 1970s to sing with the group when not playing the drums. The lyrics to the songs he liked often reflected an interest in young females.

A few weeks later during Scott's team meeting, the psychologist reported that Scott had recently begun to discuss sex offenses from his past in his Phase II group that he had never talked about. Though he had discussed many of the molestations for which he had been incarcerated, these were incidences for which he had not been arrested. Scott informed the group that he had never told anyone because he felt ashamed for what he had done.

These suppressed memories surfaced while Scott was also actively playing the drums and singing in the music therapy improvisation group. Scott chose the one instrument that allows the entire body (both lower and upper extremities) to move when playing all the parts of the set. During one session, he chose the song "Smoke Gets in Your Eyes," which has lyrics that may reflect the sort of purging effects Scott was experiencing in his Phase II group. The first verse contains the line "I of course replied, something here inside, cannot be denied." This lyric reflects the very situation Scott was experiencing by finally divulging to his Phase II group the events of his past he had suppressed for many years. Later in the fourth verse, the line "Now laughing friend deride, tears I can not hide" might reflect the shame Scott had been feeling and also the type of reaction he may have feared from others when they learned of his past inappropriate sexual behavior.

This is an interesting case example because the data support the possibility that Scott had a cathartic experience while involved in two separate therapeutic groups, stemming from the lyrics of a song he chose to sing in one of the groups. His involvement in the music therapy group's improvised drumming and singing may have helped to loosen feelings and allow repressed memories to surface. His concurrent treatment in the Phase II group provided a supportive verbal group where he was encouraged to divulge information related to his past inappropriate sexual behavior. The combination of music therapy improvisation and Phase II relapse prevention group provided Scott with the therapeutic support and impetus he needed to progress in his treatment program.

Case Study 4: The Assessment of Interpersonal Skills Through Music Therapy

James was a child molester in the Phase II treatment program when he was referred to the phase music therapy improvisation group. This group is held once a week for only those patients involved in the phase treatment program. When James first came to the music group, he demonstrated that he had some piano skills and was also able to freely improvise on the piano. The piano is not usually used in this phase of the music therapy improvisation group. Due to the small size of the group and James' piano skills, he was permitted to play the piano as long as he agreed to spend equal time in the session playing percussion instruments. James also verbalized an interest in playing the guitar.

When James played the percussion instruments in the group, he was able to play in an organized and expressive manner while also interacting spontaneously with the rest of the group. He listened and responded often to what others were playing, controlling his volume so others could be heard. During several different improvisations, James started on percussion and then moved to the piano. He was able to begin the piano playing in a manner similar to the way he had been interacting with the rest of the group on the percussion instruments.

As the improvisations continued with James playing the piano, he became more engaged with the piano and less aware of what the group was doing. He began to play in a broader style, filling more space while responding less to the group. Despite an apparent lack of awareness that others were still attempting to engage him musically, he maintained a connection to the rhythmic style and played in a creative and melodically organized manner.

Sex offenders often demonstrate demanding behaviors, insisting on getting their way and testing limits of what they can get. James demonstrated this behavior in gaining permission to use the piano. Since he had always wanted to play the electric guitar, he requested permission to add it to the group for him to play.

During the first session in which James played the guitar, he spent the first part of the group improvisation adjusting the settings on the amplifier and trying out the instrument as though he were practicing alone in the room. He constantly changed what he was playing, did not establish an organized rhythm, played at a volume that covered up other instruments, and made no attempt to engage or respond to what others were playing. Near the end of the improvisation, James finally discovered a way to make a few chord sounds. He repeated the sounds in an organized rhythm that the therapist could finally follow on the drum set. He appeared aware of this brief interaction as he made eye contact about the same time.

After the improvisation was over, James appeared very pleased with what had occurred and stated that he found the experience to be quite enjoyable. He appeared unconcerned with the lack of interaction during the improvisation. When given feedback about playing loudly and out of synch with the group when he used the guitar, James quickly disagreed. His reaction to this feedback seemed to support that he was not aware of what was occurring during the improvisation and that he might become defensive when confronted with his narcissistic playing behavior.

During the next few improvisations, James played only the guitar. The therapist finally told him to put the guitar away for one improvisation, as he made the agreement to give equal time to the percussion instruments. He put it away in a passive aggressive manner, taking a long time to remove the strap and slowly folding it as opposed to just setting the guitar down with the strap still attached.

There was very little change in the way James played the guitar during the improvisations to follow. He continued to spend much time engaging the amplifier and the tuning, paying little attention to what others were doing and how they were playing. He demonstrated that he was still capable of listening and responding to others in the group only when he returned to the percussion instruments.

During the group process discussions related to his change of behavior when playing the guitar, James continued to deny his behavior and eventually concluded that the therapist just did not like the guitar and was trying to control him. It seemed that when he was more cognitively involved in playing an instrument and more absorbed in doing what he wanted to do, he would become less empathetic toward others in the group. When confronted with his inappropriate musical behavior, he denied what he was doing and distorted reality by making himself the victim of the "guitar-hating" therapist. This type of manipulative behavior is similar to the behavior employed by a child molester when involved in grooming a potential victim.

Conclusion

An expressive, interactive music therapy group experience has the potential for addressing a combination of problems often encountered in a male forensic population. Spontaneous musical expression within a social interactive group setting creates an ideal therapeutic environment for mentally ill inmates with Axis II personality problems, substance abuse addictions, and serious anger management issues. The psychological and physiological effects of musical expression can have a positive therapeutic impact if the patient is willing to get involved. The social interactive, yet less threatening, group experience in music therapy helps these patients learn to work together successfully. For many patients, the joy of music helps to motivate them to participate in their own therapeutic process. The entire music therapy group creates their own therapeutic environment in a setting where joyful, positive experiences are rare. Musical expression lifts and refreshes the spirits of the forensic patients. When individuals are incarcerated for long periods of time in a very controlled, secure setting, the effect of producing and experiencing music is a powerful experience.

References

Allen, B., & Bosta, D. (1981). Games criminals play. Sacramento, CA: Rae John.

American Bar Association. (n.d.). Part I: Mental health, mental retardation, and criminal justice: General professional obligations. Retrieved June 15, 2004, from http://www.abanet.org/crimjust/standards/mentalhealth_blk.html

American Psychiatric Association (APA). (2000). Diagnostic and statistical manual of mental disorders (4th ed.). Washington, DC: Author.

Boone, P. (1991). Composition, improvisation, and poetry in the psychiatric treatment of a forensic patient. In K. Bruscia (Ed.), Case studies in music therapy (pp. 433–450). Gilsum, NH: Barcelona.

Bruscia, K. E. (1987). Improvisational models of music therapy. Springfield, IL: Charles C. Thomas.

Bruscia, K. E. (1998). Defining music therapy (2nd ed.). Gilsum, NH: Barcelona.

Cellini, H. R. (2002). Biopsychosocial treatment of antisocial and conduct-disordered offenders. Federal Probation, 66(2), 78–82.

Cellini, H. R., Hinze, T., Speaker, T., & Wood, R. M. (2000, March/April). The treatment and management of severe personality disordered offenders. Offender Programs Report, pp. 33–34, 92–94.

Codding, P. A. (2002). A comprehensive survey of music therapists practicing in correctional psychiatry: Demographics, conditions of employment, service provision, assessment, therapeutic objectives, and related values of the therapist. Music Therapy Perspectives, 20(2), 56–68.

Cohen, J. M. (1987). Music therapy with the overcontrolled offender: Theory and practice. The Arts in Psychotherapy, 14, 215–221.

Davis, D. L., & Boster, L. (1988). Multifaceted therapeutic interventions with the violent psychiatric inpatient. Hospital and Community Psychiatry, 39(8), 867–869.

Elliott, W. N. (2002). Managing offender resistance to counseling—The "3R's." Federal Probation, 66(3), 43–49.

Fernandez, Y. M., Anderson, D., & Marshall, W. L. (1999). *The relationship among empathy, cognitive distortions, and self-esteem in sexual offenders.* In B. K. Schwartz (Ed.), The sex offender: Theoretical advances, treating special populations and legal developments *(pp. 41–49).* Kingston, NJ: Civic Research Institute.

Fulford, M. (2002). *Overview of a music therapy program at a maximum security unit of a state psychiatric facility.* Music Therapy Perspectives, 20(2), 112–116.

Gallagher, L. M., & Steele, A. L. (2002). *Music therapy with offenders in a substance abuse/mental illness treatment program.* Music Therapy Perspectives, 20(2), 117–122.

Jacobson, E. (1974). Progressive muscle relaxation. *Chicago: University of Chicago Press, Midway Reprint.*

Hakvoort, L. (2002). *A music therapy anger management program for forensic offenders.* Music Therapy Perspectives, 20(2), 123–132.

Kaser, V. (1991). *Music therapy treatment of pedophilia using the drum set.* The Arts in Psychotherapy, 18, 7–15.

Kaser, V. (1993). *Music expressions of subconscious feelings: A clinical perspective.* Music Therapy Perspectives, 11, 16–23.

Loewy, J. (2000). *Music psychotherapy assessment.* Music Therapy Perspectives, 18, 47–58.

Loth, H. (1996). *Music therapy.* In C. Cordess & M. Cox (Eds.), Forensic psychotherapy: Crime, psychodynamics and the offender patient *(pp. 561–566). London: Jessica Kingsley.*

McMurran, M., Egan, V., Blair, M., & Richardson, C. (2001). *The relationship between social problem solving and personality in mentally disordered offenders.* Personality and Individual Differences, 30(3), 517–534.

Nolan, P. (1983). *Insight therapy: Guided imagery and music in a forensic psychiatric setting.* Music Therapy, 3, 43–51.

Nolan, P. (1991). *Group improvisation therapy for a resistant woman with bipolar disorder–manic.* In K. E. Bruscia (Ed.), Case studies in music therapy *(pp. 451–564). Phoenixville, PA: Barcelona.*

Parker, R., Ellison, C., Kirby, T., & Short, M. J. (1988). Comprehensive evaluation in recreational therapy–Psych/behavioral, revised. *Enumclaw, WA: Idyll Arbor.*

Priestley, M. (1994). Essays on analytical music therapy. *Phoenixville, PA: Barcelona.*

Reed, K. J. (2000). Music is the master key. *Orlando, FL: Rivercross.*

Reed, K. J. (2002). *Music therapy treatment groups for mentally disordered offenders (MDO) in a state hospital setting.* Music Therapy Perspectives, 20(2), 98–104.

Sloboda, A. (1997). *Music therapy and psychotic violence.* In E. V. Welldon & C. V. Velsen (Eds.), A practical guide to forensic psychotherapy *(pp. 121–129). London: Jessica Kingsley.*

Smeltekop, R. A., & Houghton, B. A. (1990). *Music therapy and psychopharmacology.* In R. Unkefer (Ed.), Music therapy in the treatment of adults with mental disorders *(pp. 109–125). New York: Schirmer Books.*

Summer, L. (1988). *The use of GIM with various populations.* In L. Summer, Guided imagery and music in the institutional setting *(pp. 35–39). St. Louis, MO: MMB Music.*

Thaut, M. H. (1987). *A new challenge for music therapy: The correctional setting.* Music Therapy Perspectives, 4, 44–50.

Thaut, M. H. (1999). *Group music psychotherapy in correctional psychiatry.* In W. B. Davis, K. E. Gfeller, & M. H. Thaut (Eds.), An introduction to music therapy theory and practice *(2nd ed., pp. 248–258). Boston: McGraw-Hill College.*

Watson, D. M. (2002). *Drumming and improvisation with adult male sexual offenders.* Music Therapy Perspectives, 20(2), 105–111.

Section 5:

Music Therapy for Children and Adolescents With Emotional/Behavioral Disturbances

Chapter 13

Diagnostic Categories for Children and Adolescents with Mental Disorders Classified as Emotionally/Behaviorally Disturbed
Barbara J. Crowe

The *Diagnostic and Statistical Manual* (4th ed.) (American Psychiatric Association [APA], 1994) summarizes the full range of mental disorders of children/adolescents, including mental retardation, learning disorders, motor skills disorders, communication disorders, and pervasive developmental delay (autism). However, these disorders are not addressed in this book. Only those disorders considered "psychiatric" whether with or without organic cause are included. For the purpose of this book children and adolescents diagnosed with "mental disorders" are those who can be categorized as having emotional and/or behavioral disturbances. The classification, *emotional disturbance,* is recognized under the Individuals with Disabilities Education Act (IDEA), but does not represent an actual diagnosis as identified by the DSM-IV.

Children and adolescents diagnosed with emotional/behavioral disorders are those who "consistently exhibit behaviors that are personally or socially deviant, maladaptive. or inappropriate" (Peters, 2000, p. 208). These clients have a higher frequency of inappropriate behaviors and comparably lower amounts of appropriate behaviors (Paul, 1982). These clients have been variously labeled:

- behavior disabled;
- childhood schizophrenic;
- conduct disordered;
- emotionally handicapped;
- hyperactive (ADHD);
- socially maladjusted;
- juvenile offender/delinquent;
- mentally disturbed;
- emotionally disturbed (Peters, 2000).

Though the *DSM-IV* (APA, 1994) designates specific diagnoses of mental disorders for children and adolescents, diagnoses associated with adults also can be observed. This is especially true for anxiety and mood disorders and for childhood onset schizophrenia. Other common diagnoses of adults seen in children/adolescents include substance abuse, schizophreniform and schizoaffective disorders, somatoform disorders, personality and adjustment disorders, psychosomatic disorders, and eating disorders. Regardless of the diagnosis, all disorders of children, and to some extent, adolescents, are marked by behavior problems. These "acting-out behaviors" are external behavioral manifestations expressing the emotional pain, conflicts, or stress being experienced by the child. Acting out behaviors typically include:

- poor impulse control and age inappropriate behavior such as temper tantrums, physical striking out (hitting, kicking, biting), verbal hostility and swearing, and destructiveness (breaking and smashing things);
- behavior that occurs for no reason such as catastrophic reactions (over reaction to situations), sudden emotional or behavioral outbursts, and functioning at a younger developmental level for no apparent reason;
- social acting out such as gang involvement, illegal behavior, fire setting, violence against person and property, and running away;
- poor frustration tolerance and an inability to delay gratification;
- sudden change in school performance, inability to learn, poor concentration;
- anxiety, fears, panic attacks, irritability;
- depression, suicide thoughts and actions;
- hyper- or hypoactivity;
- deterioration in relationships with peers, parents, and authority figures;
- personality changes including pre-occupation, inability to experience happiness, masochism (hurts self, solicits punishment), sadism (bullying, harming animals), and unpleasant, nasty disposition.

It is behavior that is unacceptable to the community that brings a child or adolescent to inpatient treatment (T. Winn, personal communication, January 4, 2005). Brooks (1989) identifies the following behaviors that can bring a child or adolescent into the hospital for psychiatric treatment:

- suicide attempt
- anger/rage outbursts
- withdrawal from family/social group
- social isolation from peers
- aggressive behavior/gang involvement
- school failure
- running away
- substance abuse
- criminal behavior

Doak (2003) notes that children and adolescents can experience depression, high levels of anxiety, and low self-esteem. They often self-medicate with drugs and alcohol to deal with these problems (See the section on substance abuse in Chapter 10 for more in-depth exploration of this topic.)

Specific Diagnoses of Children and Adolescents With Mental Disorders

The specific mental disorders first diagnosed in children or adolescents include:

- *Attention-deficit/hyperactivity disorder* (ADHD) characterized by incessant, non-goal directed activity, poor concentration, impulsivity and inattention, labile mood, and low self-esteem;

- *Conduct disorder* characterized by violation of the rights of others, poor relationships, manipulative behavior, criminal activity, gang involvement, and physical aggression to people and animals;
- *Oppositional defiant disorder* characterized by patterns of negative, hostile, and defiant behavior;
- *Separation anxiety disorder* characterized by excessive anxiety concerning separation, unrealistic worries and fears, refusal to go to school, and panic attacks;
- *Selective mutism* characterized by social anxiety and refusal to speak in social situations;
- *Reactive attachment disorder* of infancy characterized by marked disturbance in social relatedness, violent behavior, and labile mood;
- *Stereotypic movement disorder* characterized by repetitive, nonfunctional motor behavior (rocking, head banging, etc.);
- *Feeding and eating disorders* of early childhood, including pica (eating non-food items), rumination (repeated regurgitation and re-swallowing of food), and failure to eat;
- *Tic disorders* characterized by abnormality of gross motor movement and vocalizations, including Tourette's disorder, chronic motor or vocal tic, and transient tic disorder (APA, 1994).

Assessment of Children and Adolescents

The music therapy assessment of children and adolescents with emotional/behavioral disturbance follows the same general procedure and domains of functioning to be assessed as was previously explored for adults (see Chapter 2). However, two areas of assessment are of particular importance for children and adolescents. First, the music therapist needs to assess the side effects of medications that the clients are taking. It is important to note the impact on motor and cognitive functioning and general energy level. Secondly, the assessment of musical skills, personal history with music, and preferences are of particular importance, especially with adolescents.

A good assessment activity is to ask the client to bring an example of his or her music to the music therapy session. The music therapist and client listen to the selection, while the therapist encourages the client to talk about the music, explore what it means to him/her, and why s/he is drawn to this particular type of music. When the music therapist really listens to the client's music, it becomes a bonding process, building trust because an adult listened to his/her music without judgment. During this interaction, the therapist can assess the client's musical preferences, ability to relate to an adult, ability to verbally express, and general affect level.

Another assessment activity is to ask the client to freely improvise on musical instruments. Have the client choose an instrument and "do something with it." Do not ask them to "play" the instrument, which implies a "right way" to use that particular instrument. As an assessment activity, observe how they use the instrument, their willingness to try, levels of creativity, and attention span (T. Winn, personal communication, January 4, 2005).

Music Therapy for Children With Emotional/Behavioral Disturbance

Music therapy practice for children with emotional/behavioral disturbances is different from that of adults and adolescents in terms of goals and activity interventions.

General Goals for Music Therapy for Children with Mental Disorders

Goals will vary greatly based on the individual assessment of the client. Typical music therapy goals include, but are not limited to, the following:

- improve reality testing
- increase impulse control
- improve behavioral control
- increase attention to task
- increase frustration tolerance
- improve body-image and body awareness
- improve verbal and nonverbal communication skills
- improve organizational skills
- learn appropriate way of dealing with problems
- support normal developmental markers that may become arrested
- develop appropriate means for energy release through sublimation in performance
- develop relaxation strategies to decrease anxiety
- develop emotional behavior, including nonverbal expression of emotions, identification and labeling of emotions, and emotional awareness
- improve social skills and interpersonal relationships, including group behaviors
- support pre-academic and academic learning

Music Therapy Interventions for Children with Emotional/Behavioral Disturbances

Music therapy interventions for children fall primarily into the first two levels of Wheeler's (1983) levels of therapeutic interventions—supportive, activity therapy and insight music therapy with re-educative goals.

Supportive activity therapy (product-oriented). A number of music therapy activity interventions fall under this category:

- Rhythm activities—Use of rhythm instruments, rhythm band activities, group drumming, Orff chants (Bitcon, 2000), echo activities, body percussion, and rhythmic "naughtiness in music," where the music therapist uses sound making and "naughty" sounds produced by the children in organized rhythmic ensembles;
- Singing and action songs to promote body part identification and body usage, name recognition and personal identity, reinforcement of pre-academic and academic skills, and awareness and expression of emotions;
- Use of musical instruments including skill building and small ensemble playing;
- Drumming activities and rhythmic ensembles including existing drumming ensemble programs (Schmidt, 1998);
- Musical conversations on Orff instruments or slit drums;

- Movement to music including gross motor locomotion to music (marching, hopping, skipping, sliding, etc.), rhythmic mirroring to music, use of props (parachute, streamers, scarves, etc.), and structured children's dances and dance songs.

Insight music therapy with re-educative goals (process-oriented music therapy). Activity interventions for this area include:

- expressive movement to music for emotional expression, use of imagination, and creativity;
- auditory discrimination activities for auditory awareness, auditory figure-ground, and reality orientation through sensory usage and recognition;
- concrete, active listening for emotional awareness and expression. Activities could include:
  - create a story to music;
  - draw or choose a picture to music followed by verbal discussion appropriate to the child's age;
  - use of adjective lists to begin the process of labeling emotions and moods;
  - directed discussion to music including use of fill-in the phrase, e.g. "this music makes me feel _____";
  - music-directed creative dramatics, e.g., have a small group "make a machine" to do a job they hate;
  - song-writing or song parody.

Musical instruments and equipment. Instruments and equipment useful for work with children with emotional/behavioral disturbance include:

- Orff instruments;
- child-sized hand percussion instruments;
- guitars;
- Q Chords and autoharps;
- child-size versions of drums from world percussion traditions;
- props including scarves, streamers, parachutes, stuffed animals, and music boxes;
- electric keyboards, drum machines, karaoke machines, multi-effects boards;
- novelty instruments, e.g., ocean drum, slit drums, vibroslap, ratchet, and other sound effects instruments.

References

American Psychiatric Association (APA). (1994). Diagnostic and statistical manual (4th ed.). Washington, DC: Author.

Bitcon, C. (2000). Alike and different. Gilsum, NH: Barcelona.

Brooks, D. (1989). Music therapy enhances treatment with adolescents. Music Therapy Perspectives, 6, 37–39.

Doak, B. A. (2003). Relationship between adolescents psychiatric diagnoses, music preferences, and drug preferences. Music Therapy Perspectives, 21(2), 69–76.

Paul, D. (1982). Music therapy for handicapped children: Emotionally disturbed. Washington, DC: National Association for Music Therapy.

Peters, J. S. (2000). Music therapy: An introduction (2nd ed.). Springfield, IL: Charles C. Thomas.

Schmidt, W. (1998). World music drumming: A cross cultural curriculum. Milwaukee, WI: Hal Leonard.

Wheeler, B. L. (1983). A psychotherapeutic classification of music therapy practices: A continuum of procedure. Music Therapy Perspectives, 1, 8–16.

The author wishes to thank Tomas Winn, MT-BC, and Joel de la Houssaye, MT-BC, for their help in writing this section. Tomas Winn worked for many years as a music therapist on the adolescent unit of the Oregon State Hospital. Similarly, Joel de la Joussaye is a private practice music therapist in Phoenix who has done extensive work with adolescents diagnosed with emotional/behavioral disturbances.

Chapter 14

Music Therapy with Children with Emotional Disturbances
Rick Soshensky

Music Therapy With Psychotherapeutic, Analytically-Oriented Goals

The following chapter provides an overview of a psychotherapeutic, re-constructive approach for analytical and cathartic-oriented music therapy practice for children with emotional disturbance.

A child considered emotionally disturbed typically exhibits extreme behavioral symptoms such as rage and aggression, injurious behavior (toward self and others), isolation and withdrawal, inability to sustain attention or respond to limits, chronic dishonesty, criminal activity (such as shoplifting), acute anxiety, aural or visual hallucinations in the case of underlying psychosis, among others. Although many children display some of these problems to various degrees at times, to categorize a child as having an emotional disturbance, the behaviors must severely interfere with the ability to function socially in the family or in school and extend over a significant period of time. Roughly, 8 to 12% of children in the school system are identified as being emotionally disturbed according to the U.S. Department of Education (2001). Law provides children who cannot function in a regular classroom setting with special education and related services. Psychiatric services and various forms of therapy (including music therapy) may be warranted, possibly entailing diagnostic testing and medication.

There is growing understanding by mental health organizations that families, as well as their children, benefit from support, case management, and a collaborative, multi-agency approach. Parents need help in coping with a child's emotional disturbance, and the child's mental health problems cannot be isolated from his or her family system and history. Family therapy may be indicated if the parents are open to the idea, and a wealth of services exist to assist parents with their children. Clearly, serious dysfunction and/or breakdown of the family itself hinder the family system approach. Parents may be overwhelmed by their own serious problems such as mental illness, addiction, abusive tendencies, domestic violence, and poor parenting skills.

Laymen, Hussey, and Laing (2002a) report that nearly half a million children in the United States have been removed from their birth family and placed in the foster care system due to abuse or neglect. Many never return to their birth families and, even if adopted, the foster family may be no better than the birth families, requiring the child to be removed again. A child could conceivably be transferred through several foster family placements. This cycle of disruption, discontinuity, and additional trauma can lead to a compounding of psychological maladjustment (Bohman, 1990). Even under the best of conditions, complications can emerge representing an incomplete mourning process in which unresolved loss plays a major part in the maladjustment.

Due to the complexity of the problems involved, children with emotional disturbances may be quite complicated to treat. By the time an emotional disturbance is recognized, often by a child's inability to function in school, the emotional damage and psychiatric impairment are deeply entrenched. If behavioral problems are critical and the majority of the child's experience (school problems, home stressors, difficulty with peers, etc.) continues to entangle the child in a web of ongoing distress, services beyond community-based outpatient treatment and special education may be needed. Unfortunately, there is more need than availability for specialized educational/day-treatment programs for children requiring a higher level of care. Inpatient psychiatric hospitalization or long-term residential treatment (again, if available) may be necessary, even though removing the child from the family and social milieu can cause further identity trauma and stigmatization.

Music Therapy Assessment

Music therapy literature reflects diverse assessment scales designed for work with children. Bruscia (1987) outlines assessment methods from numerous music therapy models as well as his own *Improvisation Assessment Profiles* that remains a comprehensive and invaluable resource. Some assessments for children were developed primarily for children with developmental delays or disabilities while others are more specific to those with emotional disturbances. However, Nordoff and Robbins (1977) found that, in the case of music therapy, such stratification of clinical populations might not be so clear-cut.

> *No single fundamental division existed in our experiences of these two groups [autistic/non-autistic]—they merged, interconnected, and in the case of musically active autistic children, widely overlapped. The procedure adopted, therefore, was to treat our overall clinical experience as an integral body of music therapy phenomena and to differentiate and classify its entire range. (p. 178)*

Nordoff and Robbins (1977) note that the musical responses of children with disabilities may be initially fragmentary in various ways. I have found this also to be true with some children with emotional disabilities, although it generally seems to represent resistance more than incapacity. Such children may play for a moment and then pull back, or they may play instruments seemingly to exasperate (such as in an excessively loud, chaotic, possibly even destructive manner). While nonnegotiable limits must be placed on maltreatment of instruments (or people), such provocative playing can be noted for assessment purposes. It may be that entering into the flow of music represents a loss of cognitive control or breach in interpersonal boundaries that can be extremely threatening. Whitfield (1995) delineates some "core issues" of traumatized children, including the need for control, problems with trust, low self-esteem, and fear of abandonment. Consequently, they may hold off from an uninhibited musical relationship with the therapist for quite a while.

Exploring the nature of the child-therapist relationship and ability to communicate as assessed by the Nordoff-Robbins' *Scales I & II* (1977), respectively, can be enlightening. *Scale I* identifies 10 levels of participation and qualities of resistance, ranging from the level of least participation, noted as "total obliviousness," to the optimum level of participation, with the "establishment of functional independence in group work." The deepest resistance is noted as "imperviousness—rage reaction when pressed" and the quality of least resistance occurs when the client "resists own regressive tendencies."

Scale II also has 10 levels, from "no communicative response" through to the most advanced level of communicative behavior, which Nordoff and Robbins (1977) consider to be "musical-social intercommunication in group activities." Nordoff and Robbins consider group work as representative of the most advanced levels of participation and communication, because "any personal dependence upon the therapists an individual child might still have diminishes under these conditions. He becomes an independently contributing member of a working group, sharing pleasure and interest with others and feeling pride in his own accomplishments" (p. 188). *Scale II* is also designed to analyze various forms of musical communication—instrumental, vocal, and body movement—according to the 10 levels.

Layman, Hussey, and Laing (2002b) developed an assessment instrument for children with severe emotional disturbance that measures four relevant domains: behavior/social functioning, emotional responsiveness, language/communication abilities, and musical skills with sub-categories within each domain. A child's responses are coded according to three possible interpretations: defensive/withdrawn, target behavior, or disruptive/intrusive. As compared to the more open-ended Bruscia (1987) and Nordoff-Robbins (1977) models, this assessment seems to reflect a behavioral orientation through its design and terminology, such as its emphasis on the achievement of "target behaviors." The authors note that the subjects of the pilot study of this assessment instrument were found to display significantly more behaviors in the disruptive/intrusive range.

Loewy (2000) notes, with the exception of Bruscia's *Improvisation Assessment Profiles* and the Nordoff-Robbins scales, "the majority of assessment tools currently being utilized by music therapists appear as forms with specific behavioral tasks that are seemingly unrelated to the dynamic musical relationship that naturally occurs between client and therapist" (p. 48). With that in mind, Loewy developed 13 Areas of Inquiry used to assess a variety of clients, including children with emotional disturbances:

- Awareness of self, others, and of the moment
- Thematic expression
- Listening
- Performing
- Collaboration/relationship
- Concentration
- Range of affect
- Investment/motivation
- Use of structure
- Integration
- Self-esteem
- Risk taking
- Independence

Loewy believes these categories reflect the essential components of *music psychotherapy assessment*. Each area is considered as a unique entity, but also there is a degree of interaction and overlap. Loewy contends, "Essential to the understanding of music therapy is the recognition of how one assigns meaning to an experience through the process of interpretation and translation" (p. 47). Charts, scales, and checklists may quantify the experience of music (and may be fast and convenient), but, according to Loewy, the true music therapy experience is better understood through more descriptive notation.

> *Music may be the medium under which healing can occur, but words are the tools that can assist in how we comprehend and communicate what we are doing. The more we can offer each other an illustrative text that is our own, the more we can build upon a strong, well-defined foundation of understanding. (Loewy, 2000, p. 57)*

Goals for Music Therapy

Layman, Hussey, and Laing (2002b) delineate five general areas of functioning that music therapists typically address in the treatment of children with emotional disturbance: affective function, communication, social function, cognitive function, and musical response. Ordinarily, clinical goals are considered to be areas where a transfer of gains is possible from music therapy to generalized behavior. Accordingly, most music therapy goals tend to apply to functioning in day-to-day life as well as music therapy. A sampling of such goals might be as follows:

Affective

- Increase confidence
- Stabilize moods
- Increase frustration tolerance
- Identify range of emotions
- Increase commitment (to task, relationship)
- Increase initiative

Communication

- Improve self-expression
- Improve nonverbal communication (eye contact, body language)
- Increase receptivity to others
- Indicate choice/preferences

Socialization

- Increase reciprocal and cooperative behaviors
- Maintain appropriate boundaries with others
- Increase empathy for others
- Increase engagement in group activity
- Increase compliance with rules and expectations of group

Cognitive

- Increase ability to concentrate/focus
- Improve attention span
- Improve organization of ideas
- Improve integration of thought

These goals serve as a general outline of work and can be personalized or made more specific, as necessary. There is a trend in contemporary medical and managed-care models to create goals that are measurable and observable. An example includes "Client will demonstrate ability to stay on-task for five continuous minutes." Loewy (1994) found that most music therapists working with children with emotional disturbance focus on the technical aspects of music (behavioral) or other disciplines' measurements (OT, PT, speech therapy), rather than the musical relationship between client and therapist. In considering a more *music-centered* approach, Turry and Marcus (2003) submitted:

> *The music that is created spontaneously by and for the clients in each session is a vibrant interpersonal interaction in which music is the major, and sometimes the only, means of communication, regardless of the population. With the skillful intervention of the therapist, this ongoing collaboration and the songs and improvisations that are its products become the basis of the therapy and define its course. Gains in areas such as socialization, communication, motor skills, or self-esteem can ensue and be mirrored in personal and family life. (p. 199)*

From such a perspective, musical "symptoms" include:
- chaotic, isolated, fragmented or dissonant playing;
- refusing to play;
- difficulty sustaining rhythms or varying dynamics;
- pitch and phrasing problems while singing;
- disconcerting imagery in improvised song lyrics.

These may reflect areas of concern. Turry and Marcus (2003) maintain, "The process of identifying and addressing these musical tendencies in the series of musical encounters that make up a course of music therapy can result in behavioral and personality change that extends far beyond the sphere of musical behavior" (p. 199). Consequently, strictly musical goals may also be considered to impact nonmusical personality functioning, as shown in the example in Figure 14.1.

Musical Goals and Their Impact on Nonmusical Personality Functioning	
Musical Goals	Generalized Domains
Increase ability to convey ideas and feelings musically	*Affective, communication, cognitive*
Increase ability to listen and respond musically to others	*Communication, socialization*
Increase ability to initiate and structure musical form	*Affective, cognitive*
Expand expressive range (use of dynamics, idioms, etc.)	*Cognitive, affective, communication*
Improve awareness/appreciation of musical aesthetics	*Affective, communication*
Figure 14.1 Musical Goals and Their Impact on Nonmusical Personality Functioning	

Music Therapy and Child Development

Children are in an ever-changing, dynamic process of development. The underlying structures and transformation involved in this process are delineated by many theoretical constructs. One of these, developmental theory, is based on the belief that as personality and cognitive formation unfolds, each level of the process establishes the foundation for the ensuing one. Accordingly, insufficient resolution or disruption at any point would tend to impair effective realization of subsequent development, creating a cumulative and increasingly distorting effect. Understanding a child's developmental experience can, undoubtedly, assist a music therapist in making informed clinical interpretations and interventions.

Although the first four stages that trace preadolescent development in Erikson's (1963) Eight Stages of Ego Development bear some relationship to Freud's oral, anal, phallic, and latency stages, Erikson placed less emphasis on sexually based conflicts than did Freud. Erikson focused more on the child's fundamental social dilemmas at each stage.

Stage 1 (Birth–1)—Basic trust versus mistrust. This stage stems from the baby's experience of loving availability, or lack thereof, of the mother/primary caretaker. A poor experience at this primal stage could color a person's self-concept and worldview for a lifetime, possibly leading to serious psychopathology.

Stage 2 (Ages 2–3)—Autonomy versus shame and doubt. This arises from whether parental supervision is firm and reliable, allowing appropriate exploration, or neglectful/overly harsh.

Stage 3 (Ages 4–5)—Initiative versus guilt. This stage also has to do with whether the child is appropriately guided or severely punished for his or her inquiries and investigations, particularly in the area of early sexual awareness.

Stage 4 (Ages 6–12)—Industry versus inferiority. This encompasses the influence of peers and teachers, as well as parents, in helping the child develop a sense of competence in accomplishing tasks and succeeding socially.

Object Relations

Theorists also diverged from Freud's idea that individuals seek relationships principally to gratify sexual and aggressive impulses. Object relations perceives the satisfaction of libidinal needs as secondary or derivative of the more basic needs for relatedness, contact, and affiliation with others. This bears relationship to Erikson's theories, since the basic premise is that relationships, beginning with the mother-infant dyad, are primary, and the individual's interpretation of the quality and fulfillment of these relationships—both conscious and unconscious—becomes the foundation for all subsequent relationships and identity development (Westen, 1990).

Children's understanding of their experiences must be interpreted according to the nature of their thought process at any particular age. Piaget's (1972) *Stages of Cognitive Development* suggest that, at least until the age of 7, a child's thought-process must be considered. The stages are as follows:

- Sensimotoric (infancy) is primarily concrete and based on sensual/physical interactions/ experiences.
- Pre-operational (toddler and early childhood) is nonlogical, nonreversible (the child cannot analyze or reconstruct his or her thinking), and egocentric.
- Concrete operational stage (age 7 and beyond) is when children begin to have some ability to logically interpret and, thus, separate their ego (internal) experience from their real-world (external) experience.

Because the antecedents for emotional disturbance often occur prior to the age of 7, a significant portion of the psychic disturbance to be reconciled is internalized in the personality at a pre-analytical level, rendering insight-oriented approaches to therapy relatively ineffectual. Additionally, Whitfield (1995) claims that children who are abused or mistreated frequently become numb to their inner life. In Whitfield's words, "the child goes into hiding" (p. 21).

Thus, to accomplish therapeutic progress, it becomes necessary to assist the child in re-experiencing and renegotiating, to the degree possible, deficiently accomplished developmental milestones of which the child is not only unaware but actively denying at an unconscious level. Freud (1961) recognized the rich expression of unconscious process in children's play. He writes, "We see that children repeat in their play everything that has made a great impression on them in actual life" (p. 147). Klein, Lowenfield, Erikson, and others later formalized the concepts of *play therapy* for psychoanalytic work with children (Gitlin-Weiner, Sandgrund, & Schaefer, 2000). Engagement in music is certainly a form of play from a child's perspective. However, from a therapist's vantage point, music becomes an overt and perceptible manifestation of inner processes. Once revealed and tangible, formerly inaccessible material intertwines with conscious expression, becoming available for processing and healing with the aid of the therapist. According to Lehtonen (1994):

> *Music is engulfing us and at the same time spontaneously bringing to our mind meaningful memories, mental pictures and experiences from our past without pain and anxiety. The patterns of music provoke references to the past, and already forgotten experiential material, and these references intertwine with the present and lead the listener to anticipate something of the future. In the process of receiving, performing and creating music, there is always a continuous movement between the past, present and future. (p. 5)*

Case Study 1

JeanMarie was 9 years old. At age 7, she was found living in squalid conditions with her two younger brothers. The only adult in the apartment was JeanMarie's mother, who lay incapacitated in bed and near death from advanced AIDS. Rotting food, human and animal waste, and dirty clothes lay strewn about the apartment. The minimum survival needs of the young children were attended to by several adolescent sisters, who were mostly absent but who would drop by to order take-out food and occasionally engage in sexual activities to which the children were witness. Although unclear, it is probable that the children were victims of sexual abuse themselves. It was, in fact, one of the teen sisters who eventually called emergency services and fled permanently, leading to the discovery of JeanMarie and her brothers.

The children were removed from the home and placed in foster care. Their mother died shortly thereafter. JeanMarie was referred to psychiatric services for behaviors exhibited in foster care, including tearfulness, withdrawal, depressed mood, sexual acting out, enuresis, aggressive behavior, and complete inability to follow directions or respond to limits. She could not read or manage activities of daily living (ADL) like dressing herself. Her initial psychiatric diagnosis was psychosis not otherwise specified (NOS). She was selectively mute in psychotherapy sessions and exhibited bizarre behavior, such as slithering on the floor. She eventually began to respond to treatment and show some improvement. She and her brothers were placed in two successive foster homes and, both times, removed due to inappropriate care, including further physical and emotional abuse. A third foster home seemed to work out, although JeanMarie had to be separated from her brothers, one of whom was also diagnosed with psychosis NOS. After 2 years of verbal and play psychotherapy, JeanMarie's diagnostic profile was noted as follows:

Axis I - Depression NOS, Reactive-Attachment Disorder, ADHD, Enuresis

Axis II - Learning Disability Not Otherwise Specified

Axis III - R/O Seizure Disorder (due to brief periods of seeming disassociation)

Axis IV - Severe disruption of family, death of mother, history of abuse/neglect, psychosis of sibling, disruption of social milieu

JeanMarie was referred to music therapy and immediately showed herself as someone who could utilize the modality to great advantage. She was most drawn to singing and not only was she able to improvise highly personal song lyrics quite fluently, but she could spontaneously create cohesive thematic compositions. In contrast to her typically highly impulsive, evasive, and pressured presentation, when singing she was capable of great focus and fearless insight, although it appeared she was not fully conscious of the poignancy of her expressions. It has been suggested that singing is closely related to early speech. Kennair (2000) proposed that singing might contain a phylogenetic basis for language development, citing, among other things, the universal phenomenon of mothers singing to their babies. Loewy (1995) also noted that "Virtually each and every sound that infants make from the moment of their birth up until the time in which they express their first morphemes can be understood in a musical context" (p. 71). Words that are sung, then, may not only have the capacity to link cognitive and emotional functions, but also conceivably connect to primal levels of being that cannot be accessed at all by purely verbal means. Bruscia (1998) writes:

> *Songs are the ways that human beings explore emotions. They express who we are and how we feel, they bring us closer to others, they keep us company when we are alone. They articulate our beliefs and values. As the years pass, songs bear witness to our lives. They allow us to relive the past, to examine the present, and to voice our dreams for the future. Songs weave tales of our joys and sorrows, they reveal our innermost secrets, and they express our hopes and disappointments, our fears and triumphs. They are our musical diaries, our life stories. They are the sounds of our personal development. (p. 9)*

One of JeanMarie's first major compositions occurred approximately 2 months after beginning music therapy. One day, with no particular structuring or encouragement, she began to spontaneously sing with a voice that was barely able to contain the depth of her emotion. Although her conception of the song was clearly a ballad, she propelled herself into it with immense force, rushing phrasing, overshooting pitches, and practically screaming in parts. Her impassioned delivery communicated how important this was to her, though at the same time she was not quite in control of her artistic impetus. I attempted to show my support by accompanying on piano and assisting in the definition of the piece, but JeanMarie raced ahead of me, as if to shut me out or render me irrelevant. Her hesitance to trust me or integrate with me was apparent. She clearly had an arrangement in mind, including a well-formed melodic structure and introductory section with extended rubato phrasing.

Family

Above the stars—Someone's out there to save me
Family, family—Come and help me
Above the stars to help me—Family, family—To help me
You're the only family I need
You are out there, my only family I ever had
Family, family—You're my little brother that I always had
You are my two little brothers that I always had
You are my mother—I always help you cook in the kitchen
Family, family—You are my father—You always go to work and pick me up
Family, family—I will always be your family and you will always be my family
Family, family—You are all my sisters—You're all my brothers

My mom and my dad and my step-sister and my half-brother
Family—You are my uncle, you are my brothers, you are my sisters
And you are my cousins
Family, family, family—Come back together, we will have some fun like we used to do
Family, family—You are my best family
Family, family

JeanMarie's song simultaneously mourns the loss of her family and yearns for the idealized (even mythical, i.e., "above the stars") family she never had. Poetically speaking, her mother really was "above the stars," since she had passed away. Her affect and imagery seemed to reflect a view of Melanie Klein (1936), wherein music is related to the integration and healing of beloved object relationships. Through the use of such *musical object relationships,* the self aims at reaching harmony and balance by joining together psychic structures and attempting to preserve the internal symbolic representation of the beloved object. To take that concept one step further, Dewey (1934) believed that the distinguishing feature of the artistic experience is that "no such distinction of self and object exists in it, since it is aesthetic in the degree in which organism and environment cooperate to institute an experience in which the two are so fully integrated that each disappears" (p. 250). In the *creative now,* to use Clive Robbins' term (cited in Turry, 2001), the fragmentation between self and other, loss and desire, reality and fantasy do not exist. In essence, in that moment, we are whole; we are healed.

As this session was coming to an end, JeanMarie reprised the family theme. She had a difficult time with endings and would resist the conclusion of sessions with enormous intensity. We were in the habit of improvising a good-bye song to ease with the transition, although we had not yet hit on a recurring good-bye song. As she had been singing in gospel style, she continued with that, but instead of singing good-bye to me or to the music session, in general, she gave her final song a heartbreaking twist as she sang the following with up-tempo gospel fervor:

> *C'mon put your hands together*
> *We are family*
> *We got power—We got joy—We got anything you need*
> *Family*
> *Put your hands together with the family*
> *We are strong. We are tough—We're everything you can think of, yeah*
>
> > *Good-bye family . . .**

*(As she came to this line, I intuitively played a decrescendo in my gospel piano accompaniment and JeanMarie slowed with me as she soulfully sang a final lament...)

> *I will always remember you*
> *Bye-bye heart, bye-bye love*
> *Family*
> *I will always remember you*

When JeanMarie did establish an ongoing good-bye song about 3 months later, it was even more tragic. As we moved toward the end of the session, she began passionately singing,

We will say good-bye for the rest of our life
Good-bye, good-bye, good-bye

She sang the lines over and over for more than 10 minutes, increasing in intensity, eventually moving herself to tears. Bowlby and Parkes (1970) contend, "Yearning for the impossible, intemperate anger, impotent weeping, horror at the prospect of loneliness, pitiful pleading for sympathy and support—these are feelings that a bereaved person needs to express and sometimes first, to discover" (p. 210). Once she hit on this idea, she would have no other good-bye song. Week after week, I attempted to intervene by singing about how I would see her next time, but she would not integrate it. For JeanMarie, good-bye was final.

JeanMarie's tumultuous feelings were often revealed in a controlling and occasionally abusive manner toward me, giving me orders regarding what and when I could play and calling me names like "stupid" and "ugly." I did not attempt to censure this insulting and domineering behavior. Nor did I react as a punitive adult or engage in a power struggle with her. Rather, I held my own as a stable and secure ego presence. I asserted my right to play too, despite her recurrent desire to be the only one singing or playing. An example of how this played itself out in music occurred when I attempted to help JeanMarie tune a guitar that she wanted to play. She made it clear that she had no use for my assistance, demanding that I go away and leave her alone, adding that I was a "loser." Affecting exaggerated outrage, I disputed her, but JeanMarie insisted that, my opinion notwithstanding, I was indeed a loser. Rather than perpetuating a verbal debate, I launched into a strong "hip-hop" beat on a conga and improvised my "rapped" reply. JeanMarie immediately stopped arguing with me and began dancing as a musical debate ensued.

Therapist:	*People say that I'm a loser but I don't care—that's okay*
	I know that I'm really special so you can say just what you want to say
	It don't matter to me—I ain't no loser—I can sit here and sing my song
	She can play guitar if she wants, but I know that I can't go wrong
Therapist:	*I ain't no loser**
JeanMarie:	*Yes you are**

*This recurring chorus went back and forth with slight variations in the wording for several minutes.

JeanMarie:	*'Cause I'm singing in your face*
	'Cause I'm special—I'm all that you're not, 'cause I'm all that
	You can't sing—You can't play the drums—You can't do anything like I can do it, too
Therapist:	*I just like to do the things . . .*
JeanMarie	(interrupting): *But you can't do it*
Therapist :	*Anything I like to do—I can do it—How 'bout you?*
JeanMarie:	*But you can't play—But you can't rate*
	'Cause you can't rhyme—Can't tell time
	Can't come on time—Always late—Can't rate
Therapist:	*I ain't no loser**
JeanMarie:	*Yes you are**

The song continued with additional points on either side for quite a while. JeanMarie's fight for validity and superiority, although played out at my expense, seemed to reflect the struggle for competence connected with Erickson's Stage 4, industry versus inferiority. With her line, "I'm special," she took her cue from my similar assertion in the first verse, thus utilizing me as a role model for healthy self-esteem. Other lines such as "I'm all that you're not" also reveal her need to find a sense of competence and self-esteem while deflecting feelings of shame identified with trauma at early stages of development.

An important breakthrough for JeanMarie occurred about 2 months later with an improvisation called *Nobody Just Like You.* This tribute to individuality rolled along with a sprightly folk-rock feel as we traded lines such as, "Nobody even talk like you," "Nobody even sing like you," "Nobody in the world exactly like you," etc. Through this song, she found some ego separation. She was, indeed, "special," despite her history as an abused child. Her willingness to collaborate improved as did her pitch and dynamic control. Her singing became more regulated, without the frantic, pressured quality of her earlier pieces, indicating a more intact and confident presentation. Crowe (2004) points out that music therapy develops ego strength and improved self-concept

> through engagement in successful playing experiences with real and obvious standards of achievement. Progress made in music skill building is overt and obvious to the client. No external feedback is needed. We can hear for ourselves when our playing gets better. (p. 279)

One more piece seemed to build on the foundations of the previous pieces. As I played a slow, but rhythmic minor blues on the guitar, JeanMarie improvised a song with the refrain, "I Didn't Know Rick Was Like This (He's Nothing But Trouble)." Although reverting back to the device of utilizing me as the "bad" object, she sang this "funky" ballad with restraint and excellent pitch control. Her dark vocal tone and world-weary resignation recalled blues and gospel influenced singers such as Bessie Smith and Aretha Franklin. This piece, grieving the true nature of my flawed character, coincided with an uncertainty surrounding her adoption status and increase of acting-out behavior at home and at school. She projected on me what she might have imagined her foster mother and teachers (as well as her lost birth mother) were saying about her. Most significantly, however, her song did not reject me, perhaps indicating an enhancement of her own sense of hope, self-acceptance, and further healing related to internalized guilt and shame. The transformation of her earlier oppositional stance into a well-related artistic collaboration also could be interpreted as demonstrating a strengthening of basic trust, the most critical of ego strengths. For her to acknowledge her acceptance of me, as imperfect and as much trouble as I was, would have to imply at least some belief that the feeling was mutual.

Structure, Chaos, and Transformation

When music therapists working with children with emotional disturbances refer to the need for structure, they usually mean one or both of two things:

- A particular individual or group requires an explicit sense of behavioral expectations (perhaps with consequences for transgressions); and/or
- The parameters for participation in a musical piece (exactly where, how, when to sing/play) or overall session format (what happens and in what order) must be absolutely clear.

Without such definition, the potential for chaotic music and/or behavior would seem to be very high. An earnest concern on the part of a therapist might be that children with severe behavioral disturbances cannot handle too much freedom and that it would be contraindicated to place them in a situation that encouraged maladaptive responses.

Providing limits can be akin to offering auxiliary ego strength to enhance the experience of meaningful expression. As Igor Stravinsky (1942) observed, increasing constraints frees one from the chains that hinder the spirit. It is, undoubtedly, an aspect of the music therapist's role to evaluate the degree of clinical need and apply this form of support as necessary (but not more). However, helping children to cultivate their own sense of aesthetics, their unique musical style, in music therapy is also essential. I have found children to be quite capable of developing the ability to make musical choices based on their own unique sensibilities without the therapist imposing his/her need for more ordered and conventional musical form. It imparts to them not only that their feelings are valid, but also that we want to hear about them. Nordoff and Robbins (2004) point out:

> Fundamentally, the way a person feels is more important to his life than the way he thinks. Feelings are of primary importance to children [and] it is what he feels about what he knows that determines what he does with his knowledge and its ultimate value to himself and the world. . . . Children do not do anything well unless they want to do it. Want is an emotional condition. The way a child goes about an action is a function of the way he feels about it. (pp. 49–50)

If a creative environment (allowing for appropriate choice-making, discovery, and responsibility) is extended for a time, children usually discover a way to utilize it in accordance with internal structures involved in their powerful self-actualization drives. According to Carl Rogers (1961), "The mainspring of creativity appears to be the same tendency which we discover so deeply as the curative force in psychotherapy—man's tendency to actualize himself, to become his potentialities" (p. 350).

Though the fear of *chaos* relates to the pejorative sense of the word as a total breakdown of order, the new theory in physics, *the science of complexity*, changes the meaning of this word and gives chaos much to recommend it. Music therapist Barbara Crowe (2004) referred to *chaos theory* stemming from the modern science of complex systems in motion within the macro- or big word, as opposed to action at the quantum or subatomic level. In chaos theory, complex systems in motion, known as *dynamical systems*, only appear to be chaotic because they are so supremely complex. "Beyond a certain threshold of complexity, systems go in unpredictable directions; they lose their initial conditions and cannot be reversed or recovered" (Briggs & Peat, 1989, p. 155). Though these chaotic systems appear random and without order, they do, in fact, have well established patterns of underlying order, which could be considered *archetypal patterns* since they are universal and predictable. Additionally, dynamical systems are open systems. They can and are changed and influenced by even the smallest "information" being added to the system. With added information, something entirely new will emerge out of the swirling pool of variables, always changing, evolving, and moving forward. In music therapy, dynamical systems include the music itself with its movement, energy and patterns of relationships, all aspects of human functioning (physical, cognitive, behavioral), and the process of therapy itself, including the thoughts and intentions of the therapist. A wealth of discussion in music therapy and related literature refers to the inherent structures of music as embodying and reflecting this underlying universal archetypal patterning (Aigen, 1998; Berendt, 1983; Crowe, 2004; Jenny, 1974; Robbins & Robbins, 1998; Sekeles, 1996; Turry,

1998). According to Turry (1998), "The music that is created reaches beyond the client's present self to elicit developmental potentials and assist in the integration of the personality in a way unique to music" (p. 162). In this way, music is uniquely situated to provide new information with inherent, organizing patterns to move the complex system, the client and his or her behavior and response into a new, more adaptive direction.

Such views do not dislocate us, as clinicians, from our role as active facilitators making decisions and helping to shape the clinical environment. Rather, it calls us to an even greater level of presence to a process beyond our ability to fully control, one into which we must be willing to enter along with our clients. Bruscia (1995) reflects on the crucial nature of being there for his clients and how it necessitates a fluidity of consciousness.

> If we are to grasp the uniqueness of each client, and if we are to understand him as a subject who has the freedom to shape his own life, then we must go beyond the laws of objects, and we must begin to approach the unfathomable depths of his psyche. To do so, we as therapists must be prepared to move our consciousness—with courage, humility, and respect—into uncharted regions of the client's world, our own world as a person, and our world together as a client and therapist. (p. 197)

Winnicott (1966) describes the effects of early trauma and deprivation on a child as damaging the experience of "continuity of existence," giving rise to an "archaic conflict of meanings." According to Winnicott, for a small child this means chaos in developing psychic structures and an inability to calm down or ease the situation. Perhaps this shattering of internal consistency could be characterized, in musical terms, as atonal, rhythmically erratic, or harmonic tension without resolution. A piece of aesthetically pleasing music is generally seen as having a tonal center of some sort and predictable pulse. Likewise, harmonic tension is commonly seen as transitional. What if, for a child with damaged ego structures, organized, consonant music does not represent internal reality? What if the experience of tension is not transitional but constant? It may be necessary to first assist such children in expressing what is real for them, before they can be ready to expand their affective range. Nordoff and Robbins (2004) discussed the turbulent expression of their clients' emotional lives in music that was often wild and dissonant, noting that

> The music therapist would have to take hold of the child's disordered life . . . and work with this musically. Therapy would then lie in leading the child into the experiences of mobility and organization latent in the world of music. The child could only accompany me into this world and gain these experiences through his own activity. (p. 41)

This brings up an important question. If we cannot always utilize a conventional aesthetic sensibility in evaluating the potency of clinical music, how does one differentiate between noise and healing music? Aigen (1995) acknowledged that tension in therapy and life is not only unavoidable, but, in fact, a necessary precursor to growth. He also proposed that "the artist within the child, *the music child*, learns to experience tension in a positive manner when his or her *aesthetic sensitivity is engaged*" (p. 244). How, then, does one define aesthetics in the face of dissonant, chaotic sounding music? The word *aesthetic* is often considered a synonym for beautiful. However, Salas (1990) identified beauty in music as that which is analogous to "our inner world, allowing us . . . an intimation of ontological purposefulness, an intuited perception that indeed our existence has meaning" (p. 5). Thus, through the gratification inherent in artistic validation of inner reality, even music that is unrelentingly unstable can facilitate growth as one's inner response to tension transforms from negative (overwhelmed, avoidant, threatened) to positive (accepting, expressive, related). Aigen noted one more essential element in the definition of clinical aesthetics—the therapeutic relationship.

> What I am saying is that as regards musical activity, there is always some external element in terms of which the discharge acquires communicative significance which voids its nature as pure discharge. To consider a musical act in a therapy session as pure catharsis is to ignore the ever-present clinical and relational context which orients all activities taking place within it. (p. 245)

Case Study 2

Danielle was 7 years old. Until the age of 3, she lived with her mother, who was a drug-addict and dealer, intermittently homeless, and a prostitute. Danielle was severely neglected, in addition to being sexually and physically abused during this time. When her mother was incarcerated, Danielle was placed in a foster home. Danielle's mother occasionally wrote letters expressing her intent to regain custody upon release from prison, a prospect that filled Danielle with great anxiety and ambivalence.

Her temporary foster mother referred Danielle to therapy services due to escalating behavioral problems. It was reported that Danielle consistently lied and stole, both at home and at school. She exhibited violent and antisocial behaviors, including superficially cutting her foster mother several times with a knife and attempting to strangle the family cat. The foster mother described Danielle as lacking in remorse, and that, in fact, she seemed to derive pleasure from doing "bad things." Danielle did not deny these actions but tended to minimize them and deflect responsibility, blaming other people (even the cat) for provoking her. In contrast to this profile, Danielle initially presented as a "sweet little girl," very bright and friendly but also a bit inappropriately familiar, as if she had known someone for years that she actually just met. She was diagnosed by her psychotherapist with conduct disorder and reactive attachment disorder.

Danielle was referred to music therapy as part of her treatment. At first, she appeared amiable and compliant. She also seemed quite musical, being able to initiate and maintain strong rhythms on a drum and create well-realized melodic and harmonic improvisations on the piano. This superficial facade rapidly faded as she became acclimated to the expressive freedom available to her in the session. Her music became angry and confrontational. She would pound out dissonant clusters on the piano keyboard with no discernable rhythm, then abruptly stop and stare at me defiantly. Any music I made was always "too loud" according to Danielle, no matter how sensitively I attempted to play or how violently she played. If I endeavored to engage in a collaborative musical improvisation, her music would become even more impenetrable, with tumultuous sounds on the piano or drum, or else she would stop playing entirely. Although she would acquiesce to limit-setting regarding how savagely she could treat an instrument, she also made it clear, in no uncertain terms, that she had no sympathy or caring for my needs or sensibilities. She barely knew me, she would say. Why should it matter to her how I felt or what I wanted? At one point, she emphasized the magnitude of her contempt by saying she hated me. Although I believed these feelings were real for Danielle, I also sensed that she recognized the creative forum available to her and was utilizing it as a sounding board. From that viewpoint, her expressions could be more effectively understood as an intuitive understanding of the symbolic nature of art, making it once removed from the directly personal, as opposed to interpreting it strictly as *transference.*

Weekly sessions proceeded in, more or less, this manner for about 5 months at which point Danielle took the summer off to attend camp. When she returned in the fall, she seemed less petulant. Her musicality was more evident, and she was more open to collaboration. Then, one day, after a few weeks, Danielle reverted back to her earlier persona with a vengeance. Disdainful, vociferous, and inaccessible, she was in the process of smashing two hand-cymbals together as loudly as she could when the attached handle came off, and the cymbal fell to the floor. Danielle thought she had broken the cymbal, although she had merely loosened a screw. Adopting the metaphorically confrontational tone that had been transpiring between us, I quipped, "Uh, oh, that cymbal cost 60 billion dollars." Danielle was astute and defiant. I expected her to easily perceive my facetiousness and reply with indifference, "I don't care," or "That's your problem." Instead, to my surprise, she looked distraught. I soon realized she was not feigning (as I first thought), as she slumped down in a chair and began to weep. I was taken aback and suddenly aware of an unsettling countertransference, feeling myself a perpetrator of further emotional abuse of this already deeply traumatized little girl.

Extensive verbal processing ensued as I ascertained the degree of her distress over her belief that she had broken this astronomically expensive instrument and her possible responsibility for replacing it. I confirmed the realities of the situation. First of all, I was joking. Second, she had not actually damaged the instrument. Third, it probably cost about $5. And fourth, even if she had broken it, she would not be expected to pay for it. When she was a little more composed, I said, "Wow, Danielle. You're not so tough, after all, are you?" She sadly shook her head. "No," she whimpered. I assured her that her vulnerability was honored and safe in the session and suggested we try to play "the most sensitive music we can together," a proposal to which she never would have previously agreed, but which she now accepted. I played a pentatonic scale on piano to avoid any harmonic dissonance as Danielle reflectively strummed an open-tuned acoustic guitar. Our delicate, quiet improvisation was unlike anything we had ever done before. I intermittently added the improvised lyrics in a pentatonic melody:

> *It's okay to be sensitive. It's okay to cry.*
> *It's okay to be sensitive when you're warm and dry.*

Regarding that second line, it did not occur to me until later that I was singing to a little girl who had periodically lived on the street. When we completed this music, we sat in silence for a few minutes.

According to the clock, the session was technically over, but Danielle did not seem to want to leave. As I had no client directly after her, I thought it important that this pivotal session be brought to an organic sense of completion that was humanistic, not chronological. Danielle wanted to play more. We exchanged instruments, and she started to play a rapid succession of notes on the piano utilizing all the keys, black and white, across practically the full-length of the keyboard. Technically, it was impressive, and there was a resemblance to her previously unapproachable music, but there was also a difference. Rather than clusters, she played mostly single notes. Although atonal and speedy, this music was still melodic and organized by a well-defined 8-to-the bar swing-like rhythm.

I accompanied on guitar, utilizing a whole-tone scale and augmented harmonies to avoid establishing a centered tonality. This music went on for several minutes and never once achieved any harmonic stability. It was wild and dissonant but also revealed growth in its accessibility and artistic points of contact. It contextualized her previously tempestuous and distancing musical statements, without denying them, as it transformed their meaning and intent into a boldly honest expression of unrelenting tension. We continued this challenging, yet unified, music until we simultaneously hit one final note. The music seemed to take a breath (as did we), and Danielle proclaimed us, "Done."

Following that session, Danielle and I engaged in many collaborative efforts that seemed more conventional for a 7-year-old, including various tonal improvisations and singing children's songs together. She remains an intense and troubled little girl but is increasingly vulnerable and honest with her feelings, exhibiting increased trust as she makes progress in untangling her complex and guarded emotional patterns. Recently, Danielle played piano using primarily the white keys as she led us in a beautiful, classically tinged improvisation with just enough chromatic dissonance to make it interesting and keep me on my toes. I accompanied on guitar, framing the piece essentially in a C-based Ionian mode to maintain the diatonic tonality. Danielle also designated approximately an octave and a half at the top-end of the keyboard as her solo territory, and I was to stop playing altogether when she played any of those tones. Scheiby (1991) noted that any musical structure a client presents serves as a mirror of the client's psychological organization. Danielle's composition offered a symbolic representation of a personality far more functional than previously observed. This personality is primarily able to relate with a degree of unpredictable individuality and encompassing boundaries that established personal space, rather than needing to shut me out altogether.

Conclusion

Children who have faced the depth of trauma such as those described in the preceding case studies face grueling challenges and precarious futures. Escalona (1974) identified the conditions that constitute the greatest risk factors for psychopathology as (a) children without families, (b) children grossly neglected or abused, and (c) children raised in settings of severe poverty. Sadly, many children considered emotionally disturbed need to deal with significant psychiatric problems in their later life. However, a contemporary biopsychosocial perspective does not consider early traumatic experiences to be the inevitable origins of ongoing pathology. This construct cites a broad analysis of intrinsic and environmental interactions, within which pathology may be caused by genetic vulnerability or acquired vulnerability, but resilience is also typical as is the child's active influence on his or her environment (Scarr, 1992). Dawes (1994) claims no incubation effect based on early childhood problems. Clearly, childhood trauma may create deep psychic wounds that can be quite difficult to overcome, but there are additional variables at work.

Many a person has risen above a profoundly troubled youth to become a functional and successful adult. Therefore, the power and potential latent in creative transcendence can never be underestimated. In Nordoff-Robbins practice, positive change is interpreted as "a transcendence of the pathological by the clients whose motivation has been strengthened and whose range of expression has been broadened through participation in the creative process" (Turry & Marcus, 2003, p. 199). By going into a room with our clients and the instruments, we offer, as Salas (1990) put it:

> the opportunity to distill the expression of emotion into aesthetic form. This is a profound experience. Far transcending the simple discharge of feelings, it is a way to feel oneself part of the pattern that connects, even to feel one's participation in its creation. (p. 14)

Neumann (1959) wrote, "The creative process is generation and birth as well as transformation and rebirth" (p. 202). These children have known so much trauma and devastation at such a young age that it has become deeply integrated into the fabric of their being. The opportunity of affording them a chance to re-create themselves is to honor the promise and optimism of childhood.

References

Aigen, K. (1995). An aesthetic foundation of clinical theory: An underlying basis for Creative Music Therapy. In C. Kenny (Ed.), Listening, playing, creating: Essays on the power of sound (pp. 233–258). Albany, NY: State University of New York Press.

Aigen, K. (1998). Paths of development in Nordoff-Robbins music therapy. Gilsum, NH: Barcelona.

Berendt, J. (1983). The world is sound: Nada Brahma. Rochester, VT: Destiny Books.

Bohman, D. O. (1990). Outcome in adoption: Lessons from longitudinal studies. In D. Brodzinsky & M. Schecter (Eds.), The psychology of adoption (pp. 93–106). Oxford, England: Oxford University Press.

Bowlby, J., & Parkes, C. M. (1970). Separation and loss within the family. In E. Anthony & C. Koupernik, (Eds.), The child in his family (Vol. 1). New York: John Wiley & Sons.

Briggs, J., & Peat, F. D. (1989). Turbulent mirror. New York: Harper & Row.

Bruscia, K. (1987). Improvisational models of music therapy. Springfield, IL: Charles C. Thomas.

Bruscia, K. (1995). Modes of consciousness in guided imagery and music (GIM): A therapist's experience of the guiding process. In C. Kenny. (Ed.), Listening, playing, creating: Essays on the power of sound (pp. 165–198). Albany, NY: State University of New York Press.

Bruscia, K. (1998). An introduction to music psychotherapy. In K. Bruscia. (Ed.), The dynamics of music psychotherapy (pp. 1–15). Gilsum, NH: Barcelona.

Crowe, B. (2004). Music and soulmaking: Toward a new theory of music therapy. Lanham, MD: Scarecrow Press.

Dawes, R. M. (1994). House of cards: Psychology and psychotherapy built on myth. New York: The Free Press.

Dewey, J. (1934). Art as experience. New York: Wideview/Perigee.

Erikson, E. H. (1963). Childhood and society. New York: Norton.

Escalona, S. (1974). Intervention programs for children at psychiatric risk: The contribution of child psychology and developmental theory. In E. Anthony & C. Koupernik, (Eds.), The child in his family (Vol. III). New York: John Wiley & Sons.

Freud, S. (1961). Beyond the pleasure principle. New York: Norton.

Gitlin-Weiner, K., Sandgrund, A., Schaefer, C., (Eds.). (2000). Play diagnosis and assessment. New York: John Wiley & Sons.

Jenny, H. (1974). Cymatics: The structure and dynamics of waves and vibrations (Vols. I & II). Basel, Switzerland: Basilius Press.

Kennair, L. (2000). Developing minds for pathology and musicality. Nordic Journal of Music Therapy, 9(1), 26–37.

Klein, M. (1936). The psychogenesis of manic-depressive states. International Journal of Psychoanalysis, 16, 145–175.

Laymen, D., Hussey, D., & Laing, S. (2002a). Foster care trends in the United States: Ramifications for music therapists. Music Therapy Perspectives, 20(2), 38–46.

Laymen, D., Hussey, D., & Laing, S. (2002b). Music therapy assessment for severely emotionally disturbed children: A pilot study. Journal of Music Therapy, 39(3), 164–184.

Lehtonen, K. (1994). Is music an archaic form of thinking? Nordic Journal of Music Therapy, 3(1), 3–12.

Loewy, J. (1994). A hermeneutic panel study of music therapy assessment with an emotionally disturbed boy (Doctoral dissertation, New York University, 1994). Dissertation Abstracts International, 55(9-A), 2631.

Loewy, J. (1995). The musical stages of speech. Music Therapy, 13(1), 47–74.

Loewy, J. (2000). Music psychotherapy assessment. Music Therapy Perspectives, 18(1), 47–58.

Neumann, E. (1959). Art and the creative unconscious. Princeton, NJ: Princeton University Press.

Nordoff, P., & Robbins, C. (1977). Creative music therapy. New York: John Day.

Nordoff, P., & Robbins, C. (2004). Therapy in music for handicapped children. Gilsum, NH: Barcelona.

Piaget, J. (1972). The psychology of the child. New York: Basic Books.

Robbins, C., & Robbins, C. (Eds.). (1998). Healing heritage. Gilsum, NH: Barcelona.

Rogers, C. (1961). On becoming a person. New York: Houghton Mifflin.

Salas, J. (1990). Aesthetic experience in music therapy. Music Therapy, 9(1), 1–15.

Scarr, S. (1992). Developmental theories for the 1990's: Development and individual differences. Child Development, 63, 1–19.

Scheiby, B. (1991). Mia's fourteenth—the symphony of fate: Psychodynamic improvisation therapy with a music therapy student in training. In K. Bruscia (Ed.), Case studies in music therapy (pp. 271–290). Phoenixville, PA: Barcelona.

Sekeles, C. (1996). Music: Motion and emotion. St Louis, MO: MMB Music.

Stravinsky, I. (1942). The poetics of music. Cambridge, MA: Harvard University Press.

Turry, A. (1998). Transference and countertransference in Nordoff-Robbins music therapy. In K. Bruscia (Ed.), The dynamics of music psychotherapy. Gilsum, NH: Barcelona.

Turry, A. (2001). Supervision in the Nordoff-Robbins training program. In M. Forinash (Ed.), Music therapy supervision (pp. 351–378). Gilsum, NH: Barcelona.

Turry, A., & Marcus, D. (2003). Using the Nordoff-Robbins approach to music therapy with adults diagnosed with autism. In L. K. Oxford & D. J. Wiener (Eds.), Action therapy with families and groups: Using creative arts improvisation in clinical practice (pp. 197–228). Washington, DC: American Psychological Association.

U.S. Department of Education. (2001). Twenty-third annual report to Congress on the implementation of the Individuals with Disabilities Education Act. Washington, DC: U.S. Government Printing Office.

Westen, D. (1990). Psychoanalytic approaches to personality. In L. A. Pervin (Ed.), Handbook of personality: Theory and research (pp. 21–65). New York: Guilford Press.

Whitfield, C. L. (1995). Memory and abuse. Remembering and healing the effects of trauma. Deerfield Beach, FL: Health Communications.

Winnicott, D. W. (1966). The location of the cultural experience. International Journal of Psychoanalysis, 48, 368–372.

Chapter 15

Music Therapy for Adolescents with Emotional/Behavioral Disturbances
Barbara J. Crowe

Though adolescents and children are given the same diagnostic designation and can be assessed in a similar fashion, music therapy practice for adolescents is very different than that for children. These differences are delineated below.

Music and Adolescents

Music is of particular importance in the adolescent subculture. Moran (1985) found that adolescents listen to music from 4 to 6 hours a day. They tend to listen to music with which they personally identify (Wooten, 1992). Music is a basic way for adolescents to communicate. "Music is often the only tool that enhances communication with this population" (Brooks, 1989, p. 38). Wooten (1992) suggests that using the musical preferences of adolescents helps the music therapist understand the emotional issues of the client, provides for introducing and discussing alternative coping skills and behavioral responses, and provides a bridge to the client. For the adolescent, music represents power, control, and, frequently, rebellion against adults and society (Brooks, 1989). Adolescents use music, particularly popular music, in a variety of ways:

- To relax and relieve stress (Doak, 2003)
- To pass the time and relieve boredom
- To get their mind off problems
- To deal with psychological pain
- To increase sensitivity to others
- To help deal with other people
- To explore learning a musical skill (Gantz, Gartenberg, Pearson, & Schiller, 1978).

Doak (2003) notes that adolescents use music and drugs for the same purpose—to alleviate psychological pain. For adolescents, music acts as a psychoactive drug to change emotions and mood states. They may be using music to escape their emotional turmoil or to "fix" their problems by altering their mood (Wooten, 1992).

Exploring the musical preferences of adolescent clients can also provide information on their possible diagnoses. Doak (2003) reports that research has established a significant correlation between preferred music and psychiatric diagnosis. She writes, "Adolescents with the same diagnoses may be drawn to the same type of music but are not in agreement about why they listen to this music" (Doak, 2003, p. 21). In general, the following correlations between genre of music preferred and diagnosis have been drawn:

- Depression = rap, heavy metal, techno
- Mood disorders = rap, classic rock, hard rock, heavy metal, and alternative
- Oppositional/defiant disorder = only rap and techno (Doak, 2003, p. 71)

For the music therapist working with adolescents with emotional/behavioral disorders, it is vital to listen to and be familiar with current adolescent music. This becomes a constant process of learning and knowing what music is popular with adolescents. The music therapist must be genuinely open to their music and must find a way to join with them in experiencing and appreciating the music. For the adolescents, music is the projection of themselves outwardly. If the music therapist accepts their music, he or she accepts the clients. To reject their music is to reject them. However, because of highly inappropriate and objectionable lyrics of some current popular music, some editing of music to be used may be necessary, especially if the facility has a policy about inappropriate language (T. Winn, personal communication, January 4, 2005).

Problem Areas for Adolescents With Emotional/Behavioral Disturbance

Adolescents also display acting-out behaviors, though these tend to be more in the area of social acting out. Specific problem areas include:

- age-inappropriate behaviors;
- hyperactivity;
- aggression, gang involvement;
- problems in peer and adult relationships;
- depression;
- psychosomatic disorders;
- poor academic performance;
- poor self-concept, including negative self-image and failure-oriented self-view;
- poor body image;
- unrealistic goals and inappropriate fantasy;
- narcissism;
- criminal behavior and social acting out, including vandalism, fire setting, and assault;
- interpersonal problems (Brooks, 1989; Haines, 1989; Paul, 1982).

Goals for Adolescents in Music Therapy

Music therapy makes a unique contribution to the overall therapeutic effort for adolescents with emotional/behavioral problems. Music creates a freer environment for the adolescents to be themselves. A music therapy session can provide an opportunity for a client's free creative expression compared to other therapeutic disciplines.

Many of the goals appropriate for children with mental disorders are appropriate for adolescents. Typical goals for adolescents with emotional/behavioral disturbance in music therapy include the following:

- Improve self-esteem, which is the internalized process that involves the formation of beliefs, concepts, and evaluation about one's worth and self-concept through successful experiences, acceptance, respectful attention, and well-defined and enforced limits (Haines, 1989).
- Improve body-image as a means to decrease sexual acting out through expressive movement to music, learning personal boundaries by exploring space, and appropriate expression of energy (Brooks, 1989).
- Develop sense of empowerment, directing power in acceptable ways and developing appropriate forms of attention seeking.
- Provide for identity formation through a process of trial and error.
- Develop positive peer identification.
- Develop a means for self-expression.
- Develop better integration of affect and behavior.
- Develop communication skills. Development of verbal communication skills first requires the nonverbal skills of listening, eye contact, attention span, voice tone and timbre discrimination skills, and means of appropriate expression (Haines, 1989).
- Develop social skills, positive group behaviors, and appropriate interactions with peers including cooperation. Adolescents need to find ways to positively be individuals in a group (T. Winn, personal communication, January 4, 2005). Music provides adolescents with age-appropriate parallel play experiences as the first step toward group behaviors (Haines, 1989).
- Develop care and concern for others.
- Increase emotional awareness and self-expression.
- Develop relaxation strategies to decrease anxiety.
- Develop emotional behavior, including nonverbal expression of emotions, identification and labeling of emotions, and emotional awareness.
- Develop problem-solving skills.
- Develop effective coping techniques.
- Develop personal insight as to underlying causes of problems.
- Uncover repressed memories and emotions.
- Promote reality testing.
- Improve interpersonal relationships, especially with authority figures.
- Develop positive, appropriate leisure activities and interests (Edgerton, 1990; Haines, 1989; Wells, 1988; T. Winn, personal communication, January 4, 2005; Wooten, 1992).

Emunah (1990) sees a three-fold purpose for music therapy with adolescents with emotional/behavioral disturbance:

- Expression with an emphasis on creativity.
- Containment with a balance and interplay between expression and behavioral containment. This includes a sense of mastery over emotion and musical skill development to help exercise control and experience mastery.

- Expansion involving the ability to think beyond the present. In the music therapy experience, the adolescent vision is externalized and made concrete through the art expression such as songwriting.

Music Therapy Interventions for Adolescents

Group music therapy interventions are often emphasized because adolescents live within groups. A client can be included in a group intervention if he has enough social skills. These include the ability to listen and stay in a chair and the presence of minimal attention-seeking behaviors. Whatever the specific intervention used, the music and the music therapy session must always be fun, pleasurable, and interesting to the client. One way to structure a session is to have several activity interventions prepared and let the group come to a consensus as to what they will do for any particular session. Adolescents need some sense of autonomy and control. Two rules are essential for a group music therapy session for adolescents—safety and respect. All other session "rules" derive from these two principles (T. Winn, personal communication, January 4, 2005).

A large portion of the therapeutic effort for adolescents with emotional/behavioral disturbance falls in Wheeler's (1983) first two levels of music therapy—supportive activity therapy (product-oriented), and insight therapy with re-educative goals (process-oriented). The third level, re-constructive, analytical/catharsis-oriented therapy primarily focuses on musical improvisation.

Supportive Activity Therapy

A number of music therapy interventions fall under this category. These include the following:
- *Musical skill building.* Learning a musical skill is highly valued by adolescents. Skill building provides an adolescent with musical skills that are socially acceptable, positive, and esteemed by the adolescent culture (T. Winn, personal communication, January 4, 2005). Skill-building sessions can involve individual instruction or the use of cooperative play during small groups or combos (J. de la Houssaye, personal communication, January 5, 2005). Adolescents are particularly interested in electric guitars and basses, acoustic guitars, drum sets, electric keyboards, synthesizers, multi-effects boards, and drums and percussion from world music traditions (African, Afro-Caribbean). Rhythms as close to "house music" (based on African rhythms) as possible should be emphasized. Musical skill-building activities support improved self-esteem, develop a means for positive peer relations, and can sublimate tension and anxiety.
- *Music appreciation.* The music therapist can compare current music to traditional music (such as African) and investigate and expose the clients to the history of rock and roll leading to hip-hop and rap. A rate-a-record activity can be done to determine the clients' musical preferences and to develop a tolerance for preferences different from their own. To structure a rate-a-record activity, short excerpts of music should be used (30 seconds) and a written rating scale provided for responses. Discussion of preferences should follow.
- *Musical performance groups.* These foster appropriate interpersonal interaction, group behaviors, responsibility, and care and concern for others. Existing musical skills can be used as the basis of a performance group or skills can be taught. Rock, blues, jazz, and rap groups

are most appealing to adolescents, though specialized performance groups using handbells, tone chimes, and large drums for expression of power and mastery are effective (Rio & Tenney, 2002). The music therapists can use existing percussion ensemble music, including African drum and Afro Caribbean forms and modern drum ensembles like the Will Schmidt World Drumming Curriculum (Schmidt, 1998).

- *Public performance groups.* Performing for others helps clients control inappropriate behaviors, provides for self-esteem, and fosters group cohesion (Michel & Martin, 1970).

- *Structured rhythmic improvisation.* In this intervention, the group as a whole holds a steady beat. Then each client improvises a rhythm over 8 counts. A variation of this activity is to have the clients take turns improvising a short rhythm pattern that the group then echoes. This call-and-response activity gives clients experiences in leadership, supports self-esteem, and helps with impulse control (ability to produce a short, replicable pattern).

- *Singing and vocal instruction.* These interventions can involve individual vocal instruction or group singing. Current music or songs that are popular with their parents (as they will be familiar with this music) are used (J. de la Houssaye, personal communication, January 5, 2005). With adolescents, singing is most successful when the therapist-supplied accompaniment (piano or guitar) is of high quality and as close to the sound on the recording as possible. Use of a karaoke machine can also be useful.

- *Name That Tune.* This intervention can serve as an introductory session for music therapy. Clients are divided into two groups with a designated leader. The group gets a point for a correct answer only if the leader speaks for them. This fosters group cooperation, impulse control, peer identification, and group feeling (J. de la Houssaye, personal communication, January 5, 2005).

- *Movement to music.* Emphasis should be on pre-dance movement at first with bodily reflection of rhythm and beat. Structured movement experiences using rhythm and beat are usually most successful initially. Structured dance may also be introduced. Some structured forms of expressive movement evoked by music help with poor body image (Brooks, 1989). Note: A group of male-only adolescent clients do not usually participate in a group movement experience due to anxiety and embarrassment.

- *Use of technology.* Adolescents are completely comfortable with all aspects of musical technology and are attracted to anything with power. Interventions could include use of videotape or digital recording to make a music video; use of multitrack recording devices to record songs, rap songs, or other compositions; use of microphone and amplifier for singing; and the use of computers and computer software for musical composition. Work with technology gives adolescents a sense of empowerment and an opportunity to work on how to have and manage power in appropriate ways (T. Winn, personal communication, January 4, 2005).

- *Musical composition.* These interventions can involve simple techniques based on a basic rhythm pattern with improvised melodic fragments, fill-in-the-blanks songs, and chants with accompaniments.

- *Music for relaxation.* (See the section on music and relaxation techniques in Chapter 4.)

- *Music and imagery.* Basic, structured music and imagery experiences may be useful with adolescents. (See the section on music and imagery in Chapter 6.) Having the clients draw their images provides a concrete expression of the experience for them and serves as a basis for group discussion.

Insight Music Therapy with Re-Educative Goals

In insight music therapy with re-educative goals for adolescents, the music therapist should facilitate group discussions so the clients learn about their behavior from peers, not from the adult therapist. These activities do not involve therapist-directed insight psychotherapy (T. Winn, personal communication, January 4, 2005).

- *Songwriting.* Precomposed melodies or song forms like rap or blues can be used. Adolescents need written structure to produce appropriate song lyrics. (See section on song writing in Chapter 2.) Song writing can also involve song parody, where the lyrics of a song are changed to reflect personal issues, beliefs, or concerns.

- *Instrumental improvisation.* The emphasis in these interventions is not on musical product but on appropriate self-expression of emotions, issues, and concerns, especially the behavior that brought the clients to therapy. (See the section on clinical improvisation in Chapter 5 and music therapy for children with emotional disability in Chapter 14.) A version of this intervention is to have a client improvise and then have the group reflect on one special musical element presented or the overall mood and character of the improvisation (Haines, 1989). This becomes a form of musical empathy.

- *Song improvisation.* This involves having clients improvise a song about themselves or another group member. Using a specific song form like 12-bar blues facilitates this intervention (Haines, 1989).

- *Listening exercise.* This intervention involves listening to various forms of music while emphasizing mood recognition and emotional awareness. The experience includes group discussion (Henderson, 1983).

- *Lyric analysis.* The music therapist should try to use "their" music whenever possible. For adolescents, this should be approached with some structure; for example, have them circle the words in the lyrics that have meaning for them (see section on lyric analysis in Chapter 5), or provide them with a sheet of paper that has a series of questions to stimulate discussion.

- *Music combined with other creative arts.* These interventions can include picking a picture or drawing to music with verbal discussion, storytelling evoked by music, and sound illustration of a story or poem. Another form of combined creative arts expression is the album/CD cover. In this intervention, the music therapist shows how album/CD covers reflect the message or personality of the artist. Clients are asked to pick songs (a list of song titles is often supplied) and create the cover art for "their" album/CD. Verbal sharing and processing follows the creation of the covers.

Musical Instruments and Equipment Needed for Work With Adolescents

The following musical instruments and equipment are particularly useful to have for music therapy sessions for work with adolescents with emotional/behavioral disturbance:

- Full-size drum set

- Large ethnic and world drums—African tubanos, djembe, Kinkini; Afro Caribbean drums, maracas, and rattles; Japanese Tai Ko drums, etc.
- Electric guitar and electric bass
- Acoustic guitars
- Electric keyboards and synthesizers
- Sound system with microphones and amplifiers
- Multi-effects boards and pedal effects equipment for microphones and electric guitars
- Recording and music-processing technology, including multitrack recording; digital audio and video recording; CD burner; computers and computer programs for music composition, editing, and mixing; and loop stations
- Hand percussion specific to world music traditions; use authentic instruments from any given culture

Re-Constructive, Analytical/Catharsis-Oriented Music Therapy

The re-constructive, analytical and catharsis-oriented music therapy proposed by Wheeler (1983) is also used to great effect with adolescent clients. Much of this work with adolescents is achieved through musical improvisation interventions. (See section on clinical improvisation in Chapter 5.) A good example of re-constructive, analytical approach in music therapy for adolescents can to found in the article, "Symbol and Structure: Music Therapy for the Adolescent Psychiatric Inpatient," by Andrea Frisch (1990).

References

Brooks, D. M. (1989). Music therapy enhances treatment with adolescents. Music Therapy Perspectives, 6, 37–39.

Doak, B. A. (2003). Relationship between adolescent psychiatric diagnoses, music preferences, and drug preferences. Music Therapy Perspectives, 21(2), 69–76.

Edgerton, C. D. (1990). Creative group songwriting. Music Therapy Perspectives, 8, 15–19.

Emunah, R. (1990). Perspectives: Expression and expansion in adolescence: The significance of creative arts therapy. The Arts in Psychotherapy, 17(2), 101–107.

Frisch, A. (1990). Symbol and structure: Music therapy for the adolescent psychiatric inpatient. Music Therapy, 9(1), 16–34.

Gantz, W., Gartenberg, H. H., Pearson, M. L., & Schiller, S. O. (1978). Gratifications and expectations associated with pop music among adolescents. Popular Music and Society, 6, 81–89.

Haines, J. H. (1989). The effects of music therapy on the self-esteem of emotionally disturbed adolescents. Music Therapy, 8(1), 78–91.

Henderson, S. M. (1983). Effects of a music therapy program upon awareness of mood in music, group cohesion, and self-esteem among hospitalized adolescent patients. Journal of Music Therapy, 20(1), 14–20.

Michel, D. E., & Martin, D. (1970). Music and self-esteem: Research with disadvantaged, problem boys in an elementary school. Journal of Music Therapy, 7(4), 124–127.

Moran, T. (1985). Sounds of sex. The New Republic, 193, 14–16.

Paul, D. (1982). Music therapy for handicapped children: Emotionally disturbed. Washington, DC: National Association for Music Therapy.

Rio, R. E, & Tenney, K. S. (2002). Music therapy for juvenile offenders in residential treatment. Music Therapy Perspectives, 29(2), 89–97.

Schmidt, W. (1998). World music drumming. A cross cultural curriculum. Milwaukee, WI: Hal Leonard.

Wells, N. F. (1988). An individual music therapy assessment procedure for emotionally disturbed young adolescents. The Arts in Psychotherapy, 15(1), 47–54.

Wheeler, B. L. (1983). A psychotherapeutic classification of music therapy practices: A continuum of procedure. Music Therapy Perspectives, 1, 8–16.

Wooten, M. A. (1992). Towards a group analytic music therapy. Journal of British Music Therapy, 1, 16–21.

The author wishes to thank Tomas Winn, MT-BC, and Joel de la Houssaye, MT-BC, for their valuable assistance.

Section 6:

Resources

Comprehensive Bibliography

Music/Music Therapy for Clients with Mental Disorders

Abrams, B. (2002). Methods for analyzing music programs used in the Bonny Method. In K. E. Bruscia & D. E. Gorcke (Eds.), Guided imagery and music: The Bonny Method (pp. 318–335). Gilsum, NH: Barcelona.

Abrams, B. (2002). Transpersonal dimensions of the Bonny Method. In K. E. Bruscia & D. E. Gorcke (Eds.), Guided imagery and music: The Bonny Method (pp. 339– 358). Gilsum, NH: Barcelona.

Adelman, E. J. (1985). Multimodal therapy and music therapy: Assessing and treating the whole person. Music Therapy, 5(1), 12–21.

Ahonen-Eerikainen, H. (2002). Group-analytic music therapy: Using dreams and musical images as a pathway to the unconscious levels of the group matrix. Nordic Journal of Music Therapy, 11(1), 48–53.

Aigen, K. (1990). Echoes of silence. Music Therapy, 9(1), 44–61.

Aigen, K. (1996). Being in music: Foundations of Nordoff-Robbins music therapy. St. Louis, MO: MMB Music.

Aigen, K. (1997). Here we are in music: One year with an adolescent music therapy group. St. Louis, MO: MMB Music.

Aigen, K. (1999). The true nature of music-centered therapy theory. British Journal of Music Therapy, 13(2), 77–82.

Aigen, K. (2005). Music-centered music therapy. Gilsum, NH: Barcelona.

Ainlay, G. W. (1948). The place of music in military hospitals. In D. M. Schullian & M. Schoen (Eds.), Music and medicine (pp. 322–351). New York: Henry Schuman.

Albersnagel, F. A. (1988). Velten and musical mood induction procedures: A comparison with accessibility of thought associations. Behavior Research and Therapy, 26(1), 79–96.

Aldridge, D. (1993). The music of the body: Music therapy in clinical settings. Journal of Mind-Body Health, 9(1), 17–35.

Aldridge, D. (2003). Case study designs in music therapy. London: Jessica Kingsley.

Alexander, H. (1954). An investigation on the effects of music on personality by way of figure drawings. American Journal of Psychotherapy, 8, 687–702.

Allen, W. R., & White, W. F. (1966). Psychodramatic effects of music as a psychotherapeutic agent. Journal of Music Therapy, 3(1), 69–71.

Altschuler, I. M. (1939). Rational music therapy of the mentally ill. Music Teachers National Association Proceedings, 33, 153–157.

Altschuler, I. M. (1940). One year's experience with group psychotherapy. Mental Hygiene, 24, 190–196.

Altschuler, I. M. (1941). The part of music in resocialization of mental patients. Occupational Therapy and Rehabilitation, 20(2), 75–86.

Altschuler, I. M. (1941). The role of music in resocialization of mental patients. American Journal of Physical Medicine, 20, 75–86.

Altschuler, I. M. (1944). Four years experience with music as a therapeutic agent at the Eloise Hospital. American Journal of Psychology, 100(7), 792–794.

Altschuler, I. M. (1944). Music in the treatment of neurosis, theoretical considerations and practical experiences. Music Teachers National Association Proceedings, 154–163.

Altschuler, I. M. (1945). Report of the sub-committee on music in psychotherapy. Music Teachers National Association Proceedings, 39, 186–188.

Altschuler, I. M. (1948). A psychiatrist's experiences with music as a therapeutic agent. In D. M. Schullian & M. Schoen (Eds.), Music and medicine (pp. 266–281). New York: Henry Schuman.

Altschuler, I. M. (1954). Some neuropsychiatric considerations of music therapy in children. In M. Bing (Ed.), Music therapy 1953 (pp. 88–90). Lawrence, KS: Allen Press.

Altschuler, I. M. (1956). Music potentiating drugs. In E. T. Gaston (Ed.), Music therapy 1955 (pp. 120–126). Lawrence, KS: Allen Press.

Altschuler, I. M., & Shebesta, B. H. (1941). Music (alone or with hydrotherapy): Aid in management of the psychotic patient. The Journal of Nervous and Mental Disorder, 94, 179–183.

Alvin, J. (1966). Music therapy. New York: Basic Books.

Alvin, J. (1968). *Changing patterns in music therapy—Mental patient and community care in England.* In E. T. Gaston (Ed.), Music in therapy (pp. 389–393). Macmillan.

Alvin, J. (1975). *The identity of the music therapy group: A developmental process.* Journal of British Music Therapy, 6(3), 9–17.

Alvin, J. (1975). *Music therapy. London: Hutchinson.*

Alvin, J. (1977). *The musical instrument as an intermediary object.* British Journal of Music Therapy, 8(2), 7–12.

Alvin, J. (1981). *Regressional techniques in music therapy.* Music Therapy, 1(1), 3–8.

Alvin, J. (1982). *Free improvisation in individual therapy.* British Journal of Music Therapy, 13(2), 9–12.

Alward, E., & Rule, B. (1960). *An experiment in musical activities with disturbed children.* In E. H. Schneider (Ed.), Music therapy 1959 (pp. 153–168). Lawrence, KS: Allen Press.

American Music Therapy Association. (2004). *Standards of clinical practice.* In A. Elkins (Ed.), AMTA member sourcebook (pp. 18–22). Silver Spring, MD: Author.

Amir, D. (1993). *Moments of insight in the music therapy experience.* Music Therapy, 12(1), 85–100.

Amir, D. (1999). *Moments of insight in the music therapy experience.* Music Therapy, 12(1), 85–100.

Anderson, J. M., Cholden, L., Des Lauriers, A., & Miller, M. H. (1953). *Panel—Psychiatric concepts of music therapy.* In E. G. Gilliland (Ed.), Music therapy 1952 (pp. 25–33). Lawrence, KS: Allen Press.

Ansdell, G. (1990). *Limitations and potential—A report on a music therapy group for clients referred from a counseling services.* British Journal of Music Therapy, 14(1).

Ansdell, G. (1995). *Music for life: Aspects of creative music therapy with adult clients. London: Jessica Kingsley.*

Ansdell, G. (1997). *Musical elaborations: What has the new musicology to say to music therapy?* British Journal of Music Therapy, 13(2).

Ansdell, G. (1999). *Challenging premises: A response to Elaine Streeter's "Finding a balance between psychological thinking and musical awareness in music therapy"—A psychoanalytical perspective.* British Journal of Music Therapy, 13(2), 72–76.

Ansdell, G. (2002). *Community music therapy and the winds of change—A discussion paper.* In C. Kenny & B. Slige (Eds.), Contemporary voices in music therapy (pp. 109–142). Oslo, Norway: Unipubforlag.

Anshel, A., & Kipper, D. A. (1988). *The influence of group singing on trust and cooperation.* Journal of Music Therapy, 25(3), 145–155.

Apprey, Z. R., & Apprey, M. (1975). *Applied music therapy: Collected papers on a technique and a point of views. London: Institute of Music Therapy and Humanistic Psychology, International University.*

Arnold, M. (1975). *Music therapy in a transactional analysis setting.* Journal of Music Therapy, 12(3), 104–120.

Asmus, E. P., Jr., & Gilbert, J. P. (1981). *A client-centered model of therapeutic intervention.* Journal of Music Therapy, 18(1), 41–51.

Aten, E. L. (1954). *Psychiatric concepts of music therapy for children.* In M. Bing (Ed.), Music therapy 1953 (pp. 85–88). Lawrence, KS: Allen Press.

Atlee, E. A. (1804). *An inaugural essay on the influence of music in the cure of disease. Philadelphia, PA: Graves, Printer.*

Austin, D. (1989). *The healing sound: Sound, song and psychotherapy. Unpublished master's thesis, New York University.*

Austin, D. (1991). *The musical mirror: Music therapy for the narcissistically injured.* In K. E. Bruscia (Ed.), Case studies in music therapy (pp. 291–307). Phoenixville, PA: Barcelona.

Austin, D. (1993). *Projection of parts of the self onto music and musical instruments.* In M. Rolla (Ed.), Your inner music (pp. 93–99). Wilmette, IL: Chiron.

Austin, D. (1996). *The role of improvised music in psychodynamic music therapy with adults.* Music Therapy, 14(1), 29–43.

Austin, D. (1998). *When the psyche sings: Transference and countertransferrence in improvised singing with individual adults.* In K. E. Bruscia (Ed.), The dynamics of music psychotherapy (pp. 315–333). Gilsum, NH: Barcelona.

Austin, D. (1999). *Many stories, many songs.* In J. Hibben (Ed.), Inside music therapy: Client experiences (pp. 119–128). Gilsum, NH: Barcelona.

Austin, D. (1999). *Vocal improvisation in analytically oriented music therapy with adults.* In T. Wigram & J. DeBacker (Eds.), Clinical applications of music therapy in psychiatry (pp. 141–157). London: Jessica Kingsley.

Austin, D. (2001). *In search of the self: The use of vocal holding techniques with adults traumatized as children.* Music Therapy Perspectives, 19(1), 22–30.

Austin, D. (2002). *The voice of trauma. A wounded healer's perspective.* In J. Sutton (Ed.), Music, music therapy and trauma: International perspectives (pp. 231–259). London: Jessica Kingsley.

Austin, D. (2004). *When words sing and music speaks: A qualitative study of in depth music psychotherapy with adults.* (Doctoral dissertation, New York University, 2004). Dissertation Abstracts International, AAT 3110989.

Austin, D. S., & Dvorkin, J. M. (1993). *Resistance in individual music therapy.* The Arts in Psychotherapy, 20(5), 423–429.

Baines, S. (2000). *A consumer-directed and partnered community mental health program: Program development and evaluation.* Canadian Journal of Music Therapy, 7(1), 51–70.

Baker, E. K., & Hornyak, L. M. (Eds.). (1989). *The handbook of techniques in the treatment of eating disorders. New York: Guilford.*

Baker, F., & Wigram, T. (Eds.). (in press). *Song writing methods, techniques and clinical applications for music therapy clinicians, educators and students. London: Jessica Kingsley.*

Ballard, M., & Coates, S. (1995). *The immediate effects of homicidal, suicidal, and nonviolent heavy metal and rap songs on the moods of college students.* Youth and Society, 27, 148–168.

Band, J. P., Quilter, S. M., & Miller, G. M. (2002). The influence of selected music and inductions on mental imagery: Implications for practitioners of guided imagery and music. Journal of the Association for Music and Imagery, 8, 13–33.

Barclay, M. W. (1987). A contribution to a theory of music therapy: Additional phenomenological perspective on Gestalt Qualitat and transitional phenomena. Journal of Music Therapy, 24(4), 224–238.

Barnard, R. (1953). The philosophy and theory of music therapy as an adjunct therapy. In E. G. Gilliland (Ed.), Music therapy 1952 (pp. 45–49). Lawrence, KS: Allen Press.

Baron, R. (1955). Music in penal institutions. Bulletin of NAMT, 4(2), 5–6.

Batcheller, J., & Monsour, S. (1972). Music in recreation and leisure. Dubuque, IA: Wm. C. Brown.

Baumel, L. (1973). Psychiatrist as music therapist. Journal of Music Therapy, 10(2), 83–85.

Bean, K. L., & Moore, J. R. (1964). Music therapy from auditory inkblots. Journal of Music Therapy, 1(4), 143–147.

Bean, L. J. (1969). Music at Indiana State Prison. Music Journal, 27, 31.

Bednarz, L. F., & Nikkel, B. (1992). The role of music therapy in the treatment of young adults diagnosed with mental illness and substance abuse. Music Therapy Perspectives, 10(1), 21–26.

Beekley, L. H. (1959). Pantomime, music drama and therapy. Bulletin of NAMT, 8(3), 10–11.

Behrens, G. A. (1988). An objective approach to the expression of feelings. Music Therapy Perspectives, 5, 16–22.

Behrens, G. A., & Green, S. (1993). Ability to identify emotional content of solo improvisations performed vocally and on three different instruments. Psychology of Music, 21(1), 20–33.

Benedict, L. (1957). Music in a correctional setting. Bulletin of NAMT, 6, 9.

Benenzon, R. (1978). Music therapy in child psychosis. (W. Grabia, Trans.). Springfield, IL: Charles C. Thomas.

Benenzon, R. (1981). Music therapy manual (W. Grabia, Trans.). Springfield, IL: Charles C. Thomas.

Benenzon, R. (1982). Music therapy in child psychosis (2nd ed.). (W. Grabia, Trans.). Springfield, IL: Charles C. Thomas.

Benenzon, R. (1997). Music therapy theory and manual: Contributions to the knowledge of nonverbal context (2nd ed.). Springfield, IL: Charles C. Thomas.

Biller, J. D., Olson, P. J., & Breen, T. (1974). The effect of "happy" versus "sad" music and participation on anxiety. Journal of Music Therapy, 11(2), 68–73.

Bitcon, C. H. (2000). Alike and different (2nd ed.). Gilsum, NH: Barcelona.

Blackwell, E., & Neal, G. A. (1946). Music in mental hospitals. Occupational Therapy and Rehabilitation, 25, 243–246.

Blair, D., Werner, T. A., & Brooking, M. (1960). The value of individual music therapy as an aid to individual psychotherapy. In E. H. Schneider (Ed.), Music therapy 1959 (pp. 169–184). Lawrence, KS: Allen Press.

Blake, R. L. (1994). The Bonny Method of Guided Imagery and Music (GIM) in the treatment of post-traumatic stress disorder (PTSD) with adults in the psychiatric setting. Music Therapy Perspectives, 12(2), 125–129.

Blake, R. L. (1994). Vietnam veterans with post-traumatic stress disorder: Findings from a music and imagery project. Journal of the Association for Music and Imagery, 3, 5–17.

Blake, R., & Bishop, S. (1994). Bonny Method of Guided Imagery and Music (GIM) in the treatment of posttraumatic stress disorder with adults in the psychiatric setting. Music Therapy Perspectives, 12, 125–129.

Bluestone, H. (1957). Music as an aid in insulin therapy. In E. T. Gaston (Ed.), Music therapy 1956 (pp. 112–114). Lawrence, KS: Allen Press.

Blumer, G. A. (1891–1892). Music in its relation to the mind. American Journal of Insanity, 5, 350–364.

Boehneim, C. (1966). Music and group psychotherapy. Journal of Music Therapy, 3(2), 49–53.

Boenheim, C. (1967). The importance of creativity in contemporary psychotherapy. Journal of Music Therapy, 4(1), 3–6.

Boenheim, C. (1968). The position of music and art therapy in contemporary psychotherapy. Journal of Music Therapy, 5(3), 85–87.

Boguslawski, M. (1932). Music as a cure for mental depression. Etude, 50, 469+.

Bolduc, T. E. (1962). A psychologist looks at music therapy. Proceedings of the NAMT, 1962, 11, 40–42.

Bolwerk, C. (1990). Effects of relaxing music on state anxiety in myocardial infarction patients. Critical Care Nursing Quarterly, 13(2), 63–72.

Bonde, L. O. (2000). Metaphor and narrative in guided imagery and music. Journal of the Association for Music and Imagery, 7, 59–76.

Bonde, L. O. (2001). Steps toward a meta-theory of music therapy? An introduction to Ken Wilbur's integral psychology and a discussion of its relevance for music therapy. Nordic Journal of Music Therapy, 10(2), 176–187.

Bonny, E. (1988). Clinical treatment of adult children of alcoholics with guided imagery and music. Salina, KS: Bonny Foundation.

Bonny, H. L. (1968). Preferred loudness of recorded music of hospitalized psychiatric patients and hospital employees. Journal of Music Therapy, 5(2), 44–52.

Bonny, H. L. (1975). Music and consciousness. Journal of Music Therapy, 12(3), 121–135.

Bonny, H. L. (1978). Facilitating GIM sessions. GIM Monograph No. 1. Baltimore: ICM Books.

Bonny, H. L. (1978). The role of taped music programs in the GIM process. GIM Monograph No. 2. Baltimore: ICM Books.

Bonny, H. L. (1980). GIM therapy: Past, present and future implications. GIM Monograph No. 3. Baltimore: ICM Press.

Bonny, H. L. (1987). Reflections: Music: The language of immediacy. The Arts in Psychotherapy, 14(3), 255–262.

Bonny, H. L. (1989). Sound as symbol: Guided imagery and music in clinical practice. Music Therapy Perspectives, 6, 7–10.

Bonny, H. L. (1993). Body listening: A new way to review the GIM tapes. Journal of the Association for Music and Imagery, 2, 3–10.

Bonny, H. L. (1994). Twenty-one years later: A GIM update. Music Therapy Perspectives, 12(2), 70–74.

Bonny, H. L. (2002). Music consciousness: The evaluation of guided imagery and music. Gilsum, NH: Barcelona.

Bonny, H. L., Cistrunk, M., Makuch, R., Stevens, E., & Tally, J. (1965). Some effects of music on verbal interactions in groups. Journal of Music Therapy, 2(2), 61–64.

Bonny, H. L., & Keiser Mardis, L. (1994). Music resources for GIM facilitators. Olney, MD: Archedigm.

Bonny, H. L., & Pahnke, W. N. (1972). The use of music in psychedelic (LSD) psychotherapy. Journal of Music Therapy, 9(2), 64–83.

Bonny, H. L., & Savary, L. M. (1973). Music and your mind: Listening with a new consciousness. New York: Harper & Row.

Bonny, H. L., & Savary, L. M. (1990). Music and your mind (2nd ed.). Barrytown, NY: Station Hill Press.

Bonny, H. L., & Tansill, R. B. (1977). Music therapy: A legal high. In G. G. Waldorf (Ed.), Counseling therapies and the addictive client. Baltimore: School of Social Work and Community Planning.

Boone, P. (1980). Diagnostic assessment of music-related expression of behavior. Washington, DC: National Association for Music Therapy.

Boone, P. (1991). Composition, improvisation and poetry in the psychiatric treatment of a forensic patient. In K. E. Bruscia (Ed.), Case studies in music therapy (pp. 433– 449). Phoenixville, PA: Barcelona.

Borczon, R. (1997). Music therapy group vignettes. Gilsum, NH: Barcelona.

Borling, J. E. (1992). Perspectives on growth with a victim of abuse: A guided imagery and music (GIM) case study. Journal of the Association for Music and Imagery, 1, 85–98.

Bowe, H., Mudge, M. B., & Frisch, A. (1999). When words are not enough. In J. Hibben (Ed.), Inside music therapy: Client experiences (pp. 3–6). Gilsum, NH: Barcelona.

Boxberger, R. (1962). Historical bases for the use of music in therapy. In E. R. Schneider (Ed.), Music therapy 1961 (pp. 125–166). Lawrence, KS: Allen Press.

Boxberger, R. (1963). A historical study of the National Association for Music Therapy. In E. H. Schneider (Ed.), Music therapy 1962 (pp. 133–197). Lawrence, KS: National Association for Music Therapy.

Boxill, E. (n.d.). Students against violence everywhere through music therapy. New York: Music Therapists for Peace.

Boyce-Tillman, J. (2000). Constructing musical healing. London: Jessica Kingsley.

Boyer, L. B. (1992). Roles played by music as revealed during countertransference facilitated transference regression. International Journal of Psychoanalysis, 73, 55–67.

Braswell, C. (1960). The goal-directed hospital music program. In E. H. Schneider (Ed.), Music therapy 1959 (pp. 47–53). Lawrence, KS: Allen Press.

Braswell, C. (1962). The future of psychiatric music therapy. In E. H. Schneider (Ed.), Music therapy 1961 (pp. 65–76). Lawrence, KS: Allen Press.

Braswell, C. (1962). Psychiatric music therapy: A review of the profession. In E. H. Schneider (Ed.), Music therapy 1961 (pp. 53–64). Lawrence, KS: Allen Press.

Braswell, C. (1967). Changing concepts in treatment. Journal of Music Therapy, 4(2), 63–66.

Braswell, C. (1968). Clinical uses of music in the community. In E. T. Gaston (Ed.), Music in therapy (pp. 401–402). New York: Macmillan.

Braswell, C. (1968). Development of music therapy in the community: Overview. In E. T. Gaston (Ed.), Music in therapy (pp. 346–349). New York: Macmillan.

Braswell, C. (1968). Social facility and mental illness. In E. T. Gaston (Ed.), Music in therapy (pp. 364–371). New York: Macmillan.

Braswell, C., Brooks, D., Decuir, A., Humphreys, T., Jacobs, K., & Smith, K. (1983). Development and implementation of a music/activity therapy intake assessment for psychiatric patients. Part I: Initial standardization procedures in data from university students. Journal of Music Therapy, 20(2), 88–100.

Braswell, C., Brooks, D., Decuir, A., Humphreys, T., Jacobs, K., & Smith, K. (1986). Development and implementation of a music/activity therapy intake assessment for psychiatric patients. Part II: Standardization procedures in data from psychiatric patients. Journal of Music Therapy, 23(3), 126–141.

Braswell, C., Maranto, C., & Decuir, A. (1979). A survey of clinical practice in music therapy: Part I. Journal of Music Therapy, 16(1), 2–16.

Bright, R. (2002). Supportive elective music therapy for grief and loss. St. Louis, MO: MMB Music.

Brooke, S. L. (1996). A therapist's guide to art therapy assessments: Tools of the trade. Springfield, IL: Charles C. Thomas.

Brooking, M. (1960). Music therapy in British mental hospitals. In E. H. Schneider (Ed.), Music therapy 1959 (pp. 38–46). Lawrence, KS: Allen Press.

Brooks, D. M. (1989). Music therapy enhances treatment with adolescents. Music Therapy Perspectives, 6, 37–39.

Brooks, D. M. (2000). Anima manifestations of mean using guided imagery and music: A case study. Journal of the Association for Music and Imagery, 7, 77–87.

Brooks, H. B. (1973). The role of music in a community drug abuse prevention program. Journal of Music Therapy, 10(1), 3–6.

Brown, M. E., & Selinger, M. (1969). A nontherapeutic device for approaching therapy in an institutional setting. International Journal of Group Psychotherapy, 19, 88– 95.

Brown, S., & Pavlicevic, M. (1996). Clinical improvisation in creative music therapy: Musical aesthetic and the interpersonal dimension. The Arts in Psychotherapy, 23(5), 397–405.

Browne, H. E. (1961). Psychiatric treatment with the drug LSD and music therapy for alcoholics. In E. H. Schneider (Ed.), Music therapy 1960 (pp. 154–162). Lawrence, KS: Allen Press.

Brunner-Orne, M., & Flinn, S. S. (1961). Music therapy at Westwood Lodge. In E. H. Schneider (Ed.), Music therapy 1960 (pp. 44–46). Lawrence, KS: Allen Press.

Bruscia, K. E. (1987). Improvisational models of music therapy. Springfield, IL: Charles C. Thomas.

Bruscia, K. E. (1988). Standards for clinical assessment in the arts therapies. The Arts in Psychotherapy, 15(1), 5–10.

Bruscia, K. E. (1988). A survey of treatment procedures in improvisational music therapy. Psychology of Music, 16(1), 10–24.

Bruscia, K. E. (1989). The practical side of improvisational music therapy. Music Therapy Perspectives, 6, 11–15.

Bruscia, K. E. (Ed.). (1991). Case studies in music therapy. Phoenixville, PA: Barcelona.

Bruscia, K. E. (1991). Embracing life with AIDS: Psychotherapy through guided imagery and music. In K. E. Bruscia (Ed.), Case studies in music therapy (pp. 581–602). Phoenixville, PA: Barcelona.

Bruscia, K. E. (1995). Manifestations of transference in guided imagery and music. Journal of the Association for Music and Imagery, 4, 16–35.

Bruscia, K. E. (1996). Music for the imagination: Rationale, implications and guidelines for its use in guided imagery and music (GIM). Santa Cruz, CA: Association for Music and Imagery.

Bruscia, K. E. (1998). Defining music therapy (2nd ed.). Gilsum, NH: Barcelona.

Bruscia, K. E. (Ed.). (1998). The dynamics of music psychotherapy. Gilsum, NH: Barcelona.

Bruscia, K. E. (2000). A scale for assessing responsiveness to guided imagery and music. Journal of the Association for Music and Imagery, 7, 1–7.

Bruscia, K. E. (2002). The boundaries of guided imagery and music (GIM) and the Bonny Method. In K. E. Bruscia & D. E. Gorcke (Eds.), Guided imagery and music: The Bonny Method and beyond (pp. 38–61). Gilsum, NH: Barcelona.

Bruscia, K. E. (2002). Client assessment in the Bonny Method of Guided Imagery and Music (BMGIM). In K. E. Bruscia & D. E. Gorcke (Eds.), Guided imagery and music: The Bonny Method (pp. 273–295). Gilsum, NH: Barcelona.

Bruscia, K. E. (2002). Developments in music programming for the Bonny Method. In K. E. Bruscia & D. E. Gorcke (Eds.), Guided imagery and music: The Bonny Method (pp. 307–315). Gilsum, NH: Barcelona.

Bruscia, K. E. (2002). A psychodynamic orientation to the Bonny Method. In K. E. Bruscia & D. E. Gorcke (Eds.), Guided imagery and music: The Bonny Method (pp. 225–243). Gilsum, NH: Barcelona.

Bruscia, K. E., & Gorcke, D. E. (Eds.). (2002). Guided imagery and music: The Bonny Method and beyond. Gilsum, NH: Barcelona.

Bryant, D. (1987). A cognitive approach to therapy through music. Journal of Music Therapy, 24(1), 27–34.

Buchanan, J. (2000). The effects of music therapy interventions in short-term therapy with teens at risk: An opportunity for self-expression in a group setting. Canadian Journal of Music Therapy, 7(1), 39–50.

Bunt, L. (1994). Music therapy: An art beyond words. New York: Routledge.

Bunt, L. (1997). Clinical and therapeutic uses of music. In D. J. Hargreaves & A. C. North (Eds.), The social psychology of music (pp. 250–267). New York: Oxford University Press.

Bunt, L. (2000). Transformational processes in guided imagery and music. Journal of the Association for Music and Imagery, 7, 44–58.

Bunt, L. (2002). Transformation, Ovid and guided imagery and music (GIM). In L. Bunt & S. Hoskysn (Eds.), The handbook of music therapy (pp. 290–307). East Sussex, England: Brummer-Routledge.

Bunt, L., & Hoskyns, S. (Eds.). (2002). The handbook of music therapy. East Essex, England: Brummer-Routledge.

Bunt, L, Pike, D., & Wren, V. (1987). Music therapy in a general hospital's psychiatric unit—A pilot evaluation of an eight week programme. British Journal of Music Therapy, 1(2), 22–27.

Burkhardt-Mramor, K. M. (1996). Music therapy and attachment disorder: A case study. Music Therapy Perspectives, 14(2), 77–82.

Burleson, S. J., Center, D. B., & Reeves, H. (1989). The effect of background music on task performance in psychotic children. Journal of Music Therapy, 26(4), 198–205.

Burns, D., & Woolrich, J. (2004). The Bonny Method of Guided Imagery and Music. In A.-A. Darrow (Ed.), Introduction to approaches in music therapy (pp. 53–62). Silver Spring, MD: American Music Therapy Association.

Burns, D. S. (2000). The effect of classical music on absorption and control of mental imagery. Journal of the Association for Music and Imagery, 7, 35–43.

Burns, J. L., Labbe, E., Arke, B., Capeless, K., Cooksey, B., Steadman, A., & Gonzales, C. (2002). The effects of different types of music on perceived and physiological measures of stress. Journal of Music Therapy, 39(2), 101–116.

Burt, J. W. (1995). Distant thunder: Drumming with Vietnam veterans. Music Therapy Perspectives, 13(2), 110–112.

Burton, R. (1651). The anatomy of melancholy. Oxford, England: Henry Cripps, Printer.

Bush, C. (1988). Dreams, mandalas and music imagery: Therapeutic uses in a case study. The Arts in Psychotherapy, 15(3), 219–226.

Bush, C. (1992). Dreams, mandalas and music imagery: Therapeutic uses in a case study. Journal of the Association for Music and Imagery, 1, 33–42.

Bush, C. (1995). Healing imagery and music: Pathways to the inner self. Portland, OR: Rudra Press.

Butler, B. (1966). Music group psychotherapy. Journal of Music Therapy, 3(2), 53–57.

Caplan, L. M. (1965). The disturbed adolescent and problems in his treatment. Journal of Music Therapy, 2(3), 92–95.

Carlson, E. T., Wollock, J. L., & Noel, P. S. (Eds.). (1981). Benjamin Rush's lectures on the mind. Philadelphia, PA: Philadelphia Philosophical Society.

Carroccio, D., Latham, S., & Carroccio, B. (1976). Rate-contingent guitar rental to decelerate stereotyped head/face-touching of an adult male psychiatric patient. Behavior Therapy, 7, 104–109.

Carroccio, D. F., & Quattlebaum, L. F. (1969). An elementary technique for manipulation of participation in ward dances at a neuropsychiatric hospital. Journal of Music Therapy, 6(4), 108.

Carter, E., & Oldfield, A. (2002). Music therapy group to assist clinical diagnosis in child and family psychiatry. In A. Davies & E. Richards (Eds.), Music therapy and group work: Sound company (pp. 149–163). London: Jessica Kingsley.

Cassity, M. D. (1976). The influence of music therapy activity upon peer acceptance, group cohesiveness and interpersonal relationships of adult psychiatric patients. Journal of Music Therapy, 12(2), 66–75.

Cassity, M. D. (1981). The influence of a socially valued skill on a peer acceptance in a music therapy group. Journal of Music Therapy, 18(3), 148–154.

Cassity, M. D., & Cassity, J. E. (1994). Psychiatric music therapy assessment and treatment in clinical training facilities with adults, adolescents, and children. Journal of Music Therapy, 31(1), 2–30.

Cassity, M. D., & Cassity, J. E. (1995). Multimodal psychiatric music therapy of adults, adolescents and children: A clinical manual, second ed. St. Louis, MO: MMB Music.

Cassity, M. D., & Theobold, K. A. K. (1990). Domestic violence: Assessment and treatments employed by music therapy. Journal of Music Therapy, 27(4), 179–194.

Castellano, J. A., & Wilson, B. L. (1970). The generalization of institute therapy to classroom behavior of an electively mute adolescent. Journal of Music Therapy, 7(4), 139–147.

Cattanach, A. (Ed.). (1999). Process in the arts therapies. London: Jessica Kingsley.

Cattell, R. B., & Anderson, J. C. (1953). The measurement of personality and behavioral disorders by the IPAT music preference test. Journal of Applied Psychology, 37, 446–454.

Cattell, R. B., & Kline, P. (1977). The scientific analysis of personality and maturation. New York: Academic Press.

Cattell, R. B., & McMichael, R. E. (1960). Clinical diagnosis by the IPAT music preference test. Journal of Consulting Psychology, 24, 333–341.

Cattell, R. B., & Saunders, D. (1954). Musical preferences and personality diagnosis: A factorization of one hundred and twenty themes. Journal of Social Psychology, 39, 3–24.

Cavallin, B. J., & Cavallin, H. W. (1968). Group music therapy to develop socially acceptable behavior among adolescent boys and girls. In E. T. Gaston (Ed.), Music in therapy (pp. 218–228). New York: Macmillan.

Cevasco, A. M., & Kennedy, R. (2005). Comparison of movement-to-music, rhythm activities, and competitive games on depression, stress, anxiety, and anger of females in substance abuse rehabilitation. Journal of Music Therapy, 42(1), 64– 80.

Chace, M. (1954). Report of a group project: St. Elizabeth Hospital. Music Therapy, 187–190.

Chambliss, C., McMichael, H., Tyson, K., Monaco, C., & Tracy, J. (1996). Motor performance after mellow and frenetic antecedent music. Perceptual and Motor Skills, 82, 153–154.

Chambliss, C., Tyson, K., & Tracy, J. (1996). Performance on the Purdue pegboard and finger tapping by schizophrenics after mellow and frenetic antecedent music. Perceptual and Motor Skills, 83, 1161–1162.

Charlesworth, E. (1982). Music, psychology, and psychotherapy. The Arts in Psychotherapy, 9(3), 191–202.

Chase, K. M. (2002). The music therapy assessment handbook. Columbia, MS: Southern Pen.

Choi, B.-C. (1997). Professional and patient attitudes about the relevance of music therapy as a treatment modality in NAMT approved psychiatric hospitals. Journal of Music Therapy, 43(4), 277–292.

Chumacero, C. L. D. (1998). Consciously induced song recall: Transference and countertransference implications. In K. E. Bruscia (Ed.), The dynamics of music therapy (pp. 364–385). Gilsum, NH: Barcelona.

Clark, M., & Mardis, L. (1992). The Bonny Method of Guided Imagery and Music. Olney, MD: Archedigm.

Clark, M. F. (1991). Emergence of the adult self in guided imagery and music (GIM) therapy. In K. E. Bruscia (Ed.), Case studies in music therapy (pp. 321–331). Phoenixville, PA: Barcelona.

Clark, M. F. (1995). The hero's myth in BMGIM therapy. Journal of the Association for Music and Imagery, 4, 49–65.

Clark, M. F. (1998–99). The Bonny Method of Guided Imagery and Music and spiritual development. Journal of the Association for Music and Imagery, 6, 55–62.

Clark, M. F. (2002). Evolution of the Bonny Method of Guided Imagery and Music (BMGIM). In K. E. Bruscia & D. E. Gorcke (Eds.), Guided imagery and music: The Bonny Method and beyond (pp. 5–27). Gilsum, NH: Barcelona.

Clarkson, G. (1994). Learning through mistakes: Guided imagery and music (BMGIM) with a student in a hypomanic episode. Journal of the Association for Music and Imagery, 3, 77–93.

Clarkson, G. (1998). I dreamed I was normal. St. Louis, MO: MMB Music.

Clarkson, G. (2002). Combining Gestalt dreamwork and the Bonny Method. In K. E. Bruscia & D. E. Gorcke (Eds.), Guided imagery and music: The Bonny Method (pp. 257–270). Gilsum, NH: Barcelona.

Clarkson, G., & Geller, J. (1996). The Bonny Method from a psychoanalytic perspective: Insights from working with a psychoanalytic psychotherapist in a guided imagery and music series. The Arts in Psychotherapy, 23(4), 311–319.

Clemtson, B. C., & Chen, R. (1968). Music therapy in a day-treatment program. In E. T. Gaston (Ed.), Music in therapy (pp. 394–400). New York: Macmillan.

Clendenon-Wallen, J. (1991). The use of music therapy to influence the self-confidence of adolescents who are sexually abused. Music Therapy Perspectives, 9, 73–81.

Codding, P. A. (2002). A comprehensive survey of music therapists practicing in correctional psychiatry: Demographics, conditions of employment, service provision, assessment, therapeutic objectives, and related values of the therapist. Music Therapy Perspectives, 20(2), 56–68.

Cohen, G., & Gericke, O. L. (1972). Music therapy assessment: Prime requisite for determining patient objectives. Journal of Music Therapy, 9(4), 161–189.

Cohen, J. M. (1986). Rhythm and tempo in mania. Music Therapy, 6A(1), 13–29.

Cohen, J. M. (1987). Music therapy with the overcontrolled offender: Theory and practice. The Arts in Psychotherapy, 14(3), 215–221.

Conrad, J. (1962). A music therapy program for short-term psychiatric patients. Bulletin of NAMT, 11(3), 7–12.

Conway, J. L. (1949). A rhythm band for mental patients. American Journal of Occupational Therapy, 3, 246–249.

Cook, M., & Freethy, M. (1973). The use of music as a positive reinforces to eliminate complaining behavior. Journal of Music Therapy, 10(4), 213–216.

Cooke, R. M. (1969). The use of music in play therapy. Journal of Music Therapy, 6(3), 66–75.

Cordobis, T. K. (1997). Group songwriting as a method for developing group cohesion for HIV-seropositive adults patients with depression. Journal of Music Therapy, 34(1), 46–67.

Coriat, I. H. (1945). Some aspects of psychoanalytic interpretation of music. Psychoanalytic Review, 32, 408–418.

Corning, J. L. (1899). The use of musical vibrations before and during sleep—A contribution to the therapeutics of emotions. Medical Record, 14, 79–86.

Courtright, P., Johnson, S., Baumgartner, M. A., Jordan, M., & Webster, J. C. (1990). Dinner music: Does it affect the behavior of psychiatric inpatients? Journal of Psychosocial Nursing, 28(3), 37–40.

Crigler, C. (1966). The role of the music therapist in the therapeutic community. Journal of Music Therapy, 10(1), 19–21.

Critchley, N., & Hensen, R. A. (Eds.). (1977). Music and the brain. London: Camelot.

Crocker, D. B. (1953). Techniques in the use of music as therapy for the emotionally maladjusted child. In E. Gilliland (Ed.), Music therapy 1952 (pp. 175–180). Lawrence, KS: Allen Press.

Crocker, D. B. (1956). Music as a projective technique. In E. T. Gaston (Ed.), Music therapy 1955 (pp. 86–97). Lawrence, KS: Allen Press.

Crocker, D. B. (1957). The therapeutic value of music. Southwestern Musician and Texas Music Educator, 25, 23.

Crocker, D. B. (1958). Music as a therapeutic experience for the emotionally disturbed child. In E. T. Gaston (Ed.), Music therapy 1957 (pp. 114–119). Lawrence, KS: Allen Press.

Crocker, D. B. (1968). Clinical experiences with emotionally disturbed children. In E. T. Gaston (Ed.), Music in therapy (pp. 202–214). New York: Macmillan.

Crocker, D. B. (1968). Music therapy in a private music studio. In E. T. Gaston (Ed.), Music in therapy (pp. 372–378). New York: Macmillan.

Crowe, B. J. (2004). Music and soulmaking: Toward a new theory of music therapy. Lanham, MD: Scarecrow Press.

Dalton, T. A., & Krout, R. E. (2005). Development of the grief process scale through music therapy songwriting with bereaved adolescents. The Arts in Psychotherapy, 32(2), 131–143.

Darbes, A., & Shrift, D. (1957). The effect of music therapy on three groups of hospitalized psychiatric patients as measured by some clinical and observational methods. Bulletin of NAMT, 6, 7–8.

Darnley-Smith, R., & Patey, H. M. (2003). Music therapy. London: Page.

Darrow, A-A. (Ed.). (2004). Introduction to approaches in music therapy. Silver Spring, MD: American Music Therapy Association.

Daughtery, K. (1984). Music therapy in the treatment of the alcoholic client. Music Therapy, 1, 47–54.

Daveson, B. A., & Edwards, J. (2001). A descriptive study exploring the role of music therapy in prisons. The Arts in Psychotherapy, 28(2), 137–141.

Davies, A., & Richards, E. (1998). Music therapy in acute psychiatry. Our experience of working as co-therapists with a group for patients from two neighboring wards. British Journal of Music Therapy, 13(2), 53–59.

Davies, A., & Richards, E. (Eds.). (2002). Music therapy and group work: Sound company. London: Jessica Kingsley.

Davis, W. B. (1987). Music therapy in nineteenth-century America. Journal of Music Therapy, 24(2), 76–87.

Davis, W. B. (1992). The music therapy treatment process. In W. B. Davis, K. E. Gfeller, & M. H. Thaut (Eds.), An introduction to music therapy (pp. 287–301). Dubuque, IA: William C. Brown.

Davis, W. B. (2003). Ira Maximilian Altschuler: Psychiatrist and pioneer music therapist. Journal of Music Therapy, 40(3), 247–263.

Davis, W. B., & Gfeller, K. E. (1992). Music therapy: A historical perspective. In W. B. Davis, K. E. Gfeller, & M. H. Thaut (Eds.), An introduction to music therapy (pp. 16–37). Dubuque, IA: William C. Brown.

Davis, W. B., Gfeller, K. E., & Thaut, M. H. (Eds.). (1992). An introduction to music therapy theory and practice. Dubuque, IA: William C. Brown.

Davis, W. B., Gfeller, K. E., & Thaut, M. H. (Eds.). (1999). An introduction to music therapy theory and practice (2nd ed.). Boston: McGraw-Hill College.

Davis, W. B., & Thaut, M. H. (1989). The influence of preferred relaxing music on measures of state anxiety, relaxation, and physiological responses. Journal of Music Therapy, 26(4), 168–187.

DeBacker, J. (1993). Containment in music therapy. In M. Heal & T. Wigram (Eds.), Music therapy in health and education (pp. 32–39). London: Jessica Kingsley.

DeBacker, J. (1996). Regression in music therapy with psychotic patients. Nordic Journal of Music Therapy, 5(1), 24–30.

DeBacker, J. (1999). Specific aspects of music therapy's relationship to psychiatry. In T. Wigram & J. DeBacker (Eds.), Clinical applications of music therapy in psychiatry (pp. 11–23). London: Jessica Kingsley.

DeBacker, J., & Van Camp, J. (2004). The case of Marianne: Repetition and musical form in psychosis. In S. Hadley (Ed.), Psychodynamic music therapy: Case studies (pp. 273–297). Gilsum, NH: Barcelona.

De l'Etoile, S. K. (2002). The effectiveness of music therapy in group psychotherapy for adults with mental illness. The Arts in Psychotherapy, 20, 69–78.

Deschenes, B. (1995). Music and symbols. Music Therapy Perspectives, 15(1), 40–45.

Deutsch, A. (1949). The mentally ill in America: A history of their care and treatment from colonial times (2nd ed.). New York: Columbia Press.

Devlin, H. J., & Sawatzky, D. D. (1987). The effects of background music in a simulated initial counseling session with female subjects. Canadian Journal of Counseling, 21, 125–132.

Diaz de Chumaceiro, C. L. (1990). Dynamic implication of opera training in psychotherapy. The Arts in Psychotherapy, 17(2), 19–28.

Diaz de Chumaceiro, C. L. (1990). Songs of the countertransference in psychotherapy dyads. American Journal of Psychoanalysis, 50, 75–89.

Diaz de Chumaceiro, C. L. (1992). Induced song recall. The Arts in Psychotherapy, 19(5), 325–332.

Diaz de Chumaceiro, C. L. (1992). Transference-countertransference in psychology integrations for music therapy in the 1970's and 1980's. Journal of Music Therapy, 29(4), 217–235.

Diaz de Chumaceiro, C. L. (1992). What song comes to mind? Induced song recall: Transference/countertransference in dyadic music associations in treatment and supervision. The Arts in Psychotherapy, 19(5), 325–332.

Diaz de Chumaceiro, C. L. (1993). Parapraxes in song recall: A neglected variable. American Journal of Psychoanalysis, 53, 225–235.

Diaz de Chumaceiro, C. L. (1995). Lullabies are "Transferential Transition Songs": Further considerations on resistance in music therapy. The Arts in Psychotherapy, 22(4), 353–357.

Dickens, G., & Sharpe, M. (1970). Music therapy in the selling of a psychotherapeutic centre. British Journal of Medical Psychology, 43(1), 83–89.

Dickenson, M. (1957). Music as a tool in psychotherapy for children. Music Therapy, 97–104.

Diephouse, J. W. (1986). Music therapy: A valuable adjunct to psychotherapy with children. Psychiatric Quarterly Supplement, 42, 75–85.

di France, G. (1993). Music therapy—A methodological approach in the mental health field. In M. Heal, & T. Wigram (Eds.), Music therapy in health and education (pp. 82–90). London: Jessica Kingsley.

Dillard, L. M. (2006). Musical countertransference experiences of music therapists: A phenomenological study. The Arts in Psychotherapy, 33(3), 208–217.

Doak, B. A. (2003). Relationship between adolescent psychiatric diagnoses, music preferences, and drug preferences. Music Therapy Perspectives, 21(2), 69–76.

Dokter, D. (Ed.). (1995). Arts therapies and clients with eating disorders. London: Jessica Kingsley.

Dollins, C. N. (1957). The use of background music in a psychiatric hospital to increase group conversational frequency. In E. T. Gaston (Ed.), Music therapy 1956 (pp. 229–230). Lawrence, KS: Allen Press.

Donais, D. (1943). Music sets the stage for recovery from mental disease. The Modern Hospital, 61, 68–69.

Doughtery, K. M. (1984). Music therapy in the treatment of the alcoholic client. Music Therapy, 1, 47–54.

Douglass, D., & Wagner, M. K. (1965). A program for the activity therapist in group psychotherapy. Journal of Music Therapy, 2(2), 56–61.

Drabes, A., & Shrift, D. (1957). The effects of music therapy on three groups of hospitalized psychiatric patients as measured by some clinical and observational methods. Bulletin of NAMT, 6(2), 7–8.

Dreikurs, R. (1954). The dynamics of music therapy. Bulletin of NAMT, 3(10), 9.

Dreikurs, R. (1954). Psychiatric concepts of music therapy for children. In M. Bing (Ed.), Music therapy 1954 (pp. 81–84). Lawrence, KS: Allen Press.

Dreikurs, R. (1961). The psychological and philosophical significance of rhythm. Bulletin of the NAMT, 10, 8–17.

Dreikurs, R., & Crocker, D. B. (1956). Music therapy with psychotic children. In E. T. Gaston (Ed.), Music therapy 1955 (pp. 62–73). Lawrence, KS: Allen Press.

Duey, C. J. (1991). Group music therapy for women with multiple personalities. In K. E. Bruscia (Ed.), Case studies in music therapy (pp. 512–526). Phoenixville, PA: Barcelona.

Dutcher, J. (1992). Tape analysis: Creativity I. Journal of the Association for Music and Imagery, 1, 107–118.

Dvorkin, J. (1982). Piano improvisation: A therapeutic tool in acceptance and resolution of emotions in a schizo-affective personality. Music Therapy, 2(1), 53–62.

Dvorkin, J. (1991). Individual music therapy for an adolescent with borderline personality disorder: An object relations approach. In K. E. Bruscia (Ed.), Case studies in music therapy (pp. 251–268). Phoenixville, PA: Barcelona.

Eagle, C. T., Jr. (1972). Music and LSD: An empirical study. Journal of Music Therapy, 9(1), 23–36.

Eagle, C. T., Jr. (1973). Effects of existing mood and order presentation of vocal and instrumental music on rated responses to that music. Council for Research in Music Education, 32, 55–59.

Eby, J. (1943). The value of music in a psychiatric institution. Occupational Therapy and Rehabilitation, 22, 31–35.

Edgerton, C. D. (1990). Creative group songwriting. Music Therapy Perspectives, 8, 15–19.

Edwards, L. B. (1877–1878). Music as mind medicine. Virginia Medical Monthly, 4, 920–923.

Eidson, C. E. (1989). The effect of behavioral music therapy in the generalization of interpersonal skills form session to classroom by emotionally handicapped middle school students. Journal of Music Therapy, 27(4), 206–221.

Eifert, G. H., Craill, L., Carey, E., & O'Connor, C. (1988). Affect modification through evaluative conditioning with music. Behavior, Research, and Therapy, 26(4), 321–330.

Elliot, T. G., & McGahan, C. (1987). The power of music in prison. In R. B. Pratt (Ed.), The fourth international symposium on music: Rehabilitation and human well- being (pp. 170–175). Lanham, MD: University Press of America.

Ellis, A. (1981). The use of rational humorous songs in psychotherapy. Voices, 16(4), 29–36.

Elston, A. (1948). The musician's approach to musical therapy. In D. M. Schullian & M. Schoen (Eds.), Music and medicine (pp. 282–292). New York: Henry Schuman.

Emunah, R. (1990). Perspectives: Expression and expansion in adolescence: The significance of creative arts therapy. The Arts in Psychotherapy, 17(2), 101–107.

Erdonmez, D. (1992). Clinical applications of guided imagery and music. Australian Journal of Music Therapy, 3, 37–44.

Eschen, J. T. (Ed.). (2002). Analytical music therapy. London: Jessica Kingsley.

Eschen, J. T. (2002). Analytical music therapy—Introduction. In J. T. Eschen (Ed.), Analytical music therapy (pp. 17–33). London: Jessica Kingsley.

Euper, J. A. (1970). Contemporary trends in mental health work. Journal of Music Therapy, 7(1), 20–26.

Fagen, T. S., & Wool, C. A. (1999). Conjoint therapy: Psychiatry and music therapy in the treatment of psychosomatic illness. International Journal of Arts Medicine, 6(1), 4–9.

Farmer, R. (1963). A musical activities program with young psychotic girls. American Journal of Occupational Therapy, 17, 116–119.

Farnan, L. A. (1987). Composing music for use in therapy. Music Therapy Perspectives, 4, 8–12.

Feder, E., & Feder, B. (1981). The "expressive" arts therapies: Art, music and dance as psychotherapy. New Jersey: Prentice-Hall.

Feder, S., Karmel, R. L., & Pollock, G. H. (Eds.). (1990). Psychoanalytic explorations in music, First Series. Madison, CT: International Universities Press.

Ficken, T. (1976). The use of songwriting in a psychiatric setting. Journal of Music Therapy, 13(4), 163–172.

Fleshamn, B., & Fryrear, J. L. (1981). The arts in therapy. Chicago: Nelson-Hall.

Folsom, G. S. (1968). The developing situation. In E. T. Gaston (Ed.), Music in therapy (pp. 350–363). New York: Macmillan.

Forrest, C. (1968). Music in psychiatry. Nursing Mirror, 127, 22–23.

Forrest, C. (1972). Music and the psychiatric nurse. Nursing Times, 68, 410–411.

Forsyth, A. J., Barnard, M., & McKeganey, N. (1997). Musical preference as an indication of adolescent drug use. Addiction, 92(10), 1317–1325.

Frederiksen, B. V. (1999). Analysis of musical improvisations to understand and work with elements of resistance in a client with anorexia nervosa. In T. Wigram & J. DeBacker (Eds.), Clinical applications of music therapy in psychiatry (pp. 211–230). London: Jessica Kingsley.

Freed, B. S. (1989). Songwriting with the chemically dependent. Music Therapy Perspectives, 4, 13–18.

Fried, R. (1990). Integrating music in breathing training and relaxation: I. Background, rationale, and relevant elements. Biofeedback Self-Regulator, 19, 161–169.

Friedlander, L. H. (1994). Group music psychotherapy in an inpatient psychiatric setting for children: A developmental approach. Music Therapy Perspectives, 12(2), 92–97.

Friedlander, M. (1954). Some experiences in music therapy. Psychoanalysis, 2(4), 59–63.

Friedman, E. R. (1968). Psychological aspects of folk music. American Psychological Proceedings of the Annual Convention, 3, 449–450.

Frisch, A. (1990). Symbol and structure: Music therapy for adolescent psychiatric inpatients. Music Therapy, 9(1), 16–34.

Froelich, M. (1985). An annotated bibliography for the creative arts therapies. Journal of Music Therapy, 22(4), 218–226.

Fulford, M. (2002). Overview of a music therapy program at a maximum security unit of a state psychiatric facility. Music Therapy Perspectives, 20(2), 112–116.

Furman, C. E. (Ed.). (1988). Effectiveness of music therapy procedures: Documentation of research and clinical practice. Washington, DC: National Association for Music Therapy.

Furman, C. E. (Ed.). (2000). Effectiveness of music therapy procedures: Documentation of research and clinical practice (3rd ed.). Silver Spring, MD: American Music Therapy Association.

Gallagher, A. G., Dinan, T. G., & Baker, L. J. V. (1994). The effects of varying auditory input on schizophrenic hallucinations: A replication. British Journal of Medical Psychiatry, 67, 67–75.

Gallagher, L. M., & Steele, A. L. (2002). *Music therapy with offenders in a substance abuse/mental illness treatment program.* Music Therapy Perspectives, 20(2), 117–122.

Gantt, L. (2000). *Assessments in the creative arts therapies: Learning from each other.* Music Therapy Perspectives, 18(1), 41–46.

Gantz, W., Gartenberg, H. H., Pearson, M. L., & Schiller, S. O. (1978). *Gratifications and expectations associated with pop music among adolescents.* Popular Music and Society, 6, 81–89.

Gardstrom, S. C. (1987). *Positive peer culture: A working definition for the music therapist.* Music Therapy Perspectives, 4, 19–23.

Gardstrom, S. C. (1996). *Music therapy for juvenile offenders in a residential treatment setting.* In B. L. Wilson (Ed.), Models of music therapy interventions in school settings: From institution to inclusion (pp. 127–141). Silver Spring, MD: National Association for Music Therapy.

Gardstrom, S. C. (1999). *Music exposure and criminal behavior: Perceptions of juvenile offenders.* Journal of Music Therapy, 36(3), 207–221.

Gaston, E. T. (1951). *Dynamic music factors in mood change.* Music Educators Journal, 37, 42.

Gaston, E. T. (Ed.). (1968). *Music in therapy.* New York: Macmillan.

Gaston, E. T., & Eagle, C. T., Jr. (1970). *The function of music in LSD therapy for alcoholic patients.* Journal of Music Therapy, 7(1), 3–19.

Gerwitz, H. (1964). *Music therapy a form of supportive psychotherapy with children.* Journal of Music Therapy, 1(2), 61–66.

Gfeller, K., Asmus, E., & Eckert, M. (1991). *An investigation of emotional responses to music and text.* Psychology of Music, 19(2), 128–141.

Gfeller, K. E., & Thaut, M. H. (1999). *Music therapy in the treatment of mental disorders.* In W. B. Davis, K. E. Gfeller, & M. H. Thaut (Eds.), An introduction to music therapy theory and practice (2nd ed.) (pp. 89–117). Boston: McGraw-Hill College.

Giacobbe, G. A., & Graham, R. M. (1978). *The responses of aggressive emotionally disturbed and normal boys to selected musical stimuli.* Journal of Music Therapy, 15(3), 188–135.

Gibbons, A. (1957). *The development of a square dancing activity in a music therapy program at Rockland State Hospital.* In E. T. Gaston (Ed.), Music therapy 1956 (pp. 140–147). Lawrence, KS: Allen Press.

Gibbons, A. C. (1983). *Rhythm responses in emotionally disturbed children with differing needs for external structure.* Music Therapy, 3(1), 94–102.

Giles, M. M., Cogan, D., & Cox, C. (1991). *A music and art program to promote emotional health in elementary school children.* Journal of Music Therapy, 28(3), 135–148.

Gilliland, E. G. (1958). *Music as a tool in psychotherapy for children: Introductory remark.* In E. T. Gaston (Ed.), Music therapy 1957 (pp. 93–96). Lawrence, KS: Allen Press.

Gilman, L., & Paperte, F. (1952). *Music as a psychotherapeutic agent.* In E. A. Gutheil (Ed.), Music and your emotions (pp. 25–55). New York: Liveright.

Gilroy, A., & Lee, C. A. (Eds.). (1995). Art and music: Therapy and research. *London: Routledge.*

Girard, J. (1954). *Moderating anger with music.* In E. Podolsky (Ed.), Music therapy (pp. 107–111). New York: Philosophical Library.

Girard, J. (1954). *Music therapy in the anxiety states.* In E. Podolsky (Ed.), Music therapy (pp. 101–106). New York: Philosophical Library.

Glickson, J., & Cohen, Y. (2000). *Can music alleviate cognitive dysfunction in schizophrenics?* Psychopathology, 33, 43–47.

Glover, R. (1962). *New concepts in psychiatric treatment.* In E. H. Schneider (Ed.), Music therapy 1961 (pp. 48–49). Lawrence, KS: Allen Press.

Glover, R. G. (1968). *Immediate psychiatric service.* In E. T. Gaston (Ed.), Music in therapy (pp. 405–406). New York: Macmillan.

Glyn, J. (2002). *Drummed out of mind: A music therapy group with forensic patients.* In A. Davies & E. Richards (Eds.), Music therapy and group work: Sound company (pp. 43–62). London: Jessica Kingsley.

Goericelaya, F. (1988). *The role of music therapy in the eating disorders programme at St. Mary's Hill psychiatric hospital.* Australian Music Therapy Association Conference Proceedings.

Goldberg, F. S. (1989). *Music psychotherapy in acute psychiatric inpatient and private practice settings.* Music Therapy Perspectives, 6, 40–43.

Goldberg, F. S. (1992). *Images of emotion: The role of emotion in guided imagery and music.* Journal of the Association for Music and Imagery, 1, 5–17.

Goldberg, F. S. (1992). *Introduction to the special issue on psychiatric music therapy.* Music Therapy Perspectives, 12(2), 67–69.

Goldberg, F. S (1994). *The Bonny Method of Guided Imagery and Music as individual and group treatment in a short-term acute psychiatric hospital.* Journal of the Association for Music and Imagery, 3, 18–33.

Goldberg, F. S. (1995). *The Bonny Method of Guided Imagery and Music.* In T. Wigram, B. Saperston, & R. West (Eds.), The art and science of music therapy: A handbook (pp. 112–128). Chur, Switzerland: Harwood Academic.

Goldberg, F. S. (2000). *I am the creator and the created: A women's journey from loss to wholeness.* Beitrage Musiktherapie, 10, 47–58.

Goldberg, F. S. (2002). *A holographic field theory model of the Bonny Method of Guided Imagery and Music (BMGIM).* In K. E. Bruscia & D. E. Gorcke (Eds.), Guided imagery and music: The Bonny Method (pp. 359–377). Gilsum, NH: Barcelona.

Goldberg, F. S., Hoss, T., & Chesney, T. (1988). *Music and imagery as psychotherapy with a brain injured patient: A case study.* Music Therapy Perspectives, 5, 41–45.

Goldberg, F. S., McNeil, D., & Binder, R. (1988). *Therapeutic factors in two forms of inpatient group psychotherapy: Music therapy and verbal therapy.* Group: The Journal of the Eastern Group Psychotherapy Society, 12, 145–156.

Goldstein, C., Lingas, C., & Sheafor, D. (1965). Interpretive or creative movements as a sublimination tool in music therapy. Journal of Music Therapy, 2(1), 11–15.

Goldstein, S. L. (1990). A songwriting assessment for hopelessness in depressed adolescents: A review of literature and a pilot study. The Arts in Psychotherapy, 17(2), 117–124.

Goodman, K. D. (1989). Music therapy assessment of emotionally disturbed children. The Arts in Psychotherapy, 16(3), 179–192.

Gouk, P. (2000). Musical healing in cultural contexts. Aldershot, England: Ashgate.

Graham, R. M. (1959). Procedures for conducting rhythmic activities on wards of chronic and regressed mental patients. In E. H. Schneider (Ed.), Music therapy 1958 (pp. 157–161). Lawrence, KS: Allen Press.

Graham, R. M. (1975). Music education of emotionally disturbed children. In R. M. Graham (Ed.), Music for the exceptional child (pp. 111–129). Reston, VA: Music Educators National Conference.

Graham, R. M. (Ed.). (1975). Music for the exceptional child. Reston, VA: Music Educators National Conference.

Greenberg, M. (1970). Musical achievement and self-esteem. Journal of Research in Music Education, 18, 57–64.

Greenberg, R., & Fischer, S. (1971). Some differential effects of music in projective and structured psychological tests. Psychological Reports, 28, 817–818.

Gregory, D. (2000). Test instruments used by Journal of Music Therapy authors from 1984–1997. Journal of Music Therapy, 39(2), 79–94.

Gregory, J. S. (1956). Music therapy with mental patients. In E. T. Gaston (Ed.), Music therapy 1955 (pp. 189–192). Lawrence, KS: Allen Press.

Gresham, E. (1955). A program of music therapy in a neuropsychiatric hospital. In E. T. Gaston (Ed.), Music therapy 1954 (pp. 195–199). Lawrence, KS: Allen Press.

Greven, G. M. (1958). Music as a tool in psychotherapy for children. In E. T. Gaston (Ed.), Music therapy 1957 (pp. 105–108). Lawrence, KS: Allen Press.

Grimmett, J. O. (1952). Personality diagnosis through music—An apperceptive dynamic approach to personality diagnosis. Bulletin of NAMT, 1(2), 10.

Grocke, D. E. (1999). The music which underpins pivotal moments in guided imagery and music. In T. Wigram & J. DeBacker (Eds.), Clinical applications of music therapy and psychiatry (pp. 197–210). London: Jessica Kingsley.

Grocke, D. E. (1999). Pivotal moments in guided imagery and music. In J. Hibben (Ed.), Inside music therapy: Client experiences (pp. 296–305). Gilsum, NH: Barcelona.

Grocke, D. E. (2002). The Bonny music programs. In K. E. Bruscia & D. E. Grocke (Eds.), Guided imagery and music: The Bonny Method (pp. 99–133). Gilsum, NH: Barcelona.

Grocke, D. E. (2002). The evolution of Bonny's music programs. In K. E. Bruscia & D. E. Grocke (Eds.), Guided imagery and music: The Bonny Method (pp. 85–98). Gilsum, NH: Barcelona.

Grocke, D. E. (2003). A case study in guided imagery and music (BMGIM). In D. Aldridge (Ed.), Case study designs in music therapy. London Jessica Kingsley.

Grogan, K., & Knak, D. (2002). A children's group: An exploration of the framework necessary for therapeutic work. In A. Davies & E. Richards (Eds.), Music therapy and group work: Sound company (pp. 202–215). London: Jessica Kingsley.

Grossman, S. (1978). An investigation of Crocker's music projective technique for emotionally disturbed children. Journal of Music Therapy, 15(4), 179–184.

Grubler, E. (1958). The effect of a specific music listening program on depressed patients. Bulletin of NAMT, 7(2), 7–8, 10.

Gutheil, E. A. (Ed.). (1952). Music and your emotions. New York: Liveright.

Gutheil, E. A. (1959). Music as adjunct to psychotherapy—Proceedings from the advancement of psychotherapy. American Journal of Psychotherapy, 8(1), 94–109.

Guze, V. S. (1957). The drawings of normal and psychotic women as affected by music. In E. T. Gaston (Ed.), Music therapy 1956 (pp. 119–124). Lawrence, KS: Allen Press.

Hadley, S. (2001). Exploring relationships between Mary Priestley's life and work. Nordic Journal of Music Therapy, 10(2), 116–131.

Hadley, S. (2002). Theoretical basis of Analytical music therapy. In J. T. Eschen (Ed.), Analytical music therapy (pp. 34–50). London: Jessica Kingsley.

Hadley, S. (2003). Psychodynamic music therapy: Case studies. Gilsum, NH: Barcelona.

Hadsell, N. (1974). A sociological theory and approach to music therapy with adult psychiatric patients. Journal of Music Therapy, 11(3), 113–124.

Hahn, M. E. (1952). A proposed technique for investigating the relationship between personality structure and musical preference. Bulletin of NAMT, 1(2), 10.

Haines, J. H. (1989). The effects of music therapy on the self-esteem of emotionally disturbed adolescents. Music Therapy, 8(1), 78–91.

Hakvoort, L. (2002). A music therapy anger management program for forensic offenders. Music Therapy Perspectives, 20(2), 123–132.

Hall, D. (1955). Recorded music and insulin shock therapy. Bulletin of NAMT, 4(2), 7–8, 10.

Hammer, S. E. (1996). The effects of guided imagery through music on state and trait anxiety. Journal of Music Therapy, 33(1), 47–70.

Hanks, K. J. (1992). Music, affect and imagery: A cross-cultural exploration. Journal of the Association of Music and Imagery, 1, 19–31.

Hanser, S. B. (1974). Group contingent music listening with emotionally disturbed boys. Journal of Music Therapy, 11(4), 220–225.

Hanser, S. B. (1984). Music group psychotherapy: An evaluation model. Music Therapy Perspectives, 1(4), 14–16.

Hanser, S. B. (1985). Music therapy and stress reduction research. Journal of Music Therapy, 22(4), 193–206.

Hanser, S. B. (1987). Music therapist's handbook. St. Louis, MO: Warren H. Green.

Hanser, S. B. (1990). A music therapy strategy for depressed older adults in the community. Journal of Applied Gerontology, 9, 283–298.

Hanser, S. B., & Thompson, L. W. (1994). Effects of music therapy strategy on depressed older adults. Journal of Gerontology, 49(6), 265–269.

Hanson, H. (1948). Emotional expression in music. In D. M. Schullian & M. Schoen, (Eds.), Music medicine (pp. 244–265). New York: Henry Schuman.

Harbert, W. K. (1957). Treatment of emotionally disturbed children in a music therapy clinic. In E. T. Gaston (Ed.), Music therapy 1956 (pp. 156–164). Lawrence, KS: Allen Press.

Hargreaves, D. J., & North, A. C. (Eds.). (1997). The social psychology of music. New York: Oxford University Press.

Harrington, A. H. (1939). Music as a therapeutic aid in a hospital for mental disease. Mental Hygiene, 23, 601–609.

Harris, C., Bradley, R., & Tutus, S. (1992). A comparison of the effects of hard rock and easy listening on the frequency of observed inappropriate behavior: Control of environmental antecedents in a large public area. Journal of Music Therapy, 29(1), 6–17.

Hatta, T., & Nakamura, M. (1991). Can antistress music tapes reduce mental stress? Stress Medicine, 7, 181–184.

Hauck, L. P., & Martin, P. L. (1970). Music as a reinforcer in patient-controlled duration of time out. Journal of Music Therapy, 11(1), 43–53.

Heal, M. (1989). In time with the mind: How music therapy allows the expression of inner feelings. Surbiton: Good Impressions, Ltd.

Heal, M. (1989). The use of pre-composed songs with a highly defended client. Journal of British Music Therapy, 3(1), 10–15.

Heal, M., & O'Hara, J. (1993). The music therapy of an anorectic mentally handicapped adult. British Journal of Medical Psychology, 66, 33–41.

Heal, M., & Wigram, T. (Eds.). (1993). Music therapy in health and education. London: Jessica Kingsley.

Healey, B. (1973). Pilot study in the applicability of the music preference test of personality. Journal of Music Therapy, 10(1), 36–45.

Heaney, C. J. (1992). Evaluation of music therapy and other treatment modalities by adult psychiatric inpatients. Journal of Music Therapy, 29(2), 70–86.

Heimlich, E. P. (1960, June). Music as therapy with emotionally disturbed children. Child Welfare, pp. 7–11.

Heimlich, E. P. (1965). The specialized use of music as a mode of communication in the treatment of disturbed children. Journal of the American Academy of Child Psychiatry, 4(1), 86–122.

Heimlich, E. P. (1983). The metaphoric use of song lyrics as paraverbal communication. Child Psychiatry and Human Development, 14(2), 67–75.

Heller, G. N. (1987). Ideas, initiatives, and implementation: Music therapy in America, 1789–1848. Journal of Music Therapy, 24(1), 35–46.

Henderson, H. (1991). Improvised song stories in the treatment of a 13-year old sexually abused girl from the Xhosa tribe in South Africa. In K. E. Bruscia (Ed.), Case studies in music therapy (pp. 207–218). Phoenixville, PA: Barcelona.

Henderson, S. M. (1983). Effects of a music therapy program upon awareness of mood in music, group cohesion, and self-esteem among hospitalized adolescent patients. Journal of Music Therapy, 20(1), 14–20.

Herman, E. P. (1954). Music therapy in depression. In E. Podolsky (Ed.), Music therapy (pp. 112–115). New York: Philosophical Library.

Herman, F. (1991). The boy that nobody wanted: Creative experience for a boy with severe emotional problems. In K. E. Bruscia (Ed.), Case studies in music therapy (pp. 99–108). Phoenixville, PA: Barcelona.

Hernandez-Ruiz, E. (2005). Effect of music therapy on the anxiety levels and sleep patterns of abused women in shelters. Journal of Music Therapy, 42(2), 140–158.

Hibben, J. (Ed.). (1999). Inside music therapy: Client experiences. Gilsum, NH: Barcelona.

Hilliard, R. E. (2001). The effects of music therapy-based bereavement groups on mood and behavior of grieving children: A pilot study. The Journal of Music Therapy, 38(4), 291–306.

Hilliard, R. E. (2001). The use of cognitive-behavioral music therapy in the treatment of women with eating disorders. Music Therapy Perspectives, 19(2), 109–113.

Hoffman, J. (1995). Rhythmic medicine: Music with a purpose. Leawood, KS: Jamillan Press.

Holligan, F. (1992). Case study: Guided imagery and music. The Australian Journal of Music Therapy, 3, 27–36.

Holligan, F. (1994). Using guided imagery and music in retreat. Journal of the Association for Music and Imagery, 3, 59–63.

Hong, M., Hussey, D., & Heng, M. (1998). Music therapy with children with severe emotional disturbances in a residential treatment setting. Music Therapy Perspectives, 16, 61–66.

Horden, P. (2000). Music as medicine: The history of music therapy since antiquity. Aldershot, England: Ashgate.

Hoskyns, S. L. (1988). Studying group music therapy with adult offenders: Research in progress. Psychology of Music, 16(1), 25–41.

Hoskyns, S. L. (1995). Observing offenders: the use of simple rating scales to assess changes in activity during group music therapy. In A. Gilroy & C. Lee (Eds.), Art and music therapy research (pp. 138–151). London: Routledge.

Hoskyns, S. L. (1995). The use of simple rating scales to assess changes in activity during group music therapy. In A. Gilroy & C. Lee (Eds.), Art and music: Therapy and research. London: Routledge.

Howe, A. W. (1960). Music therapy in the psychiatric treatment program. Journal of the South Carolina Medical Association, 56, 59–65.

Hudson, W. C. (1973). Music: A physiologic language. Journal of Music Therapy, 10(3), 137–140.

Hustig, H. H., Tran, D. B., Hafner, R. J., & Miller, R. J. (1990). The effect of headphone music on persistent auditory hallucinations. Behavioral Psychotherapy, 18, 273–281.

Isenberg-Grzeda, C. (1988). Music therapy assessment: A reflection of professional identity. Journal of Music Therapy, 25(3), 156–169.

Isenberg-Grzeda, C. (1995). The sound image: Music therapy in the treatment of the abused child. In C. B. Kenny (Ed.), Listening, playing, creating: Essays on the power of sound (pp. 137–149). Albany, NY: State University of New York Press.

Isenberg-Grzeda, C., Goldberg, F. S., & Dvorkin, J. M. (2004). Psychodynamic approach to music therapy. In A.-A. Darrow (Ed.), Introduction to approaches in music therapy (pp. 79–101). Silver Spring, MD: American Music Therapy Association.

Isham, A. C. (1945). The use of song parodies as recreational therapy for mental patients. Occupational Therapy and Rehabilitation, 24, 259–261.

Ishiyama, T. (1963). Music as a psychotherapeutic tool in the treatment of catatonic. Psychiatric Quarterly, 37, 437–461.

Iwanga, M., Ikeda, M., & Iwaki, T. (1996). The effects of repetitive exposure to music on subjective and physiological responses. Journal of Music Therapy, 33(3), 219–230.

Jacobson, H. L. (1956). The effects of sedative music on the tension, anxiety, and pain experienced by mental patients during dental procedures. Bulletin of NAMT, 5(3), 9–11.

Jahn-Langenberg, M. (2002). Some considerations on the treatment techniques of psychoanalytically-established music therapy. In J. T. Eschen (Ed.), Analytical music therapy (pp. 51–63). London: Jessica Kingsley.

Jahn-Langenberg, M., & Schmidt, H. U. (2003). A comparison for first encounters: Diagnostic impressions of a music therapy session and the analytic first interview. Nordic Journal of Music Therapy, 12(1), 91–99.

James, M. R. (1987). Implications of selected social psychology theories on life-long skill generalization. Music Therapy Perspectives, 4, 29–33.

James, M. R. (1988). Music therapy and alcoholism: Part I – An overview of addiction. Music Therapy Perspectives, 5, 60–65.

James, M. R. (1988). Music therapy and alcoholism: Part II – Treatment services. Music Therapy Perspectives, 5, 65–68.

James, M. R. (1988). Music therapy values clarification: A positive influence on perceived locus of control. Journal of Music Therapy, 25(4), 206–215.

James, M. R. (1988). Self-monitoring inclinations and adolescent clients with chemical dependency. Journal of Music Therapy, 25(2), 94–102.

James, M. R., & Freed, B. S. (1989). A sequential model for developing group cohesion in music therapy. Music Therapy Perspectives, 7, 28–34.

Jarvis, J. (1988). Guided imagery and music (GIM) as a primary psychotherapeutic approach. Music Therapy Perspectives, 5, 69–72.

Jenkins, R. (1962). Common problems in child psychiatry. In E. H. Schneider (Ed.), Music therapy 1961 (pp. 116–122). Lawrence, KS: Allen Press.

Jensen, B. (1999). Music therapy with psychiatric in-patients: A case study with a young schizophrenic man. In T. Wigram & J. DeBacker (Eds.), Clinical applications of music therapy in psychiatry (pp. 44–60). London: Jessica Kingsley.

Jensen, K. L. (2001). The effects of selected classical music on self-disclosure. Journal of Music Therapy, 38(1), 2–27.

Joel, C. (1957). New developments in psychiatry and their relations to music therapy. Bulletin of NAMT, 6(2), 1–6.

John, D. (1992). Towards music psychotherapy. Journal of British Music Therapy, 6(1), 10–11.

John, D. (1995). The therapeutic relationship in music therapy as a tool in the treatment of psychosis. In T. Wigram, B. Saperston, & R. West (Eds.), The art and science of music therapy: A handbook (pp. 157–166). Chur, Switzerland: Harwood Academic.

Johnson, D. R. (1987). The role of the creative arts therapies in the diagnosis and treatment of psychological trauma. The Arts in Psychotherapy, 14(1), 7–13.

Johnson, D. R. (1990). Introduction to the special issue on creative arts therapies in the treatment of substance abuse. The Arts in Psychotherapy, 17(4), 295–298.

Johnson, E. R. (1981). The role of objective and concrete feedback in self-concept treatment of juvenile delinquents in music therapy. Journal of Music Therapy, 18(3), 137–147.

Johnson, J. M. (1968). Evaluating patients in music therapy. Journal of Music Therapy, 5(4), 108–110.

Jones, J. D. (2005). A comparison of songwriting and lyric analysis techniques to evoke emotional change in a single session with people who are chemically dependent. Journal of Music Therapy, 42(2), 94–110.

Joseph, H., & Heimlich, E. P. (1959). The therapeutic use of music with treatment resistant children. American Journal of Mental Deficiency, 64, 41–49.

Justice, R. W. (1994). Music therapy interventions for people with eating disorders in an inpatient setting. Music Therapy Perspectives, 12(2), 104–110.

Kahans, D., & Calford, M. B. (1982). The influence of music on psychiatric patients' immediate attitude change toward therapists. Journal of Music Therapy, 19(3), 179–187.

Kalms, M. A. (1931). Music in mental hospitals. Occupational Therapy and Rehabilitation, 10, 381–385.

Kalms, M. A. (1942). Differences in the music program of private and state hospitals. Occupational Therapy and Rehabilitation, 21, 294–296.

Kantor, M., & Pinsker, H. (1973). Musical repression of psychopathology. Perspective in Biology and Medicine, 16, 263–269.

Kasayka, R. E. (2002). A spiritual orientation to the Bonny Method: To walk the mystical path on practical feet. In K. E. Bruscia & D. E. Gorcke (Eds.), Guided imagery and music: The Bonny Method (pp. 257–270). Gilsum, NH: Barcelona.

Kaser, V. (1991). *Music therapy treatment of pedophilia using the drum set.* The Arts in psychotherapy, 18(1), 7–15.

Kaser, V. (1993). *Musical expressions of subconscious feelings: A clinical perspective.* Music Therapy Perspectives, 11(1), 16–23.

Katsh, S., & Merle-Fishman, C. (1987). *Metaphorical improvisation therapy.* In K. E. Bruscia (Ed.), Improvisational models of music therapy (pp. 319–335). Springfield, IL: Charles C. Thomas.

Katsh, S., & Merle-Fishman, C. (1998). *The music within you* (2nd ed.). Gilsum, NH: Barcelona.

Kennair, L. (2000). *Developing minds for pathology and musicality.* Nordic Journal of Music Therapy, 9(1), 26–37.

Kenny, C. B. (1991). *The use of musical space with an adult in psychotherapy.* In K. E. Bruscia (Ed.), Case studies in music therapy (pp. 333–356). Phoenixville, PA: Barcelona.

Kenny, C. B. (Ed.). (1995). Listening, playing, creating: Essays on the power of sound. *Albany, NY: State University of New York Press.*

Kenny, C. B., & Slige, B. (Eds.). (2002). Contemporary voices in music therapy. *Oslo, Norway: Unipubforlag.*

Kenny, D., & Faunce, G. (2004). *The impact of group singing on mood, coping, and perceived pain in chronic pain patients attending a multidisciplinary pain clinic.* Journal of Music Therapy, 41(3), 241–258.

Kerr, T., Walsh, J., & Marshall, A. (2001). *Emotional change processes in music- assisted reframing.* Journal of Music Therapy, 38(3), 193–211.

Kibler, V. E., & Rider, M. S. (1983). *Effects of progressive muscle relaxation and music on stress as measured by finger temperature response.* Journal of Clinical Psychology, 32, 213–215.

King, P. (1988). *Heavy metal music and drug abuse in adolescents.* Drug Abuse, 83, 295–304.

Kivland, M. J. (1986). *The use of music to increase self-esteem in a conduct disordered adolescent.* Journal of Music Therapy, 23(1), 25–29.

Koh, S. D., & Shears, G. (1970). *Psychophysical scaling by schizophrenics and normals: Line lengths and music preferences.* Archives of General Psychiatry, 23, 249–259.

Kohut, H. (1952). *The psychological significance of musical activity.* In (Ed.), Music therapy 1951 (pp. 151–157). Lawrence, KS: Allen Press.

Korlin, D. (2002). *A neuropsychological theory of traumatic imagery in the Bonny Method of Guided Imagery and Music (BMGIM).* In K. E. Bruscia & D. E. Gorcke (Eds.), Guided imagery and music: The Bonny Method (pp. 379–415). Gilsum, NH: Barcelona.

Korlin, D., Nyback, H., & Goldberg, F. (2002). *Creative arts groups in psychiatric care: Development and evaluation of a therapeutic alternative.* Nordic Journal of Psychiatry, 54, 333–340.

Korlin, D., & Wrangsjo, B. (2001). *Gender differences in outcome of guided imagery and music (GIM) therapy.* Nordic Journal of Music Therapy, 10(2), 132–143.

Kortegaard, H. M. (1993). *Music therapy in the psychodynamic treatment of schizophrenia.* In M. Heal & T. Wigram (Eds.), Music therapy in health and education (pp. 55–65). London: Jessica Kingsley.

Kotler, W. (1955). *A study of the relationship between music and post-electroshock awakening.* In E. T. Gaston (Ed.), Music therapy 1954 (pp. 211–215). Lawrence, KS: Allen Press.

Kovach, A. M. S. (1985). *Shamanism and guided imagery and music: A comparison.* Journal of Music Therapy, 22(3), 154–165.

Krout, R. E. (1999). *Songs from sorrow, song from joy: Original music to facilitate creative grief processing with bereaved children and youth* (Book accompanying compact disc recording). St. Louis, MO: MMB Music.

Krout, R. E. (2002). *The use of therapist-composed songs to facilitate multi-modal grief processing and expression with bereaved children in group music therapy.* Annual Journal of the New Zealand Society for Music Therapy, 21–35.

Krout, R. E. (in press). *The music therapist as singer-songwriter: Applications with bereaved teens.* In F. Baker, & T. Wigram (Eds.), Song writing methods, techniques and clinical applications for music therapy clinicians, educators and students. *London: Jessica Kingsley.*

LaMaster, R. J. (1947). *Music therapy as a tool for treatment of mental patients in the hospital.* Hospital Management, 62–63, 110–114.

Langdon, G. S., Pearson, J., Stastny, P., & Thorning, H. (1989). *The integration of music therapy into a treatment approach in the transition of adult psychiatric patients from institution to community.* Music Therapy, 8(1), 92–107.

Langenberg, M. (1999). *Music therapy and the meaning of affect regulation for psychosomatic patients.* In T. Wigram & J. DeBacker (Eds.), Clinical applications of music therapy in psychiatry (pp. 232–243). London: Jessica Kingsley.

Langenberg, M., Frommer, J., & Trees, W. (1993). *A qualitative research approach to Analytical music therapy.* Music Therapy, 12(1), 59–84.

Langenberg, M., Frommer, J., & Trees, W. (1995). *From isolation to bonding: A music therapy study with a patient with chronic migraines.* The Arts in Psychotherapy, 18(1), 47–58.

Larson, B. A. (1981). *Auditory and visual rhythmic pattern recognition by emotionally disturbed and normal adolescents.* Journal of Music Therapy, 18(3), 128–136.

Latham, W. (1981). *Role of music therapy in the education of handicapped children and youth.* Lawrence, KS: National Association for Music Therapy.

Latham, W. (1982). *Survey of current functions of a music therapist.* Journal of Music Therapy, 19(1), 2–27.

Latham-Radocy, W. (2002). Pediatric music therapy. *Springfield, IL: Charles C. Thomas.*

Layman, D. L., Hussey, D. L., & Laing, S. J. (2002). *Foster care trends in the United States: Ramifications for music therapists.* Music Therapy Perspectives, 20(2), 38–46.

Layman, D. L., Hussey, D. L., & Laing, S. J. (2002). *Music therapy assessment for severely emotionally disturbed children: A pilot study.* Journal of Music Therapy, 39(3), 164–187.

Lee, C., & Gilroy, A (Eds.). (1995). *Art and music: Therapy and research. London: Routledge.*

Lee, C. A. (1989). Structural analysis of therapeutic improvisatory music. Journal of British Music Therapy, 3(2), 11–19.

Lee, C. A. (1990). Structural analysis of post-tonal improvisatory music. Journal of British Music Therapy, 4(1), 6–20.

Lee, C. A. (1995). The analysis of therapeutic improvisatory music. In A. Gilroy & C. A. Lee (Eds.), Art and music: Therapy and research (pp. 35–50). London: Routledge.

Lee, C. A. (2000). A method for analyzing improvisation in music therapy. Journal of Music Therapy, 37(2), 147–167.

Lee, C. A. (2003). The architecture of aesthetic music therapy. Gilsum, NH: Barcelona.

Lee, R. E. (1956). Music therapy at Rockland State helps to resocialize patients. Bitter times, 37(18), 13–20.

Lehman, R., & Farberow, N. (1994). Pop-rock music as precipitating cause in youth suicide. Journal of Forensic Science, 39(2), 494–499.

Lehman, W. E. (1962). Music therapy in a maximum security setting. In E. H. Schneider (Ed.), Music therapy 1961 (pp. 91–96). Lawrence, KS: Allen Press.

Lehrer, P. M., & Woolfolk, R. L. (Eds.). (1993). Principles and practice of stress management. New York: The Guilford Press.

Lehrer-Casle, I. (1971). Group dynamics as applied to the use of music with schizophrenic adolescents. Journal of Contemporary Psychotherapy, 3(2), 111–116.

Levine, D. (1960). Music therapy as part of the total hospital program. Bulletin of NAMT, 9(3), 7–11.

Lewis, D. (1964). Chamber music–proposed as a therapeutic medium. Journal of Music Therapy, 4, 126–127.

Lewis, G. H. (1980). Popular music, musical preference and drug use among youth. Popular Music and Society, 7, 176–181.

Lewis, K. (1998–99). The Bonny Method of GIM: Matrix for transpersonal experience. Journal of the Association for Music and Imagery, 6, 63–86.

Lindberg, K. A. (1995). Songs of healing: Songwriting with an abused adolescent. Music Therapy, 13(1), 93–108.

Lindecker, J. M. (1954). Music therapy in a juvenile detention home. In M. Bing (Ed.), Music therapy 1953 (pp. 108–114). Lawrence, KS: Allen Press.

Lindecker, J. M. (1955). Music therapy for juvenile delinquents. In E. T. Gaston (Ed.), Music therapy 1954 (pp. 117–123). Lawrence, KS: Allen Press.

Loewy, J. V. (1995). A hermeneutic panel study of music therapy assessment with an emotionally disturbed boy (Doctoral dissertation, New York University, 1995). Dissertation Abstracts International, 55(9-A), 2631.

Loewy, J. V. (2000). Music psychotherapy assessment. Music Therapy Perspectives, 18(1), 47–58.

Logan, T. G., & Roberts, A. R. (1984). The effects of different types of relaxation music on tension level. Journal of Music Therapy, 21(4), 177–183.

Lord, W. (1971). Communication of activity therapy rationale. Journal of Music Therapy, 8(2), 68–71.

Loth, H. (1994). Music therapy and forensic psychiatry—Choice, denial and the law. Journal of British Music Therapy, 8(2), 10–18.

Loth, H. (2002). There's no getting away from anything in here: A music therapy group within an inpatient programmed for adults with eating disorders. In A. Davies & E. Richards (Eds.), Music therapy and sound work: Sound company (pp. 90–104). London: Jessica Kingsley.

Lowe, J. C. (1973). Conciliatory response to music as a reciprocal inhibitor. Journal of Behavior Therapy and Experimental Psychiatry, 4(3), 297–299.

Luce, D. W. (2001). Cognitive therapy and music therapy. Music Therapy Perspectives, 19(2), 96–103.

Luce, G. C. (1970). Biological rhythms in psychiatry and medicine. Public Health Service Monograph #2088. Chevy Chase, MD: National Institute of Mental Health.

Luetje, V. M. (1989). Music therapy in crisis intervention. Music Therapy Perspectives, 7, 35–39.

MacIntosh, H. B. (2003). Sounds of healing: Music in group work with survivors of sexual abuse. The Arts in Psychotherapy, 30(1), 17–23.

Madsen, C. K., & Madsen, C. H., Jr. (1968). Music as a behavior modification technique with juvenile offenders. Journal of Music Therapy, 5(3), 72–76.

Mahns, W. (2002). The psychodynamic function of music in analytical music therapy with children. In J. T. Eschen (Ed.), Analytical music therapy (pp. 95–103). London: Jessica Kingsley.

Maranto, C. D. (1993). Music therapy and stress management. In P. M. Lehrer & R. L. Woolfolk (Eds.), Principles and practice of stress management (pp. 407–442). New York: The Guilford Press.

Margo, A., Hemsley, D. R., & Slade, P. D. (1981). The effects of varying auditory input on schizophrenic hallucinations. British Journal of Psychiatry, 157, 913–914.

Margolis, P. M. (1972). Community mental health: Harmony or cacophony? Journal of Music Therapy, 9(3), 123–129.

Mark, A. (1986). Adolescents discuss themselves and drugs through music. Journal of Substance Abuse Treatment, 3(4), 242–246.

Marr, J. (2001). The use of guided imagery and music in spiritual growth. Journal of Pastoral Care, 55(4), 397–406.

Marsh, C. W. (1968). A hospital-community music therapy program. In E. T. Gaston (Ed.), Music in therapy (p. 404). New York: Macmillan.

Marshman, A. T. (2003). The power of music: A Jungian aesthetic. Music Therapy Perspectives, 21(1), 21–26.

Martin, M. A., & Metha, A. (1997). Recall of early childhood memories through musical mood induction. The Arts in Psychotherapy, 24(5), 447–454.

Mary, Miller, L., & Miller, E. (1999). Playing music in the group. In J. Hibben (Ed.), Inside music therapy: Client experiences (pp. 83–86). Gilsum, NH: Barcelona.

Masserman, J. H. (1954). Music and the child. American Journal of Psychotherapy, 8(1), 63–67.

Matto, H. C. (1997). An integrative approach to the treatment of women with eating disorders. The Arts in Psychotherapy, 24(4), 347–354.

Maultsby, M. (1977). Combining music therapy and rational behavior therapy. Journal of Music Therapy, 14(2), 89–97.

Mazza, N., & Price, B. D. (1985). When time counts: Poetry and music in short-term group treatment. Social Work and Groups, 8(2), 53–68.

McClean, M. (1974). One therapist; one patient: A success story. Hospital and Community Psychiatry, 25, 153–156.

McCraty, R., Atkinson, M., Rein, G., & Watkins, A. D. (1996). Music enhances the effect of positive emotional states on salivary IgA. Stress Medicine, 12, 167–175.

McDonald, M. (1990). Transitional times and musical development. In S. Feder, R. L. Karmel, & G. H. Pollock (Eds.), Psychoanalytic explorations in music (Applied Psychoanalysis Monograph Series) (pp. 79–95). Madison, CT: International Universities Press.

McDonnell, L. (1979). Paraverbal therapy in pediatric cases with emotional complications. American Journal of Orthopsychiatry, 49(1), 44–52.

McDonnell, L. (1984). Music therapy with trauma patients and their families in a pediatric service. Music Therapy, 4(1), 47–54.

McFarland, R. A. (1984). Effects of music upon emotional content of TAT stories. Journal of Psychology, 116, 227–234.

McFerran-Skewes, K., & Gorcke, D. E. (2000). What do grieving young people and music therapy have in common: Exploring the match between creativity and younger adolescents. European Journal of Palliative Care, 7(6), 227–230.

McGinty, J. (1980). Survey on duties and responsibilities of current music therapy positions. Journal of Music Therapy, 12(3), 148–166.

McGuire, M. G. (2004). Psychiatric music therapy in the community: The legacy of Florence Tyson. Gilsum, NH: Barcelona.

McKay, L. A. (1945). Music as a group therapeutic agent in the treatment of convalescents. In Group psychotherapy: A symposium. Sociometry, 8(3/4), 233–237.

McKinney, C. H. (1990). The effect of music on imagery. Journal of Music Therapy, 27(1), 34–46.

McKinney, C. H. (1993). The case of Therese: Multidimensional growth through guided imagery and music. Journal of the Association for Music and Imagery, 2, 99–110.

McKinney, C. H., Antoni, M. H., Kumar, A., & Kumar, M. (1995). The effects of guided imagery and music on depression and beta-endorphin levels. Journal of the Association for Music and Imagery, 4, 67–78.

McKinney, C. H., Antoni, M. H., Kumar, A. M., Tims, F. C., & McCabe, P. M. (1997). Effects of guided imagery and music (GIM) therapy on mood and cortisol in healthy adults. Health Psychology, 16, 390–400.

McKinney, C. H., & Tims, F. C. (1995). Differential effects of selected classical music on the imagery of high versus low imagers: Two studies. Journal of Music Therapy, 32(1), 22–45.

McKinnis, I. G. (1952). The construction of a list for the selection of neuropsychiatric patients for music therapy. In E. G. Gilliland (Ed.), Music therapy 1951 (pp. 190–191). Lawrence, KS: Allen Press.

Meadows, A. (2000). The validity and reliability of the Guided Imagery and Music Responsiveness Scale. Journal of the Association for Music and Imagery, 7, 8–33.

Meadows, A. (2002). Distinctions between the Bonny Method of Guided Imagery and Music (BMGIM) and other imagery techniques. In K. E. Bruscia & D. E. Gorcke (Eds.), Guided imagery and music: The Bonny Method (pp. 63–83). Gilsum, NH: Barcelona.

Meadows, A. (2002). Psychotherapeutic application of the Bonny method. In K. E. Bruscia & D. E. Gorcke (Eds.), Guided imagery and music: The Bonny Method (pp. 187–204). Gilsum, NH: Barcelona.

Merle-Fishman, C. R., & Marcus, M. I. (1982). Musical behaviors and preferences in emotionally disturbed and normal children: An exploratory study. Music Therapy, 2, 1–12.

Merritt, S. (1990). Music, mind, and imagery: Unlocking the treasures of your mind. New York: Penguin Books.

Merritt, S., & Schulberg, C. (1995). GIM and collective grief. Journal of the Association for Music and Imagery, 6, 37–54.

Metzger, L. K. (1986). The selection of music for therapeutic use with adolescents and young adults in a psychiatric facility. Music Therapy Perspectives, 3, 20–24.

Metzner, S. (1999). Psychoanalytically informed music therapy in psychiatry: In T. Wigram & J. DeBacker (Eds.), Clinical applications of music therapy in psychiatry (pp. 102–118). London: Jessica Kingsley.

Metzner, S. (2004). The significance of triadic structures in patients undergoing therapy for psychosis in a psychiatric ward. In S. Hadley (Ed.), Psychodynamic music therapy: Case studies (pp. 257–271). Gilsum, NH: Barcelona.

Mezzano, J., & Preuter, B. (1974). Background music and counseling interaction. Journal of Counseling Psychology, 21, 84–86.

Michel, D. E. (1952). A study of the sedative effects of music for acutely disturbed patients in a mental hospital. In E. G. Gilliland (Ed.), Music therapy 1951 (pp. 182–183). Lawrence, KS: Allen Press.

Michel, D. E. (1953). Music in mental hospitals panel: Philosophy and theory. In E. G. Gilliland (Ed.), Music therapy 1952 (pp. 36–69). Lawrence, KS: Allen Press.

Michel, D. E. (1955). Some applications of group therapy methods with music therapy. In E. T. Gaston (Ed.), Music therapy 1954 (pp. 205–208). Lawrence, KS: Allen Press.

Michel, D. E. (1958). A study to determine potential music therapy needs in a federal correctional institution. In E. T. Gaston (Ed.), Music therapy 1957 (pp. 206–214). Lawrence, KS: Allen Press.

Michel, D. E. (1959). A survey of 375 cases in music therapy at a mental hospital. In E. H. Schneider (Ed.), Music therapy 1958 (pp. 166–176). Lawrence, KS: Allen Press.

Michel, D. E. (1960). Concluding report: A survey of 375 case records in music therapy. In E. H. Schneider (Ed.), Music therapy 1959 (pp. 137–152). Lawrence, KS: Allen Press.

Michel, D. E. (1965). Professional profile: The NAMT member and his clinical practice in music therapy. Journal of Music Therapy, 2(4), 124–129.

Michel, D. E. (1968). Adolescents. In E. T. Gaston (Ed.), Music in therapy (pp. 215– 228). New York: Macmillan.

Michel, D. E. (1968). Music therapy for children and adolescents with behavior disorder. In E. T. Gaston (Ed.), Music in therapy (pp. 175–180). New York: Macmillan.

Michel, D. E. (1968). The psychiatric approach and music therapy. In E. T. Gaston (Ed.), Music in therapy (pp. 175–180). New York: Macmillan.

Michel, D. E. (1971). Self-esteem and academic achievement in black junior high school students: Effects of automated guitar instruction. Council for Research in Music Education, 24, 15–23.

Michel, D. E. (1976). Music therapy: An introduction to therapy and special education through music. Springfield, IL: Charles C. Thomas.

Michel, D. E. (1985). Music therapy: An introduction (2nd ed.). Springfield, IL: Charles C. Thomas.

Michel, D. E., & Farrell, D. M. (1973). Music and self-esteem: Disadvantaged problem boys in an all-black elementary school. Journal of Research in Music Education, 21(1), 80–84.

Michel, D. E., & Martin, D. (1970). Music and self-esteem: Research with disadvantaged, problem boys in an elementary school. Journal of Music Therapy, 7(4), 124–127.

Michel, D. E., & Rohrbacher, M. (Eds.). (1982). The music therapy assessment profile for severely/profoundly handicapped persons, research draft III (0–27 month level). Denton, TX: Texas Women's University.

Migliore, M. J. (1991). The Hamilton Rating Scale for depression and rhythmic competency: A correlational study. Journal of Music Therapy, 28(4), 211–221.

Miles, C. (1958). The treatment of a hospitalized adolescent patient by the method of individual music therapy. In E. T. Gaston (Ed.), Music therapy 1957 (pp. 65–80). Lawrence, KS: Allen Press.

Miller, A. S. (1970). Music therapy for alcoholics at a Salvation Army center. Journal of Music Therapy, 7(4), 136–138.

Miller, E. B. (1994). Musical intervention in family therapy. Music Therapy, 12(2), 39– 57.

Miller, H. O. (1991). Group improvisation therapy: The experience of one man with schizophrenia. In K. E. Bruscia (Ed.), Case studies in music therapy (pp. 417– 431). Phoenixville, PA: Barcelona.

Mitchell, G. C. (1966). Bedtime music for psychotic children. Nursing Mirror, 122, 453.

Mitchell, S. D. (1958). Music in mental hospitals. Hospital (London), 44, 431–436.

Mitchell, S. D., & Zanker, A. (1949). Musical styles and mental disorders. Occupational Therapy and Rehabilitation, 28, 411–422.

Moe, T., Roesen, A., & Rabin, H. (2000). Restitutional factors in group music therapy with psychiatric patients based on a modification of guided imagery and music (GIM). Nordic Journal of Music Therapy, 9(2), 36–50.

Montello, L. M. (1996). A psychoanalytic music therapy approach to treating adults traumatized as children. Proceedings of the World Congress of Music Therapy, Hamburg, Germany.

Montello, L. M. (1998). Relational issues in psychoanalytic music therapy with traumatized individuals. In K. E. Bruscia (Ed.), The dynamics of music therapy (pp. 299–313). Gilsum, NH: Barcelona.

Montello, L. M. (1999). A psychoanalytic music therapy approach to treating adults traumatized as children. Music Therapy Perspectives, 17(2), 74–81.

Montello, L. M. (2002). Essential musical intelligence. Wheaton, IL: Quest Books.

Montello, L., & Coons, E. (1998). Effects of active versus passive group music therapy on preadolescents with emotional, learning, and behavioral disorders. Journal of Music Therapy, 35(1), 49–67.

Moran, T. (1985). Sounds of sex. The New Republic, 193, 14–16.

Moreno, J. J. (1980). Musical psychodrama: A new direction in music therapy. Journal of Music Therapy, 17(1), 34–42.

Moreno, J. J. (1984). Musical psychodrama in Paris. Music Therapy Perspectives, 1(4), 2–6.

Moreno, J. J. (1985). Music play therapy: An integrated approach. The Arts in Psychotherapy, 12(1), 17–23.

Moreno, J. J. (1987). The therapeutic role of the blues singer and considerations for the clinical application of the blues form. The Arts in Psychotherapy, 14(4), 333–340.

Moreno, J. J. (1999). Acting your own inner music. St. Louis, MO: MMB Music.

Morgan, E. (1975). Music—A weapon against anxiety. How music builds self-esteem in a psychiatric ward. Music Educators Journal, 61(5), 38–40.

Morgenstern, A. M. (1982). Group therapy: A timely strategy for music therapists. Music Therapy Perspectives, 1(1), 16–20.

Mornhinwey, G. C. (1992). Effects of music preference and selection on stress reduction. Journal of Holistic Nursing, 10, 101–109.

Murdock, H. M., & Eaton, M. T., Jr. (1952). Music as an adjunct to electroshock therapy. Journal of Nervous and Mental Disorders, 116, 336–339.

Murdock, H. M., & Eaton, M. T., Jr. (1954). Music as an adjunct to electroshock therapy. In E. Podolsky (Ed.), Music therapy (pp. 89–94). New York: Philosophical Library.

Murphy, M. E. (1983). Music therapy: A self-help group experience for substance abuse patients. Music Therapy, 3(1), 52–66.

Murphy, M. E. (1991). Group music therapy in acute psychiatric care: The treatment of a depressed woman following neurological trauma. In K. E. Bruscia (Ed.), Case studies in music therapy (pp. 465–478). Phoenixville, PA: Barcelona.

Murphy, M. E. (1992). Coping in the short-term: the impact of acute care on music therapy practice. Music Therapy, 11(1), 99–119.

Murray, W. E. (1959). The music therapist as special educator in the public schools. In E. H. Schneider (Ed.), Music therapy 1958 (pp. 94–99). Lawrence, KS: Allen Press.

Muskatevc, L. C. (1961). The role of music therapy in the clinical setting. In E. H. Schneider (Ed.), Music therapy 1960 (pp. 41–43). Lawrence, KS: Allen Press.

Myers, K. F. (1985). The relationship between degree of disability and vocal range, vocal range midpoint, and pitch-matching ability of mentally retarded and psychiatric clients. Journal of Music Therapy, 22(1), 35–45.

Nass, M. L. (1971). Some considerations of a psychoanalytic interpretation of music. Psychoanalytic Quarterly, 40, 303–316.

National Music Council. (1944). Report on a survey on the use of music in hospitals for mental and nervous disease. National Music Council Bulletin, 5.

Nelson, A. (1958). Mental patients can like new music! Bulletin of NAMT, 7(3), 7–8.

Newham, P. (1997). Therapeutic voice work. London: Jessica Kingsley.

Newham, P. (1999). Using voice and movement in therapy. London: Jessica Kingsley.

Newham, P. (1999). Using voice and song in therapy. London: Jessica Kingsley.

Nielson, M., & Moe, T. (1999). Chaos, crisis, development, cosmos. In J. Hibben (Ed.), Inside music therapy: Client experiences (pp. 53–60). Gilsum, NH: Barcelona.

Nielzen, S., & Cesarec, Z. (1982). Emotional experience of music by psychiatric patients compared with normal subjects. Acta Psychiatric Scandavian, 65, 450–460.

Nolan, P. (1983). Insight therapy: Guided imagery and music in a forensic psychiatric setting. Music Therapy, 3(1), 43–51.

Nolan, P. (1989). Music as a transitional object in the treatment of bulimia. Music Therapy Perspectives, 6, 49–51.

Nolan, P. (1989). Music therapy improvisation techniques with bulimic patients. In E. K. Baker & L. M. Hornyak (Eds.), The handbook of techniques in the treatment of eating disorders. New York: Guilford.

Nolan, P. (1991). Group improvisation therapy for a resistant woman with bipolar disorder–manic. In K. E. Bruscia (Ed.), Case studies in music therapy (pp. 451– 565). Phoenixville, PA: Barcelona.

Nolan, P. (1991). Music therapy with bone marrow patients: Reaching beyond the symptoms. In R. Spintge & R. Droh (Eds.), MusicMedicine. St. Louis, MO: MMB Music.

Nolan, P. (1994). The therapeutic response in improvisational music therapy: What goes on inside? Music Therapy Perspectives, 12(2), 84–91.

Nolan, P. (1995). The integration of mental health concepts in the education of the music therapist. In T. Wigram, B. Saperston, & R. West (Eds.), The art and science of music therapy: A handbook. Chur, Switzerland: Harwood Academic.

Nolan, P. (1997). Music therapy improvisation in the treatment of a resistant woman. In K. Bruscia (Ed.), Case studies in music therapy (pp. 451–464). Phoenixville, PA: Barcelona.

Nolan, P. (1998). Countertransference in clinical song-writing. In K. E. Bruscia (Ed.), The dynamics of music therapy (pp. 387–406). Gilsum, NH: Barcelona.

Nolan, P. (2003). Through music to therapeutic attachment: Psychodynamic music psychotherapy with a musician with dysthymic disorder. In S. Hadley (Ed.), Psychodynamic music therapy: Case studies (pp. 319–338). Gilsum, NH: Barcelona.

Nolan, P. (2005). Verbal processing in the music therapy relationship. Music Therapy Perspectives, Special Issue: The Role of the Music Therapist in the Music Therapy Process, 23, 18–23.

Nordoff, P., & Robbins, C. (1977). Creative music therapy. New York: John Day.

North, E. F. (1966). Music therapy as an important treatment modality with psychotic children. Journal of Music Therapy, 3(1), 22–24.

Nowicki, A. L., & Trevisan, L. A. (1978). Beyond the sound. Porterville, CA: Nowicki & Trevisan.

Noy, P. (1966). The psychodynamic meaning of music—Part I: A critical review of the psychoanalytic and related literature. Journal of Music Therapy, 3(4), 126–134.

Noy, P. (1967). The psychodynamic meaning of music—Part II–IV: A critical review of the psychodynamic and related literature. Journal of Music Therapy, 4(1), 7–23, 45–51, 81–94, 128–131.

O'Brien, N., & Goldstein, A. (1985). A systematic approach to developing a private practice in music therapy. Music Therapy, 5, 37–43.

Odell, H. (1988). A music therapy approach in mental health. Psychology of Music, 16(1), 52–61.

Odell-Miller, H. (1995). Approaches to music therapy in psychiatry with specific emphasis upon a research project with the elderly mentally ill. In T. Wigram, B. Saperston & R. West (Eds.), The art and science of music therapy: A handbook (pp. 83–111). Chur, Switzerland: Harwood Academic.

Odell-Miller, H. (1995). Why provide music therapy in the community for adults with mental health problems? British Journal of Music Therapy, 9(1), 4–10.

Odell-Miller, H. (1999). Investigating the value of music therapy in psychiatry: Developing research tools arising from clinical perspectives. In T. Wigram & J. DeBacker (Eds.), Clinical applications of music therapy in psychiatry (pp. 119–140). London: Jessica Kingsley.

Odell-Miller, H. (2001). Music therapy and its relationship to psychoanalysis. In Y. Seale & I. Streng (Eds.), Where analysis meets the arts (pp. 129-163). London: Karnac.

Odell-Miller, H. (2002). One man's journey and the importance of time: Music therapy in an NHS mental health day centre. In A. Davies & E. Richards (Eds.), Music therapy and group work: Sound company (pp. 63–76). London: Jessica Kingsley.

Oldfield, A. (1995). *Communicating through music: The balance between following and initiating*. In T. Wigram, B. Saperston, & R. West (Eds.), The art and science of music therapy: A handbook *(pp. 226–237)*. Chur, Switzerland: Harwood Academic.

Oldfield, A. (2000). *Music therapy as a contribution to the diagnosis made by the staff team in child and family psychiatry—An initial description of a methodology that is still emerging through clinical practice*. In T. Wigram (Ed.), Assessment and evaluation in the arts therapies. *St. Albans, NY: Harper House.*

Oldfield, A. (2001). *Mum can play too—Short-term music therapy with mothers and young children*. British Journal of Music Therapy, 15*(1)*, 27–36.

Osborne, J. W. (1981). *The mapping of thoughts, emotions, sensations, and images as responses to music*. Journal of Mental Imagery, 5, 133–136.

Parente, A. B. (1989). *Feeding the hungry soul: Music as a therapeutic modality in the treatment of anorexia nervosa*. Music Therapy Perspectives, 6, 44–48.

Parker, A. B. (1998). How to choose music to support physiological and emotional processes: A neuropsychological approach. *Unpublished masters thesis, Prescott College, Prescott, AZ.*

Patterson, W. (1972). *Our own thing*. Journal of Music Therapy, 9, 119.

Paul, D. (1982). Music therapy for handicapped children: Emotionally disturbed. *Washington, DC: National Association for Music Therapy.*

Pavlicevic, M. (n.d.). *Inter-personal processes in clinical improvisation*. In B. Saperston, R. West, & A. Wigram (Eds.), Music and the healing process. *Chichester, England: Carden.*

Pavlicevic, M. (1987). *Reflections on the pre-musical moment*. Journal of British Music Therapy, 1*(1)*, 22–24.

Pavlicevic, M. (1988). *Describing critical moments*. In S. Hoskyns (Ed.), The case study as research: Proceedings of the fourth music therapy conference. *London: City University.*

Pavlicevic, M. (1990). *Dynamic interplay in clinical improvisation*. Journal of British Music Therapy, 4*(2)*, 5–10.

Pavlicevic, M. (1994). *Between chaos and creativity: Music therapy with traumatized children in South Africa*. Journal of British Music Therapy, 8*(2)*, 4–9.

Pavlicevic, M. (1995). *Growing into sound and soundmaking into growth: Improvisation groups with adults*. The Arts in Psychotherapy, 22*(4)*, 359–367.

Pavlicevic, M. (1995). *Interpersonal processes in clinical improvisation: Towards a subjectively objective systematic definition*. In T. Wigram, B. Saperston, & R. West (Eds.), The art and science of music therapy: A handbook *(pp. 167–176)*. Chur, Switzerland: Harwood Academic.

Pavlicevic, M. (1995). *Music and emotion*. In A. Gilroy & C. A. Lee (Eds.), Art and music: Therapy and research. *London: Routledge.*

Pavlicevic, M. (1997). Music therapy in context: Music, meaning and relationships. *London: Jessica Kingsley.*

Pavlicevic, M. (1999). Music therapy intimate notes. *London: Jessica Kingsley.*

Pavlicevic, M. (1999). *With listeners in mind: Creating meaning in music therapy dialogues*. The Arts in Psychotherapy, 26*(2)*, 85–94.

Pavlicevic, M. (2000). *Improvisation in music therapy: Human communication in sound*. Journal of Music Therapy, 37*(4)*, 269–285.

Pavlicevic, M. (2003). Groups in music: Strategies from music therapy. *London: Jessica Kingsley.*

Pavlicevic, M., & Ansdell, G. (2004). Community music therapy: International initiatives. *London: Jessica Kingsley.*

Pavlicevic, M., & Trevarthen, C. (1989). *A musical assessment of psychiatric states in adults*. Psychopathology, 22, 325–334.

Pavlicevic, M., Trevarthen, C., & Duncan, J. (1994). *Improvisational music therapy and the rehabilitation of persons suffering from chronic schizophrenia*. Journal of Music Therapy, 31*(2)*, 86–104.

Payne, H. (Ed.). (1993). Handbook of inquiry in the arts therapy. *London: Jessica Kingsley.*

Peach, S. (1984). *Some implications for the clinical use of music facilitated imagery*. Journal of Music Therapy, 21*(1)*, 27–34.

Pederson, I. N. (1999). *Music therapy as holding and re-organizing work with schizophrenic and psychotic patients*. In T. Wigram & J. DeBacker (Eds.), Clinical applications of music therapy in psychiatry *(pp. 24–43)*. London: Jessica Kingsley.

Pederson, I. N. (2002). *Analytical music therapy with adults in mental health and counseling*. In J. T. Eschen (Ed.), Analytical music therapy *(pp. 64–84)*. London: Jessica Kingsley.

Pederson, I. N. (2002). *Music therapy with psyciatric clients*. In T. Wigram, I. Nygaard Pedersen, & L. O. Bonde (Eds.), A comprehensive guide to music therapy: Theory, clinical practice, research and training. *London: Jessica Kingsley.*

Perilli, G. G. (1991). *Integrated music therapy with a schizophrenic woman*. In K. E. Bruscia (Ed.), Case studies in music therapy *(pp. 403–416)*. Phoenixville, PA: Barcelona.

Perilli, G. G. (1995). *Subjective tempo in adults with and without psychiatric disorders*. Music Therapy Perspectives, 13*(2)*, 104–109.

Perilli, G. G. (2002). *The role of metaphor in the Bonny Method of Guided Imagery and Music (BMGIM)*. In K. E. Bruscia & D. E. Gorcke (Eds.), Guided imagery and music: The Bonny Method *(pp. 417–448)*. Gilsum, NH: Barcelona.

Peters, J. S. (1987). Music therapy an introduction. *Springfield, IL: Charles C. Thomas.*

Peters, J. S. (2000). Music therapy an introduction *(2nd ed.)*. Springfield, IL: Charles C. Thomas.

Peterson, D. J. (1973). *Guest editorial: A place for music in drug education*. Journal of Music Therapy, 10*(1)*, 1–2.

Phillips, W. G. (1965). *Community mental health—A new challenge*. Journal of Music Therapy, 2*(1)*, 16–18.

Pickett, E. (1991). *Guided imagery and music (GIM) with a dually diagnosed woman having multiple addictions*. In K. E. Bruscia (Ed.), Case studies in music therapy *(pp. 497–512)*. Phoenixville, PA: Barcelona.

Pickett, E. (1992). *Guided imagery and music (GIM) with a dually diagnosed woman having multiple addictions.* Journal of the Association for Music and Imagery, 1, *55–68.*

Pickett, E. (1995). *The Bonny Method of Guided Imagery and Music: A technique for healing trauma.* Journal of the Association for Music and Imagery, 5, *51–60.*

Pickett, E. (1995). *The Bonny Method of Guided Imagery and Music: A technique for healing trauma.* In E. S. Cluft (Ed.), Experimental and functional therapies in the treatment of multiple personality disorders. *Springfield, IL: Charles C. Thomas.*

Pickett, E. (2002). *A history of the literature on guided imagery and music (GIM).* In K. E. Bruscia & D. E. Gorcke (Eds.), Guided imagery and music: The Bonny Method *(pp. xxv–xxxv).* Gilsum, NH: Barcelona.

Pickett, E., & Sonnen, C. (1993). *Guided imagery and music: A music therapy approach to multiple personality disorder.* Journal of the Association for Music and Imagery, 2, *49–72.*

Pierce, A. H. (1934). *The therapeutic value of music for psychotic patients.* U.S. Veteran's Administration Medical Bulletin, 11, *142–147.*

Pikler, A. G. (1962). *Music as an aid in psychotherapy.* In E. H. Schneider (Ed.), Music therapy 1961 *(pp. 23–39).* Lawrence, KS: Allen Press.

Plach, T. (1980). *The creative use of music in group therapy. Springfield, IL: Charles C. Thomas.*

Podolsky, E. (1954). *Music and mental health.* Mental Health, 13, *99–109.*

Podolsky, E. (1954). *Music and mental health.* In E. Podolsky (Ed.), Music therapy *(pp. 11–23).* New York: Philosophical Library.

Podolsky, E. (1954). *Music therapy. New York: Philosophical Library.*

Powell, A. (1983). *The music of the group: A musical inquiry into group analysis.* Group Analysis, 16, *3–19.*

Pratt, R. B. (1987). *The fourth international symposium on music: Rehabilitation and human well-being. Lanham, MD: University Press of America.*

Pratt, R. B. (1992). *Healing and art.* The International Journal of Arts Medicine, 1 *(2), 3.*

Pratt, R. B. (1993). *Music therapy and music education for the handicapped. St. Louis, MO: MMB Music.*

Presti, G. M. (1984). *A levels system approach to music therapy with severely behaviorally handicapped children in the public school system.* Journal of Music Therapy, 21 *(3), 117–125.*

Preston, M. J. (1950). *The organization of a music program as a rehabilitation measure for the mentally ill.* Psychiatric Quarterly, 24, *119–127.*

Preston, M. J. (1954). *The organization of a music program as a rehabilitation measure for the mentally ill.* In E. Podolsky (Ed.), Music therapy *(pp. 79–88).* New York: Philosophical Library.

Price, H. G. (1949). *The use of music as therapy in the treatment of psychiatric patients.* Hospital Music Newsletter, 1 *(3).*

Price, H. G., Mountney, V., & Knouss, R. (1954). *Selection of music to accompany electroshock therapy.* In E. Podolsky (Ed.), Music therapy *(pp. 107–111).* New York: Philosophical Library.

Priestley, M. (1975). *Music therapy in action. New York: St. Martin's Press.*

Priestley, M. (1976). *Music, Freud and the port of entry.* Nursing Times, 72 *(49), 1940–1941.*

Priestley, M. (1977). *Music, Freud and recidivism.* Journal of British Music Therapy, 8 *(3), 10–14.*

Priestley, M. (1978). *Countertransference in Analytical music therapy.* Journal of British Music Therapy, 9 *(3), 2–5.*

Priestley, M. (1980). *Analytical music therapy and the "detour through phantasy."* British Journal of Projective Psychology, 25 *(1), 11–14.*

Priestley, M. (1983). *Music therapy in action (2nd ed.). St. Louis, MO: MMB Music.*

Priestley, M. (1985). *Music therapy and love.* Journal of British Music Therapy, 16 *(3), 2–7.*

Priestley, M. (1987). *Music and the shadow.* Music Therapy, 6 *(2), 20–27.*

Priestley, M. (1988). *Music and the listeners.* Journal of British Music Therapy, 2 *(2), 9–13.*

Priestley, M. (1994). *Essays on Analytical music therapy. Phoenixville, PA: Barcelona.*

Priestley, M. (1995). *Linking sound and symbol.* In T. Wigram, B. Saperston, & R. West (Eds.), The art and science of music therapy: A handbook *(pp. 129–138).* Chur, Switzerland: Harwood Academic.

Priestley, M., & Eschen, J. T. (2002). *Analytical music therapy—Origin and development.* In J. T. Eschen (Ed.), Analytical music therapy *(pp. 11–16).* London: Jessica Kingsley.

Procter, S. (2004). *Playing politics: Community music therapy in a non-medical mental health setting.* In M. Pavlicevic & G. Ansdell (Eds.), Community music therapy: International initiatives. *London: Jessica Kingsley.*

Prueter, B. A., & Mezzano, J. (1973). *Effects of background music upon initial counseling interaction.* Journal of Music Therapy, 10 *(4), 205–212.*

Pulliam, J. C., Somerville, P., Prebluda, J., & Warja-Danielson, M. (1988). *Three heads are better than one: The expressive arts group assessment.* The Arts in Psychotherapy, 15 *(2), 71–77.*

Purdon, C. (2002). *The role of music in analytical music therapy—Music as a carrier of stories.* In J. T. Eschen (Ed.), Analytical music therapy *(pp. 104–114).* London: Jessica Kingsley.

Purvis, J., & Sanet, S. (Eds.). (1976). *Music in developmental therapy. Baltimore: University Park Press.*

Quittner, A., & Gluckauf, R. (1983). *The facilitative effects of music on visual imagery: A multiple measures approach.* Journal of Mental Imagery, 7, *105–119.*

Racker, H. (1951). *Contribution to the psychoanalysis of music.* American Imago, 8, *129-163.*

Racker, H. (1965). *Psychoanalytic considerations on music and the musician.* Psychoanalytic Review, 52, *75–94.*

Ragland, Z., & Apprey, M. (1974). Community music therapy with adolescents. Journal of Music Therapy, 11(3), 147–155.

Ragland, Z. S. (1973). Categorizing music therapy groups and session plans. Journal of Music Therapy, 10(4), 194–200.

Redinbough, E. M. (1988). The use of music therapy in developing a communication system in a withdrawn, depressed older adults resident: A case study. Music Therapy Perspectives, 5, 82–85.

Reed, K. J. (2000). Music is the master key. Orlando, FL: Rivercross.

Reed, K. J. (2002). Music therapy treatment groups for mentally disordered offenders (MDO) in a state hospital setting. Music Therapy Perspectives, 20(2), 98–104.

Reinhardt, V., & Large, M. (1982). Effect of music on depressed patients. Psychiatric Nerologie und Medizinische Psychology, 34(7), 414–421.

Reinke, J. H. (1956). The use of unfamiliar music as stimulus for a projective test of personality. In E. T. Gaston (Ed.), Music therapy 1955 (pp. 224–230). Lawrence, KS: Allen Press.

Rickson, D. J., & Watkins, W. G. (2003). Music therapy to promote prosocial behaviors in aggressive adolescent boys—A pilot study. Journal of Music Therapy, 49(4), 283–301.

Rigg, M. G. (1964). The mood effects of music: A comparison of data from investigators. The Journal of Psychology, 58, 427–438.

Rio, R. E., & Tenney, K. S. (2002). Music therapy for juvenile offenders in residential treatment. Music Therapy Perspectives, 20(2), 89–97.

Ritchey Vaux, D. (1993). GIM applied to the 50-minute hour. Journal of the Association for Music and Imagery, 2, 29–34.

Ritchie, F. (1991). Behind closed doors: A case study. Journal of British Music Therapy, 5(2), 4-9.

Ritholz, M., & Robbins, C. (1999). Themes for therapy. New York: Carl Fischer.

Robarts, J. (1994). Towards autonomy and a sense of self: Music therapy and the individuation process in relation to children and adolescents with early onset anorexia. In D. Dokter (Ed.), Arts therapies and clients with eating disorders (pp. 229–246). London: Jessica Kingsley.

Robarts, J. Z. (2000). Music therapy and adolescents with anorexia nervosa. Nordic Journal of Music Therapy, 9(1), 3–12.

Robarts, J. Z., & Sloboda, A. (1994). Perspectives on music therapy with people suffering from anorexia nervosa. Journal of British Music Therapy, 8(1), 7–14.

Robb, S. L. (1996). Techniques in song writing: Restoring emotional and physical well being in adolescents who have been traumatically injured. Music Therapy Perspectives, 14(1), 30–37.

Robb, S. L. (2000). Music assisted progressive muscle relaxation, progressive muscle relaxation, music listening, and silence: A comparison of relaxation techniques. Journal of Music Therapy, 37(1), 2–21.

Robbins, A. (1980). Expressive therapy. New York: Human Sciences Press.

Robbins, L. (1966). Role of music therapy in psychiatric treatment. Journal of Music Therapy, 7(1), 79.

Robinson, D. (1970). Is there a correlation between rhythmic response and emotional disturbance? Journal of Music Therapy, 7(2), 54.

Robinson, W. C. (1976). The musical preferences of mental patients based on Cattell's interpretations of factors associated with certain aspects of personality. Dissertation Abstracts International, 38 (01), 149A. (UMI No. 7713931)

Rogers, P. (1992). Issues in working with sexually abused clients in music therapy. Journal of British Music Therapy, 6(2), 5–15.

Rogers, P. (1993). Research in music therapy with sexually abused clients. In. H. Payne (Ed.), Handbook of inquiry in the arts therapy (pp. 197–217). London: Jessica Kingsley.

Rogers, P. J. (1995). Childhood sexual abuse: Dilemmas in therapeutic practice. Music Therapy Perspectives, 13(1), 24–30.

Rogers, P. J. (1995). Sexual abuse and eating disorders: A possible connection indicated through music therapy. In D. Dokter (Ed.), Arts therapies and clients with eating disorder (pp. 262–278). London: Jessica Kingsley.

Rogers, P. J. (1996). New directions in music therapy practice with abused clients. Music Therapy International Report, 10, 59–63.

Rogers, P. J., & Smeyatsky, N. (1995). Short-term verbal and musical memory in schizophrenia: Implications for theories of working memory and cerebral dominance. In T. Wigram, B. Saperston, & R. West (Eds.), The art and science of music therapy: A handbook (pp. 139–156). Chur, Switzerland: Harwood Academic.

Rohner, S. J., & Miller, R. (1980). Degrees of familiar and affective music and their effects on state anxiety. Journal of Music Therapy, 17(1), 2–15.

Rolla, M. (Ed.). (1993). Your inner music. Wilmette, IL: Chiron.

Rollin, H. R. (1960). Music therapy in a mental hospital. In E. H. Schneider (Ed.), Music therapy 1959 (pp. 25–37). Lawrence, KS: Allen Press.

Rollin, H. R. (1962). Therapeutic use of music in a mental hospital. Transactions of the College of Physicians of Philadelphia, 29, 130–136.

Rollin, H. R. (1964). Music therapy in a mental hospital. Nursing Times, 60, 1219–1222.

Romano, G., & Perilli, G. G. (1999). Freedom, emotions, togetherness. In J. Hibben (Ed.), Inside music therapy: Client experiences (pp. 41–44). Gilsum, NH: Barcelona.

Rosenbaum, J., & Prinsky, L. (1991). The presumption of influence: Recent responses to popular music subculture. Crime and Delinquency, 30(3), 317–330.

Rosenbaum, J. B. (1963). Songs of the transference. American Imaga, 20, 257–269.

Rosenfeld, A. H. (1985, December). Music, the beautiful disturber. Psychology Today, 48–56.

Roy, M. (1996–1997). Guided imagery and music group experiences with adolescent girls in a high school setting. Journal of the Association for Music and Imagery, 5, 67–74.

Ruben, B. (1973). Music therapy as an outreach station of the Milwaukee County Mental Health Center. Journal of Music Therapy, 10(4), 201–204.

Ruben, B. (1975). Music therapy in a community mental health program. Journal of Music Therapy, 12(2), 59–66.

Ruben, B. (1976). Handbells in therapy. Journal of Music Therapy, 13(1), 49–53.

Ruegnity, M. J. (1946). Applied music on disturbed wards. Occupational Therapy and Rehabilitation, 25, 203–206.

Rugenstein. L. (1996). Wilber's spectrum model of transpersonal psychology and its application to music therapy. Music Therapy, 14, 9–28.

Ruppenthal, W. (1952). A study of the rhythmic responses of normal subjects and neuropsychiatric patients. In E. G. Gilliland (Ed.), Music therapy 1951 (pp. 194–196). Lawrence, KS: Allen Press.

Ruppenthal, W. (1965). Scribbling in music therapy. Journal of Music Therapy, 2(1), 8–10.

Rupracht, M. S., & Cohrasen, C. (1957). Music therapy study on a hyperactive ward. In E. T. Gaston (Ed.), Music therapy 1956 (pp. 125–129). Lawrence, KS: Allen Press.

Russell, L. A. (1992). Comparisons of cognitive, music, and imagery techniques on anxiety reduction with university students. Journal of College Student Development, 33, 516–523.

Ruud, E. (1978). Music therapy and its relationship to current treatment theories. St. Louis, MO: Magnamusic Baton.

Ruud, E. (1995). Improvisation as a liminal experience: Jazz and music therapy as modern "rite de passage." In C. Kenny (Ed.), Listening, playing, creating: Essays on the power of sound (pp. 91–110). Albany, NY: State University of New York Press.

Ruud, E. (1998). Music therapy: Improvisation, communication, and culture. Gilsum, NH: Barcelona.

Samaroff, O. (1947). Music: Crime cure? Journal of Criminal Law, Criminology and Police Science, 43, 578–591.

Sandrock, D., & James, M. R. (1989). Assessment instruments for music-assisted relaxation training. Music Therapy Perspectives, 7, 44–50.

Saperston, B., West, R., & Wigram, T. (Eds.). (n.d.). Music and the healing process. Chichester, England: Carden.

Scalenghe, R., & Murphy, K. M. (2002). Music therapy assessment in the managed care environment. Music Therapy Perspectives, 18(1), 23–30.

Scartelli, J. P. (1989). Music and self-management. St. Louis, MO: MMB Music.

Scheiby, B. (1991). Mia's fourteenth—the symphony of fate: Psychodynamic improvisation therapy with a music therapy student in training. In K. E. Bruscia (Ed.), Case studies in music therapy (pp. 271–290). Phoenixville, PA: Barcelona.

Schipkowensky, W. (1977). Music therapy in the field of psychiatry and neurology. In N. Critchley & R. A. Hensen (Eds.), Music and the brain (pp. 433–445). London: Camelot.

Schmidt, J. (1983). Songwriting as a therapeutic procedure. Music Therapy Perspectives, 1(2), 4–7.

Schneider, C. W. (1961). The effects of Dalcroze eurhythmics upon the motor processes of schizophrenics. In E. H. Schneider (Ed.), Music therapy 1960 (pp. 132–140). Lawrence, KS: Allen Press.

Schulberg, C. H. (1986). The music therapy sourcebook. New York: Human Sciences Press.

Schulberg, C. H. (1997). An unwanted inheritance: Healing transgenerational trauma of the Nazi holocaust through the Bonny Method of Guided Imagery and Music. The Arts in Psychotherapy, 24(4), 323–345.

Schulberg, C. H. (1999). Out of the ashes: Transforming despair into hope with music and imagery. In J. Hibben (Ed.), Inside music therapy: Client experiences (pp. 7–12). Gilsum, NH: Barcelona.

Schullian, D., & Schoen, M. (Eds.). (1948). Music and medicine. New York: Henry Schuman.

Scott, T. J. (1970). Use of music to reduce hyperactivity in children. American Journal of Orthopsychiatry, 40(5), 677–680.

Scovel, M. A. (1990). Music therapy within the context of psychotherapeutic models. In R. F. Unkefer (Ed.), Music therapy in the treatment of adults with mental disorders (pp. 96–108). New York: Schirmer Books.

Seale, Y., & Streng, I. (Eds.) (2001). Where analysis meets the arts. London: Karnac.

Sears, W. (1968). Processes in music therapy. In E. T. Gaston (Ed.), Music in therapy (pp. 30–46). New York: Macmillan.

Seely, M. C. (1960). Problems and techniques of a public radio broadcast from a mental hospital. Bulletin of NAMT, 9(2), 7–8, 11.

Sekeles, C. (1996). Music: Motion and emotion. St. Louis, MO: MMB Music.

Sekeles, C. (1999). Working through loss and mourning in music therapy. In T. Wigram & J. DeBacker (Eds.), Clinical applications of music therapy in psychiatry (pp. 176–196). London: Jessica Kingsley.

Shatin, J. (1970). Alteration of mood via music: A study of the vectoring effect. The Journal of Psychology, 75, 81–86.

Shatin, L. (1958). The application of rhythmic music stimuli to long-term schizophrenic patients. In E. T. Gaston (Ed.), Music therapy 1957 (pp. 169–178). Lawrence, KS: Allen Press.

Shatin, L., & Kotter, W. (1957). Rhythm groups in rehabilitation: Hospitalized mental patients. Recreation, 50, 263–264.

Shatin, L., Kotter, W. L., & Douglas–Longmore, G. (1961, September/October). Music therapy for schizophrenics. Journal of Rehabilitation, pp. 30–31.

Shatin, L., Kotter, W. L., & Douglas-Longmore, G. (1962). Music therapy for schizophrenics. In E. H. Schneider (Ed.), Music therapy 1961 (pp. 99–104). Lawrence, KS: Allen Press.

Shatin, L., Kotter, W. L., & Douglas-Longmore, G. (1964). A psychological study of the music therapist in rehabilitation. Journal of General Psychology, 71, 193–205.

Shatin, L., Kotter, W. L, & Longmore, G. (1967). Psycho-social prescription for music therapy in hospital. Diseases of the Nervous System, 4, 231–233.

Shatin, L., & Zimet, C. (1958). The influence of music upon verbal participation in group psychotherapy. Diseases of the Nervous System, 19, 66–72.

Sheppard, T. (1977). Relationship therapy through music with maladjusted boys. British Journal of Music Therapy, 8(3), 6–10.

Sherman, L. J. (1963). Group dynamics for the music therapist. In E. H. Schneider (Ed.), Music therapy 1962 (pp. 50–59). Lawrence, KS: Allen Press.

Sherwin, A. C. (1958). A consideration of the therapeutic use of music in psychiatric illness. Journal of Nervous and Mental Disease, 127(1), 84–90.

Short, A. (1996–97). Jungian archetypes in GIM therapy: Approaching the client's fairy tale. Journal of the Association for Music and Imagery, 5, 37–49.

Silverman, M. J. (2006). Psychiatric patients' perception of music therapy and other psychoeducational programming. Journal of Music Therapy, 43(2), 111–122.

Silverman, M. J. (2003). Contingency songwriting to reduce combativeness and non- cooperation in a client with schizophrenia: A case study. The Arts in Psychotherapy, 30(1), 25–33.

Silverman, M. J. (2003). Music therapy and clients who are chemically dependent: A review of literature and pilot study. The Arts in Psychotherapy, 30(5), 273–281.

Silverman, M. J. (2003). The influence of music on the symptoms of psychosis: A meta-analysis. Journal of Music Therapy, 40(1), 27–40.

Silverman, M. J. (2005). Using music therapy games with adult psychiatric patients. The Arts in Psychotherapy, 32(2), 121–129.

Silverman, M. J., & Marcionetti, M. J. (2004). Immediate effects of single music therapy intervention with persons who are severely mentally ill. The Arts in Psychotherapy, 31(5), 291–302.

Simon, B., Holzberg, J. D., & Alessi, S. L. (1951). The recognition and acceptance of mood in music by psychotic patients. Journal of Nervous and Mental Disease, 114, 66–78.

Simon, B., Holzber, J. D., Alessi, S. L., & Garrity, D. A. (1954). The recognition and acceptance of mood in music by psychotic patients. In E. Podolsky (Ed.), Music therapy (pp. 62–78). New York: Philosophical Library.

Simon, W. (1945). The value of music in the resocialization and rehabilitation of the mentally ill. Military Surgeon, 97, 498–500.

Singer, S. (1962). Music therapy: Its applications to emotionally disturbed children in a cottage-plan treatment center. Bulletin of NAMT, 11(3), 19–22.

Skaggs, R. (1992). Music as co-therapist: Creative resource for change. Journal of the Association for Music an Imagery, 1, 77–83.

Skaggs, R. (1997). Finishing strong: Treating chemical addictions with music and imagery. St. Louis, MO: MMB Music.

Skaggs, R. (1997). Music-centered arts in a sex offender treatment program for male juveniles. Music Therapy Perspectives, 15(2), 73–78.

Skelly, C. G., & Haslerud, G. M. (1952). Music and the general activity of apathetic schizophrenics. Journal and the General Activity of Apathetic Schizophrenics, 47, 188–192.

Skelly, C. G., & Haslerud, G. M. (1954). Music and general activity in apathetic schizophrenics. In E. Podolsky (Ed.), Music therapy (pp. 231–240). New York: Philosophical Library.

Skewes, K. (2000). From the mouths of babes: The response of six younger, bereaved teenagers to the experience of psychodynamic group music therapy. The Australian Journal of Music Therapy, 11, 3–22.

Skewes, K., & Grocke, D. E. (2000). What does group music therapy offer to bereaved young people: A rounded approach to the grieving adolescent. Grief Matters: The Australian Journal of Loss and Grief, 3(3), 54–61.

Slaughter, F. (1958). A transition from individual to group music therapy. In E. T. Gaston (Ed.), Music therapy 1957 (pp. 85–90). Lawrence, KS: Allen Press.

Slaughter, F. (1960). Some concepts concerning the therapeutic use of music in a psychiatric setting. Bulletin of NAMT, 9(1), 11.

Slaughter, F. (1968). Approaches to the use of music therapy. In E. T. Gaston (Ed.), Music in therapy (pp. 238–244). New York: Macmillan.

Sloboda, A. (1993). Individual therapy with a man who has an eating disorder. In M. Heal, & T. Wigram (Eds.), Music therapy in health and education (pp. 103–111). London: Jessica Kingsley.

Sloboda, A. (1995). Individual music therapy with anorexic and bulimic patients. In D. Dokter (Ed.), Arts therapies and clients with eating disorders (pp. 247–261). London: Jessica Kingsley.

Sloboda, A. (1996). Music therapy and psychotic violence. In E. Weldon & C. Van Velson (Eds.), A practical guide to forensic psychotherapy (pp. 121–130). London: Jessica Kingsley.

Sloboda, A., & Bolton, R. (2002). Music therapy in forensic psychiatry: A case study with musical commentary. In L. Bunt & S. Hoskysn (Eds.), The handbook of music therapy (pp. 132–148). East Sussex, England: Brummer-Routledge.

Sloboda, J. (1991). Music structure and emotional response: Some empirical findings. Psychology of Music, 19(2), 110–127.

Slotoroff, C. (1994). Drumming techniques for assertiveness and anger management in the short-term psychiatric setting for adult and adolescent survivors of trauma. Music Therapy Perspectives, 12(2), 111–116.

Smeijsters, H. (1993). Music therapy and psychotherapy. The Arts in Psychotherapy, 20(3), 223–230.

Smeijsters, H. (1999). Feelings of doubt, hope, and faith. In J. Hibben (Ed.), Inside music therapy: Client experiences (pp. 277–305). Gilsum, NH: Barcelona.

Smeijsters, H., & van der Hurk, J. (1993). Research in practice in the music therapeutic treatment of a client with symptoms of anorexia nervosa. In M. Heal & T. Wigram (Eds.), Music therapy in health and education (pp. 255–263). London: Jessica Kingsley.

Smeijsters, H., & van der Hurk, J. (1999). *Music therapy to work through grief and finding a personal identity*. Journal of Music Therapy, 36*(3)*, 222–252.

Smeijsters, H., Wijzenbeek, G., & van Nieuwenhuizen, N. (1995). *The effect of musical excerpts on the evocation of values for depressed patients*. Journal of Music Therapy, 32*(3)*, 167–188.

Smeltekop, R. A., & Houghton, B. A. (1990). *Music therapy and psychopharmacology*. In R. F. Unkefer (Ed.), Music therapy in the treatment of adults with mental disorders *(pp. 109–125)*. New York: Schirmer Books.

Smith, B. (1996–97). *Uncovering and healing wounds: Using GIM to resolve complicated and disenfranchised grief*. Journal of the Association for Music and Imagery, 5, 1–23.

Smith, G. H. (1991). *The song-writing process: A woman's struggle against depression and suicide*. In K. E. Bruscia (Ed.), Case studies in music therapy *(pp. 479–496)*. Phoenixville, PA: Barcelona.

Smith, S. M. (1975). *Using music therapy with short-term alcoholic and psychiatric patients*. Hospital and Community Psychiatry, 26*(7)*, 420–421.

Sobey, K., & Woodcock, J. (1999). *Psychodynamic music therapy: Considerations in training*. In A. Cattanach (Ed.), Process in the arts therapies *(pp. 132–154)*. London: Jessica Kingsley.

Sommer, D. T. (1958). *The effect of background music on frequency of interaction in group psychotherapy*. In E. T. Gaston (Ed.), Music therapy 1957 *(pp. 167–168)*. Lawrence, KS: Allen Press.

Sommer, D. T. (1961). *Music in the autobiographies of mental patients*. Mental Hygiene, 45, 401–407.

Sommer, D. T. (1962). *Treating the second illness*. Bulletin of NAMT, 11*(1)*, 4–12.

Sommer, D. T. (1968). *Individual music therapy with adolescent patients*. In E. T. Gaston (Ed.), Music in therapy *(pp. 215–218)*. New York: Macmillan.

Soshensky, R. (2001). *Music therapy and addiction*. Music Therapy Perspectives, 19*(1)*, 45–52.

Stack, S., Gundlach, J., & Reeves, J. (1994). *The heavy metal subculture and suicide*. Suicide and Life-Threatening Behavior, 24*(1)*, 15–23.

Standley, J. (1991). *Music techniques in therapy, counseling and special education*. St. Louis, MO: MMB Music.

Stanford, G. A. (1964). *Orchestration of the new mental hospital theme*. Journal of Music Therapy, 4, 124–128.

Stankovic, P. J. (1957). *Musical psychotherapy*. Bulletin of NAMT, 6, 5–6.

Staum, M. J. (1993). *A music/nonmusic intervention with homeless children*. Journal of Music Therapy, 30*(4)*, 238–262.

Staum, M. J., & Brotons, M. (1995). *Issues in music for children in a homeless shelter: Social objectives and choice reinforcement*. Journal of Music Therapy, 32*(4)*, 248–264.

Staum, M. J., & Brotons, M. (2000). *The effect of music amplitude on the relaxation response*. Journal of Music Therapy, 37*(1)*, 22–39.

Steele, A. L. (1972). *The community music school: Flexibility and accessibility*. Journal of Music Therapy, 9*(3)*, 111–118.

Steele, A. L. (1975). *Three year study of a music therapy program in a residential treatment center*. Journal of Music Therapy, 12*(2)*, 67–83.

Steele, A. L., & Smith, L. L. (1996). *Music therapy in a center for juvenile offenders*. Cleveland, OH: The Cleveland Music School Settlement.

Steele, A. L., Vaughan, M., & Dolan, C. (1976). *The school support program: Music therapy for adjustment problems in elementary schools*. Journal of Music Therapy, 6*(4)*, 98–104.

Steele, P. H. (1984). *Aspects of resistance in music therapy: Theory and technique*. Music Therapy, 4*(1)*, 64–72.

Stein, J. (1963). *Problem cases in individual music therapy*. Bulletin of NAMT, 12*(1)*, 9–12.

Stein, J. (1965). *The music therapist's role in work with severely disturbed patients*. Journal of Music Therapy, 2*(2)*, 53–60.

Stein, J. (1977). *Tempo errors and mania*. American Journal of Psychiatry, 134*(4)*, 454–456.

Stein, J., & Euper, J. A. (1974). *Advances in music therapy*. In J. H. Masserman (Ed.), Current psychiatric therapies *(Vol. 14, pp. 107–113)*. New York: Grune and Stratton.

Stein, J., & Thompson, S. V. (1971). *Crazy music: Theory*. Psychotherapy: Theory, Research, and Practice, 8, 137–145.

Steinberg, R., Kimmsig, V., Raith, L., Gunther, W., Bogner, J., & Timmerman, J. (1991). *Music psychopathology: The course of musical expression during music therapy with psychiatric inpatients*. Psychopathology, 24, 121–129.

Steinberg, R., & Raith, L. (1985). *Music psychopathology: Musical tempo and psychiatric disease*. Psychopathology, 18, 254–264.

Steinberg, R., Raith, L., Rossinagl, G., & Eben, R. (1985). *Music psychopathology: Musical expression and psychiatric disease*. Psychopathology, 18, 274–285.

Stephens, G. (1981). *Adele: A study in silence*. Music Therapy, 1*(1)*, 24–31.

Stephens, G. (1983). *The use of improvisation for developing relatedness in the adult client*. Music Therapy, 3*(1)*, 29–42.

Sterba, R. F. (1965). *Psychoanalysis and music*. American Image, 22, 96–111.

Sterne, S. B. (1956). *The validity of music as an effective group psychotherapeutic technique*. In E. T. Gaston (Ed.), Music therapy 1955 *(pp. 130–140)*. Lawrence, KS: Allen Press.

Stevens, E. A. (1968). *Music therapy in a mental health institute*. In E. T. Gaston (Ed.), Music in therapy *(pp. 379–388)*. New York: Macmillan.

Stewart, D. (1996). *Chaos, noise, and a wall of silence: Working with primitive affects in psychodynamic group music therapy*. British Journal of Music Therapy, 10*(2)*, 21–33.

Stewart, D. (2002). *Sound company: Psychodynamic group music therapy as facilitating environment, transformational object and therapeutic playground*. In A. Davies & E. Richards (Eds.), Music therapy and sound work: Sound company *(pp. 27–42)*. London: Jessica Kingsley.

Stige, B. (1999). The meaning of music—From the client's perspective. In T. Wigram & J. DeBacker (Eds.), Clinical applications of music therapy in psychiatry (pp. 61– 83). London: Jessica Kingsley.

Stige, B. (2002). Culture-centered music therapy. Gilsum, NH: Barcelona.

Stith, G. K. (1965). Functions of a music therapist in a day hospital. Journal of Music Therapy, 2(4), 121–123.

Stokes-Stearns, S. J., Bush, C. A., & Borling, J. (1998a). Level II guided imagery and music training. Annapolis, MD: Mid-Atlantic Institute.

Stokes-Stearns, S. J., Bush, C. A., & Borling, J. (1998b). Music and transpersonal. Virginia Beach, VA: Mid-Atlantic Training Institute.

Stoudenmire, J. (1975). A comparison of muscle relaxation training and music in the reduction of state and trait anxiety. Journal of Clinical Psychology, 31, 490–492.

Stratton, V. N. (1992). Influences of music and socializing on perceived stress while waiting. Perceptual and Motor Skills, 75, 334.

Stratton, V. N., & Zalanowski, A. (1984). The effects of background music on verbal interaction in groups. Journal of Music Therapy, 21(1), 16–26.

Stratton, V., & Zalanowski, A. (1989). The effects of music and paintings on mood. Journal of Music Therapy, 26(1), 30–41.

Stratton, V., & Zalanowski, A. (1991). The effects of music and cognition on mood. Psychology of Music, 19(2), 121–127.

Stratton, V., & Zalanowski, A. (1991/1992). The interfering effects of music with imagery. Imagination, Cognition and Personality, 11, 381–388.

Stratton, V. H., & Zalanowski, A. H. (1994). Affective impact of music v. lyrics. Empirical Studies in the Arts, 12(2), 173–184.

Stratton, V. H., & Zalanowski, A. (1997). The relationship between characteristic moods and most commonly listened to types of music. Journal of Music Therapy, 34(2), 129–140.

Streeter, E. (1999). Definition and use of the musical transference relationship. In T. Wigram & J. DeBacker (Eds.), Clinical applications of music therapy in psychiatry (pp. 84–101). London: Jessica Kingsley.

Streeter, E. (1999). Finding a balance between psychological thinking and musical awareness in music therapy theory—A psychoanalytical perspective. British Journal of Music Therapy, 13(1), 5–20.

Summer, L. (1981). Imagery and music. Journal of Mental Imagery, 9, 83–90.

Summer, L. (1988). Guided imagery and music in the institutional setting. St. Louis, MO: MMB Music.

Summer, L. (1992). Music: The aesthetic elixir. Journal of the Association for Music and Imagery, 1, 43–53.

Summer, L. (1994). Considering classical music for use in psychiatric music therapy. Music Therapy Perspectives, 12(2), 130–133.

Summer, L. (1995). Melding musical and psychological processes: The therapeutic musical space. Journal of the Association for Music and Imagery, 4, 37–48.

Summer, L. (2002). Group music and imagery therapy: Emergent receptive techniques in music therapy practice. In K. E. Bruscia & D. E. Gorcke (Eds.), Guided imagery and music: The Bonny Method (pp. 297–306). Gilsum, NH: Barcelona.

Sutton, J. P. (2002). Music, music therapy and trauma: International perspectives. London: Jessica Kingsley.

Suzuki, A. I. (1998). The effects of music therapy on mood and congruent memory of elderly adults with depressive symptoms. Music Therapy Perspectives, 16(2), 75–80.

Sylwester, K., Barg, M., Frueh, B., Baker, K. A., Patrick, F. D., & Shaffer, S. (1971). Music therapy in a decentralized hospital. Journal of Music Therapy, 8(2), 53–67.

T, & Caughman, J. M.. (1999). Tools of recovery: a year of guided imagery and music. In J. Hibben (Ed.), Inside music therapy: Client experiences (pp. 27–40). Gilsum, NH: Barcelona.

Tang, W., Yao, X., & Zheng, Z. (1994). Rehabilitative effects of music therapy for residual schizophrenia: A 1-month randomized controlled trial in Shanghai. British Journal of Psychiatry, 165 (Suppl. 24), 38–44.

Tasney, K. (1993). Beginning the healing of incest through guided imagery and music: A Jungian perspective. Journal of the Association for Music and Imagery, 2, 35–48.

Taylor, D. (1969). Expressive emphasis in the treatment of intropunitive behaviors. Journal of Music Therapy, 6(2), 41–43.

Taylor, D. (1997). Biomedical determinants of control reversal therapy. In D. Taylor (Ed.), Biomedical foundations of music as therapy (pp. 76–83). St. Louis, MO: MMB Music.

Terwogt, M. M., & Van Grinsven, F. (1991). Musical expression of mood states. Psychology of Music, 19(2), 99–109.

Thaut, M. (1987). A new challenge for music therapy: The correctional setting. Music Therapy Perspectives, 4, 44–50.

Thaut, M. H. (1989). Music therapy, affect modification and therapeutic change: Towards an integrative model. Music Therapy Perspectives, 7, 55–62.

Thaut, M. H. (1989). The influence of music therapy interventions on self-rated changes in relaxation, affect, and thought in psychiatric prisoner-patients. Journal of Music Therapy, 26(3), 155–166.

Thaut, M. H. (1992). Music therapy in correctional psychiatry. In W. B. Davis, K. E. Gfeller, & M. H. Thaut (Eds.), An introduction to music therapy theory and practice (pp. 273–301). Dubuque, IA: William C. Brown.

Thaut, M. H. (1999). Group music psychotherapy in correctional psychiatry. In W. B. Davis, K. E. Gfeller, & M. H. Thaut (Eds.), An introduction to music therapy theory and practice (2nd ed.) (pp. 248–258). Boston: McGraw-Hill College.

Thaut, M. H., & Davis, W. B. (1993). The influence of subject-selected versus experimenter-chosen music on affect, anxiety, and relaxation. Journal of Music Therapy, 30(4), 210–223.

Thaut, M. H., & Gfeller, K. E. (1992). Music therapy in the treatment of mental disorder. In W. B. Davis, K. E. Gfeller, & M. H. Thaut (Eds.), An introduction to music therapy theory and practice (pp. 93–132). Dubuque, IA: William C. Brown.

Thomas, M. W. (1976). *Implications for music therapy as a treatment modality for the mentally ill deaf.* Voice of the Lakes, 76, *19–22*.

Thompson, M. F. (1955). *Piano ensembles for schizophrenic patients.* In E. T. Gaston (Ed.), Music therapy 1954 *(pp. 91–94).* Lawrence, KS: Allen Press.

Thompson, M. F. (1958). *Present trends in using psychotherapy potentials of music activities.* In E. T. Gaston (Ed.), Music therapy 1957 *(pp. 49–55).* Lawrence, KS: Allen Press.

Thompson, M. F. (1968). *Music and creative art therapies in a hospital setting.* In E. T. Gaston (Ed.), Music in therapy *(pp. 259–267).* New York: Macmillan.

Toedter, A. D. (1955). *Music therapy for the criminally insane and the psychopath.* In E. T. Gaston (Ed.), Music therapy 1954 *(pp. 95–103).* Lawrence, KS: Allen Press.

Took, K., & Weiss, D. (1994). *The relationship between heavy metal and rap music and adolescent turmoil: Real or artifact?* Adolescence, 25(115), 613–621.

Toomey, L. (1991). *Musical improvisation and GIM: A comparative study.* Journal of the New Zealand Society of Music Therapy, 13(1), 20–31.

Towse, E. (1991). *Relationships in music therapy: Do music therapy relationships discourage the emergence of the transference?* British Journal of Psychotherapy, 7(4), 323–330.

Towse, E., & Flower, C. (1993). *Levels of interaction in group improvisation.* In M. Heal & T. Wigram (Eds.), Music therapy in health and education *(pp. 73–81).* London: Jessica Kingsley.

Treder-Wolff, J. (1990). *Affecting attitudes: Music therapy in addiction treatment.* Music Therapy Perspectives, 8, 67–71.

Treder-Wolff, J. (1990). *Music therapy as a facilitator of creative process in addictions treatment.* The Arts in Psychotherapy, 17(4), 319–324.

Trevarthen, C., & Malloch, S. (2000). *The dance of well-being: Defining the musical therapeutic effect.* The Nordic Journal of Music Therapy, 9(2), 3–17.

Tunks, J. L. (1983). *The ward music therapy group and the integral involvement of nursing aides.* Music Therapy Perspectives, 2, 23–24.

Turrey, A. (1998). *Transference and countertransference in Nordoff-Robbins music therapy.* In K. E. Bruscia (Ed.), The dynamics of music psychotherapy *(pp. 161–212).* Gilsum, NH: Barcelona.

Turrey, A. (2004). *Music psychotherapy and community music therapy: Questions and considerations. Voices: A world forum for music therapy.* Retreived from http://www.voices.no/mainissues/mie0005000171.html

Tyler, H. M. (2002). *Working, playing and relating: Issues in group music therapy for children with special needs.* In A. Davies & E. Richards (Eds.), Music therapy and group work: Sound company *(pp. 216–230).* London: Jessica Kingsley.

Tyson, F. (1959). *The development of an out-patient music therapy referral service.* In E. H. Schneider (Ed.), Music therapy 1958 *(pp. 129–134).* Lawrence, KS: Allen Press.

Tyson, F. (1963). *Therapeutic elements in outpatient music therapy.* In E. H. Schneider (Ed.), Music therapy 1962 *(pp. 81–93).* Lawrence, KS: Allen Press.

Tyson, F. (1965, April). *Therapeutic elements in out-patient music therapy.* The Psychiatric Quarterly, 315–327.

Tyson, F. (1966). *Music therapy in private practice: Three case histories.* Journal of Music Therapy, 3(1), 8–18.

Tyson, F. (1966). *Music therapy practice in the community—Three case histories.* The Psychiatric Quarterly Supplement, Part I, 45–64.

Tyson, F. (1968). *The community music therapy center.* In E. T. Gaston (Ed.), Music in therapy *(pp. 382–388).* New York: Macmillan.

Tyson, F. (1973). *Guidelines toward the organization of clinical music therapy programs in the community.* Journal of Music Therapy, 10(3), 113–124.

Tyson, F. (1979). *Child at the gate: Individual music therapy with a schizophrenic woman.* The Arts in Psychotherapy, 6, 77–83.

Tyson, F. (1981). *Psychiatric music therapy: Origins and development.* New York: Fred Weidner and Sons.

Tyson, F. (1982). *Individual singing instruction: An evolutionary framework for psychiatric music therapists.* Music Therapy Perspectives, 1(1), 5–15.

Tyson, F. (1984). *Music therapy as a choice for psychotherapeutic intervention: A preliminary study of motivational factors among adult psychiatric patients.* Music Therapy Perspectives, 2(1), 2–8.

Tyson, F. (1987). *Analytically-oriented music therapy in a case of generalized anxiety disorders.* Music Therapy Perspectives, 4, 51–55.

Ulfarsdotter, L. O., & Erwin, P. G. (1999). *The influence of music on social cognitive skill.* The Arts in Psychotherapy, 26(2), 81–84.

Unkefer, R. F. (1952). *The effect of music in insulin coma therapy.* In E. G. Gilliland (Ed.), Music therapy 1951 *(pp. 184–187).* Lawrence, KS: Allen Press.

Unkefer, R. F. (1968). *Adult behavior disorders.* In E. T. Gaston (Ed.), Music in therapy *(pp. 231–237).* New York: Macmillan.

Unkefer, R. F. (1968). *Clinical practices.* In E. T. Gaston (Ed.), Music in therapy *(pp. 238–258).* New York: Macmillan.

Unkefer, R. F. (Ed.). (1990). Music therapy in treatment of adults with mental disorders: Theoretical bases and clinical interventions. *New York: Schirmer Books.*

Unkefer, R. F., & Thaut, M. H. (2002). Music therapy in the treatment of adults with mental disorders: Theoretical bases and clinical interventions (2nd ed.). St. Louis, MO: MMB Music.

Unwin, M. M., Kenny, D. T., & Davis, P. J. (2002). *The effects of group singing on mood.* Psychology of Music, 30(2), 164–174.

van der Hurk, J., & Smeijsters, H. (1991). *Musical improvisation in the treatment of a man with obsessive compulsive personality disorder.* In K. E. Bruscia (Ed.), Case studies in music therapy *(pp. 387–401).* Phoenixville, PA: Barcelona.

van den Daele, L. (1967). A music projective techniques. Journal of Projective Techniques and Personality Assessment, 31(5), 47–57.

Van de Wall, W. (1923). Music in correctional institutions. Albany, NY: J. B. Lyon.

Van de Wall, W. (1926). A systematic music program for mental hospitals. American Journal of Psychiatry, 6, 279–291.

Van de Wall, W. (1936). Music in institutions. New York: Russell Sage Foundation.

Van de Wall, W. (1948). Music in hospitals. In D. M. Schullian & M. Schoen (Eds.), Music and medicine (pp. 293–321). New York: Henry Schuman.

Van Stone, J. K. (1960). The effects of instrumental tone quality upon mood response to music. In E. H. Schneider (Ed.), Music therapy 1959 (pp. 196–202). Lawrence, KS: Allen Press.

Ventre, M. (1994). Guided imagery and music in process: The interweaving of the archetype of the mother, mandala, and music. Music Therapy, 12(2), 19–38.

Ventre, M. (1994). Healing the wounds of childhood abuse: A guided imagery and music case study. Music Therapy Perspectives, 12(2), 98–103.

Ventre, M. (1999). A tape from Lilly. In J. Hibben (Ed.), Inside music therapy: Client experiences (pp. 135–140). Gilsum, NH: Barcelona.

Ventre, M. (2002). The individual form of the Bonny Method of Guided Imagery and Music (BMGIM). In K. E. Bruscia & D. E. Gorcke (Eds.), Guided imagery and music: The Bonny Method (pp. 29–35). Gilsum, NH: Barcelona.

Verdeau-Pailles, J. (2004). Le bilan psychomusicale et le personalité (3rd ed., Rev.). Paris: Fuzeau Editions.

Vescelius, E. A. (1918). Music and health. The Musical Quarterly, 4(3), 376–401.

Volkman, S. (1993). Music therapy and the treatment of trauma-induced dissociative disorders. The Arts in Psychotherapy, 20(3), 243–251.

Wagner, R. (1978). Study of the emotional and association effects of music. Psychologie in Erziehung und Unterricht, 25, 374–376.

Waldorff, G. G. (Ed.). (1977). Counseling therapies and the addictive client. Baltimore: School of Social Work and Community Planning.

Walker, A. (1980). Music and the unconscious. The Music Therapy Association Bulletin, 3(3), 3–7.

Walker, J. (1995). Music therapy, spirituality, and chemically dependent clients. Journal of Chemical Dependency Treatment, 5(2), 145–166.

Walker, V. (1993). Integrating guided imagery and music with verbal psychotherapy. Journal of the Association for Music and Imagery, 2, 111–121.

Walworth, D. D. (2003). The effect of preferred music genre selection versus preferred song selection on experimentally induced anxiety levels. Journal of Music Therapy, 40(1), 2–14.

Wang, R. P. (1968). Psychoanalytic theories and music therapy practice. Journal of Music Therapy, 5(4), 114–117.

Wannamaker, C., & Rznikoff, M. (1989). Effects of aggressive and nonaggressive rock songs on projective and structured tests. Journal of Psychology, 123, 561–570.

Ward, K. M. (2002). A Jungian orientation to the Bonny Method. In K. E. Bruscia & D. E. Gorcke (Eds.), Guided imagery and music: The Bonny Method (pp. 208–224). Gilsum, NH: Barcelona.

Wardle, M. (1979). Music therapy in a women's prison. Part I: The old prison. British Journal of Music Therapy, 19(2), 11–13.

Wardle, M. (1980). Music therapy in a women's prison. Part II: The new prison. British Journal of Music Therapy, 11(2), 2–7.

Warja, M. (1994). Sounds of music through the spiraling path of individuation: A Jungian approach to music psychotherapy. Music Therapy Perspectives, 12(2), 75–83.

Warren, J. (1968). Paired-associate learning in chronic institutionalized subjects using synthesized sounds, nonsense syllables, rhythmic sounds. Journal of Music Therapy, 17(1), 16–25.

Warrington, O. (1961). Volunteer classical music programs: Suggestions. Bulletin of NAMT, 10(1), 9.

Wasserman, N. M. (1972). Music therapy for the emotionally disturbed in a private hospital. Journal of Music Therapy, 9(2), 99–104.

Watson, D. (2002). Drumming and improvisation with adult male sexual offenders. Music Therapy Perspectives, 20(2), 105–111.

Wayne, M. (1944). Instrumental music for the maladjusted child. Music Educators Journal, 31, 33–36.

Webner, N. (1966). The practice of music therapy with psychotic children. Journal of Music Therapy, 3(1), 25–31.

Weidenfeller, E. W., & Zinny, G. H. (1962a). Effects of music upon GSR of children. Child Development, 33, 891–896.

Weidenfeller, E. W., & Zinny, G. H. (1962b). Effects of music upon GSR of depressives and schizophrenics. Journal of Abnormal Psychology, 64, 307–312.

Weintraub, I. G. (1961). Emotional responses of schizophrenics to selected musical compositions. Delaware Medical Journal, 33, 186–187.

Weiss, D. M., & Margolin, R. J. (1953). The use of music as an adjunct to group therapy. American Archives of Rehabilitation Therapists, 3, 13–26.

Wells, N. F. (1988). An individual music therapy assessment procedure for emotionally disturbed young adolescents. The Arts in Psychotherapy, 15(1), 47–54.

Wells, N. F., & Stevens, T. (1984). Music as a stimulus for creative fantasy in group psychotherapy with young adolescents. The Arts in Psychotherapy, 11(2), 71–76.

Werbner, N. (1966). The practice of music therapy with psychotic children. Journal of Music Therapy, 3(1), 25–31.

Wesley, S. B. (2001). Within these walls: Auditory consciousness in a psychiatric hospital for inpatient children for the new millenium. Karolinska Institute Proceedings—Integrating design and care in hospital planning for the new millenium. Stockholm: Karolinska Institute.

Wesley, S. B. (2002). Guided imagery and music with children and adolescents. In K. E. Bruscia & D. E. Gorcke (Eds.), Guided imagery and music: The Bonny Method (pp. 138–149). Gilsum, NH: Barcelona.

Weir, L. (1952). *Music therapy at Devereux Ranch school*. In E. G. Gilliland (Ed.), Music therapy 1951 (pp. 22–25). Lawrence, KS: Allen Press.

Weiss, L. (1994). *Accessing the inner family through guided imagery and music*. Journal of the Association for Music and Imagery, 3, 49–58.

West, B. (1981, January). *A music therapy technique for psychiatric patients*. Quodlibet, p. 16.

Wexler, M. M. (1989). *The use of song in grief therapy with Cibecue White Mountain Apaches*. Music Therapy Perspectives, 7, 63–66.

Wheeler, B. L. (1981). *The relationship between music therapy and theories of psychotherapy*. Music Therapy, 1(1), 9–16.

Wheeler, B. L. (1983). *A psychotherapeutic classification of music therapy practices: A continuum of procedure*. Music Therapy Perspectives, 1, 8–16.

Wheeler, B. L. (1985). *Relationship of personal characteristics to mood and enjoyment after hearing live and recorded music to musical taste*. Psychology of Music, 13, 81–92.

Wheeler, B. L. (1985). *The relationship between musical and activity elements of music therapy sessions and client responses: An exploratory study*. Music Therapy, 5(1), 52–60.

Wheeler, B. L. (1987). *Levels of therapy: The classification of music therapy goals*. Music Therapy, 6(2), 39–49.

White, W. F., & Allen, W. R. (1966). *Psychodramatic effects of music as a psychotherapeutic agent*. Journal of Music Therapy, 3(2), 89–71.

Wigram, A. L. (1988). *Music therapy—Developments in mental handicap*. Psychology of Music, 16(1), 42–51.

Wigram, T. (1999). *Assessment methods in music therapy. A humanities or natural science framework?* Nordic Journal of Music Therapy, 8(1), 7–25.

Wigram, T. (Ed.). (2000). *Assessment and evaluation in the arts therapies*. St. Albans, NY: Harper House.

Wigram, T. (2004). *Improvisation: Methods and techniques for music therapy clinicians, educators and students*. London: Jessica Kingsley.

Wigram, T., & DeBacker, J. (Eds.). (1999). *Clinical applications of music therapy in psychiatry*. London: Jessica Kingsley.

Wigram, T., Pederson, I. N., & Bonde, L. O. (2002). *A comprehensive guide to music therapy*. London: Jessica Kingsley.

Wigram, T., Saperston, B., & West, R. (1995). *The art and science of music therapy: A handbook*. Chur, Switzerland: Harwood Academic.

Wijzenbeek, G., & van Nieuwenhuizen, N. (1993). *Receptive music therapy with depressive and neurotic patients*. In R. R. Pratt (Ed.), Music therapy and music education for the handicapped (pp. 174–175). St. Louis, MO: MMB Music.

Wilke, M. (1960). *Music therapy at work in the short-term psychiatric setting at Charity Hospital of New Orleans*. Bulletin of NAMT, 9(2), 5–6, 10.

Wilke, M. (1961). *The disc jockey jamboree*. In E. H. Schneider (Ed.), Music therapy 1960 (pp. 41–43). Lawrence, KS: Allen Press.

Williams, G., & Dorrow, L. (1983). *Changes in complaints and non-compliance of a chronically depressed psychiatric patient as a function of an interrupted music/verbal feedback package*. Journal of Music Therapy, 20(3), 143–155.

Wilson, A. (1964). *Special education for the emotionally disturbed child*. Journal of Music Therapy, 1(1), 16–18.

Wilson, A. E. (1968). *Music in the treatment and education of emotionally disturbed children*. In E. T. Gaston (Ed.), Music in therapy (pp. 293–313). New York: Macmillan.

Wilson, B. L. (1990). *Assessment of adult psychiatric clients: The role of music therapy*. In R. F. Unkefer (Ed.), Music therapy in the treatment of adults with mental disorders (pp. 126–144). New York: Schirmer Books.

Wilson, B. L. (1990). *Music therapy in hospital and community programs*. In R. F. Unkefer (Ed.), Music therapy in the treatment of adults with mental disorders (pp. 88–95). New York: Schirmer Books.

Wilson. B. L. (Ed.). (1996). *Models of music therapy interventions in school settings: From institution to inclusion*. Silver Spring, MD: National Association for Music Therapy.

Wilson, C. V. (1976). *The use of rock music as a reward in behavior therapy with children*. Journal of Music Therapy, 13(1), 39–48.

Wilson, C. V., & Aiken, L. S. (1977). *The effect of intensity levels upon physiological and subjective affective responses to rock music*. Journal of Music Therapy, 14(2), 60–76.

Winkelman, M. (2003). *Drumming out drugs*. American Jouranl of Public Health, 94(4), 674–679.

Winter, W. D. (1955). *The psychologist asks: How can the music therapy help me perform my job more effectively?* Bulletin of NAMT, 4(3), 7–8.

Wolfe, D. E. (1988). *Group music therapy in short-term psychiatric care*. In C. E. Furman (Ed.), Effectiveness of music therapy procedures: Documentation of research and clinical practice (pp. 175–205). Washington, DC: National Association for Music Therapy.

Wolfe, D. E. (2000). *Group music therapy in acute mental health care: Meeting the demands of effectiveness and efficiency*. In American Music Therapy Association (Ed.), Effectiveness of music therapy procedures: Documentation of research and clinical practice (3rd ed., pp. 265–296). Silver Spring, MD: American Music Therapy Association.

Wolfe, D. E., Burns, S., Stoll, M., & Wichmann, K. (1975). *Analysis of music therapy group procedures*. Minneapolis, MN: Golden Valley Health Center.

Wolfe, D. E., & O'Connell, A. (1999). *Specifying and recording treatment objectives within a group music therapy setting*. Music Therapy Perspectives, 17(1), 37–41.

Wolfgram, B. J. (1978). *Music therapy for retarded adults with psychotic overlay: A day treatment approach*. Journal of Music Therapy, 15(4), 199–207.

Woodcock, J. (1987). *Towards a group analytic music therapy*. Journal of British Music Therapy, 1, 16–21.

Wooten, M. A. (1992). *The effects of heavy metal music on affective shifts of adolescents in an inpatient psychiatric setting*. Music Therapy Perspectives, 10(2), 93–98.

Worden, M. C. (1998). The effects of music on difference in body movement of college music majors, dance, majors, and survivors of sexual abuse. Journal of Music Therapy, 35(4), 259–273.

Wortis, R. P. (1960). Music therapy for the mentally ill: The effect of music on emotional activity and the value of music as a resocializing agent. Journal of General Psychology, 62, 311–318.

Wrangsjo, B. (1994). Psychoanalysis and guided imagery and music: A comparison. Journal of the Association for Music and Imagery, 3, 35–48.

Wrangsjo, B., & Korlin, D. (1995). Guided imagery and music (GIM) as a psychotherapeutic method in psychiatry. Journal of the Association for Music and Imagery, 4, 79–92.

Wright, B. (1976). A study in the use of music therapy techniques for behavior modification at St. Thomas Psychiatric Hospital, Ontario. Journal for the Canadian Association for Music Therapy, 4, 2–4.

Wright, P. (1980). A case study. British Journal of Music Therapy, 11(3), 2–5.

Wright, P., & Priestley, M. (1972). Analytical music therapy. British Journal of Music Therapy, 3(2), 20–15.

Wrobel, A. M. (1963). Roles of the music therapist in the open institution. In E. H. Schneider (Ed.), Music therapy 1963 (pp. 43–49). Lawrence, KS: Allen Press.

Wyatt, J. G. (2002). From the field: Clinical resources for music therapy with juvenile offenders. Music Therapy Perspectives, 20(2), 80–87.

Zalanowski, A. H., & Stratton, V. N. (1993). The effects of music and cognition on mood. In R. R. Pratt (Eds.), Music therapy and music education for the handicapped (pp. 178–179). St. Louis, MO: MMB Music.

Zanker, A., & Glatt, M. M. (1956). Individual reaction of alcoholics and neurotic patients to music. Journal of Nervous and Mental Disorders, 123, 395–402.

Zharinova-Sanderson, O. (2004). Promoting integration and socio-cultural change: Community music therapy with traumatized refugees in Berlin. In M. Pavlicevic & G. Ansdell (Eds.), Community music therapy: International initiatives. London: Jessica Kingsley.

Zwerling, I. (1979). The creative arts therapies as "real therapies." Hospital and Community Psychiatry, 30(12), 841–844.

Appendices

Appendix C: Music Therapy and Mental Health Fact Sheet

Appendix D: Music Therapy for Persons In Correctional and Forensic Settings Fact Sheet

Appendix E: Music Therapy in Response to Crisis and Trauma Fact Sheet

Fact Sheets retrieved from the web site of The American Music Therapy Association, Inc., www.musictherapy.org, on September 1, 2007.

Music Therapy and Mental Health Fact Sheet

What is Music Therapy?

Music Therapy is the clinical and evidence-based use of music interventions to accomplish individualized goals within a therapeutic relationship by a credentialed professional who has completed an approved music therapy program. It is an established health service similar to occupational therapy and physical therapy and consists of using music therapeutically to address physical, psychological, cognitive and/or social functioning for patients of all ages. Because music therapy is a powerful and non-invasive medium, unique outcomes are possible. In addition to its applications in mental health, music therapy is used successfully in a variety of additional healthcare and educational settings.

How Does Music Therapy Make a Difference for Persons with Mental Health Needs?

Music therapy is an efficacious and valid treatment for persons who have psychosocial, affective, cognitive and communicative needs. Research results and clinical experiences attest to the viability of music therapy even in those who are resistive to other treatment approaches. Music is a form of sensory stimulation that provokes responses due to the familiarity, predictability and feelings of security associated with it. Music therapy for clients with mental health concerns uses musical interaction as a means of communication and expression. The aim of therapy is to help individuals develop relationships and address issues they may not be able to address using words alone. Music therapy sessions include the use of active music making, music listening, and discussion.

What do Music Therapists Do?

Music therapists use music strategies, both instrumental and vocal, which are designed to facilitate changes that are non-musical in nature. Music selections and certain active music making activities are modified for client preferences and individualized needs (i.e., song selection and music may vary). Music therapy programs are based on individual assessment, treatment planning, and ongoing program evaluation. Frequently functioning as members of an interdisciplinary team, music therapists implement programs with groups or individuals that display a vast continuum of needs, from reduction of anxiety to deeper self-understanding.

What Can One Expect From a Music Therapist?

Music therapists work with the interdisciplinary team to assess emotional well being, physical health, social functioning, communication abilities, and cognitive skills through musical responses. When individualized music experiences are designed by the music therapist to fit functional abilities and needs, responses may be immediate and readily apparent. Clients need not have a music background to benefit from music therapy. Music therapy intervention provides opportunities to:

- Explore personal feelings and therapeutic issues such as self-esteem or personal insight
- Make positive changes in mood and emotional states
- Have a sense of control over life through successful experiences
- Enhance awareness of self and environment
- Express oneself both verbally and non-verbally

- Develop coping and relaxation skills
- Support healthy feelings and thoughts
- Improve reality testing and problem solving skills
- Interact socially with others
- Develop independence and decision making skills
- Improve concentration and attention span
- Adopt positive forms of behavior
- Resolve conflicts leading to stronger family and peer relationships

Who is Qualified as a Music Therapist?

Graduates of colleges or universities from more than 70 approved music therapy programs are eligible to take a national examination administered by the Certification Board for Music Therapists (CBMT), an independent, non-profit certifying agency fully accredited by the National Commission for Certifying Agencies. After successful completion of the CBMT examination, graduates are issued the credential necessary for professional practice, Music Therapist-Board Certified (MT-BC). In addition to the MT-BC credential, other recognized professional designations are Registered Music Therapists (RMT), Certified Music Therapists (CMT), and Advanced Certified Music Therapist (ACMT) listed with the National Music Therapy Registry. Any individual who does not have proper training and credentials is not qualified to provide music therapy services.

Where do Music Therapists Work?

Music therapists offer services in psychiatric treatment centers, outpatient clinics, community mental health centers, substance abuse programs, group homes, rehabilitation facilities, medical hospitals, senior centers, schools, hospice and other facilities. Some music therapists specialize in mental health and have additional training in advanced music therapy techniques and psychology. Some music therapists are self-employed and may be hired on a contractual basis to provide assessment, consultation, and treatment services for children and adults.

What Research And Resources Are Available To Substantiate And Support Music Therapy?

AMTA has promoted a vast amount of research exploring the benefits of music as treatment through publication of the *Journal of Music Therapy, Music Therapy Perspectives*, and other resources. The CD-ROM "Music Therapy Research - Quantitative and Qualitative Foundations" offers a complete collection of research published by the music therapy associations in the United States from 1964 through 2003.

What Outcomes are Documented in Music Therapy Research?

- Reduced muscle tension
- Improved self-image/Increased self-esteem
- Decreased anxiety/agitation
- Increased verbalization
- Enhanced interpersonal relationships
- Improved group cohesiveness
- Increased motivation
- Successful and safe emotional release

Selected Research Samples

Music therapy as an addition to standard care helps people with schizophrenia to improve their global state and may also improve mental state and functioning if a sufficient number of music therapy sessions are provided.

Gold, C., Heldal, T.O., Dahle, T., Wigram, T. (2005). *Music Therapy for Schizophrenia or Schizophrenia-like Illnesses.* The Cochrane Database of Systematic Reviews, 3. *Accession: 00075320-100000000-03007 PMID: 15846692*

Music therapy significantly diminished patients' negative symptoms, increased their ability to converse with others, reduced their social isolation, and increased their level of interest in external events. As music therapy has no side-effects and is relatively inexpensive, it merits further evaluation and wider application.

Tang W, Yao X, Zheng Z. *Rehabilitative effect of music therapy for residual schizophrenia: A one-month randomised controlled trial in Shanghai.* British Journal of Psychiatry 1994;165(suppl. 24):38-44. *PMID: 7946230*

Results indicated that music has proven to be significantly effective in suppressing and combating the symptoms of psychosis.

Silverman, M.J. *The Influence of Music on the Symptoms of Psychosis: A Meta-Analysis.* Journal of Music Therapy 2003; XL(1) 27-40.

Depressed adolescents listening to music experienced a significant decrease in stress hormone (cortisol) levels, and most adolescents shifted toward left frontal EEG activation (associated with positive affect).

Field, T., Martinez, A., Nawrocki, T., Pickens, J., Fox N.A., & Schanberg, S. (1998). *Music shifts frontal EEG in depressed adolescents.* Adolescence, 33(129), 109-116.

Music therapy clients significantly improved on the Aggression/Hostility scale of Achenbach's Teacher's Report Form, suggesting that group music therapy can facilitate self-expression and provide a channel for transforming frustration, anger, and aggression into the experience of creativity and self-mastery.

Montello, L.M., & Coons, E.E. (1998). *Effect of active versus passive group music therapy on preadolescents with emotional, learning, and behavioral disorders.* Journal of Music Therapy, 35, 49-67.

Additional References

Burns, J. L., Labbé, E. Arke, B., Capeless, K., Cooksey, B., Steadman, A., & Gonzales, C. (2002). *The effects of different types of music on perceived and physiological measures of stress.* Journal of Music Therapy, 39(2), 101-116.

Cevasco, A. M., Kennedy, R., & Generally, N. R. (2005). *Comparison of Movement-to-Music, Rhythm Activities, and Competitive Games on Depression, Stress, Anxiety, and Anger of Females in Substance Abuse Rehabilitation.* Journal of Music Therapy, 42(1), 64-80.

Hammer, S. E (1996). *The effects of guided imagery through music on state and trait anxiety.* Journal of Music Therapy, 33(1), 47-70.

Hernández-Ruiz, E. (2005). *Effect of Music Therapy on the Anxiety Levels and Sleep Patterns of Abused Women in Shelters.* Journal of Music Therapy, 42(2), 140-158.

Hsu, W., & Lai, H. (2004). *Effects of Music on Major Depression in Psychiatric Inpatients.* Archives of Psychiatric Nursing, 18(5), 193-199.

Jones, N., & Field, T. (1999). *Massage and music therapies attenuate frontal EEG asymmetry in depressed adolescents.* Adolescence, 34(135), 529-534.

Kerr, T., Walsh, J., & Marshall, A. (2001). *Emotional change processes in music-assisted reframing.* Journal of Music Therapy, 38(3), 193-211.

Mayers, K. S. (1995).*Songwriting as a way to decrease anxiety and distress in traumatized children.* Arts in Psychotherapy, 22(5), 495-498.

Reilly, J. (1997). LIGHTNING strikes: A correlational study of the gesturo-musical responses of in-patients with acute manic or depressive symptomatology using the LIGHTNING module. Journal of Music Therapy, 34(4), 260-276.

Tornek, A., Field, T., Hernandez-Reif, M., Diego, M., & Jones, N. (2003). Music Effects on EEG in Intrusive and Withdrawn Mothers with Depressive Symptoms. Psychiatry: Interpersonal and Biological Processes, 66(3), 234-243.

What is AMTA?

The American Music Therapy Association (AMTA) represents over 5,000 music therapists, corporate members, and related associations worldwide. AMTA's roots date back to organizations founded in 1950 and 1971. Those two organizations merged in 1998 to ensure the progressive development of the therapeutic use of music in rehabilitation, special education, and medical and community settings. AMTA is committed to the advancement of education, training, professional standards, and research in support of the music therapy profession. The mission of the organization is to advance public knowledge of music therapy benefits and increase access to quality music therapy services. Currently, AMTA establishes criteria for the education and clinical training of music therapists. Professional members of AMTA adhere to a Code of Ethics and Standards of Practice in their delivery of music therapy services.

How Can You Find a Music Therapist or Get More Information?

American Music Therapy Association
8455 Colesville Road, Suite 1000
Silver Spring, MD 20910
Phone: (301) 589-3300
Fax: (301) 589-5175
Web: www.musictherapy.org
Email: info@musictherapy.org

Music Therapy for Persons In Correctional and Forensic Settings Fact Sheet

What is Music Therapy?

Music Therapy is the clinical and evidence-based use of music interventions to accomplish individualized goals within a therapeutic relationship by a credentialed professional who has completed an approved music therapy program. It is a well-established healthcare profession in which various music-based methods are used to address the specific needs of individuals with illnesses, disabilities and special needs. The music therapist assesses the needs of the clients, develops and implements a treatment plan based on assessment findings, and evaluates the treatment process. Because music is a powerful and non-threatening medium, unique outcomes are possible with a variety of populations

How Does Music Therapy Make A Difference for Persons in Correctional and Forensic Settings?

In correctional and forensic settings, clients may include adolescents and adults who are incarcerated, individuals adjudicated for treatment in secure mental health facilities, persons living in half-way houses, group homes, and intensive sanctions programs, and individuals on probation and parole who live independently in the community. Research in the field and clinical anecdotes attest to the validity and efficacy of music therapy with these individuals, many of whom have physical, psychological, emotional, social, behavioral, cognitive, communicative, and/or spiritual needs and challenges.

What Do Music Therapists Do?

Music therapists use four basic methods to help clients achieve predetermined treatment goals and objectives:

- *Receptive* methods involve listening and responding to live or recorded music. For example, the use of music as a rhythmic support and motivation for exercise, movement, and dance may be helpful for individuals living in confined spaces. Listening to and discussing popular songs provide opportunities for clients to express themselves in safe and socially accepted ways and to examine personal issues. Music-assisted relaxation can aid in the reduction of anxiety.

- *Improvisation* revolves around the spontaneous creation of music using media such as voice, instruments, and body sounds. Engagement in this form of active music-making allows for creative expression, the release of energy, the development of personal insight, and a redirection of difficult or counterproductive emotions in individual and/or group settings.

- *Recreative* experiences focus on singing and playing precomposed music. In corrections and forensic settings, this method allows individuals to develop skills that lead to a sense of mastery and increased confidence. Experiences in ensembles such as choruses, popular music combos, and chime choirs provide opportunities for meaningful social interaction and can contribute to the productive use of leisure time.

- *Composition* methods involve creating vocal and instrumental pieces. Songwriting can be an effective means of expression and a source of self-satisfaction in individual and group treatment settings, as well as a vehicle for learning foundational music concepts. This generative process also encourages thoughtful work over time, ideally leading to completion of a musical product which may be preserved in tangible form (songsheet, audiotape, etc.).

As with all populations, the trusting and respectful relationship that develops between the therapist and the forensic client serves as the basis for therapeutic change through shared music experience. When individualized experiences are designed by the music therapist to support and challenge the client's unique abilities and needs, desired results may be immediate and readily apparent.

Clients need not have prior music training or experience in order to benefit from music therapy treatment.
- Specific goals in correctional and forensic settings may include the following:
- Increase self-awareness
- Improve reality testing and problem-solving skills
- Improve respect for others, including peers and authority figures
- Develop healthy verbal and non-verbal communication skills
- Decrease impulsivity through practical techniques
- Accept responsibility for thoughts and feelings
- Learn relaxation and coping skills
- Improve physical conditioning
- Develop effective leisure skills
- Explore feelings and make positive changes in mood states

Who is Qualified as a Music Therapist?

Graduates of colleges or universities from more than 70 approved music therapy programs are eligible to take a national examination administered by the Certification Board for Music Therapists (CBMT), an independent, non-profit certifying agency fully accredited by the National Commission for Certifying Agencies. After successful completion of the CBMT examination, graduates are issued the credential necessary for professional practice, Music Therapist-Board Certified (MT-BC). In addition to the MT-BC credential, other recognized professional designations are Registered Music Therapists (RMT), Certified Music Therapists (CMT), and Advanced Certified Music Therapist (ACMT) listed with the National Music Therapy Registry. Any individual who does not have proper training and credentials is not qualified to provide music therapy services.

Where do Music Therapists Work with Correctional and Forensic Clients?

Music therapists offer services in a variety of correctional and forensic settings, including: maximum security hospitals, jails, prisons, detention centers, group homes, sanctions programs, and community-based probation and parole programs. Music therapists may also encounter forensic clients in homeless shelters, missions, refuge houses, substance abuse treatment centers, volunteer training programs, churches, aftercare programs, mental health facilities, medical hospitals, schools, skilled nursing facilities, rehabilitation centers, and private practice. Some professionals in these settings acquire advanced training in psychology or forensic medicine.

Is There Research to Support Music Therapy?

A vast amount of clinical- and research-based information exists to support the use of music therapy with forensic populations. Both quantitative and qualitative research studies have been published in forensic journals, as well as in peer-reviewed journals within the creative arts therapies, including the *Journal of Music Therapy, Music Therapy, Music Therapy Perspectives, Arts in Psychotherapy*, and the *Nordic Journal of Music Therapy*.

Why Music Therapy?

Mike Morgan, Chaplain at Fremont Correctional Facility in Canon City, Colorado comments:

> *"The use of music therapy in corrections facilitates a connection with people from every socio-economic level and race. By entering their world through music, principles and values can be communicated so that the people who are incarcerated can live, love, learn, and leave a legacy. Music therapy in corrections is not an undocumented fad. It works and creates positive change in a very negative environment."*

Joy Prelznik, Asst. Deputy Warden, Ionia Temporary Correctional Facility in Michigan states:

> *"Music Therapy is very helpful in a prison setting with psychiatric patients. These patients often have had no life experiences with music and positive emotions or with bodily movement related to music. The patients find themselves responding to music therapy when they cannot cooperate with conventional therapy."*

James Neville, Chief of Rehabilitation at Atascadero State Hospital in California comments:

> *"Here at Atascadero, music therapy provides an opportunity for our patients to learn cognitive, social, and functional skills using a non-threatening and an expressive modality."*

Susan Davis, Deputy Warden at Scott Correctional Facility in Plymouth, Michigan writes:

> *"Music therapy is an integral part of our residential treatment program. Many of the women articulate their problems and needs through songs and channel their physical energy through instrumental music lessons and performances. The unit is a positive and more peaceful environment because of music therapy."*

What is AMTA?

The American Music Therapy Association (AMTA) represents over 5,000 music therapists, corporate members, and related associations worldwide. AMTA's roots date back to organizations founded in 1950 and 1971. Those two organizations merged in 1998 to ensure the progressive development of the therapeutic use of music in rehabilitation, special education, and medical and community settings. AMTA is committed to the advancement of education, training, professional standards, and research in support of the music therapy profession. The mission of the organization is to advance public knowledge of music therapy benefits and increase access to quality music therapy services. Currently, AMTA establishes criteria for the education and clinical training of music therapists. Members of AMTA adhere to a Code of Ethics and Standards of Practice in their delivery of music therapy services.

How Can You Find a Music Therapist or Get More Information?

American Music Therapy Association
8455 Colesville Road, Suite 1000
Silver Spring, MD 20910
Phone: (301) 589-3300
Fax: (301) 589-5175
Web: www.musictherapy.org
Email: info@musictherapy.org

Music Therapy in Response to Crisis and Trauma Fact Sheet

What Is Music Therapy?

Music Therapy is the clinical and evidence-based use of music interventions to accomplish individualized goals within a therapeutic relationship by a credentialed professional who has completed an approved music therapy program. It is the structured use of music to assist people of all ages in times of need. A well-established, healthcare profession, music therapy uses carefully selected music and music interventions to address physical, emotional, cognitive and social needs. While music therapy will not cure or solve problems brought on by crisis, music therapy can help children and adults in crisis learn and use positive coping skills and express difficult feelings and emotions. Because music therapy is a powerful and non-invasive medium, unique outcomes are possible.

How Does Music Therapy Make A Difference In Response To Crisis Situations?

The work of the AMTA New York City Music Therapy Relief Project, combined with over fifty years of practice and research in music therapy, has demonstrated the impact of music therapy as 'second-wave' relief in helping to cope with events surrounding a crisis and its aftermath. The directed use of music and music therapy is highly effective in developing coping strategies, including understanding and expressing feelings of anxiety and helplessness, supporting feelings of self-confidence and security, and providing a safe or neutral environment for relaxation. Research results and clinical experiences attest to the viability of music therapy even in situations outside of traditional therapeutic settings. Music is a form of sensory stimulation, which provokes responses due to the familiarity, predictability, and feelings of security associated with it. Feedback from relief workers and caregivers indicates that music therapy sessions helped to develop a stronger sense of readiness to cope with day-to-day stressors and potential future crisis situations.

How Does Music Therapy Help Those Affected By Crisis Or Trauma?

Music therapy has been shown to have a significant effect on an individual's relaxation, respiration rate, self-reported pain reduction, and behaviorally observed and self-reported anxiety levels. A coordinated program of music and music therapy interventions in response to crisis or trauma, designed and implemented by a qualified music therapist, provides opportunities for:

- Non-verbal outlets for emotions associated with traumatic experiences
- Anxiety and stress reduction
- Positive changes in mood and emotional states
- Active and positive participant involvement in treatment
- Enhanced feelings of control, confidence, and empowerment
- Positive physiological changes, such as lower blood pressure, reduced heart rate, and relaxed muscle tension

In addition, music therapy may allow for:

- Emotional intimacy with peers, families, caregivers
- Relaxation for family groups or other community and peer groups

Meaningful time spent together in a positive, creative way

What Was The New York City Music Therapy Relief Project?

The New York City Music Therapy Relief Project was a program of the American Music Therapy Association, with generous underwriting support from The Recording Academy. The project was designed to provide direct music therapy services to children and adults in the New York metropolitan area struggling with the aftermath of the attacks of September 11, 2001. The 8-month program encompassed 25 community programs and 33 professional music therapists, facilitating over 7,000 music therapy interventions in schools, senior centers, healthcare facilities, and other locations throughout the metropolitan area. Five music therapy programs were specifically designed for caregivers and relief workers—including doctors, nurses, counselors, social workers, teachers, guidance counselors, crisis workers, and therapists—responding to the needs of others. Eleven music therapy programs, including eight schools, served over 3,000 children and teachers. Three community-based music therapy programs in Manhattan, Westchester County, NY and Hoboken, NJ provided individual and group music therapy programs, serving adults and families affected by the attacks.

What Services Does AMTA Provide When Crises Occur?

AMTA raises funds through donations and other sources for disaster response and coordinates the delivery of programs and services for individuals affected by disaster. In response to the 2005 hurricane season, AMTA initiated several support activities for music therapy professionals and students impacted by the storms. Phase I involved welfare inquiries and contact updates for individuals dealing with relocations, job loss, transportation challenges, housing problems, and/or serious financial stressors. Technical assistance and references were provided regarding PTSD, acute stress response, psychological first aid, critical incident stress management, and training in post-disaster mental health services. Phase II hurricane relief work has aimed to provide support to members who are working with those affected by the 2005 hurricanes including provision of music therapy services to first and second responders. Specific programs have included caregiver workshops and music therapy services and consultation with social workers and teachers serving young children in daycare programs. In addition, the Gulf Coast Youth orchestra participated in a youth and parent hurricane recovery music therapy experience and recording session of original music.

What Do Music Therapists Do?

Music therapists use music and music therapy interventions, both instrumental and vocal, designed to facilitate changes that are non-musical in nature. Music therapy programs are based on individual assessment, treatment planning, and ongoing program evaluation. The professionally trained music therapist utilizes individualized music experiences and interventions to assess, treat, and evaluate patients. Frequently functioning as members of an interdisciplinary team, music therapists implement programs with groups or individuals addressing a vast continuum of outcomes, including reduction of anxiety, stress management, communication, and emotional self-expression.

Who Is Qualified As A Music Therapist?

Graduates of colleges or universities from more than 70 approved music therapy programs are eligible to take a national examination administered by the Certification Board for Music Therapists (CBMT), an independent, non-profit certifying agency fully accredited by the National Commission for Certifying Agencies. After successful completion of the CBMT examination, graduates are issued the credential necessary for professional practice, Music Therapist-Board Certified (MT-BC). In addition to the MT-BC credential, other recognized professional designations are Registered Music Therapists (RMT), Certified Music Therapists (CMT), and Advanced Certified Music Therapist (ACMT) listed with the National Music Therapy Registry. Any individual who does not have proper training and credentials is not qualified to provide music therapy services.

Where Do Music Therapists Work?

Music therapists offer services in medical hospitals, skilled and intermediate care facilities, rehabilitation hospitals, adult day care centers, senior centers, hospices, psychiatric treatment centers, drug and alcohol programs, schools and other facilities. In crisis situations, it is important for music therapy services to be available and accessible to the community in need. Music therapists mobilize to provide services locally, working in schools, hospitals, community centers, corporate offices, senior centers, universities and colleges, etc. Some music therapists are self-employed and work as independent contractors, while others may be full or part time employees.

What Research And Resources Are Available To Substantiate And Support Music Therapy?

Through the Journal of Music Therapy, Music Therapy Perspectives, and other resources, the American Music Therapy Association has promoted research exploring the benefits of music therapy with children and adults. The CD-ROM "Music Therapy Research - Quantitative and Qualitative Foundations" offers a complete collection of research published by the music therapy associations in the United States from 1964 through 2003.

Why Music Therapy?

"Music therapy enables people to sometimes put words together in ways that are hard for them to do otherwise. ...The music seems to get through to the patient and in many ways it enables [the patient] to get through to us which [may be] very hard to do with any other modality."

- Susan Shurin, MD

"...music therapy (particularly improvisation and guided imagery and music) can be most helpful in identifying with the feelings as a pre-cursor to verbal dialogue. One who is trained to elicit, reflect, and interpret non-verbal responses can be most helpful in these beginning stages of recovery."

- Music Therapist from the New York City Music Therapy Relief Project

"Families reported having reclaimed a sense of joy through participation in a music activity with one another."

- Music Therapy Institute, Westchester, NY

"Music gives all a chance to express ourselves, to share our souls, to share our feelings with each other."

- Participant, Nordoff-Robbins Center for Music Therapy, New York University

"The training reinforced and reminded me of how much music plays such an important part in my life and how it can be used as a therapeutic tool whenever the need arises. I valued the times I played the drums and so much energy was released. I felt a sense of calm afterwards... Music was a way for us to bring the emotions or energy to the forefront, which could then possibly release some of the residue, discharging the energy from the body."

- New York City Relief Worker

"During the Caring for the Caregiver sessions I felt some of that tension melt away, evidence of the magical way music can seep into the nooks and crannies of our souls and psyches, not to mention that raw collective nervous system we have all been carrying with us. By connecting with a community of caregivers seeking out healing for themselves through music and expression, I was able to move forward, inward and outward simultaneously in the way I needed to. I became better equipped to care."

- New York City Nurse

"...[in music therapy] We learned not to keep in your feelings or else your stomach will twist in knots and you will get very hurt..."

- New York City Fourth Grade Student

"Thank you for helping me to understand everything... You taught me to cool down when I was mad. You taught me to solve my problems. You were there when I needed help. The music that played soothed my pain. When I was feeling sad, you were always there to comfort me. I could talk to you about anything."

- New York City Fourth Grade Student

What is AMTA?

The American Music Therapy Association (AMTA) represents over 5,000 music therapists, corporate members, and related associations worldwide. AMTA's roots date back to organizations founded in 1950 and 1971. Those two organizations merged in 1998 to ensure the progressive development of the therapeutic use of music in rehabilitation, special education, and medical and community settings. AMTA is committed to the advancement of education, training, professional standards, and research in support of the music therapy profession. The mission of the organization is to advance public knowledge of music therapy benefits and increase access to quality music therapy services. Currently, AMTA establishes criteria for the education and clinical training of music therapists. Members of AMTA adhere to a Code of Ethics and Standards of Practice in their delivery of music therapy services.

How Can You Find A Music Therapist or Get More Information?

American Music Therapy Association

8455 Colesville Road, Suite 1000

Silver Spring, MD 20910

Phone: (301) 589-3300

Fax: (301) 589-5175

Web: www.musictherapy.org

Email: info@musictherapy.org